MORE THAN MAOISM

The Institute of South Asian Studies was established in July 2004 as an autonomous research institute within the National University of Singapore (NUS).

The Institute is dedicated to the study of contemporary South Asia. It aims to generate knowledge and insights about the region, and to disseminate them in a manner that is useful to policy-makers, the business community, academia and civil society.

The Institute is actively engaged in developing key multidisciplinary research programmes and generating publication pertaining to economic, political and social developments in South Asia. It also organises regular conferences, seminars, public lectures and roundtable sessions to promote general, academic and professional awareness of South Asia. At the same time, it interacts with government and international bodies, and the business community as well as establishes linkages with centres of South Asia research worldwide and think-tanks in South Asia. Lastly, it assists NUS to develop research on South Asia.

MORE THAN MAOISM

Politics, Policies and Insurgencies in South Asia

Edited by

ROBIN JEFFREY
RONOJOY SEN
PRATIMA SINGH

Institute of South Asian Studies

MANOHAR
2013

First published 2012

Reprinted 2013

ISBN 978-81-7304-933-0

Published by

Ajay Kumar Jain *for*
Manohar Publishers & Distributors
4753/23 Ansari Road, Daryaganj
New Delhi 110 002

Typeset at

Digigrafics
New Delhi 110 049

Printed at

Salasar Imaging Systems
Delhi 110 035

Contents

'CAUSES' AND 'INDICATORS'

PERCEPTIONS

SECURITY

MEDIA

INTERVIEWS

Illustrations

MAPS

FIGURES

PLATES *between pages 240-1*

Tables

Glossary

adivasi	tribal person
anganwadi	childcare centre
annaj	grains
Arakshak	a constable
ashram	residential schools set up by the Indian government
Balak Sangathan	CPI(Maoist) youth wing: a roving network of young members who are involved in health care, education, and cultural activities
bandh	a strike
Bhoomiporatam	land struggle
Bhumiswami	a landholder who pays revenue to government and has permanent right to the land
bidi	cottage-industry cigarette popular in India and rolled in a *tendu* leaf
chowki	a guard post; a gatehouse
COBRA commandos	Commando Battalion for Resolute Action; specially trained anti-guerrilla units of the CRPF
Communist Party of India (Maoist)	formed in 2004 by bringing together different insurgent groups sharing an affinity for the revolutionary analysis of Mao Zedong
Communist Party of India (Marxist-Leninist)	Maoist-inspired revolutionary organization formed from the merger of the People's War Group with the Party Unity group; the CPI(ML) united with the Maoist Communist Centre in 2004 to form the CPI (Maoist)
Dainik Bhaskar	one of India's largest circulation Hindi-language daily newspapers, based in Bhopal
dalams	cells; units

Dalit	recent, preferred term for an 'untouchable'; in Gandhi's word, 'Harijan'; literal meaning, 'oppressed person'; 'Scheduled Caste' in official language
dasta	an armed guerrilla squad
eminent domain	legal concept enabling governments to expropriate land for the 'greater good'
'the Emergency'	17-month period of authoritarian rule instituted by Prime Minister Indira Gandhi from June 1975 to January 1977
Gaan	a song (Bengali)
gana-sangeet	people's songs
gherao	militant action in which a group surrounds, or impedes, an individual or premises and prevents normal movement or activity
girijan	a tribal person
Gondi	a tribal language spoken by the Gond people
Gonds	a particular tribal group
Gram Panchayat	officially designated unit of local government, usually consisting of a group of villages clubbed together, whose members are elected by the Gram Sabha,
Gram Sabha	village meeting; in the official bureaucratized version all adults have a right to vote for representatives to the Gram Panchayat
Gram Sasan	village assembly
Greyhounds	anti-Maoist special police created by the government of Andhra Pradesh
Holi	spring festival, famous for the fact that celebrants throw coloured powder and water on each other
Jan Andolan	people's movement, particularly applied to Nepal
Jana Natya Mandala	cultural wing of the CPI (Maoist)
Kargil war	war between Indian and Pakistan forces fought along the Line of Control in Kashmir for two months in 1999
Koya Commandos	special police raised allegedly by the government of Chhattisgarh; a later version of the Salwa Judum

lal salaam	'red greeting', a salutation used by Maoist cadres
lathaits	lathi-wielding henchmen. Lathi is a heavy bamboo stick used by Indian police
lathi	stave
Mahatma Gandhi National Rural Employment Guarantee Act, 2005 (MGNREGA)	act of parliament, intended to improve living standards of rural poor by guaranteeing rural households, whose members volunteer, 100 days of work a year at government approved rates
mahila	woman
mahua	*Madhuca longifolia*: a fast-growing tree of north India, suited to dry climates and valued by tribal people; *mahuwa*, an intoxicating spirit, is made from the flowers
Mandal Parishad	Block Assembly
mangujars	landlords or *zamindars*
Maoist Communist Centre of India	Maoist-inspired revolutionary organization that merged with the CPI (ML) in 2004 to form the CPI (Maoist)
Maoist Unity Centre	formed 1997 out of members from Kerala and Maharashtra
mazdoor	a labourer
mukhveer	a spy
munshi	a manager employed by *tendu* contractors
nakedar	forest guard
Naxalbari	village in West Bengal where peasant insurgency began in 1967
Naxalite	term originating from Naxalbari village and used to describe peasant insurgents; often used interchangeably with 'Maoist'
Operation Green Hunt	armed offensive against the Naxalites, organized by government, particularly in Chhattisgarh
Party Unity	Maoist group, centred in Bihar, that merged with the People's War Group in 1998 to form the Communist Party of India (Marxist-Leninist)
patwari	land revenue officer
People's War Group (PWG)	Maoist group based in Andhra Pradesh that merged with the Party Unity group in 1998

	to form the Communist Party of India (Marxist-Leninist)
POSCO	Pohang Iron and Steel Company, a Korean steel-making corporation building a giant project in the state of Orissa
quintal	unit of weight equal to about 100 kilograms
raiyat	a peasant; also spelled *ryot*
rakshas	monster
Revolutionary International Movement (RIM)	loose global organization of left-wing movements
Ryot Coolie Sangham	Agricultural Labourers' Association
Salwa Judum	a militia raised largely from tribal youths to counter Maoist insurgent groups in Chhattisgarh
sangham	an organization
sarpanch	head of a village council
Sarva Shiksha Abhiyan	Government of India programme seeking to provide education for all children
Sarvodaya movement	ideas and movements, originating with M. K. Gandhi, seeking to build a fair and equal society
Schedule V Areas	the fifth appendix of the Indian Constitution outlines special provisions for areas inhabited by tribal people
Scheduled Caste	official designation of an 'ex'-untouchable caste; the practice of untouchability is outlawed, but about 15 per cent of Indians belong to 'untouchable' castes, who are entitled to affirmative action or 'reservation'
Scheduled Tribe	official designation of tribal people; about 7 per cent of India's population are classified as being members of a Scheduled Tribe, which entitles them to affirmative action or 'reservation'
Special Economic Zone	land set aside by government for industrial development and offering various incentives and benefits to the investors
tarri	alcoholic drink

Tebhaga movement	peasant uprising in West Bengal in 1946
Telangana	northern portion of the state of Andhra Pradesh, once part of the old princely state of Hyderabad; scene of rural unrest since the 1940s and focus of a demand for a separate state of the Indian Union
tendu leaves	*Diospyros melonoxylon.* Leaf from a deciduous tree found throughout central India and preferred as a wrapper for *bidis*, cottage-industry cigarettes widely smoked in India; tribal people collect and sell *tendu* leaves
ulama	Muslim religious teachers
vetti	bonded labour
Virasam	Viplava Rachayitala Sangham or Revolutionary Writers' Association
Yu Chi Chan (Pinyin: *youjizhan*)	Chinese term for guerrilla warfare
zamindar	a landlord

Abbreviations

AC	Area Committee
APSIB	Andhra Pradesh Special Intelligence Bureau
BRAC	Bangladesh Rural Advancement Committee
BSF	Border Security Force
BSKSS	Bastar Sambhag Kisan Sangharsh Samiti
CC	Central Committee
CCC	Committee of Concerned Citizens
CCOMPOSA	Coordination Committee of the Maoist Parties of South Asia
CISF	Central Industrial Security Force
CM	Chief Minister
CMC	Central Military Commission
CNM	Chaitanya Natya Manch
COBRA	Commando Battalion for Resolute Action
CPEP	Communist Party of East Pakistan
CRPF	Central Reserve Police Force
CSR	corporate social responsibility
DAKMS	Dandakaranya Adivasi Kisan Mazdoor Samiti
DGP	Director-General of Police
DK	Dandakaranya
DKSZC	Dandakaranya Special Zonal Committee
EDC	Education Committee of the CPI (Maoist)
FICCI	Federation of Indian Chambers of Commerce and Industry
GDP	Gross Domestic Product
GOI	Government of India
GPC	Gram Party Committee
IAS	Indian Administrative Service
ILPS	International League of People's Struggles
INSAS	Indian Small Arms System (the name of a rifle)
IP	Inspector of Police
IPF	Indian People's Front
ITBP	Indo-Tibetan Border Police
JKLF	Jammu and Kashmir Liberation Front
JMM	Jharkhand Mukti Morcha

JS	Janatana Sarkar
JVP	Janatha Vimukthi Peramuna
KAMS	Krantikari Adivasi Mahila Samiti
LGS	Local Guerrilla Squads
LIC	Low Intensity Conflict
LOS	Local Organizing Squad
LTR	Land Transfer Regulation
LTTE	Liberation Tigers of Tamil Eelam
LWE	Left-Wing Extremist
MAS	Mobile Academic Schools
MCCI	Maoist Communist Centre of India
MFP	Minor Forest Produce
MGNREGA	Mahatma Gandhi National Rural Employment Guarantee Act
MKSS	Mazdoor Kisan Shakti Sangathan
ML	Marxist-Leninist
MLA	Member of the Legislative Assembly (state legislature)
MLM	Marxism Leninism Maoism
MFN	Minor Forest Produce
MOPOS	Maoist Political School
MP	Member of Parliament (national parliament)
MUC	Maoist Unity Centre, formed 1997
NDA	National Democratic Alliance
NHRC	National Human Rights Commission
NRHM	National Rural Health Mission
NSCN	National Socialist Council of Nagaland
OGH	Operation Green Hunt
PCAPA	People's Committee Against Police Atrocities
PDFI	People's Democratic Front of India
PDS	Public Distribution System
PESA	Panchayats (Extension to Scheduled Areas)
PGH	Project Green Hunt
PLA	People's Liberation Army
PLGA	People's Liberation Guerrilla Army
POSCO	Pohang Iron and Steel Company
POTA	Prevention of Terrorism Act, 2002
PPW	Protracted People's War
PSBJC	Police E-Sangharsh Birodhi Janaganer Committee
PWD	Public Works Department

PWG	People's War Group
RDF	Revolutionary Democratic Front
RIM	Revolutionary International Movement
RJD	Rashtriya Janata Dal
RMA	Rural Medical Assistant
RNA	Royal Nepal Army
RPC	Revolutionary People's Committee
RSS	Rashtriya Swayamsevak Sangh
SAARC	South Asian Association for Regional Cooperation
SEZ	Special Economic Zone
SIKASA	Singareni Karmika Samakhya
SIMI	Students' Islamic Movement of India
SJ	Salwa Judum
SMC	State Military Commission
SP	Superintendent of Police
SPO	Special Police Officer
SSP	Senior Superintendent of Police
ST	Scheduled Tribe
SUCOMO	Sub-Committee on Mass Organizations
TADA	Terrorist and Disruptive Activities Act, 1985
TDP	Telugu Desam Party
TUF	Tactical United Front
UCPN	Unified Communist Party of Nepal (Maoist)
UF	United Front
ULFA	United Liberation Front of Assam
UNDP	United Nations Development Programme
UP	Uttar Pradesh
UPA	United Progressive Alliance
VCD	Video Compact Disc

Acknowledgements

The splendid support provided by the Institute of South Asian Studies (ISAS) at the National University of Singapore made this extensive collection possible – along with the generosity of our contributors in offering their work for publication in a collection of this kind.

In bringing the book together, we are particularly grateful to the administrative staff of the ISAS and to those of our contributors who took part in a workshop in Singapore in September 2010. That event provided the impetus and encouragement to create the book.

We are similarly grateful to various publications for allowing us to use material that they had published, often in different form, earlier. Specific acknowledgements are to be found with the relevant article.

Harivansh and the photographers at *Prabhat Khabar*, Shailendra Pandey at *Tehelka* (through the good offices of Kunal Majumder) and Suvojit Bagchi provided photos that enrich the book. Vimal Mishra of Allahabad translated Harivansh's remarkable reflections from Hindi into English.

We are especially grateful to Lee Li Kheng, a talented cartographer at NUS, for producing maps specially tailored for our discussions, to Minnie Doron for patience and imagination in designing the jacket and to our publisher, Ramesh Jain, for advice, care and professional knowledge.

Singapore RJ, RS, PS
November 2011

Map 1: South Asia: National Borders and States and Union Territories of India (Lee Li Kheng, Cartography, National University of Singapore)

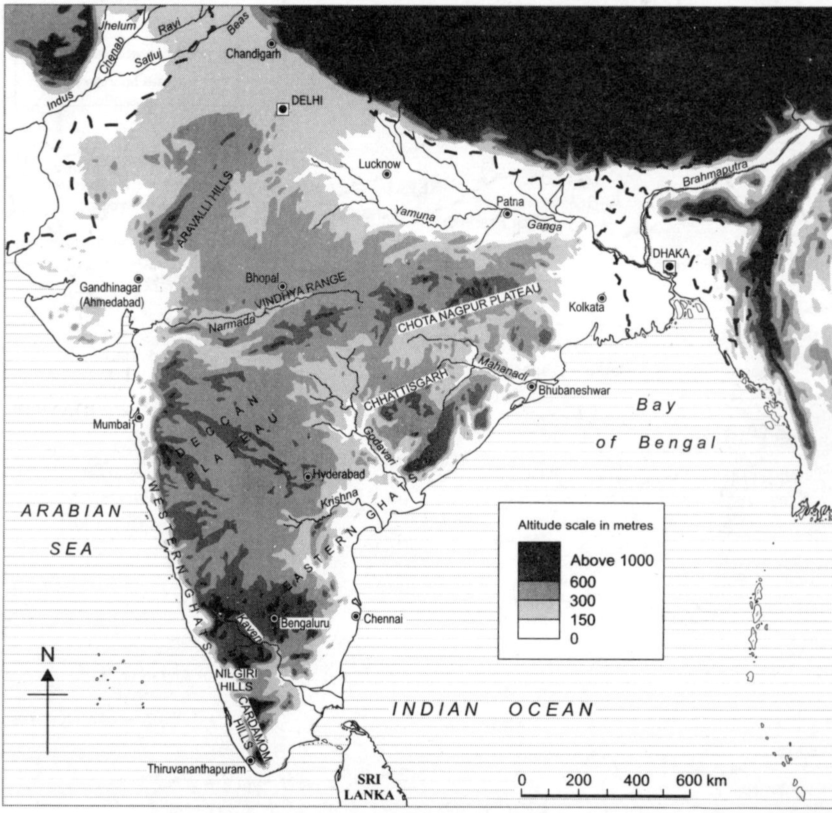

Map 2: South Asia: Physical (Lee Li Kheng, Cartography, National University of Singapore)

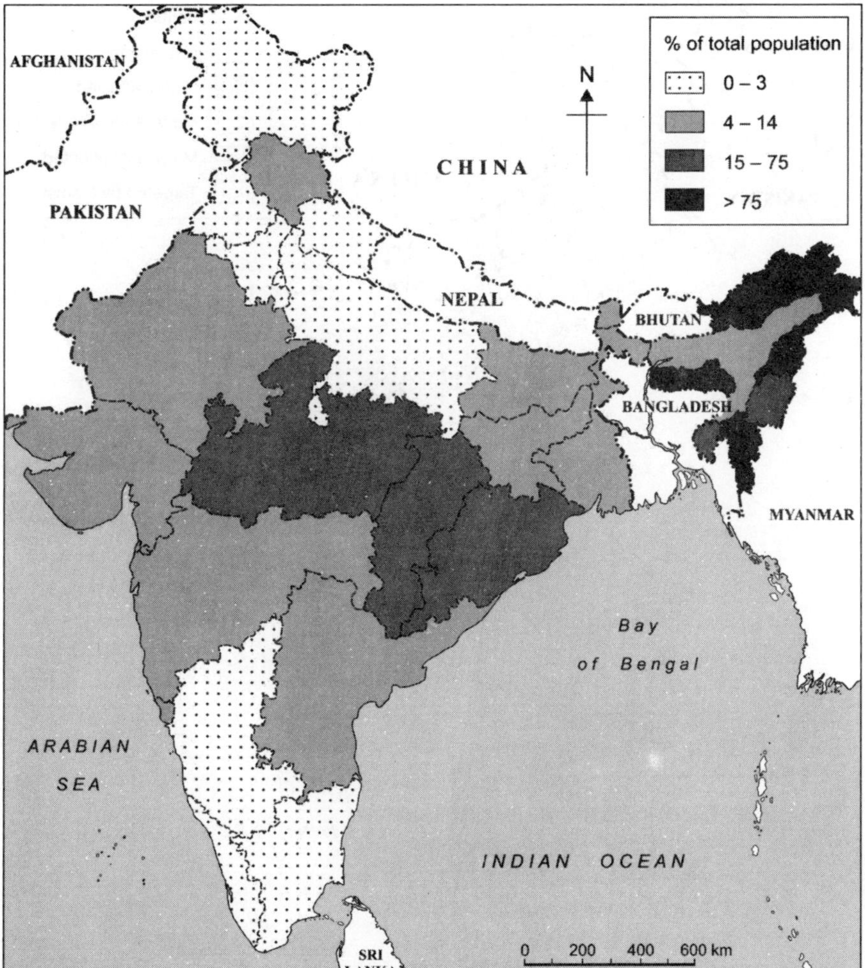

Map 3: Scheduled Tribes as Proportion of Population by States (Lee Li Kheng, Cartography, National University of Singapore, adapted from B.L.C. Johnson, *India*, London: Heinemann, 1979)

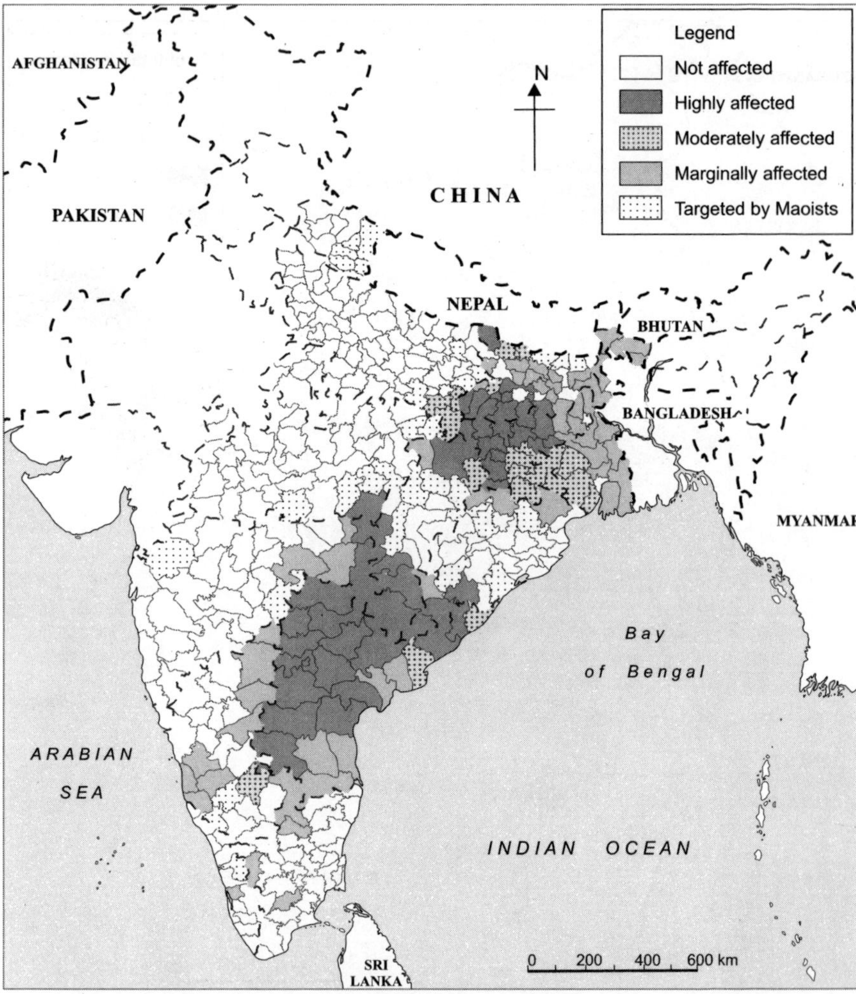

Map 4: India: 'Maoist-Affected Districts' (Lee Li Kheng, Cartography, National University of Singapore, adapted from P. V. Ramana, *The Naxal Challenge*, New Delhi: Pearson-Longman, 2008)

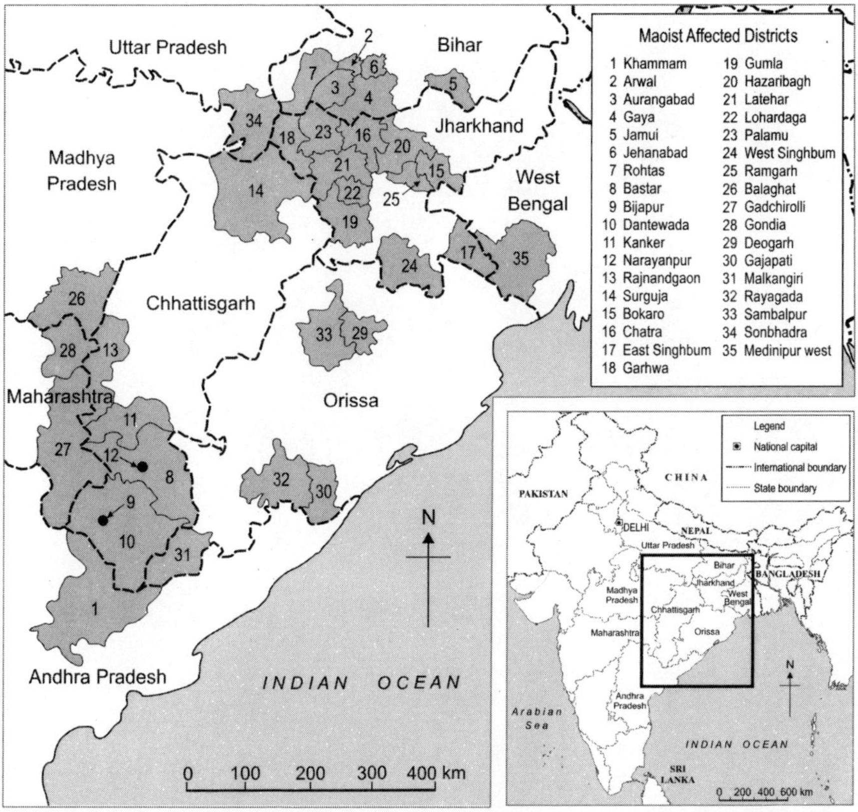

Map 5: Eastern India: 'Maoist-Affected Districts' (Lee Li Kheng, Cartography, National University of Singapore, adapted from P.V. Ramana, *The Naxal Challenge*, New Delhi: Pearson-Longman, 2008)

Introduction

ROBIN JEFFREY
RONOJOY SEN
PRATIMA SINGH

An introduction should explain why a book exists, tempt readers to delve into it and enable them to use it. 'What is this Maoist business in India?' Singaporeans frequently asked the editors who work in the Institute of South Asian Studies (ISAS) at the National University of Singapore. Didn't Mao belong to China? What was he doing in India? Why was a communist insurgency flaring up in India when the rest of the world had left communism for dead a generation ago?

An inhouse seminar in the National University of Singapore allowed us to assess our knowledge, tell our colleagues what we knew and pinpoint our deficiencies. We discovered we had significant knowledge about the varied journeys of 'Maoist ideas', not just in India and Nepal but in Bangladesh, Pakistan and Sri Lanka. We also had the capacity to analyse the economic conditions that were remaking regions of India at frighteningly varied speeds from the 1990s.

One of our deficiencies, however, lay in lack of intimate knowledge of grassroots conditions. To address this lack, we held a workshop in September 2010 that brought three close-to-the-ground authorities to Singapore in September 2010—a scholar (Nandini Sundar), a security specialist (P.V. Ramana) and a journalist (Kunal Majumder). Some of their work, and interviews with each of them, are included in this book (Chapters 9, 19, 20, 29, 30 and 34). In the course of these discussions and research, we concluded that a multi-authored book on 'the Maoist movement' that brought together various perspectives would be valuable. No single author, we believed, could write a book that captured the diverse dislocation and conflict that tormented large areas of India. What would be useful, we concluded, was a book that introduced readers to wide-ranging phenomena that involved so much 'more than Maoism'. Such a treatment needed to include various perspectives; it also needed maps to enable readers to appreciate the importance of physical and human geography.

As we planned this book, the first readers we thought about were our original interrogators in Singapore: 'What is this Maoist business all about?' We hope that in chapters such as Sumanta Banerjee's riveting account of Indian Maoism and his own involvement (Chapter 3), and in the interviews conducted by Ronojoy Sen (Chapter 4) and Avijit Ghosh (Chapter 23), readers will get a sense of the motivations and conditions that made young Indians into Maoists in the 1960s and engendered the 1960s cry: 'China's chairman is our chairman!' 'But why too in Nepal?' readers may ask. S.D. Muni's comprehensive account of Nepal (Chapter 5) provides answers and further emphasizes the importance of local structures, beliefs and terrain in any explanation for the evolution of a movement.

The book, we hope, offers more than simply a response to the basic question about 'this Maoist business'. For policy makers, media people, scholars and students, the book provides historical context, essential facts, thematic analysis and evocative writing and illustration. The six sections can be dipped into as required. 'Travels and Travails' allows readers to follow ideas of peasant-led communist revolution from their successful base in China across South Asia with particular emphasis on India. 'Causes and Indicators' presents six perspectives on the nature of insurgency in India—the effects of legislation and government policy, the effectiveness of administration, the place of women, the role of negotiations and the dislocation of social and economic structures. The sections on 'Security' and 'Media' highlight the importance of the training and morale of the people who either represent the Indian state or attempt to present events and issues to their fellow citizens through print and television.

'Perceptions' offers five pieces of powerful journalism, starting with Suvojit Bagchi's remarkable 'Red Star over Bastar?', an account of 34 days with Maoist groups in the hills of Chhattisgarh during the monsoon of 2010 (Chapter 15). Readers should be warned: they may break out in prickly heat and goose bumps as they read. These accounts are from remote places by people who have travelled and lived there and who earn their livings by navigating the dangerous rapids between involvement on one side and detachment on the other. Twelve interviews (Chapters 23-34), including the last interview given by the Maoist spokesman, Azad (Chapter 24), add an ominous richness to these accounts from people caught up in daily events. The photos by Suvojit Bagchi of the BBC, Shailendra Pandey of

Tehelka and the archives of the newspaper *Prabhat Khabar* in Ranchi capture a few of the 'more than' aspects of the book's title—on one hand, small boys with bows and arrows, and, on the other, *Do Bigha Zamin*, the 1953 film classic, played on a laptop computer in the hills of Chhattisgarh.

Marxist-inspired insurgencies since 1947 have provoked rhetoric and reactions out of proportion to the threat they have posed to the Indian State. The first amendment to the Indian Constitution, passed within months of its inauguration in 1950, was largely provoked by the ill-fated revolt led by the Communist Party of India following the 'Ranadive Line' that called for immediate armed revolt. The amendment curtailed freedom of the press. In 1970, as the term 'Naxalite' entered the vocabulary, Y.B. Chavan, home minister of the Government of India, declared that 'unless we do something about the Green Revolution, it will become the red revolution'.[1] Inspired by ideologues proclaiming 'China's chairman is our chairman', peasants attacked village landlords in eastern India and were joined for a time by idealistic urban youths. As in 1950, the movement was limited in its spread and agonizingly but readily smashed, as Sumanta Banerjee describes (Chapter 3). And from 2006, in the midst of global-capitalist enthusiasm about a 'rising' and 'shining' India, the prime minister repeatedly declared 'Naxalism and Left-wing extremism pose the greatest threat to our national security'.[2]

The insurgency provokes puzzling questions. Why should people risk their lives and kill others in the name of a dead foreign dictator? Why did such things happen at a time when so much international excitement focused on India's economic growth and 'rising power' status? Ideas and ideology are only part of a story whose essence lies in

- remote places colliding with a modernizing polity wanting to exploit the resources of those remote places as never before;
- state institutions, promising equality and justice, colliding with the failure of those institutions to honour the promises; and
- ways of life and belief of indigenous tribal people colliding with deeply based religious traditions, broadly labelled 'Hindu', based in the plains.

The resulting despair and anger created millions of people ready to listen to ascetic, true-believing intellectuals expounding Marxism-

Leninism and its elaboration for rural societies expounded by Mao Zedong. A simple version of Maoism had a beguiling relevance. Such a version could be told like this:

Once upon a time, in a poor, heavily populated country just like ours, there lived a man called Chairman Mao. He saw terrible injustice all around him. A few rich people lived off the labour of the vast majority of the poor and constantly squeezed them to extract a larger share of poor people's land and labour. He found followers in remote areas where the lackeys of the rich were afraid to go. Slowly, using clever tactics and brave struggles, he and his devoted followers fought back, their support grew and after many years of sacrifice, they encircled the cities, overthrew the corrupt, wealthy class . . . and today's envied and prosperous China is the result.

Like all bedtime stories, this one leaves out a lot. But such a story is easy to understand, as is its appeal to people who can identify with tales of impoverishment and exploitation.

This book draws together writings that wrestle with questions that the 'Maoist insurgency' pose. Prasenjit Duara sets the stage (Chapter 1) by putting 'India's Maoist insurgency' in an international context with his comparative analysis of the Chinese revolution of 1927-49 and the intellectual and geographic locations of Maoist ideas in India. Maps drawn for this book by cartographers at the National University of Singapore help in visualizing the points he makes in this provocative and incisive essay.

In the twenty-first century, with China a daily fact for anyone who wears shoes (where were they made?) or makes a phone call (where were the components of the phone produced?), it may be difficult to comprehend the attraction that Mao's ideas of peasant revolt and continuous revolution still hold. Such ideas were particularly potent in South Asia where Western imperialism, highly stratified agrarian society and stark poverty were experiences that 'British India' shared with China. In the 1960s, moreover, 'socialism' and 'Marxism' had the material backing of the Soviet Union. They were words that held out hope, rather than provoke derision.

To understand why 'the Maoist idea' endured in India and Nepal but vanished from Pakistan, Bangladesh and Sri Lanka, this book includes chapters (6, 7 and 8) on the differing experience of the four smaller countries. In Nepal, Maoist ideas took hold in the 1960s and gathered strength among a core of highly motivated and ideologically convinced men and women able to elude the state in remote regions of a rugged, loosely governed country. As economic disparity increased and inequities became more obvious, Nepal's Maoist movement grew to overthrow a regime and begin uncertainly to create a new one, as S.D. Muni details (Chapter 5).

In Pakistan, on the other hand, Maoist ideas and organization were crushed in the time of Z.A. Bhutto, who adopted Mao's cap but not his land reforms. Pakistan never had meaningful land reform.[3] Semi-feudal tenants, heavily dependent on their landlords, were less ripe for resistance than people accustomed to the independence that comes with isolation (e.g., those of western Nepal or tribal India). The military regimes that followed Bhutto eliminated any vestiges of 'Maoism'. Ishtiaq Ahmed's essay on Pakistan (Chapter 6) should be read in conjunction with Iftekhar Chowdhury's account of the Marxist and Maoist movements in Bangladesh (Chapter 7). There, the flight of Hindu landlords during partition and the Tenancy Act of 1950 produced a rural landscape of hundreds of thousands of small holders. In Sri Lanka, as Dayan Jayatilleka relates (Chapter 8), Maoist ideas, and the youthful enthusiasm they often inspired, found initial expression in the Janatha Vimukthi Peramuna (JVP), which twice attempted armed revolt, but whose members later abandoned Mao for Sinhala nationalism.

Who were the custodians of Maoism in India who lit the flame and kept it alive? Sumanta Banerjee's account (Chapter 3) of one man's journey provides readers with a history of 'Indian Maoism' from the 1960s to the 1990s. Three interviews in this book offer further personal insights. Kanu Sanyal (1929-2010) was at the village of Naxalbari on 24 May 1967, the day that gave the 'Maoist movement' its Indian name—Naxalite. There was 'a huge gathering of peasantry and tea garden workers', he told Avijit Ghosh 40 years later (Chapter 23). 'One police officer was killed there.' The following day, the police came in force, and '11 activists were killed'. Sanyal remained a committed Marxist-Leninist and admirer of Mao all his life. But when Ghosh met him in a village in West Bengal in May 2007, Sanyal believed that current Maoist leaders had abandoned crucial ideas. Other urban idealists of 1967, such as Dipanjan Rai Chaudhuri (Chapter 4) slipped back into more conventional lives for men of his urban upper-class milieu. The essence of belief for those who stayed Maoists, and stayed alive through the 1970s, 1980s and 1990s, was expressed in Azad's interview with Siddharth Varadarajan in 2010 (Chapter 24):

While all forms of struggle are legitimate in our eyes, some so-called

> revolutionaries, veterans of yesteryears, surprisingly exclude armed struggle . . . and lay one-sided emphasis on peaceful forms of struggle. They can well join the Gandhian organisations and fight for some reforms instead of calling themselves . . . Maoists aiming for the revolutionary transformation of society.

Similar views can be found in the conversations of Varavara Rao, a Maoist from Andhra Pradesh, recorded in Anand Giridharadas' *India Calling*.[4] The ideologues and idealists who survived thirty years in the wilderness (real and metaphorical) tended to be higher caste men who took their convictions to remote areas.[5] In the case of at least two leaders, their mother-tongue was Telugu, their *lingua franca* was Hindi, they spoke Gondi, the tribal language, well enough to communicate—and their message was people's war as expounded by Mao.[6]

Maoist movements were not exterminated in the mid-1970s; they endured in parts of Bihar, Andhra Pradesh and Madhya Pradesh. In 1986 one of the competing organizations, the Communist Party of India (Marxist-Leninist), was able to publish a book analysing the party's progress in Bihar. It was dedicated to 'those heroic martyrs who sacrificed their lives to transform the backward State of Bihar into a forward post of the Indian revolution'.[7] In 2011, Bihar continued to have a Maoist presence, though it was still no more than 'a forward post'. Elsewhere, however, Maoist movements spread from the 1990s as burgeoning Indian capitalism found it lucrative to push into rugged country that in the past had proved inhospitable and unprofitable. As followers of Mao's ideas, leaders of the movement took a long view. Mao could not have clearly seen the triumph of 1949 from the shambles of Shanghai after the communists were smashed in 1927. According to one policeman, India's Maoists 'have kept 2060 as the flag post [by which time] to liberate the entire country'.[8]

In 1997, half a dozen groups, mostly in eastern and central India, claimed a Maoist or Marxist-Leninist label.[9] They showed a growing confidence and common purpose in October 2003 with an assassination attempt on the chief minister of Andhra Pradesh, Chandrababu Naidu. Within a year, a number of these groups merged to form the Communist Party of India (Maoist). A failed attempt to assassinate the chief minister of West Bengal, Buddhadeb Bhattacharya, in November 2008 symbolized grievances: the chief minister had been laying the foundation stone for a steel mill on tribal land.[10]

John Harriss (Chapter 2) reviews attempts by journalists, scholars and activists to make sense of the economic forces and human reactions that interacted to vitalize 'the Maoist movement' of the 1990s and the twenty-first century. True-believers of earlier times found new supporters and relevance among the peoples of remote areas as capitalists great and small looked to the untapped water, forests and minerals of eastern India's hills and valleys. These processes had begun slowly in the 1980s (S. Narayan, Chapter 10) with the state looking for sources of energy, both coal and hydroelectricity. The effects on tribal people were accentuated by well-meaning legislation, such as the Forest (Conservation) Act of 1980, intended to protect forests but in fact depriving local people of livelihoods and opening the way for them to be exploited by officials.[11] Other national legislation, such as the Panchayats (Extension to Scheduled Areas) Act of 1996 (PESA), which were intended to give meaningful powers of local government to their communities, were impeded, ignored or diluted by state governments (Chapter 11). 'Neo-liberal land grabbing and tribal rights' are the fuel of discontent, writes journalist Shoma Chaudhury (Chapter 18). And the measures of central government to remove the fuel have been ineffectual. One of Chaudhury's informants tells her of a conversation with a 'Maoist' in Bihar: 'You can call me a Naxal or whatever you want,' he said, but 'I have picked up the gun to get my three kilos of *annaji* [grain].'

The views of police and security officials are represented in this book in the work of P.V. Ramana (Chapters 20 and 30) and interviews with a senior Chhattisgarh police officer, a district administrator and a Special Police Officer (Chapters 31, 32 and 33).[12] Officials and police broadly agreed about what was wrong and what needed to be done. Giridhari Nayak, a Chhattisgarh policeman with no time for Maoists or their sympathizers, nevertheless concluded that what was necessary to drain Maoist support was 'to distribute land to the landless poor as part of the speedy implementation of land reforms . . .'.[13] Agrawal, a senior land-reform official of West Bengal, contrasted India with China. In China, he wrote, 90 per cent of landless households had acquired access to land by 1980; in India by 2010, 'less than 28 per cent' of the landless had such access. Agrawal's 'cure', referred to in the title of his book, *Naxalism: Causes and Cure*, was land reform: 'it is high time that land reform is recognized as the basic policy of India'.[14] A former chief of the Border Security Force (BSF) said the same: 'Why are the adivasis [tribal people] ambushing security forces? That is because we have not satisfied them on basic issues of land and forest reforms.'[15] Prakash Singh, another former BSF chief, wrote: 'laws . . . enacted to disburse excess land among the landless . . . were successfully circumvented by the landlords'.[16] In Agrawal's view, the problem lay in the fact that 'political leaders' did not have 'any intention . . . to implement the land reform legislation seriously and honestly'.[17]

State police and central para-military police such as the Central Reserve Police Force (CRPF) and BSF face accusations of ruthlessness, illegality and ineptitude. P.V. Ramana's accounts (Chapters 20 and 30) examine the difficulties they confront, both from their own internal workings and from the tactics of their adversaries. Police from outside a region must cope with unfamiliar and unfriendly terrain; young recruits are far from home, poorly trained and little disciplined; officers would rather be somewhere else. 'The paramilitary and police forces are neither adequately trained nor organised', wrote a soldier experienced in anti-insurgency campaigns. 'The paramilitary and police forces,' he continued, 'have crumbled in incident after incident without giving a tough fight.'[18] In April 2010, more than 70 members of the CRPF were killed in an ambush by Maoist forces in Dantewada in Chhattisgarh. Poor procedures, discipline and morale led to almost complete annihilation.[19]

The inquiries stemming from the massacre of April 2010 highlighted key elements of a twenty-first-century insurgency in India. Television broadcasters, modelling themselves on Fox TV and radio populists in the US, called for the toughest action against 'anti-national elements'. The Government of India and state governments announced new measures to coordinate security and bring genuine improvement to the lives of people in the 'affected areas'. In such areas, angered but fearful police sometimes took revenge on anyone they could lay their hands on, thus repeating a cycle that has fed dislocation and violence for thirty years.

The insurgency of the twenty-first century is India's first violent internal challenge since television became a pervasive medium. To be sure, India experienced a television war at Kargil in Kashmir in 1999, the televized communal killings in Gujarat in 2002 and the real-time, terror-on-television attack on central Mumbai in 2008.[20] But a prolonged insurgency across vast, inaccessible country presents different challenges, opportunities and temptations for fiercely competitive media, particularly television. Divya Iyer recounts how the beheading of police inspector Francis Induwar in Jharkhand in 2009 confronted a big-city television newsroom with the need to make fast judgements about taste, journalism—and ratings (Chapter 22).

Governments and insurgents seek to use media to elicit sympathy and convince audiences—'the people'—of the rightness of their acts and the wrongness of others. In areas of conflict, journalists are often in danger and their accounts shrouded in doubt because they face threats and inducements from administrators, police, Maoist cadres and opportunistic criminals. As an example of dogged, painstaking reporting, Suvojit Bagchi's essay, 'Red Star Over Bastar?' (Chapter 15), intentionally echoes Edgar Snow's *Red Star Over China*, the American journalist's account of months spent with the Chinese communists in 1936.[21] Unlike Snow, Bagchi inserts a question mark at the end of his title. Like Arundhati Roy at the beginning of 2010,[22] Bagchi was invited to accompany Maoist groups in Chhattisgarh in August 2010. His interviews, detailed accounts and personal reflections provide rare insights into daily life among people who kill others and know that others will try to kill them.

This book contains half a dozen accounts of journalists and scholars who have interacted in various ways with Maoist leaders and followers. It includes a long memoir by Harivansh, editor of *Prabhat Khabar*, the Hindi daily based in Ranchi (Chapter 16). His free-wheeling reflections on Maoists, tribal people, governments and police forces is based on more than thirty years' experience in the heart of less-accessible India. Sudeep Chakravarti, author of *Red Sun: Travels in Naxalite Country*, reflects (Chapter 17) on changes in the political environment since his experiences of 2006.[23]

Women are combatants in the insurgency and comprise up to 40 per cent of active Maoist cadres, according to some estimates (Chapter 13).[24] Police and security officials, anxious to counteract frequent accounts of rape and assault by security forces, report sexual licence and exploitation among Maoist groups. 'As per police reports,' writes Agrawal, the civil servant, 'vices of drinking, gambling, sex-exploitation, and comforts form part of their lifestyle.'[25] In June 2011, women who had allegedly fled Maoist organizations, gave video interviews in Ranchi to expose sexual exploitation.[26] 'Most women are exploited by senior Maoists', another woman, who said she had been raped, told a journalist after she surrendered to the police in 2010.[27] On the other hand, Bagchi, who spent more than a month with Maoist groups (Chapter 15), saw no such evidence, though he is too seasoned a reporter to generalize. For Akanksha Mehta writing in this book, the fact that women form such a large component of Maoist forces indicates shifts in gender relations, even if women are still largely absent from key decision-making positions.

Some police and para-military see a vicious, conspiratorial threat to Indian democracy and nationhood. 'Naxalism is evil *per se*', wrote Giridhari Nayak. As an additional director-general of police in Chhattisgarh, he was as close to the blood and squalour as a policeman could be.[28] His views were plain in the dedication of his book: 'to all brave souls who went for heavenly abode while performing their duty'.[29] For policemen like Nayak, the Maoists had attracted 'a perverse confluence of [the] underworld, [a] few publicity-seeking intellectuals and vested interests'. They engineered 'support from the press', from 'the elites connected to Naxalites' and from 'labyrinthine frontal organisations' to generate a 'sinister nation-destroying process'.[30]

Among Nayak's 30 suggestions for overcoming the insurgencies, one was perhaps ominously prescient: 'Development of forested areas is not sustainable. . . . People living in hunting gathering stage cannot be developed by more pumping [in] of funds. The settlements of human beings in forested areas need to be changed to cluster system to make development viable and protected.'[31]

In the past 250 years, industrialization and the movement of people from the countryside to city has never been gentle, beautiful or benign, whether in Europe, North America, Japan or other parts of Asia. As early as 1770, when Britain's industrial revolution had barely begun, Oliver Goldsmith's 'Deserted Village' bemoaned the changes in rural life:

> But times are alter'd; Trade's unfeeling train
> Usurp the land, and dispossess the swain;
>
> ***
>
> Where, then, ah! where shall poverty reside,
> To 'scape the pressure of contiguous pride?
>
> ***
>
> Those fenceless fields the sons of wealth divide,
> And even the bare-worn common is denied.
> If to the city sped—what waits him there?
> To see profusion that he must not share;
> To see ten thousand baneful arts combined

> To pamper luxury and thin mankind;
> To see each joy the sons of pleasure know
> Extorted from his fellow-creature's woe . . .

In the twenty-first century, the 'profusion that he must not share' conjures up visions of the new multistoreyed mansion of the Ambanis in Mumbai, while those associated with the Narmada Bachao Andolan, or other attempts to safeguard the interests of dispossessed people, might find a soulmate in Goldsmith.

With the experience of 250 years, it ought to be possible to modify earlier paths that led to urban misery or at least to mitigate the trauma. But the Indian state has shown few signs of being able to break out of a vicious circle. The constituents of that circle are readily identified:

- rugged, forbidding terrain, inhabited often by people whose livelihoods and traditions are not closely linked to those of mainstream rural India;
- only occasional contact with the state and the commerce and law of mainstream India;
- the arrival in such havens in the 1980s of ardent Maoist intellectuals, seeking sanctuary from suppression elsewhere;
- increasing interest from industrializing India in the raw materials—water, timber and minerals—of these remote areas;
- collisions between indigenous people and industrial interests, in which indigenous people usually lose and promises of compensation are seldom fulfilled;
- a growing availability of arms and explosives leaking from wars in South Asia, from Sri Lanka to Afghanistan.

To break the circle, Indian governments proclaim a policy to 'clear, hold and build'—clear areas of Maoist influence, protect them with adequate security and build infrastructure and institutions that will woo residents to the state, not the insurgency. The plan is straightforward; execution is not. As articles in the 'Perceptions' section of this book indicate, armed Maoist units readily slip away into more remote areas when large state forces challenge them. Though 'clearing' of some areas therefore can be done, 'holding' requires a persistence, flexibility and alertness for which the Indian state is not famed. And 'building' requires motivated administrators, teachers, medical workers and engineers, willing to live in remote areas, accept low pay and face danger. To make such a programme succeed would require the administrative intensity that built the Delhi metro and an institutionalized idealism that combined the best of Mahatma Gandhi and the Peace Corps.

Maoist ideologues walk a fine line. They must stay alive. (Kishenji, a prominent Maoist leader, was killed by police in West Bengal in November 2011). They must feed, arm, educate and control their followers. They often seem to fail. The beheading of policeman Francis Induwar (Chapter 22), the murder of hostage policeman Lucas Tete (himself a tribal) and the derailment of a passenger train killing more than 140 people gave a voracious urban media plenty about which to be outraged.[32] Even those with considerable sympathy for Maoist analysis concede that 'the Maoists often appear . . . bullies—extorting money . . . brutally killing minor offenders—even innocent people—on the mere suspicion that they are police informers.'[33] Maoist leaders become media managers to try to cope with India's insatiable TV channels and retain the sympathy of sections of the middle class. They realize that their perceived martyr-ish idealism and the genuine agonies of tribal people are essential ingredients that cement the allegiance of Maoist cadres and garner sympathy—grudging or whole-hearted—from sections of urban India.

Those who call themselves Maoists often claim that idealism lies solely with them. Azad, the Maoist spokesman killed in July 2010, staked out high moral ground in his last interview with Siddharth Varadarajan (Chapter 24):

> How many of our countrymen know that three lakh adivasis [300,000 tribal people] were driven away from their homes, that half the adivasi population in our country is already living under conditions of chronic famine and even the rest of the population is now pushed into famine condition? And why? Because of the insatiable greed of the corporate sharks. . . .

Explaining the attraction of 'Maoism', Varavara Rao, one of the Telugu-speaking Brahmin leaders from Andhra Pradesh, told Anand Giridharadas:

> Maoism . . . was ultimately a revolt against what he had known in childhood: a society of barriers, . . . Brahmins and untouchables, nonpolluting and polluting, beating and beaten. He had believed for a time that independence and a new republic would bring new ideas of justice, solidarity and common humanity. But those ideas had faded. . . . From . . . the disappointment of a generation of like-minded souls, the Maoist cause was born.[34]

This combination of idealism and ideology—the willingness to believe in Marx, Mao and a science of politics and history that anticipates the future—has co-existed with the brutal realities of rural India since the 1940s. The results have often been violent, bloody and fatal. The rapidity of economic expansion, the glaring disparities of class and power that it accentuates and the promise of Maoist ideas to desperate people mean that just and prosperous harmony is not likely to replace resistance and revolt in rural India in the near future.

NOTES

1. *Time*, 13 July 1970, http://www.time.com/time/magazine/article/0,9171,909446,00.html (downloaded 22 May 2011).
2. *Telegraph* (Kolkata), 23 October 2010, http://www.telegraphindia.com/1101023/jsp/nation/story_13090790.jsp and *India Today*, 19 April 2010, http://indiatoday.intoday.in/site/story/Maoism+is+terrorism/1/92085.html (both downloaded 22 May 2011).
3. Akmal Hussain, 'Pakistan: Land Reforms Reconsidered', paper presented at Group 83 Seminar, Lahore, December 1982, http://www.akmalhussain.net/Publish%20Work/SouthAsia/PakistanLandReformsReconsidered.pdf (downloaded 24 June 2011).
4. Anand Giridharadas, *India Calling* (Melbourne: Black Inc., 2010), pp. 133-58.
5. See also the interview with Kishenji (alias Koteswar Rao), a Telugu who came to live in Bihar and West Bengal. *Frontline*, 6 November 2009, pp. 22-3.
6. Email from Kunal Majumder to R. Jeffrey, 25 June 2010, after meetings with Maoist leaders, Ramana and Ganesh, in Dantewada.
7. *Report from the Flaming Fields of Bihar: A CPI (ML) Document* (Kolkata: Prabodh Bhattacharya, 1986).
8. Giridhari Nayak, *Neo-Naxal Challenge: Issues and Options* (New Delhi: Pentagon Security International, 2011), pp. 19-20. Bibhu Prasad Routray, 'Dealing with the Rationalisation of Maoist Violence', *Aakrosh*, vol. 13, no. 48 (July 2010), p. 50, suggests the Maoists aim for 2050.
9. K. Srinivas Reddy, 'The Maoist Challenge', *Seminar*, no. 569 (January 2007), http://www.india-seminar.com/2007/569/569_k_srinivas_reddy.htm (downloaded 21 April 2010).
10. NDTV, 8 November 2008, http://www.ndtv.com/convergence/ndtv/story.aspx?id=NEWEN20080070919&ch=633612431125153750 (downloaded 21 April 2011).
11. P.K. Agrawal, *Naxalism: Causes and Cure* (New Delhi: Manas, 2010), p. 131.
12. Two senior security specialists whom the editors approached for their perspectives were not in a position to contribute. See also P.V. Ramana (ed.), *The Naxal Challenge: Causes, Linkages and Policy Options* (New Delhi: Pearson Longman, 2008).

13. Nayak, *Neo-Naxal Challenge*, p. 215.
14. Agrawal, *Naxalism*, pp. 11-12.
15. E.N. Rammohan in *Mail Today*, 22 May 2010, quoted in Anuradha M. Chenoy and Kamal A. Mitra Chenoy, *Maoist and Other Armed Conflicts* (New Delhi: Penguin, 2010), p. 76.
16. Prakash Singh, *The Naxalite Movement in India*, rev. edn. (New Delhi: Rupa, 2006), p. 221.
17. Agrawal, *Naxalism*, p. 184. He referred here specifically to Maharashtra, but his views were similar for most other states.
18. Harinder Singh, 'Countering the Naxal', *IDSA Issue Brief*, 11 June 2010, pp. 5 and 7.
19. *Outlook*, 19 April 2010, pp. 23-7. Nayak, *Neo-Naxal Challenge*, p. 238: 'good trainers . . . are becoming [a] rare species in police and paramilitary forces.'
20. Nalin Mehta, *India on Television* (New Delhi: HarperCollins, 2008), pp. 276-95.
21. Edgar Snow, *Red Star Over China* (London: Victor Gollancz, 1937).
22. Booker Prize-winner Arundhati Roy also spent an extended period with Maoists in Chhattisgarh early in 2010. Her long essay is in *Outlook*, 29 March 2010, pp. 24-59.
23. Sudeep Chakravarti, *Red Sun: Travels in Naxalite Country*, rev. edn. (New Delhi: Penguin, 2009).
24. Chenoy and Chenoy, *Maoist*, p. 201.
25. Agrawal, *Naxalism*, p. 87.
26. http://www.hindustantimes.com/audio-news-video/Women-Maoist-complain-of-sexual-exploitation-by-maoist-leaders/Article2-712139.aspx (downloaded 26 June 2011).
27. Rakhi Chakrabarty reporting on an interview with ex-Maoist, Uma, in *Times of India*, 24 August 2010, www.timesofindia.indiatimes.com/aricleshow/6423200.cms?prtpage=1 (downloaded 24 August 2010).
28. Nayak, *Neo-Naxal Challenge*, p. 34.
29. Ibid., p. v.
30. Ibid., pp. 30, 72, 156, 202. Routray, 'Dealing with the Rationalisation of Maoist Violence', pp. 50-7, offers a critique of Maoist 'front' organizations.
31. Ibid., p. 245.
32. *Governance Now*, 17 September 2010 for Tete's murder, www.governancenow.com/print8014 (downloaded 22 September 2010). *Hindu*, 22 June 2010, for the derailment of the Jnaneswari Express, beta.thehindu.com/news/national/article478921.ece?homepage=true&css=print (downloaded 22 June 2010).
33 Sumanta Banerjee, *In the Wake of Naxalbari: Four Decades of a Simmering Revolution*, 2nd edn. (Kolkata: Sahitya Samsad, 2009), p. 372.
34 Giridharadas, *India Calling*, p. 141.

'MAOISM': TRAVELS AND TRAVAILS OF AN IDEA

The term 'Maoism' has fascinated the world since the 1940s. From the publication of Edgar Snow's *Red Star Over China* (1937), a global mystique grew; it spread worldwide with the triumph of the Chinese revolution in 1949, the Korean War, the isolation of China and the Cultural Revolution. In South Asia, communist parties in the newly-independent countries of the erstwhile British Empire debated the doctrines of Mao's Chinese Communist Party (CCP) and agonized over the Sino-Soviet split of 1964.

This section provides accounts of Maoist ideas and Maoist-inspired actions in the countries of the region. It has been a chequered history. Three essays on India reveal the circumstances that have led men and women to learn about, embrace, and sometimes, later, reject, Maoist analysis. The detailed essay on Nepal explains why Maoist models and rhetoric have exerted such attraction, while the essays on Pakistan, Bangladesh and Sri Lanka offer subtle analyses of the different reasons why Maoist ideas and organizations took hold only fitfully and by the twenty-first century had largely disappeared.

CHAPTER 1

The Chinese Revolution and Insurgent Maoism in India: A Spatial Analysis*

PRASENJIT DUARA

The first Naxalite flare-up in 1967 was largely suppressed by 1972, particularly in the urban centres of Bengal. While some of the urban leadership from Kolkata continued with rural activism, the movement became fractured and remained dormant for much of the next few decades. The more recent uprising in the last decade appears to be much more widespread, better organized and moreover, to have emerged within more distinct geographical or spatial perimeters.

My goal in this brief account is not to discount or devalue the social and economic conditions leading to the Maoist uprisings. Rather, I want to identify the spatial conditions of peasant revolutionary uprisings principally by comparing the Indian Maoist movement with the Chinese peasant revolution that established the People's Republic of China (PRC) in 1949. These spatial factors were by no means sufficient to grasp the revolution, but I hypothesize that they represent necessary initial conditions.

In the last ten years or so, the Maoist movement in India has arisen in the so-called 'Red Corridor' which occupies large swathes of hilly and forest lands and is inhabited for the large part by indigenous peoples. Even in the first phase, the Naxalites found their main support among the indigenous (*adivasi*) communities such as the Santhals in the Bengal-Bihar area and the Girijans in Andhra Pradesh. Earlier communist uprisings in colonial India also took place in areas with large concentrations of indigenous and non-caste Hindu groups such

*First published in the *Economic and Political Weekly*, 30 April 2011, pp. 33-6. Reprinted with permission.

as the Telengana uprising of 1947 or the Tebhaga movement in the predominantly Muslim areas of colonial Bengal in 1946.

The advent of the modern, post-colonial state seems to have focused the uprising to a still greater extent in this kind of peripheral geographical space. While the exploitation of these spaces intensifies, at the same time the modern state apparatus and the agrarian social order appear to have limited capacity to penetrate these areas. One might say that the exploitation of these regions is external and the people typically escape domination and interdependency on an everyday basis that is more common in agrarian society. As such, they have a greater capacity for horizontal solidarity. It is beyond the scope of this paper to examine how and why agrarian caste society limits the horizontal solidarity required for peasant uprisings, but one can hazard that it has to do not simply with caste hierarchy but with the systemic exclusion that upwardly aspiring lower castes have historically adopted towards still lower groups in the hierarchy.

The intensification of uprisings in the forested and indigenous regions of India in the recent period has to do with the deepening exploitation of forest resources that has accompanied the expansion of multinational and Indian capitalist interests with collusive state interests, particularly in the mining industry. Thus not only has the independent state neglected these communities but it is now contributing to the deprivation of the resources for their livelihood. Finally, despite their relative isolation, the *adivasi* communities are very conscious of their modern rights not only in the local or Indian context but also of the rights of indigenous communities as a global phenomenon and movement. This awareness also reinforces the justness of their cause.

What do these conditions have to do with the Chinese revolution? To anticipate my conclusion here, the Chinese revolution could not have succeeded without the benefit of the peripheral geographical spaces resembling the regions of the contemporary Maoist movement in India. The revolutionary organization—the Chinese Communist Party (CCP) and the People's Army—consolidated and built-up the military and political machinery of insurgent power in the relatively protected spaces of the periphery, which were identified as base areas or Soviets.

Consider some of the arguments made about the success of the Chinese revolution. The CCP's own explanation of the peasant revolution contained in the doctrine of Marxism-Leninism and Mao

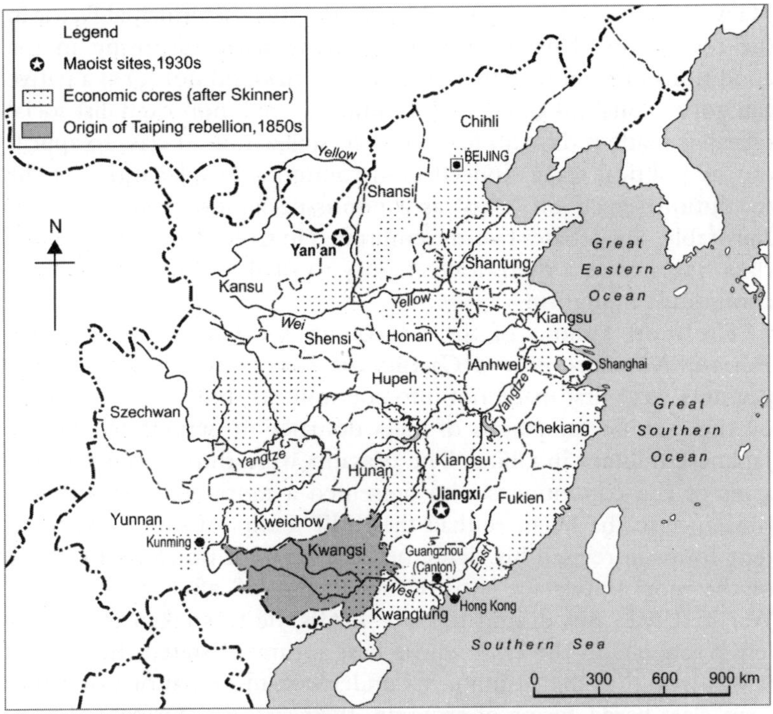

Map 1.1: China: Territorial Bases of Revolution
(Lee Li Kheng, Cartography, National University of Singapore)

Zedong Thought emphasized the importance of class struggle, the coalition of lower and middle classes and autonomous military power. The class struggle line was de-emphasized during the resistance to the Japanese invasion (1937-45) in favour of a coalition with 'bourgeois' forces led by Chiang Kai-shek. Notably though, the CCP maintained its independent military power in this United Front in contrast to the first United Front of 1923-7. After the defeat of Japan, the CCP unleashed a class revolution directed against the landed and urban propertied classes during the civil war with the Kuomintang (KMT) forces from 1946-9. With the successful establishment of the PRC, the CCP once again initiated the 'new democratic coalition' with the remaining cooperative classes until they could peacefully establish a classless society sometime in the future.

The reason I outline this narrative is to indicate that even in official accounts, the CCP registers the ambiguous role of the orthodox

Marxist notion of 'class' and 'class struggle' as the principal factor in the revolution. This is perhaps not particularly surprising in the conditions of rural society in Asia, where class did not form a native category of analysis and complex, multi-layered, non-capitalist social relations made it difficult for a clear crystallization of class to appear on the political stage. Indeed, non-communist explanations of the revolution seized on 'class' as a non-issue almost from the start. Inevitably, the debates became embroiled in Cold War politics where class was seen as a rhetorical category to mask the brutal power of communist militarism.

The most famous of these accounts was Chalmers Johnson's *Peasant Nationalism and Communist Power*,[1] which argued that peasants were first made not into communists, but into nationalists by the horrific campaigns of mass destruction perpetrated by the Japanese military in China. The peasants were thus driven into the arms of the communists who presented a more credible *national* resistance to the Japanese than the KMT. I am not sure to what extent Johnson revised his views, because he went on to become one of the most important leftist critics in the US after the first Gulf War in 1991. But during the late 1960s, he was taken to task by leftist scholars in the USA whose best argument stated that even if it was true that the communists undertook more nationalist rather than class-based forms of struggle, their success represented their championing of the economic and political interests of the masses much more satisfactorily than did the KMT or any other group in China.

By 1991, some of the leftists themselves began to recognize that there had been considerable mystification of the revolution and cover-ups of its darker aspects. Take for instance, the book, *Chinese Village, Socialist State*.[2] While it did not represent a denunciation of the revolution, it did point to considerable heterogeneity in the composition of both class enemies and good classes. It thus threw into doubt the social and economic categories crafted in the revolution. Even before that point, the French scholar Lucien Bianco's work and my own book[3] argued that in north China at least, the principal fault-line appeared between a predatory state, engaged in a dysfunctional form of modern state-building, and collective village or rural resistance to the extractions of this state (including the late Qing, the Republican and the Japanese regimes). Class, to the extent that it was an issue, was distinctly secondary; many of the state collaborators were originally lower class peasants and the *lumpen proletariat*.

The communists were able to mobilize these heterogeneous grievances in rural society because of their ***highly organized and efficient party apparatus.*** But why was the geographical space so important to them? I argue that the communists were not able to mobilize these grievances in the core regions of Chinese agrarian society precisely because of the dominance of the state and elite power networks that extended through lineages and other forms of hierarchical and dependency relationships. Indeed, the history of the Communist Party shows that they were able to mobilize and consolidate their military and party power only where elite and state structures were relatively weak. The base areas or Soviets established during the 1930s and 1940s were precisely—as in the Telangana communist region (1946-51)—in these peripheral spaces, with terrain as difficult to cultivate as it was to traverse.

The most famous base areas of the Chinese communists were the Jiangxi and Yan'an Soviets, although there were also several others located in cross provincial border peripheries. These were not only guerilla home-bases but also effectively sovereign entities where the communists could experiment with and implement both reformist and revolutionary agendas. Most, if not all, of these regions represented rugged, hardscrabble zones often beyond the reach of the state and with weak elite, market and transportation networks. Banditry and local violence ruled these spaces into which the flexible communist units were able to make forceful inroads and build their power. The KMT forced the communists under Mao and Zhu De to abandon the first Jiangxi Soviet (in inland south China) through a series of air campaigns that bombarded the Soviet in 1934. In response and in the most notable instance of turning a bad thing into a good (though costly) thing, the CCP conducted the Long March to Yan'an in the northwest where they re-established themselves in mountainous cave redoubts (and possibly also gained protection from the proximity to the Soviet Union). The Yan'an Soviet was perhaps the most important crucible for CCP military and political success.

In Chinese studies, while a group of scholars was studying the base areas, a parallel exploration was being undertaken of the study of regions and regionalism in China. An important book, edited and mostly written by G.W. Skinner entitled *The City in Late Imperial China*[4] was to change the way social historians and others would approach the vastness of China as a spatial entity. Skinner argued that most of imperial China could be divided into nine macro-regions, the boundaries of each of which could be grasped by looking at the difference in transportation costs. The relative escalation of transportation costs for people and goods in one part of China indicated the boundary of a macro-region.

Since pre-modern transport was conducted through rivers and along river valleys, the macro-regions came to be divided by physiographic barriers that occurred along the major rivers such as the Yellow, Yangzi and the West rivers. These natural barriers such as forests, mountains or otherwise rugged terrains made transportation across them hugely difficult and expensive both for trade and state control. As such, the areas around these barriers represented the peripheries of the macro-regions, whereas the dense nodes of riverine transportation and irrigation created the cores, which were cities dominated by the Confucian elite. The periphery in turn was characterized by difficulty of penetration, autonomy, banditry and a culture of competitive violence. It also had a larger share of minority, non-Han and non-Confucianized people and quasi-nomadic and other marginal groups like the Hakkas and the shed peoples.

The history of popular uprisings in China has revealed that most rebellions were started, organized and consolidated in the peripheral regions because the space afforded protection from state and elite power. For example, the leaders of the mid-nineteenth-century Christian Taiping rebellion moved away from the Pearl River delta core because they were attacked by the elites there; they moved to the deeply peripheral regions of Guangxi and began to organize among the marginal and embattled Hakka people. Once they organized a substantial military force, they were able—because of the weakness of Qing imperial power—to attack and defeat the core cities of south and central China, ending up in Nanjing (the Ming capital) from which they ruled much of China for fourteen years. The communist revolution, which as far as I know, is yet to be *fully* studied from this spatial perspective, appears to have followed a similar pattern.

What does this spatial narrative of the Chinese revolution tell us about the contemporary Maoist movement in India? Clearly India, like China, has spatial peripheries in the interior of the country occupied by peoples more likely to take to insurgency than those within the agrarian heartland. This is both because they are economically oppressed and because they have the spatial capacity to develop horizontal solidarity by a powerful mobilizing organization. Certainly, the modern Indian state is hardly like the weak KMT state in the

Republican period. Even less does the situation resemble the period in China where the Japanese invasion alienated large segments of the population in both core and peripheral regions. Nonetheless, unless the state and capitalist interests begin to pay due attention to the livelihood needs and dignity of the indigenous and marginal peoples, the 'red corridor' will fester like a wide open gash across the body politic of the Indian republic. For those unmoved by humanitarian concerns, the analysis suggests that a combination of contingent and/ or external circumstances could turn this wound into a bloody, unending war.

NOTES

1. Chalmers Johnson, *Peasant Nationalism and Communist Power: The Emergence of Revolutionary China, 1937-1945* (Stanford, CA: Stanford University Press, 1962).
2. Edward Friedman, Paul G. Pickowicz, and Mark Selden (with Kay Ann Johnson), *Chinese Village, Socialist State* (New Haven, CT: Yale University Press, 1991).
3. Prasenjit Duara, *Culture, Power and the State: Rural North China, 1900-1942* (Stanford, CA: Stanford University Press, 1988).
4. G.W. Skinner, *The City in Late Imperial China* (Stanford, CA: Stanford University Press, 1977).

CHAPTER 2

What is Going on in India's 'Red Corridor'? Questions about India's Maoist Insurgency: A Literature Review*

JOHN HARRISS

The early months of 2010 in India were marked by a whole series of serious attacks on security forces by groups of Maoist (or Naxalite, as they are sometimes still described) insurgents. In February, 24 members of the security forces were killed in an attack on a camp at Silda in West Bengal; on 4 April the BBC reported that 'Suspected Maoist rebels have killed at least ten policemen in a landmine attack in the eastern state of Orissa'; just two days later 76 paramilitaries of the Central Reserve Police Force (CRPF) were killed in a major attack in the Dantewada district of Chhattisgarh; on 17 May in the same district a mine detonated under a bus carrying both civilians and Special Police Officers, killing 44 people; on 28 May the derailment of an express train in West Bengal, killing about 150 people, was blamed on the Maoists, though denied by them; then on 29 June a further 26 CRPF men were killed in Narayanapur in Chhattisgarh. These are only the more notable events that were widely reported internationally, and many more incidents were recorded by the Indian press. The London *Economist* noted (on 27 February 2010) that '[b]oasting an estimated 14,000 full-time guerillas and many more semi-trained sympathisers, [the Maoists] loosely control tracts of Jharkhand, Orissa and Chhattisgarh. They have also overrun a smaller, but spreading area of West Bengal'. There is now what is sometimes described as the 'red corridor', stretching from the upper Gangetic

*First published in *Pacific Affairs,* vol. 84, no. 2 (June 2011), 309-27. Reprinted with permission.

plain bordering Nepal, across the plains of Bihar and through the forested hills that parallel the east coast of India down as far as northern Tamil Nadu. The corridor is twice the geographical size of the other two insurgency-affected areas of India, in the north-east and in Kashmir; and the Maoists, mobilizing more cadres than the insurgents in the other two regions, are now said by the government to operate in over a third of India's districts. The frequency and intensity of their attacks, and the geographical spread of the Maoist insurgency explain why the prime minister of India, Manmohan Singh, described the insurgency, first in 2006, and on many occasions since then,[1] as the most serious internal security threat that India has ever faced.

What explains the rise of the Maoist insurgency in India? What, if anything, does it have to do with the country's hugely successful economic growth of recent years, that seems to have followed from the adoption of neo-liberal policies and India's increased integration into the global economy? What accounts for the particular geography of the insurgency? Is it, as some senior politicians argue, a response to the grievances held by India's poorest people as a result of years of neglect by the state and what the Government of India itself has described as the 'structural violence' to which they have been subjected?[2] Has it become, in consequence, what might be described as a popular insurgency, winning widespread support? Or is it, as some observers maintain, essentially a movement driven by middle-class intellectuals, often from upper castes, who are playing out revolutionary fantasies at the expense of some of India's least privileged people?[3] Is it, indeed, affected by caste differences and tensions? Then, how do the insurgents raise resources for their campaigns? Are they, as some observers claim, deeply implicated in criminal activity, together with corrupt politicians and local power-holders? Readers who are familiar with the recent general literature concerned with explaining civil war and insurgencies across the world will recognize in these questions the alternative hypotheses about their causes that have been labelled those of 'grievance' *vs.* 'greed'.[4] How well do these general theories stand up against the facts of India's Maoist insurgency? How indeed does this insurgency compare both with those in other parts of the world (especially that in neighbouring Nepal), and with earlier peasant and other popular risings in India?

These are questions that I address in this essay. Trying to find answers to them in the literature, as I have done, is not easy. That there should be so much disinformation is inevitable, given that the movement has always been at least partly underground, and that the Communist Party of India (Maoist) [CPI (Maoist)], formed, as I go on to explain, in 2004, has been proscribed since June 2009 as a terrorist organization under the Unlawful Activities (Prevention) Act. Its leaders cover their tracks and rarely make public statements. In these circumstances it is not surprising that there is little published independent research, and that regular reporting is extremely difficult. A blogger from the central Indian state of Chhattisgarh posted the following comment:

> How does the media in Chhattisgarh report the conflict between the Naxalites and the Salwa Judum [a local militia, set up to oppose the Maoists], or the conflict between local communities and corporations? Quite simply, it doesn't. The pressures on journalists in Chhattisgarh are unique. They are paid not to report stories that are critical of the powers-that-be, whether they are industrial lobbies or state authorities.[5]

This probably is an accurate account.[6] Certainly it is extremely difficult to sift information from disinformation, fact from opinion, reason from rhetoric, as we see clearly in very different accounts that have been given of events in the Lalgarh region of West Bengal in 2009, where some hold that there was a spontaneous rising of local tribal people against repressive police actions, and others that the rising only took place because of the organizational work that had been done over many years by Maoist cadres, and where some see a brave experiment in forging an alternative path of development and others only a Maoist 'reign of terror'.[7]

In what follows I have tried to weigh alternative accounts, relying on the few ethnographic studies that exist, by Bela Bhatia and George Kunnath, who have both worked in central Bihar, by Jason Miklian from Chhattisgarh, and by Alpa Shah from Jharkhand,[8] taking note of differences relating to the time at which their research was carried out, as well as of place; on reports and articles reflecting widely differing opinions that have appeared in the pages of India's remarkable *Economic and Political Weekly*—some of them based on reports of enquiries undertaken by civil liberties and other citizens' groups—and in the quality news magazines *Frontline* and *Outlook*, as well in the *Hindu*, which I consider to be India's premier newspaper of record. Invaluable material is also available on a number of websites.[9]

THE HISTORICAL BACKGROUND TO THE PRESENT RISE OF INDIAN MAOISM

Maoism in India is not a new phenomenon, and it is recognized that its roots are in what was known as the Naxalite movement, itself born of ideological struggles in the Indian communist movement that culminated in splits in the once united CPI in the 1960s.[10] Those Marxist intellectuals who led a peasant uprising against landlords in the area of Naxalbari in northern West Bengal in 1967 argued against participation in parliamentary democracy and against mass organization, in favour of armed struggle. They sought to follow the example of the Chinese communists, led by Mao Zedong, in 'liberating' rural areas and then encircling and taking the towns. Their actions sometimes degenerated into indiscriminate violence following from the injunction of Charu Mazumdar, who had emerged as the movement's leader, to undertake 'annihilation of class enemies'. Mazumdar once wrote that the battle cry of the movement should be: 'He who has not dipped his hand in the blood of class enemies can hardly be called a communist.'[11]

Perhaps because it rejected mass organization, the Naxalite movement, though it spread quickly well beyond Naxalbari into parts of Bihar, Orissa, Andhra Pradesh and elsewhere, was very nearly crushed by the Indian state, quite rapidly, even before the death of Mazumdar in police custody in 1972. Some of the present Maoist leaders are survivors from those early days, however, and they went underground to keep their struggle alive. They and their followers were divided by varying commitments to parliamentary politics, to mass organization and to armed guerilla struggle, and the movement, never entirely unified, fragmented further. Bela Bhatia presents a complicated genealogy of groups in central Bihar in the mid-1990s when there were as many as 17 different entities, often as much at war with each other as with the state.[12] These internal struggles over varying ideas about the correct revolutionary line sometimes led to contradictory alliances, such as those described by Shashi Bhushan Singh, who found in parts of Bihar that

> the Maoist Communist Centre supported [upper caste] rajputs and opposed [low caste, "untouchable"] dalits initially in order to gain supremacy *vis-à-vis* the MKSS [the peasant organization of another group called Party Unity], and later for survival *vis-à-vis* the police and Ranvir Sena [a vigilante army formed by high caste landlords]. An organization formed to support the dalits ended up by supporting the dominant castes.[13]

It is clear from this and many other accounts that Naxalism has always been influenced and sometimes riven by caste-related tensions.

For all such conflict, and confusing alliances, the Naxalites did have some success in central Bihar, according to Bhatia and to Kunnath, in building a mass base mainly amongst Dalits and other low castes, who were mostly agricultural labourers. Bhatia describes mobilizations by Dalits against upper-caste Bhumihar landowners in the Bhojpur region, Kunnath the struggles between Maoist-led landless Dalits and middle-caste Kurmi landholders in another village in central Bihar. In both cases the accounts given show that the feudal power of the landowners has been undermined, though at a high cost in terms of human life—especially when, in this region, the Naxalites began to be opposed in the 1990s by vigilante gangs (like the Bhumihars' Ranvir Sena), set up by the landowners. Some limited gains were realized for the least privileged: land rights for some, raised wages in the areas of struggle, and perhaps above all the inspiration for poor people to assert themselves as human beings and to claim their social and political rights. Honour or self-respect (*izzat*) appears to have been for many their most important achievement through their participation in mass mobilizations.

Later, however, as Kunnath shows from his life-history of a landless Dalit friend whom he calls Rajubhai, the Naxalites' armed squads (*dastas*) increasingly included middle-class and middle-caste members, as they sought to build a wider cross-class movement in their pursuit of the goal of securing state power. Rajubhai told him that:

> When the Sanghathan [the term he used to describe the combination of the Naxalites' mass movement and their guerilla squads] came here, it began among the *mazdoor varg* [working class]. The cadres used to sleep and eat in the mud houses of the *mazdoor*. It fought for the issues of the working classes: land and wages, as well as against social abuses, exploitation and sexual abuse of women. But now that the Sanghathan has got a foothold here, its ambition has grown into one of capturing state power. So they have started taking in people from dominant castes, against whom we fought previously. As a result of the entry of the landowning castes into the Sanghathan, it is hesitant to raise the issues of land and wages. For the last twenty years, wages have remained the same: three kilos of paddy for a day's work. The working class is no longer a priority for the Sanghathan.[14]

Rajubhai's disaffection from the Sanghathan was completed by the fact that landless Dalits in the *dastas,* though they are the ones who had died or suffered physically the most, actually received less compensation in these cases than the middle-caste members. This seems a shocking denial of the moral claims of the movement.

K. Balagopal tells a comparable story from Andhra Pradesh.[15] In the 1970s the Naxalites there fought fairly successfully, in spite of police actions, against landlordism (including the practice of *begar*, or bonded labour), and then encouraged tribals to cut down reserve forests for cultivation ('far and away the most successful land struggle of the Naxalites', he says[16]), until later, in the changed circumstances of the mid-1990s imposing 'quite a successful ban on the cutting of forests'. He argues that

> the main reason for the wide popularity of the Naxalites in the entire forest region abutting the Godaveri river in Telengana, Vidharba and Chattisgarh [*sic*], is the protection they gave to the forest dwellers for cultivation in reserve forests, the substantial increase they achieved in the payment for picking tendu leaf [used in making the country cigarettes of India], and the end they put to the oppressive domination of the headmen and patwaris [village accountants].[17]

In the early period, in the northern Telengana region of Andhra Pradesh, Balagopal says, the Naxalites spread mainly through mass organizations (of agricultural labourers, students and youth). Thereafter, however, in this region and elsewhere in the state, heavy repression on the part of government forces brought an increased reliance on armed squads. This meant that 'the immediate economic and social problems of the masses took a back seat and the battle for supremacy with the state became the central instance of struggle . . . (requiring) . . . a range of acts of violence, which have no direct relation to the immediate realization of any rights for the masses, though the resulting repression invariably hits at the masses.'[18] Unsurprisingly, this has led to questioning amongst people as to whether they haven't been made into 'guinea pigs of revolution'. New generations, though they may have benefited from the earlier actions of the Maoists, are less sympathetic to them than were people of their parents' generation, while at the same time the tactics employed by the state in Andhra, including the creation of special police forces—the 'Greyhounds'—that live and operate like the Naxalites' own squads and are 'bound by no known law, including the Constitution of India', have led to serious weakening of the revolutionaries in this state.[19] 'Today, the state stands as the best example of the success of counter-revolutionary strategies of a government.'[20] The movement in Andhra Pradesh has, however, supplied leaders very widely: as to Bastar in neighbouring Chhattisgarh,[21] and nationally. Kishenji, for example, a politburo member, killed in 2011, was from Karimnagar,[22] and Azad, who was killed in 2010, came from Warangal, also in Andhra Pradesh.[23]

These accounts, from what Sumanta Banerjee thinks of as the second phase in the history of the movement,[24] after the early period and before the formation of a united party in 2004, clearly reveal contradictions that persist to the present. Tilak Gupta thinks that Naxalism/Maoism has a large mass following because 'no other political party in the country has taken up the cause of the rural poor with such single-minded zeal and devotion'.[25] His argument may be justified, but, as Gupta himself seems to recognize elsewhere in his article, the Maoists have then undone their commitment to the cause of the rural poor by giving priority to an armed struggle to overthrow the state,[26] reflecting their ideological commitments as well as their response to state repression (to which Balagopal refers, see above). This has lent credence to the accusations of those such as Aditya Nigam, who argue that the movement has been intellectually driven from the very beginning, led by middle-class ideologues who take it upon themselves to lead 'the people', and who claim 'correct knowledge' for themselves, arguing implicitly that

> [t]he *adivasis* [the 'tribal' people of India, who are generally the least privileged people of all in Indian society] cannot represent themselves; they must be represented. . . . They must be represented either by agents of the state . . . or by the revolutionaries . . . (and) . . . the voice of the revolutionary is almost always that of a Brahman/upper caste Ganapathy or Koteswara Rao or their intellectual spokespersons. So we have a Maoist-aligned intelligentsia vicariously playing out their revolutionary fantasies through the lives of *adivasis,* while the people actually dying in battle are almost all *adivasis.*[27]

It may actually be true, as the close observers of Maoism/Naxalism in central Bihar suggest, yet somewhat contrary to Nigam's point of view, that revolutionary violence can appeal to those who have been subjected to violence by their social superiors over generations. But Bela Bhatia particularly, amongst these scholars, is deeply concerned about the way in which violence corrupts the movement.[28] Her conclusion is worth quoting in full:

> The Naxalite movement will thrive only to the extent that its vision resonates with the people. The wider the gap between the two, the higher the chances

the movement will fizzle out. The present formula is a mélange of convenience between the leaders who dream of Maoist revolution and people who aspire for practical change. In order to bring about a genuine people's movement, the Naxalite leaders have to be ready to walk at the pace of the people and let their concerns guide the vision of the movement.[29]

The story of the movement in Andhra Pradesh according to Balagopal, as recounted earlier, is salutary. There, as he argues, the gap between the visions of leadership and masses has ended up seriously weakening the movement.

THE CURRENT PHASE OF INDIAN MAOISM

Banerjee argues that the movement is now in its third phase, following the agreement of leaders and cadres of scattered and divided groups to the creation of the single revolutionary party, the CPI (Maoist) in 2004, after several years of dialogue, and commitments not to take up arms again against 'class friends'.[30] According to some reports the final merger was partly facilitated by the Nepali leader Prachanda, and the Indian Maoists and their Nepali comrades, with other parties from across the region, as members of the Coordination Committee of Maoist Parties and Organisations of South Asia. Fusion was partly prompted, however, by the actions of the government of the new Jharkhand state against Naxalites, beginning in 2000. The merger, which also led to the formation of the People's Liberation Guerilla Army, has brought about a significant regeneration of the movement, and provided a large swathe of the country within which the Maoists are able to move without the problems of coordination that afflict the state police forces. They are able to think now of liberating a Compact Revolutionary Zone over much of what has been labelled the red corridor: a continuous stretch of territory under their influence and control. And as I noted at the beginning of this essay, both the scale and the frequency of incidents in which the Maoists have confronted the security forces have sharply increased.

The CPI (Maoist) has reaffirmed the programmatic line of the Naxalites of 1970, committing to a 'people's war' (referring back to Mao) for seizure of power, and the establishment of a people's democratic state. The proposed programme of the party, however, once the new people's democratic state is established, is one with which 'a large chunk of the Indian political class should have nothing to quarrel about'.[31] The party proposes to redistribute land to poor peasants and landless labourers according to the slogan 'land to the tillers'; to ensure the land rights of women; to ensure that facilities for agricultural development are available; to regulate working conditions and to ensure that wages are adequate and equal between the sexes; to guarantee the right to work and 'improved living conditions for the people'; and 'to take special measures to proceed towards the elimination of regional inequalities'. Much of this also appears in the Common Minimum Programme, which the United Progressive Alliance, headed by the Congress party, set out, also in 2004, while the major established party of the left, the Communist Party of India (Marxist) [CPI(M)], remains committed to the abolition of landlordism and to radical land reforms. Contrary to what is suggested by some commentators, the CPI (Maoist) does have a coherent programme. The party now also states that it will wage struggles against the Government of India's plans to set up Special Economic Zones, and against the displacement of tribals and forest dwellers by mining and other projects.[32] I was informed in March 2010 by a noted human rights activist who has been involved in negotiations with them, that the Maoists are now prioritizing mobilization, especially of tribals, against mining and other projects involving big displacements of people. Their prime objective, he thinks, has become that of mobilization against imperialism as reflected in India's economic liberalization, and the effects of globalization, rather than anti-feudal struggles against landlordism. Their leaders probably do recognize—in spite of the language of the Party Programme, which continues to emphasize the concept—that 'landlordism' is now less significant, given the development of capitalist relations of production in agriculture across much of the country.

This likely shift in strategic emphasis, and the Maoists' focus on military and other activity in the forested areas of central India, marks the distinct difference between this phase of their struggle and that of the late 1960s and early 1970s, when they were crushed relatively easily. Though the CPI (Maoist) has reaffirmed a commitment to 'protracted armed struggle', the Maoists are now much more deeply embedded than before, in local society. Both the state and the Maoists themselves have reasons to exaggerate their strength, of course—the former because it justifies the use of force, and the latter because it projects an impression of power, and so builds an atmosphere of fear through which they really can exercise power[33]—but ethnographic accounts like that of Alpa Shah show the extent to which Maoists are part of the fabric of society.[34] In these circumstances repression alone is unlikely to work, in the way that it did before, as some of India's senior political leaders—notably the former Congress chief minister of Madhya Pradesh, Digvijay Singh—have argued forcefully, against the emphasis placed on conventional security measures by the home minister, P. Chidambaram.[35]

THE MAOISTS AND SOCIETY

As may be seen from my brief references earlier to the work of Bhatia and Kunnath in Bihar, as well as to Balagopal's observations from Andhra, the few ethnographic studies show that the Maoists do win support amongst, and articulate the needs and aspirations of poor and landless peasants and of *adivasis*. These authors point out that there is a perception amongst poorer people that the Maoists are 'good people' who are opposed to their oppressors and who support them in a struggle for their basic rights. According to Bhatia, however, people understand the objective of the movement as being change, not revolution, and they support it because they feel that the Maoists share their sense of injustice, rather than for any ideological reasons. The appeal of class struggle is as a means of securing needs: for higher wages, land redistribution and freedom from harassment. Bhatia notes that people petition the Maoists for exactly the same things for which they may also petition government.[36]

And it would be facile to accept the argument that this is a popular movement of lower-caste and lower-class rural people. That idea is firmly quashed by Alpa Shah's ethnography from a region of Jharkhand, showing how the Maoists entered the area through the rural middle class, of upper-caste elites and educated well-to-do *adivasis*.[37] Studies also show up the tensions and contradictions in the tactics and actions of the movement. The relationship between the mainly educated middle-class and higher-caste leadership of the CPI (Maoist), and the young *adivasi* men and women (some of them very young) who are so vividly portrayed by Arundhati Roy,[38] or in Kunnath's account of the career of his Dalit friend Rajubhai[39] may well be fraught with tensions, and there certainly are contradictions, as we have seen, between the immediate tactics of changing rural power relations, which answers to the problems that their supporters confront, and on the other hand, the Maoists' military strategy.

It seems from the ethnographies that, unsurprisingly, the extent to which the leadership has been able to develop a revolutionary consciousness amongst the poor peasantry is very limited. Kunnath's research,[40] in particular, shows how support amongst Dalits for the Maoists in central Bihar weakened considerably, as the latter have sought to bring in men from the middle and upper castes in pursuit of the goal of capturing state power. The tendency on the part of the leadership to romanticize the revolutionary character of the peasantry is sometimes a problem, and it is clear that, such as this consciousness is, it is weakened when government provides adequately for the most immediate needs of the people.

The other big source of tension is between mass mobilization and the necessarily secretive, armed power of the underground movement, which is not inherently democratic at all. This relates in turn to the contradiction between the moral basis of the Maoist movement and the violence that it perpetrates, which undermines that moral base and alienates supporters (as has happened, according to Balagopal's account, summarized earlier, in Andhra Pradesh). The understandable sense of their persecution amongst Maoist cadres, confronted by the violence of the state, may lead to the indiscriminate use of force and their alienation from the people they claim to fight for, mirroring exactly the same people's alienation from the state because of the actions of police forces that, according to Human Rights Watch, 'have largely failed to evolve from the ruler-supportive, repressive forces they were designed to be under Britain's colonial rule', habitually using abuse and threats as a primary means of crime investigation and of law enforcement.[41] Maoists themselves are extremely sensitive, it seems from interviews with their leaders and with individual cadres, about accusations that they are engaged in unconstrained violence. Gautam Navlakha is one who questioned the Maoists he travelled amongst in Bastar about this:

> They said that they did not kill everyone who was considered an enemy and the party stopped its members from killing informers. It was only when they did not mend their ways despite repeated warnings that such persons were killed . . . (and). . . . They insisted that the party acted rather firmly against those responsible for acts of indiscipline or reckless violence.[42]

But it is clear, too—and also unsurprising—that there is but a thin line between the revolutionary and the criminal thug. One of the early leaders in central Bihar (one of a pair referred to colloquially as 'Marx and Engels') was a dacoit, who had served a long prison sentence for the murder of a police constable.[43]

With the partial exception of the work of Jason Miklian,[44] there are no ethnographic studies of the movement in the Bastar region of Chhattisgarh. However, Nandini Sundar, who has carried on substantial ethnographic research in the region—if not in the Maoist-dominated areas, as she says—has written on it, drawing on interviews conducted as part of a Citizens' Initiative visit there in May 2006. Sundar records that the Maoists 'claim to include 60 lakh people in the "organizational sweep" of their Dandakaranya "guerilla zone," where they have established mass organizations, colloquially called sanghams. The Maoists claim, too, to have carried on a great deal of development work, including the setting up of 135 peoples' clinics, educational facilities and a large number of minor irrigation works.'[45] Sundar points out that while these efforts—assuming that the Maoists' claims are accurate—are not equivalent to what the government might have achieved, they do show much greater commitment to people's development. They are said to have taken up women's issues,[46] and have consciously promoted Gondi language and literature. These positive efforts, however, are compromised by other Maoist activities, when they have 'resisted even genuine government initiatives'. For example, '[w]hile recognizing that traders cheat *adivasis* over minor forest produce, [the Maoists] have defended them against government attempts to introduce cooperatives to buy tamarind and tendu'.[47] Miklian, too, comments that most villagers 'are upset at Naxal opposition to government programmes and efforts to block participatory elections'.[48] But more significant than this has been the 'brute force' that has accompanied their work. Sundar argues that '[t]heir supporters need to debate whether armed struggle was necessary to their positive work, and whether peaceful mass mobilization would not work better. Certainly, the attempt to defend their guerilla zone seems now to have overtaken people's needs'.[49] Her conclusion, then, is exactly the same as Bhatia's from Bihar, or Balagopal's from Andhra, though both were writing about events happening a decade earlier.

MAOISTS AND LOCAL STRUGGLES OVER LIBERALIZATION AND GLOBALIZATION

I commented earlier on the indications of the shift in the Maoists' strategic focus to struggles over the displacement of people for mining and infrastructure projects, for the establishment of Special Economic Zones, or over the alienation of forest land for commercial projects or sometimes for wildlife conservation. Estimates of the numbers of those displaced over the history of independent India range from 20 million to as many as 60 million people.[50] They are certainly very substantial, and it is acknowledged by government as well as by independent observers that those who have been affected by displacement have only very rarely been adequately compensated or rehabilitated. The failure of the state in this regard became notorious in the case of the massive Narmada irrigation and power project in western India.[51]

The people who are now being most affected by displacement are members of the Scheduled Tribes: those people from what were thought of as backward, tribal areas who were 'scheduled' for particular protection under the Constitution of India. People of these tribes live in the forested hilly tracts of eastern and central India, in exactly the sort of terrain that is thought by Collier and Hoeffler, and by Fearon and Laitin to favour insurgency.[52] These *adivasis* (as they are also described) include many different tribes but they have in common a way of life bound up with the forest. They have suffered historically, first in the colonial period and then after India's Independence from repressive forestry policies, which have only very recently undergone reform so as to protect tribal peoples' rights.[53] They have in common, as well, their exceptional disadvantage by comparison with all other social groups in India in regard to all the key indicators of social welfare.[54] Displacement now especially affects such tribal people in the forested areas of Orissa, Jharkhand and Chhattisgarh, where there is, in the words of one observer, a kind of latter-day gold rush going on, in the context of the liberalization of the Indian economy and the opening up to private and international companies, to secure valuable resources of bauxite, iron ore and other minerals.[55] There are local movements at a number of the sites affected by these projects, opposing displacement and loss of entitlements to land and other natural resources, including at Kalinganagar in Orissa, where they are fighting the construction of a steel plant by the Tata company, opposition to the projects of the South Korean steel company POSCO around Paradeep, and campaigning against the activities of the Vedanta mining company.[56] The latter have led to the projects in question being stopped.[57]

Many, perhaps most of these movements of organized resistance to what may be described as 'the new enclosures'—movements such as Visthapan Virodhi Janmanch at Kalinganagar, or the Bastar

Sambhag Kisan Sangharsh Samiti (BSKSS) in Chhattisgarh that opposes displacement to make way for the construction of the Bodh Ghat Dam, and the privatization of mines and river water resources[58]—are branded by the authorities and a pliant media as Naxalite or Maoist. Independent evidence suggests that it is most unlikely that they really are, but equally that there is a recognition on the part of those involved that the Maoists are on their side. There is not always, or necessarily, the kind of disconnect between the Maoists and people that writers such as Aditya Nigam (reported above) think exists.

At the same time it is equally important to recognize that poor peasants, Dalits and tribal people are not inherently or naturally revolutionaries, but rather possessed of practical common sense (just as Ben Kiernan argues of the Cambodian peasantry in the period of the Khmer Rouge[59]). Bela Bhatia makes these points very strongly from her ethnographic researches in central Bihar in the 1990s. As I explained earlier, she refers to the perception amongst poorer people that Naxalites were 'good people' (exactly as was observed at the rally of the BSKSS in Bastar in 2009), but they supported the movement because they felt that the Naxalites shared their sense of injustice, rather than for any ideological reasons.[60] Smita Gupta reports in a somewhat similar vein from a visit to Bastar in the early months of 2010, though her point is that the *adivasis* there are caught between government and Maoists. The Maoists score over the government in just one respect: they are regarded as being more trustworthy and as providing some sort of justice in an area where the government has been seen as an oppressor.[61] There are, as a result, good reasons for thinking that the many movements of resistance to the new enclosure movement generally aren't Maoist, though they welcome support from the Maoists, and, up to a point, but only up to a point, support them in turn.[62]

GREED?

The fact that so much Maoist activity is now taking place in a part of India that is rich in natural resources gives rise to a further question: Isn't it possible that the insurgency is driven by what has been labelled in the wider literature as 'greed', or the quest for loot? This has been argued forcefully by Miklian and Carney, who suggest that there is a perfect correspondence geographically between those areas in which the Maoists are active and India's mining areas. They refer to interviews with mine owners who say that the only way to stop Maoist attacks is to negotiate and to hand over some share of their revenues—though they also refer to cases in which mining companies have used 'the fog of war' as a pretext for land grabs. 'The mines,' write Miklian and Carney, 'are cash registers for the Maoist war chest. Through extortion, covert attacks and plain old theft, insurgents have tapped a steady stream of mining money to pay their foot soldiers and buy arms and ammunition, sometimes from treasonous cops themselves.'[63] The Maoists, they believe, are less an organized movement 'than a loose confederation of militias, and many of their local commanders appear to be in it for money alone'.

The case may be overstated—and certainly there are major tracts in which the Maoists are strongly entrenched where there are no mines—but there is no doubt whatsoever about the fact that the Maoists are engaged in all manner of protection rackets. They have benefited in some ways from the spectacular maladministration of the new states of Jharkhand and Chhattisgarh in particular, and from political corruption. In Jharkhand, we know from work by the anthropologist Alpa Shah how at an earlier stage the MCC and the local state functioned *in tandem*, and had a kind of symbiotic relationship with each other, both materially and symbolically.[64] In the region that Shah studied the MCC spread in the first place not by mobilizing poor tribal peasants but rather amongst the rural elite, including non-tribal people from intermediate castes, by supplying protection and facilitating their acquisition of lucrative contracts for local government projects. This is an important reminder that we must not assume that there is a simple or an unmediated connection between the grievances of poor rural people and their mobilization against the state, and also that insurgent movements, like the state, require resources, and may obtain them from supplying protection in exchange for taxation, just like the state. Alpa Shah asked Gopalji, the spokesperson from Jharkhand whom she interviewed, 'It is widely reported that you finance yourself through the black economy of development schemes coming in through the state. How do you justify participation in the very systems of corruption that you oppose?' Gopalji answered: 'This is not corruption. This is taxation. . . . We are not simply collecting money for private gain.' Resources raised from the supply of protection are used, Gopalji claimed, 'for the service of the toiling masses'.[65]

CONCLUSION

The tropes of greed and of grievance are blunt instruments for capturing the complexities of the Maoists' mobilizations. Predation undoubtedly does take place, in the ways just described, and in others, such as the income/taxation that the Maoists derive from the trade in *tendu* leaves in northern Telangana.[66] And no doubt there are, as Miklian and Carney suggest, local commanders who are 'in it for money alone', but it is equally a gross generalization to say, as these authors also do, that 'Maoists have become a business as much as anything else'.[67] It is surely more sensible to conclude, as both Collier and Hoeffler, and Fearon and Laitin have done, from their large-*n* statistical analyses, that the availability of loot contributes to the feasibility of insurgency, rather than accounting for it.[68] The feasibility thesis to which these scholars now subscribe (though they propound rather different versions of it) holds that the existence of valuable natural resources that insurgents can control makes rebellion financially feasible. The presence in a population of large numbers of young men (between the ages of 15 and 29) is a further significant factor, and it is clear from accounts such as that of Arundhati Roy that this is the case with the Maoist insurgency, though here young women are very significantly involved as well.[69] The feasibility thesis also holds that insurgency is favoured by rough and mountainous terrain, as is the case here. Fearon and Laitin, however, in their version of the thesis, argue that insurgency is favoured especially by state weakness. Weak government, they posit, renders insurgency more feasible and more attractive, due to weak local policing or inept and corrupt counter-insurgency practices which 'often include a propensity for brutal and indiscriminate retaliation that helps drive non-combatant locals into rebel forces'.[70] All the accounts that are referred to in this essay bear out this general argument. The governments of Jharkhand and Chhattisgarh are especially weak and notably corrupt, while the ineptness of policing in general and the pervasiveness of police brutality are reported by Human Rights Watch.[71]

To show, however, that conditions are there to make insurgency feasible—as I think most clearly is the case in the parts of India where the Maoists are well organized—still does not explain why and when it occurs. From the more detailed reports considered here, the conclusion is inescapable: the Maoists have tapped into and to some extent, at least, have articulated the long-standing grievances of Dalits and landless peasants, as for example in central Bihar, against higher-caste landowners, and the grievances of tribal peoples, especially against the state, both for what it has done, such as bringing about or tolerating displacement, and sanctioning repressive policing, and for what it has not done, such as failing in the provision of basic services. The current conjuncture, and the impact of economic liberalization, especially in tribal areas of central and eastern India, has enhanced these tensions. The trope of grievance is not irrelevant or misapplied in this case, as indeed the Planning Commission of the Government of India has recognized in its analysis (see note 2). The accounts given by Bhatia and Kunnath or by Balagopal also recall Ranajit Guha's celebrated thesis, *Elementary Aspects of Peasant Insurgency*, in which he argued that 'the general form of insurgency . . . had its roots in the relationship of dominance and subordination characteristic of Indian society for a very long period', and against which there was always posed 'the counter tradition of defiance and revolt'.[72] Such defiance and revolt against dominance and subordination are shown in the Maoist insurgency, which is now deeply imbricated in the fabric of society in large parts of central and eastern India and will not easily be crushed, as the Naxalite movement seems to have been in the late 1960s and early 1970s.

Equally the insurgency is not to be explained as being simply a popular movement from below and there are irreducible tensions and contradictions, as sensitive and informed observers like Balagopal, Bhatia and Sundar so clearly show, between the responses of the Maoists' movement to the needs and aspirations of some of the poorest people in India, on the one hand, and their continuing commitment to armed struggle to overthrow the Indian state on the other. The tragedy is that though this armed struggle responds to the structural violence to which Dalits and *adivasis* and others have long been subject it leads to a spiral of suspicion, violence and retaliation in which these same people are most often the victims.

NOTES

1. See, for example, *The Hindu*, 12 October 2009.
2. See the report of the expert group set up by the Planning Commission, entitled 'Development Challenges in Extremist Affected Areas' (published in March 2008), discussed by Sumanta Banerjee, 'On the Naxalite Movement: A Report with a Difference', *Economic and Political Weekly*, 43, no. 21 (24 May 2008), 10-12; and in Editorial, 'Beyond the Security-Centric Approach', *Economic and Political Weekly*, 44, no. 8 (21 February 2009), 6.

3. These views are expressed by Dilip Simeon, 'Permanent Spring' and by Aditya Nigam, 'The Rumour of Maoism', both in the monthly *Seminar*, #607 March 2010 (last accessed at www.india-seminar.com on 8 December 2010).
4. Perhaps the most important contributions to this general literature have been those made by Paul Collier and Anke Hoeffler. See, for example, 'Beyond Greed and Grievance: Feasibility and Civil War', *Oxford Economic Papers*, 61, no. 1 (2009): 1-27 (with Dominic Rohner); and James Fearon and David Laitin, 'Ethnicity, Insurgency and Civil War', *American Political Science Review*, 97, no. 1 (2003): 75-90.
5. From the Kafila website, http://kafila.org. Cited by Alpa Shah, in 'India Burning: The Maoist Revolution', in Isabelle Clarke-Deces (ed.), *The Blackwell Companion to the Anthropology of India* (Oxford and Malden, MA: Blackwell, forthcoming).
6. The argument seems entirely reasonable in the light of the information given by Jason Miklian, 'The Purification Hunt: The Salwa Judum Counter-insurgency in Chattisgarh, India', *Dialectical Anthropology*, 33, nos. 3-4 (December 2009): 441-59. Miklian reports on how 'Media freedoms have suffered at the individual and institutional levels' (454).
7. For these different views see Sumit Sarkar and Tanika Sarkar, 'Notes on a Dying People', *Economic and Political Weekly*, 44, nos. 26 and 27 (27 June 2009): 10-14; Manik Bora and Budhadiya Das, 'The Movement in Lalgarh', *Economic and Political Weekly*, 44, nos. 26 and 27 (27 June 2009): 15-17; and Amit Bhattacharyya, 'Is Lalgarh Showing the Way?', *Economic and Political Weekly*, 45, no. 2 (9 January 2010): 17-21. See also Nigam, 'The Rumour of Maoism'. On rhetoric and reason see Sudhanva Deshpande's commentary on the report from the Bastar region of central India by the noted activist and writer, Arundhati Roy. Roy's long article appeared in the news magazine *Outlook*, 29 March 2010, Deshpande's critique in the same magazine, 12 April 2010.
8. Bela Bhatia, 'The Naxalite Movement in Central Bihar', *Economic and Political Weekly*, 40, no. 15 (2005): 1536-43; George Kunnath, 'Becoming a Naxalite in Rural Bihar: Class Struggle and its Contradictions', *Journal of Peasant Studies*, 33, no. 1 (2006): 89-123; George Kunnath, 'Smouldering Dalit Fires in Bihar, India', *Dialectical Anthropology*, 33, nos. 3-4 (2009): 309-25; Jason Miklian, 'The Purification Hunt', 2009; Alpa Shah, 'Markets of Protection: The "Terrorist" Maoist Movement and the State in Jharkhand, India', in *Critique of Anthropology*, 26, no. 3 (2006): 297-314; Alpa Shah, 'In Search of Certainty in Revolutionary India', *Dialectical Anthropology*, 33, nos. 3 and 4 (2009): 271-86; and Alpa Shah, *In the Shadows of the State: Indigenous Politics, Environmentalism and Insurgency in Jharkhand, India* (Durham and London: Duke University Press, 2010).
9. See notably the South Asia Terrorist Portal, at www.satp.org; and http://

sanhati.com/, which carries much information including interviews with Maoist leaders (the most recent at the time of writing being with Ganapathy, the general secretary of the CPI (Maoist), on 9 November 2010).

10. This history is recounted by several authors but the best account is that of Sumanta Banerjee, *In the Wake of Naxalbari: A History of the Naxalite Movement in India* (Calcutta: Subarnrekha, 1980). See this book, Chapter 3, pp. 47-68.
11. Cited by Simeon, 'Permanent Spring'.
12. Bhatia, 'The Naxalite Movement'.
13. Shashi Bhushan Singh, 'Limits to Power: Naxalism and Caste Relations in a South Bihar Village', *Economic and Political Weekly*, 40, no. 29 (16 July 2005): 3167-75; 3173.
14. Kunnath, 'Becoming a Naxalite', p. 110.
15. K. Balagopal, 'Maoist Movement in Andhra Pradesh', *Economic and Political Weekly*, 41, no. 29 (22 July 2006): 3183-7.
16. Balagopal, 'Maoist Movement', p. 3184.
17. K. Balagopal, 'Chhattisgarh: Physiognomy of Violence', *Economic and Political Weekly* 41, no. 22 (3 June 2006): 2183-6.
18. Balagopal, 'Maoist Movement', p. 3185.
19. This account is substantially confirmed in a *Frontline* report (vol. 26, no. 22, 6 November 2009) which says, with regard to the first 10 years or so, 'On the whole, a generation reaped the benefits of the Maoist movement', but that thereafter the movement rather fell apart, as a result of the determination of police and politicians to change the conditions in which it had thrived: 'It is this change in the conditions on the battleground and to some extent the change in the social climate [in the aftermath of India's economic reforms] that contributed to the downfall of the naxalite movement in Andhra Pradesh, and not just the military capability of the elite commando force—Greyhounds.' This report, too, comments on the changed perceptions of the Naxalites over generations.
20. *Frontline* report, vol. 26, no. 22, 6 November 2009.
21. See Arundhati Roy's account of her travels with the Maoists in Bastar, *Outlook*, 29 March 2010.
22. See the report of an interview with Koteswar Rao, alias 'Kishenji', in *Frontline*, vol. 26, no. 22, 6 November 2009.
23. From 'Ganapathy on the Current Situation of the Revolutionary Movement and Contemporary Issues: An Interview', at http://sanhati.com/ (last accessed 8 December 2010).
24. Banerjee, 'Reflections of a One-time Maoist Activist'.
25. Tilak D. Gupta, 'Maoist Movement in Andhra Pradesh: Ideology, Programme and Armed Struggle', *Economic and Political Weekly*, 41, no. 29 (22 July 2006): 3172-6, quote from p. 3174.
26. This is argued forcibly by Nirmalangshu Mukherji, 'Arms Over the

People: What Have the Maoists Achieved in Dandakaranya', *Economic and Political Weekly*, 45, no. 25 (19 June 2010): 16-20.

27. Nigam, 'The Rumour of Maoism'.
28. Bela Bhatia, 'On Armed Resistance', *Economic and Political Weekly*, 41, no. 29 (July 22, 2006): 3179-83. Bhatia writes, 'the use of violence has taken a heavy toll. The downside of violence has been so wide-ranging that it may well end up negating what the Naxalites stand for', p. 3182.
29. Bela Bhatia, 'The Naxalite Movement in Central Bihar', p. 1547.
30. Banerjeee, 'Reflections of a One-time Maoist Activist'. The negotiations between the main parties are described in an article about the CPI (Maoist) on the South Asia Terrorist Portal (www.satp.org).
31. Gupta, 'Maoist Movement in Andhra Pradesh', p. 3172.
32. See Ganapathy, 'Interview with Ganapathy, General Secretary, CPI (Maoist)', released in April 2007, accessible at www.satp.org.
33. Smita Gupta, 'Searching for a Third Way in Dantewada', *Economic and Political Weekly*, 45, no. 16 (17 April 2010): 12-14.
34. Alpa Shah, 'Markets of Protection', and 'In Search of Certainty in Revolutionary India'.
35. Venkitesh Ramakishnan, 'Flawed Opposition', *Frontline* 27, no. 9 (7 May 2010).
36. Bhatia, 'The Naxalite Movement in Central Bihar'.
37. Alpa Shah, 'Markets of Protection', and 'In Search of Certainty in Revolutionary India'.
38. Roy, *Outlook*, 29 March 2010.
39. Kunnath, 'Smouldering Dalit Fires in Bihar, India'.
40. Kunnath, 'Becoming a Naxalite in Rural Bihar: Class Struggle and its Contradictions'.
41. See Human Rights Watch, *Broken System: Dysfunction, Abuse and Impunity in the Indian Police* (New York: Human Rights Watch, 2009).
42. Gautam Navlakha, 'Days and Nights in the Maoist Heartland', *Economic and Political Weekly*, 45, no. 16 (17 April 2010): 38-47, 39-40. See also Alpa Shah, 'Annihilation is the Last Choice', *Economic and Political Weekly*, 45, no. 19 (8 May 2010): 24-9.
43. Balagopal, 'Maoist Movement in Andhra Pradesh', says with regard to Andhra Pradesh, 'strategies of militancy attract unruly types who straddle the border between rebellion and mere rowdy-ism', (3186).
44. Miklian, 'The Purification Hunt'.
45. Nandini Sundar, 'Bastar, Maoism and Salwa Judum', *Economic and Political Weekly*, 41, no. 29 (3 February 2006): 3187-92. Arundhati Roy, *Outlook*, 29 March 2010, also gives some account of the developmental work undertaken by the Maoists.
46. Arundhati Roy, *Outlook*, 29 March 2010, describes activities of the KAMS.
47. Sundar, 'Bastar, Maoism and Salwa Judum', p. 3190.

48. Miklian, 'The Purification Hunt', p. 454.
49. Sundar, 'Bastar, Maoism and Salwa Judum', 3191. And see Mukherji, 'Arms Over the People'.
50. See Judy Whitehead, 'Place, Space and Primitive Accumulation in Narmada Valley and Beyond', *Economic and Political Weekly*, 38, no. 40 (4 October 2003): 4224-6 for the lower estimates; and Walter Fernandes, 'Background Note' to Petition Against Operation Green Hunt, at www.sanhati.org (last accessed 11 June 2010), for the higher one.
51. There is a large literature on the Narmada project and on the popular movement against it. A recent contribution is by Alf Gunvald Nilsen, *Dispossession and Resistance in India: The River and the Rage* (London & New York: Routledge, 2010).
52. Collier and Hoeffler, 'Beyond Greed and Grievance: Feasibility and Civil War'; Fearon and Laitin, 'Ethnicity, Insurgency and Civil War'.
53. On forest policy a seminal source is Ramachandra Guha, 'Forestry in British and Post-British India: A Historical Analysis', *Economic and Political Weekly*, 18, no. 44 (29 October 1983): 1882-96; and nos. 45/46 (5 November 1983): 1940-7; the *Scheduled Tribes and Other Traditional Forest Dwellers (Recognition of Forest Rights) Bill* (of December 2006, implemented from the beginning of 2008), at last vested in forest dwellers inheritable rights in land that were not alienable or transferable. On this see 'Editorial: Restoring Rights', *Economic and Political Weekly* (6 January 2007): 4-5.
54. See Ramachandra Guha, 'Adivasis, Naxalites and Indian Democracy', *Economic and Political Weekly*, 42, no. 32 (11 August 2007): 3305-12.
55. The idea of the 'gold rush' is that of Banikanta Misra, 'Agriculture, Industry and Mining in Orissa in the Post Liberalisation Era: An Inter-District and Inter-State Panel Analysis', *Economic and Political Weekly*, 45, no. 20 (15 May 2010): 49-68.
56. On Kalinganagar see 'Churning in Orissa', *Hindu*, 13 January 2006, and 'Tension in Kalinga Nagar Steel Hub', *Hindu*, 20 January 2010.
57. One as a result of the recommendations of an official panel set up by the Government of India chaired by distinguished former civil servant N.C. Saxena (*Business Line*, 25 August 2010); and the second by the High Court of Orissa (*Hindu*, 17 November 2010).
58. See Gautam Navlakha and Asish Gupta, 'The Real Divide in Bastar', *Economic and Political Weekly*, 44, no. 33 (15 August 2009): 20-3.
59. Ben Kiernan, *The Pol Pot Regime: Race, Power and Genocide under the Khmer Rouge, 1975-79* (New Haven and London: Yale University Press, 1996), pp. 210-15.
60. Bhatia, 'The Naxalite Movement'; Kunnath, 'Becoming a Naxalite in Rural Bihar' and 'Smouldering Dalit Fires in Bihar, India'; Gautam Navlakha and Asish Gupta, 'The Real Divide in Bastar'.
61. Gupta, 'Searching for a Third Way'.

62. Though it is only one report, the comment of a villager quoted by Miklian and Carney does perhaps sum it up: 'It is better to die here fighting on our own land than merely survive on someone else's. If the Maoists came here, then we would ask their help to resist'. Jason Miklian and Scott Carney, 'Fire in the Hole', *Foreign Policy*, no.181 (2010): 104-12.
63. Miklian and Carney, 'Fire in the Hole', page reference not available from electronic edition of *Foreign Policy.*
64. Shah, 'Markets of Protection' and *In the Shadows of the State*, Chapter 6.
65. Alpa Shah, 'Annihilation is the Last Choice', *Economic and Political Weekly*, 45, no. 19 (8 May 2010): 24-9.
66. See Bert Suykens, 'Diffuse Authority in the Beedi Commodity Chain: Naxalite and State Governance in Tribal Telengana, India', *Development and Change*, 41, no. 1 (2010): 153-78.
67. Miklian and Carney, 'Fire in the Hole'.
68. Collier and Hoeffler, 'Beyond Greed and Grievance: Feasibility and Civil War'; Fearon and Laitin, 'Ethnicity, Insurgency and Civil War'.
69. Arundhati Roy, 'Walking with the Comrades', *Outlook*, 29 March 2010, http://www.outlookindia.com/content5147.asp. (accessed on 3 March 2011).
70. Fearon and Laitin, 'Ethnicity, Insurgency and Civil War', p. 76.
71. Human Rights Watch, *Broken System.*
72. Ranajit Guha, *Elementary Aspects of Peasant Insurgency in Colonial India* (New Delhi: Oxford University Press, 1983), p. 335.

CHAPTER 3

Reflections of a One-time Maoist Activist*

SUMANTA BANERJEE

INTRODUCTION

The Maoist movement in India articulates the deep sense of estrangement that pervades the vast backwater of the country—the alienation of the peasantry from land; the rupture between the oppressed indigenous people and depressed castes on the one hand and the oppressive upper caste/class feudal vested interests on the other; the uprooting of the urban poor from their socio-cultural moorings. The movement can be divided into three phases—the first from 1967 to 1975; the second covering the 1980–90 period; and the present phase from the late 1990s onwards. In the course of these three periods, the Indian Maoists have been able to mobilize large sections of alienated populations in certain parts of the country, and empower them with both moral and military strength to recover their land, assert their rights and reinvent themselves as dignified human beings in their quotidian existence. At the same time, the exigencies of armed struggle against the ruthless suppression launched by the security forces of the Indian state have quite often brutalized the Maoists themselves and have led them to violate the human rights of the people inhabiting the areas under their control (e.g. killing of innocent villagers as suspected spies; extortion of money from traders; destruction of public transport). The Indian Maoists therefore represent alienation at two levels—at one level, they give voice to the alienation of the deprived poor and at another level, they themselves are tending to alienate the very people whose support they need.

*First published in *Dialectical Anthropology*, vol. 33, nos. 3-4 (2009), pp. 253-69. Reprinted with permission from Springer Science+Business Media.

Their experiment harks back to the old disturbing tussle between the moral basis of revolutionary ideology and the practical compulsions of revolutionary action that has dogged—and distorted—the communist movement in other parts of the world. How will the Indian Maoists reconcile the two in their ongoing struggle? This is a challenge that faces not only the Maoists, but also other sections of Indian society—including the middle class intelligentsia—who seek to intervene in efforts to radically transform our present deplorable socio-economic order towards an egalitarian direction that would help our people to overcome their sense of alienation and provide them with the basic facilities for individual and collective development in their everyday life.

In this essay, I reflect on my own changing involvement with Maoist movement in South Asia as an active participant, an intimate observer and then a distant onlooker. I thus offer my retrospection, reappraisal and prognosis through my personal experiences of the movement.

Like some other Bengali middle-class intellectuals, I was an active participant in the movement in its first phase (1967-75), which inaugurated perhaps one of the most significant radical changes in modern India. In the movement's second phase in the 1980-90 period, I took on the role of an intimate observer, reporting developments in the movement in my capacity as a working journalist. In the present phase—due to a number of imponderables, both physical and political—I am reduced to the role of a distant onlooker, speculating about the future of the movement, depending on secondary sources like reportage by journalists who visit the Maoist guerrilla zones, and official publications by the CPI (Maoist) which describe the changes that the Maoists have brought about in the daily life of the villagers living in their zones. In a certain sense, my narrative may reflect my personal gradual distancing from the dangers and perils that I once shared with my comrades in the movement, and which are still being faced by those who chose to stick to their guns, as well as a new generation of fighters in the hills and jungles of Jharkhand, Chhattisgarh, Orissa and Andhra Pradesh. At the political level, in the course of the narrative, while admiring their courage and sacrifice, I also seek to interrogate their present strategy and tactics. In conclusion, I touch upon some of the changes in the Indian rural scene that have taken place during the last four decades since the Naxalbari uprising, the new challenges and options that are being faced by the Maoists, and I attempt a prognosis of the course that their movement is likely to take in the future. As a historian of the Maoist movement, I may also appear to represent alienation at yet another level—talking of the future of the movement while remaining estranged from the personal experiences of the ground reality. But then, distance also helps us to dispassionately look at the past as well as the future contours of the movement.

THE CONTEXT

A brief recapitulation of the history of the Maoist movement in India is necessary to provide the historical background. The movement can be traced back to the communist-led armed peasants' struggle in Telangana in Andhra Pradesh in south India, which began from the pre-Independence era of 1946 and continued until the post-Independence period of 1951.[1] The continued exploitation and oppression of the peasantry by feudal landlords, usurious money-lenders, unscrupulous government officials and a rapacious police force after two decades of Independence sparked the first rebellion led by a group of communist revolutionaries. It took place in May 1967 in Naxalbari, on the northern tip of the state of West Bengal. Adopting the Maoist strategy of agrarian revolution and tactics of guerrilla struggle, they led an armed uprising of the peasants against the local landlords. The protest soon spread to parts of Bihar and Andhra Pradesh, and inspired popular actions in other parts of rural India. It came to be known as the Naxalite movement (led by the communist revolutionaries who formed the CPI-Marxist Leninist party in 1969).[2] The Indian state's savage suppression of the Naxalites during the late 1960-early 1970 period and the imposition of the Emergency by the Indira Gandhi-led Congress government all over India in June 1975 snuffed out all opposition activities and smothered the last embers of the Naxalite movement, bringing to an end its first phase.

The second phase followed the lifting of the Emergency in 1977 and the election of a non-Congress coalition government at the centre. This initiated a process of re-thinking among the survivors of the earlier phase of the movement and led them to spread out into two different directions—one favouring participation in parliamentary elections and trade union activities, and the other returning to the policy of resorting to the old path of armed struggle to seize power. By the end of the 1980s, several Naxalite groups following the latter course succeeded in building up a militant peasant movement with strong bases in Andhra Pradesh (in the south), Madhya Pradesh (in the centre), Maharashtra (in the west) and Bihar and Orissa (in the east). In the course of the next two decades, they extended their influence to some 160 districts in at least 10 states of India, spanning some 400,000 sq km (equivalent to one-eighth of the total Indian land mass), in effective control of a long corridor of both forests and plains, stretching from the state of Bihar bordering Nepal in the north, through Jharkhand further south and Chhattisgarh, Madhya Pradesh and Maharashtra in the west, down to Orissa in the east and Andhra Pradesh and Tamil Nadu in the south. The corridor is twice the size of the geographical region of the other two insurgency-affected areas—the five states in the north-east (Assam, Manipur, Nagaland, Meghalaya, Tripura) and Jammu & Kashmir in the north-west. The population inhabiting the Maoist corridor is five times as much. Little wonder then that the Indian Prime Minister Manmohan Singh at a conference in New Delhi in July 2006 described it as the 'single biggest internal security challenge'.

The spread of the movement opened up the third phase of its history. On 21 September 2004, the leaders and cadres of the various scattered Naxalite groups, which had been leading the movement for the last two decades, met in one of their base areas and decided to form a single revolutionary party called the CPI (Maoist). In its programme, it reaffirmed its main political agenda—agrarian revolution through protracted people's war to capture state power and set up a 'people's democratic state', develop their guerrilla squads into a people's liberation army, wage struggles against the Indian government's latest plans to set up Special Economic Zones (SEZs) and resist the displacement of tribals and forest dwellers due to mining projects.

During all these three phases of the movement, the Maoist leadership had remained consistent in stressing the role of the poor and landless peasantry as the leader of the projected people's democratic revolution. But the interrelationship between the learned middle class, urban Maoist leaders (in the role of ideological vanguards) and the peasantry (in the role of political leaders) had always been fraught with tensions between symbiosis and dissonance. From the ideological perspective, the Maoist leaders' theoretical concept of a future 'people's democratic state' as an intermediary stage in the long drawn-out revolution for the establishment of socialism (according to their programme) remains a somewhat distant bookish dream for the local leaders of the peasants' movements. It is in fact the immediate tactics in the Maoist programme of guerrilla struggles to throw out the oppressive landlords and moneylenders and set-up alternative units of governance to benefit the rural poor through radical land reforms that had attracted the local peasant leaders in the areas of struggle. By resorting to those tactics in the course of their struggle, they succeeded in changing power relationships in village society by overturning the patron-client network, and enabling the rural poor and oppressed, marginalized groups (i.e. indigenous people and women) to rediscover their collective self and reassert their rights. These achievements harken back to the old Marxian concept of class formation—the transformation from class *in* itself to class *for* itself.

However, the structure of the Maoist movement also raises the crucial question of the extraneous influence of the Maoist vanguard (mainly urban middle-class intellectuals) in making the peasants take on a role that at times broke down when their interests were in dissonance with the Maoist strategy. I shall come to this issue later in the course of my retrospection. The Maoist experiment also sheds light on the complex relationship between the moral base of the ideology which initially impelled the Maoists to launch the movement on the one hand, and the excesses committed by them in the course of their armed struggle against encirclement by a repressive state apparatus on the other, that threaten to erode that moral base. While acting as a catalytic agent in Indian rural society, the Maoist movement itself has also undergone a transformation—both in a positive and in a negative sense.

IN RETROSPECT: SNIPPETS FROM A PERSONAL MEMOIR

The Maoist vanguard in the early phase of the movement primarily consisted of members of the urban educated middle class who went to the villages to ideologically initiate the peasantry into the strategy of agrarian revolution and organize them through the tactics of guerrilla warfare. A few personal remarks may be of interest in this connection, since as a participant in the movement in that phase (in the early 1970s), I can claim to be a typical representative of that urban middle class from Bengal.

Born and brought up in Kolkata in a communist family, I almost automatically drifted into the communist movement in the early 1950s, as a student activist in the then undivided CPI. I remained a member of that party till 1964 when it split, with one faction breaking away to form the CPI(M). Since politically I could not agree with either of the two parties, I withdrew from active politics.[3] Following this, after a stint as a teacher in a college, I joined the *Statesman* newspaper in Kolkata as a reporter. Paradoxically enough, while the *Statesman* was run by conservative interests (British business houses), it offered me an opportunity to visit rural areas in course of assignments and opened my eyes to the sufferings of the poor peasantry. As a communist activist in the past, I had mainly worked among urban students and middle-class people. But now, the *Statesman* sent me to cover droughts and floods in the countryside, and during my travels, I became exposed to the rural reality of continuing exploitation of landlords and the oppressive feudal hierarchy in social relations.

The 1966-7 period—when I was working as a reporter—saw an intensification of the agrarian crisis in Bengal and other parts of India, with widespread incidents of starvation deaths and pillaging of food stores by people in rags and tatters—the outcome of years of negligence of land reforms. There was a popular movement in West Bengal against the Congress government's agrarian policies, following which a coalition government of opposition parties (including the two communist parties) was elected to power in March 1967. I was again drawn to politics—and came to share this time the ideological viewpoint of the Maoists who led a peasants' uprising at Naxalbari in May that year. I got closer to some of their leaders and activists.

In September that year, I was transferred to the Delhi office of the *Statesman*, which helped me to watch from close quarters the administrative policies that were being adopted by the government to control the widely spreading Naxalite movement. The opportunity to meet ministers and senior policemen who were entrusted with the task of suppressing the Naxalites was gained in the course of my journalistic assignments—thanks to the *Statesman* again! I continued at the same time to remain in touch with my friends in the movement in West Bengal and receive their underground political literature (e.g. the CPI-ML organ *Liberation*), which kept me informed of the armed struggles that were breaking out in different parts of India.

In 1972, I was commissioned to write a book on the Naxalite movement by the publishers Orient Longman. To explain the circumstances, let me quote from the preface to the book (which was eventually brought out by another publisher, after a gap of eight years in 1980, following a series of interruptions, including my imprisonment during the 1975-6 Emergency):

> Writing the first draft was an important lesson for me. Even after the completion of the manuscript. . . . I continued to be nagged by certain doubts that had crept in while I was working on the draft. Was my journalistic fund of information and type of specialization adequate to enable me to do justice to the events and people about whom I was writing? Is it enough to write about a cause and praise it from a distance? A curiosity to probe deeper, as well as a desire for further commitment brought about by the pressures of the surrounding political reality, soon drove me in the direction of the CPI(M-L), and threw me in the company of its cadres. The unforgettable experience of sharing their adventures and living among poor and landless peasants provided me with the invaluable opportunity of understanding their problems. . . . All these helped me to look at the entire history of the CPI(M-L) and related movements from a fresh angle. I soon came to realize that my draft manuscript lying with the publishers was an incomplete and erroneous account of the movement. I withdrew it and started rewriting the entire book in the light of my new experiences and recently acquired information. . . .[4]

I resigned from the *Statesman* in 1973 and went underground, joining several of my journalist colleagues who had in the meantime left their jobs to participate in the CPI(M-L) movement. The party leadership assigned me the task of accompanying party organizers in villages, translating and typing out party literature into English for their organ *Liberation*, and often acting as a courier to carry messages from one underground shelter to another. While carrying out this new assignment—another type of journalism involving political activism this time—I had the opportunity of staying with poor peasants in Bengal and Bihar, and Girijan tribals in Srikakulam in Andhra Pradesh.

Later, my imprisonment in 1975 also threw me into the company of Naxalite peasant activists and their sympathizers who became my comrades in jail. This helped me in a certain measure to understand their varied perspectives better, to realize how responses differed from one section of the rural poor (the tribals) to another (the Dalits), and to comprehend what Maoist messages they accepted or rejected. In the process, certain beloved myths about the peasant 'psyche' that were commonly nourished by romantic middle-class communists like myself were also demolished. These questionings of received wisdoms nevertheless did not destroy my fundamental belief in the Indian peasantry's need, and my confidence in its power, to put an end to its present status of deprivation through a revolutionary transformation.

SOCIAL PRIORITIES IN A PEASANT SOCIETY

Let me first take up some of the social problems that were of concern to the peasants and were identified by the Maoist ideologues and organizers. It was not merely the economic demands of right to land and increase in wages, but also issues like justice and equal treatment in the daily existence of the peasantry that formed the leitmotif in Naxalite propaganda and actions. The Naxalites gave voice to the sense of *izzat* (the term for dignity) of the downtrodden peasantry (particularly those coming from the depressed castes—known as Dalits) who had been historically subjected to a system of social discrimination and exploitation in a hierarchical and patriarchal society. This was a system where the upper-caste landlords treated them as 'untouchables' and denied them their civic rights, and had no compunction in abducting their women and raping them. The spread of Naxalite politics inspired these sections of the poor to assert themselves as equal human beings and resist the humiliating code of conduct that had been imposed upon them by the upper classes.

Let me give an example: while visiting a village in Burdwan in West Bengal in 1969, I met an old Bauri (a depressed caste) peasant. I asked him if he felt any difference after the Naxalbari events. He said: 'Yes! I can now walk with my head straight up, and do not have to make way even when I cross the path of my landlord.' One has to put oneself in the shoes of this peasant to understand what he meant. In the Indian countryside, the poor from the depressed castes had been compelled to bow their heads whenever they came across their upper-caste neighbours—a sign of subservience rather than normal respect.

How such social customs and extra-economic pressures of a feudal society can be viewed differently by the downtrodden, and their violation can become a gesture of protest was demonstrated by events in Bhojpur in Bihar during the Naxalite movement there in the 1970s. The leaders of the movement were peasants who came from the backward and depressed castes (many among the latter considered 'untouchables'). Their own experiences in their search for human dignity, protection of their homes and womenfolk from the depredations of the upper-caste gentry, and demand for equal rights, rather than the cold and abstract theories of political science, initially motivated these people and drew them towards Naxalism.

We can take a few typical representatives of the Bihar Naxalite movement of those days who emerged and developed from among their own communities. Jagdish Mahto (from the backward Koeri caste), for instance, a teacher in his village, was hated by the local upper-caste Bhumihar landlords because he refused to get up from his cot when they passed his house. This was, in the landlords' eyes, a heinous crime! When Mahto tried to resist an upper-caste Bhumihar landlord from intimidating voters in his village during the 1967 general elections, he was beaten up and left half dead. He soon went underground to join the communist armed revolutionaries who had started propagating in the Bihar villages following the events in Naxalbari.

Rameshwar Ahir, the son of a poor peasant, was regarded by the Bhumihar landlords of his village as an upstart since he did not bow down to them—an unpardonable sin for a backward caste youth! He was implicated in a case of dacoity and sentenced to imprisonment. In jail, Rameshwar became a changed man, reading books and learning about what was happening in Vietnam. On his release in 1970, he joined Jagdish Mahto, went underground and began to build the organization in his area.

Butan, belonging to the so-called 'untouchable' Mushahar caste, was the first to complete matriculation from his community. Yet, he was denied job because of his caste. He watched his kinsmen living for years in fear of the local landlord who raped his caste's women with impunity. Butan finally decided to retaliate. He got in touch with his kinsmen in neighbouring villages who had already joined the newly formed CPI(M-L) party and formed guerrilla bands to seize power from the landlords.

People like Jagdish Mahto, Rameshwar Ahir, Butan Mushahar and others have become folk heroes among the peasants of Bhojpur who still narrate tales of how they fought the police and faced death.[5] The actions in Bhojpur reveal the priorities that the peasants had. They formed *dastas* (armed guerrilla squads), killed notorious landlords and moneylenders, occupied their land and planted red flags on them. They then set up *Krantikari* Committees (revolutionary committees) which distributed land and set up people's courts to decide disputes among the villagers and impose fines on recalcitrant landlords. These practices continue to run like a major thread through Maoist activities in the areas under their influence.

DEMYSTIFYING PEASANT MILITANCY

The Maoist ideological stress on the revolutionary role of the peasantry somehow led the urban-based Bengali middle-class Naxalite organizers to stereotype and valorize them as a fixed entity of ingrained revolutionaries. My experiences—limited though they might be—unfolded a more complex and multi-faceted world of the peasantry on which I would like to shed some light. Wriggling out from all attempts to flatten them out in one uniform mould, the peasantry assumed multiple identities to struggle and survive in a hostile environment.

First, I was led to question the unity and homogeneity of the peasantry that were usually held as axiomatic by the Naxalite leaders. Different perceptions born of differing experiences by individuals or groups within a peasant community, and the tensions generated thereafter, could split the community on issues like gender. This was brought home to me on one particular occasion: in the early 1980s (during the second phase of the movement, by when I had resumed my journalistic career as a freelancer, writing for newspapers in India and abroad), I accompanied a team of Maoist activists and trekked through a long stretch of villages in the Gaya-Aurangabad region of Bihar. The landlords had fled from those villages, their houses taken over by the Maoists, their lands distributed among the peasants. We reached a village one morning, where we found a Maoist people's court in session. The issue before the court was a charge brought by a peasant woman against the local Maoist party organizer—also from the same poor-peasant background—whom she accused of molesting her. What I found interesting was the multiplicity of opinions that were voiced by the villagers who had assembled there, particularly women. They appeared to be divided—one section supporting the woman's charges and accusing the Maoist organizer of behaving in a similar fashion with other women in the past; another section alleging that the woman herself had a dubious moral reputation and could not be trusted therefore, while the others taking a neutral stand. We could not stay back to hear the final verdict of the people's court. But what struck me was the heterogeneity of the rural poor, which we often assumed to be monolithic and responding in a uniform manner.[6]

Second, I was led to question the expectation that mere poverty could produce the revolutionary consciousness and capacity of self-sacrifice that are anticipated by the Maoist ideologues. In fact, I found that the conscious activity of many peasants I met was more shaped within the established order and aimed at ensuring two meals a day, a home, a few amenities, by any means available to him or her. I remember, when spending a few days in an underground shelter of a Naxalite peasant comrade of mine, his mother one evening said to me: 'Son, don't you ever worship the peasantry! Like you babus, we also have in our villages poor peasants who are dishonest, congenital liars, flatterers, thieves. . . .' She then whispered to me: 'Thanks to your party, this son of mine has become a revolutionary. But my other son is a dacoit—on whose earnings I live!'

Her confiding the secret to me also made me aware of a third point: there is in fact often a thin line between a potential revolutionary and a potential criminal. This point was made sharper during my days of imprisonment in 1976. Jail authorities often employed poor rural convicts—petty criminals—to beat up imprisoned Naxalite activists. They came from the same peasant class whom the Naxalites had been trying to mobilize for a revolutionary change in their conditions. Yet, these convicts were willing to terrorize the Naxalite prisoners for immediate benefits like fringe concession or remission of their sentences, as promised by the jailer.

A third issue to consider is that of the militancy of the peasantry. Contrary to the media-sponsored impression that the peasantry's brutal reprisal is peculiar only to the Maoist movement, historical records suggest that the peasantry, while often passive sufferers for years, have nevertheless also participated in violent retaliation against their oppressors. 'Memories of past oppression,' as the anthropologist Verrier Elwin (1950)[7] said, 'die slowly.' These violent histories of peasant retribution, which attributed a kind of inherent rebel savagery amongst the downtrodden peasantry, were to a certain extent used by the Maoist activists to rationalize and institutionalize the violence of their movement. For instance, there was the example of Santhali tribal peasants in eastern India, in the 1855-7 rebellion, who were reported to have chopped off the limbs of a usurer shouting, 'With these fingers you counted our money. With these hands you snatched away our food.'[8] Or, there was the example that I remember hearing—of a ghastly incident in a village in Bangladesh where I went as a reporter in 1972, immediately after liberation. The villagers were suffering from starvation, although there were enough food grain arriving from foreign donors. But the local landlord-cum-trader had cornered them and stacked away sacks of rice in his warehouse—hoping to sell them in the black market. The desperate villagers were reported to have raided his house, looted the rice, tied him up, slit his stomach—and then stuffed into it a sack of rice, shouting: 'This is for your greed!' Such examples formed a key part of the Maoist stereotype of an inherently violent peasantry that was further emphasized by reports in their organ *Liberation*. For instance, in the early 1970s, in the people's courts set up by Naxalites in villages in Birbhum in West Bengal and some other strongholds, oppressive landlords and moneylenders were brutally killed by the peasants, and the gory details used to be published in *Liberation* (1969-72).

In these representations, the tribals/*adivasis* in particular, have been stereotyped by the Maoist literature as a revolutionary class, which has also, in part, led to their focus on the tribal-populated states of Jharkhand, Chhattisgarh, Orissa and Maharashtra where they have built their revolutionary base. The image of the vengeful tribal also reproduces the impression that having had a long history of anti-colonial rebellion (particularly in eastern India in the nineteenth century), the tribals are particularly prone to violence today in the face of the new threats from incursions on their territory by industrial interests under India's neoliberal policies.

These popular representations of peasant, and especially tribal peasant, violence that are very much a part of Maoist rhetoric need to be both contextualized and questioned. Violent acts are expressions at a point of time of the belligerence of an insulted self-respect and innocence that has been violated and brutalized over years by oppressors. This should not lead us to generalize that the peasantry is inherently violent and ready to join a revolution at any moment. Even at the height of militancy, the peasants never directed violence indiscriminately. Their actions were dictated by a canny awareness of the traditional rural socio-economic life support system. Let me give an instance of their decision to refrain from violence on certain occasions. Sometime in 1973, I was living as a party activist among poor peasants in a village in Hooghly in West Bengal. At a meeting of their revolutionary committee, they decided to raid the house of a usurious landlord and set fire to it to burn all the promissory notes that they had signed when borrowing money from him, and which were growing as an incubus upon them with the rising annual interest. On a particular night, a guerrilla squad of poor peasants went on the raid. I was asked by the guerrilla commander to stay behind. Being an urban middle-class newcomer to the scene, I was not considered fit—quite rightly—to join them. I waited with bated breath for the signs of the fire to appear from the corner of the village where the landlord's house was situated. To our surprise, the guerrilla squad returned a few hours later. When I asked them what happened, they admitted, rather sheepishly, that they did not carry out the task. Why? A pair of bullocks belonging to the landlord was tied in the cowshed, they said. So what, I asked? The guerrilla squad leader—himself an agricultural labourer—said: 'But the bullocks are innocent! They would have died if the house was set on fire.' I asked them why did they not set them free? He reprimanded me: 'Stupid! If we disturbed the bullocks, they would have bellowed like hell! The landlord would have woken up.'

If we rethink some of these widely-held assumptions, it is clear as well that the Maoists' perspectives and tactics were not blindly accepted by the peasants everywhere. Individuals—whether peasants or workers, even when a part of a community that had become a 'class for itself' (in the Marxian sense)—developed their independent personalities and formed their own opinions in the course of the struggle. Not all poor peasants at every stage were willing to go the whole hog with the Maoists in their objective of capturing state power through armed revolution. If immediate economic and social benefits (like a plot of land, a home, higher returns from labour, improvement in civic facilities, schooling for their children, better medical services, end to casteist discrimination and oppression) are offered in their everyday life by any government—irrespective of its political hue—some Indian peasants may rather opt for that in exchange of a long-drawn-out armed struggle in pursuit of a distant ideological dream of a 'people's democratic state'. Only the politically committed among them would remain steadfast in the arduous path of struggle.

In Naxalbari in West Bengal, the rural poor who joined the armed Maoist insurrection that broke out there for the first time in 1967 have today dropped out from the movement and accepted instead the *status quo* of a government ruled by parliamentary Leftists, since the latter has provided them with a modicum of economic benefits:

small plots of cultivable land, higher wages for labour and a partial voice in local decision-making through self-government institutions known as Panchayats. When I travel by train or bus through the Bengal countryside, I listen to a new generation of rural people who nurture dreams of a better future within this system rather than changing it through an armed revolution.

Srikakulam in Andhra Pradesh is another example of the neutralization of the Maoist followers by the state. Here, in 1969-70, along vast stretches of hills and forests, the Maoists rallied the poor and oppressed Girijan tribals and set-up guerrilla zones in their villages. The Congress government, after suppressing the movement, undertook a few development projects in 1972 among the Girijan tribals (who formed the backbone of the insurrection) and advanced loans to them for agricultural improvement. These beneficiaries gradually distanced themselves from their erstwhile Maoist leaders. There is hardly any Maoist base in Srikakulam today.

One final issue that I want to raise in this section is that of the peasant suspicion of the vanguard (from outside) that was generated by class differences. It is evident that in order to sustain their bases, the Maoists had to make their peasant followers politically conscious of the larger ideological goal of socialism that goes beyond the temporary satisfaction of their immediate material needs. But this task of politicizing the peasants and transforming them from a class in itself to a class for itself, became more difficult due to the class character of the interventionist vanguard which took up the task—namely the urban, middle-class ideologues. The deeply entrenched suspicion of the city-bred outsider among the peasantry was the biggest hurdle that the Maoist vanguard faced.[9] I remember an incident in a village, where I accompanied our party leader (of middle-class origin) who addressed a small gathering of poor peasants. After explaining the objectives of the agrarian revolution and the need for setting up guerrilla squads, he urged the youth to be prepared for leaving their homes and sacrificing their lives. An old woman from among the listeners asked him: 'Do you have a family, wife and children?' He replied: 'Yes, but I've left my home to devote full-time to the cause of liberating the peasantry of my country from their present plight.' The woman retorted: 'Son, if you can't look after your own little home and family, and remain indifferent to their plight, how can you shoulder the responsibility of taking care of all the peasant homes and leading them to a revolution in this vast country of ours?' Her question not only reflected the down-to-earth concerns of the peasantry, but also exposed to some extent the dichotomy between the lack of individual responsibility in personal lives on the one hand and the sincerity of collective commitment to a wider ideal on the other that usually marks the participation of middle-class activists in the Maoist movement. The conflict between a sense of guilt at failing one's own family and the urgency of responding to the larger claim of a political movement had plagued the souls of all revolutionaries throughout history.

GLIMPSES OF MAOIST MOVEMENT TODAY

As I explained at the beginning, my perception and analysis of the present phase of the Maoist movement may be constrained by the distance that separates me today from the ground reality of the Maoist base areas. The peasant experience and perception, glimmerings of which I could capture during my participation in the Maoist movement in the early 1970s, must have changed after three decades of socio-economic transformation in India. As I mentioned earlier, there is a difference in the perception of the Girijan tribals who joined the Naxalite movement and with whom I spent some memorable evenings in the forests of Srikakulam in 1974 and of that of their children who had grown up in different circumstances. Among the oppressed, the far-reaching theoretical understanding of capitalist or feudal exploitation in Marxist or Maoist terms can be blunted by the mitigation of effects of such exploitation in terms of temporary material concessions and benefits by the ruling powers.

But then again, the Indian peasantry, as I have been trying to describe, is neither a fixed monolithic nor a frozen, changeless category. While some may remain quiescent in certain parts of the country, others are bursting out in revolts in different areas. Partial beneficiary measures by the Indian state—as in the earlier Maoist-affected areas of Naxalbari or Srikakulam—are mere transient healing touches to a rural society that is afflicted by a fast-moving cancerous disease.[10] Even when contained in one corner of the country, peasant unrest invariably breaks out in some other areas. It is fuelled by the economic policies of the Indian government which, as we shall describe later, are creating more and more epicentres of upheavals.

It is in this perspective that the expansion of the Maoist movement assumes importance in present-day India. Significantly, the Maoists effectively control those areas in a long stretch of territory which are inhabited by the most deprived sections of the Indian rural poor, including tribals, who had been living in a limbo, left out from all the altruistic programmes of the government. The Maoists stepped into the vacuum, mobilized the poor, formed guerrilla squads to drive out the oppressive landlords, moneylenders, forest contractors and fight the police which came to protect the latter. They then set-up parallel administrative units in their 'liberated zones' to govern these areas. It is this deeply entrenched sensitivity to the rural existential concerns that helped the peasant Maoist leaders and cadres to take roots among the poor and underprivileged in the backward areas of India and carve out guerrilla zones there. Loss of this sensitivity will alienate them from their followers, divest them of the enclaves that they occupy and deprive them of the moral sympathy that they enjoy among sections of Indian civil society (e.g., liberal intellectuals, human rights organizations).

Reports about the changes brought about by the Maoists in the living and working conditions of the people in areas which they control today—as culled from the mainstream media and the CPI(Maoist) pamphlets—indicate a record of mixed sorts. In some of the guerrilla zones, the poor peasants and agricultural labourers appear to have gained by way of occupation of land, better wages for labour, recognition of social rights and protection from oppressive landlords, corrupt forest officials and predatory policemen. But at the same time, while assuming the role of protectors, the Maoists often appear to some people as bullies—extorting money from contractors who are engaged in development projects in their areas; brutally killing minor offenders—even innocent people—on the mere suspicion that they are police informers; destroying government-run public services (e.g., railway stations) and assaulting their employees, holding them as symbols of the Indian state. Such acts can be explained—not excused—by the existential conditions faced by the Maoists in the beleaguered zones within which they are confined. The urge for revenge against the oppressor, spurred by Maoist propaganda, often explodes into such brutalities. That apart, constantly facing raids by the police and security forces, the Maoists have grown up with a persecution complex, which leads them to suspect everyone who may differ from them. As a result, quite often they resort to indiscriminate force, giving up the patience for democratic methods to spread their movement. But in the long run, this would alienate them from the people for whom they claim to fight for.[11]

We cannot deny, however, that much of the cruel streak in Maoist activities is due to the Indian state's militarist intervention in their guerrilla zones. Had they been left to themselves to run their parallel administration and follow their model of economic development and social reforms in the narrow stretch of their zone of influence, over a period of time they could have proved themselves either as failed adventurers, or as providers of a viable alternative. It could have been left to the Indian people to reject or accept their model. Instead of democratic tolerance, the Indian state has resorted to militarist methods to suppress the alternative socio-economic experiments that are being tried out in the Maoist strongholds. In Chhattisgarh, for instance, the state has created armed vigilante groups by recruiting mercenaries from among the tribal population to counter the Maoists (e.g., the Salwa Judum). This has led to further dehumanization of everyday life in the area, with one group of tribals (owing allegiance to the Maoists) fighting another (armed by the state). It has unleashed an unprecedented internecine warfare with far-reaching consequences for the daily life of the tribal population there.

In such a situation, it behoves both the Indian state and its Maoist opponents to rethink their respective strategies and plans of action. The Indian state still refuses to recognize Maoism as a strong ideological force based on the genuine popular grievance about economic inequity and social injustice. The Maoist objective of setting up a secular and socialist society in India (as outlined in the party programme issued by the CPI (Maoist) on 9 September 2004) is more in consistency with the spirit of the Indian constitution's commitment to that goal than the programmes of the various terrorist outfits (with whom the Indian state brackets the Maoists)—which follow the design of dividing the Indian people along religious, regional and linguistic lines.

A dialogue between representatives of the Indian state and the Maoists seems to be more in the fitness of things—given their proclaimed faith in the twin objectives of socialism and secularism (whatever differences they might have over their interpretation and practice). If the Indian government can engage in talks with the armed secessionist National Socialist Council of Nagaland-Isak-Muivah (NSCN) group, and open doors to the insurgent United Liberation Front of Assam (ULFA) for talks, what prevents it from taking up the threads of an interrupted dialogue with the Maoists which the Andhra Pradesh government entered into in 2004?[12]

But a dialogue can succeed only when both sides are willing to give up their maximalist positions and meet up halfway. As for the Indian state, in order to begin a dialogue with the Maoists, the state must stop using the police to restore the feudal rule of landlords in villages where the Maoists have already established a parallel socio-economic order that allows the rural poor to enjoy rights to their land and forest produce, and offers them educational and medical facilities. As for the Maoists, they will have to establish norms that conform to the well-established code of human rights and values as part of their political perception and practice. A ceasefire is necessary—not only in the Maoists' enlightened self-interest of preserving their cadres from the ruthless attack by the state, but mainly in the humanitarian interest of the thousands of poor and innocent families who have been caught in the cross-fire between the police and the Maoists in the affected areas.

THE FUTURE

The battle between the Indian state and the Maoists is being fought over two basic demands which should have been met years ago—land reforms and social justice for the rural poor. Instead, by following the neoliberal model of growth, the Indian state is creating newer explosive points of dispute between an expansive corporate sector and a shrinking habitat from which vast masses of the poor are being displaced. Establishment of SEZs on agricultural land, introduction of commercial crops (with fluctuating market value) by multinational corporations, increasing exploitation of forest reserves for industrial expansion, all are claimed by the state as signs of economic growth in statistical terms. But for those at the receiving end, in bread-and-butter terms, they mean growing impoverishment. Peasants ousted from their lands by SEZs (in West Bengal, Orissa) and farmers victimized by the inequitable terms of free market economy (which are driving many among them to commit suicide in Vidarbha in Maharashtra, and parts of Andhra Pradesh) are swelling the ranks of the disgruntled. Reports of starvation deaths and outbreaks of popular demonstrations against the government's economic policies hark back to the explosions of peasant discontent in the late 1960s which heralded the Naxalite movement. The state has responded to these demonstrations by violent retaliation, resulting in the killing of the poor participants in the agitations.[13]

This vast disaffected spectrum of Indian society is crying out for an alternative programme of radical transformation, and a responsive political leadership that will be different from the present crop of parties which are rich and consummate in crime and corruption and barren of any humanitarian ideology. Will the Maoists be able to fit the bill and respond to their cry in this political vacuum in the Indian heartland? The conditions are opening up new possibilities for Maoist intervention in areas outside their hitherto strongholds in the backward underdeveloped districts, and call for a new set of operative tactics in the planes of the advanced districts, as different from their cloistered hideouts in forests and hills.

Until now, the Maoists have been generally absent from the movements of the industrial working class, the agitations against environmental pollution and gender-discrimination, the day-to-day struggles of the large sections of urban slum dwellers for better living conditions, the protests of the middle class against corruption and crime. That apart, their major failure has been their powerlessness in putting up an effective resistance to the Hindu religious fascist forces which have imposed a reign of terror over members of the Muslim and Christian religious minorities. The indifference of the Maoist leaders to these major flashpoints of popular grievances and resistance indicates to some extent the alienation that they are prone to, an inadequacy to which I had pointed out at the beginning of this article.

This alienation is also reflected in the isolation of the Maoist bases which are confined to a narrow corridor of inaccessible forest and hill areas. These bases are vulnerable to attacks and destruction by the Indian armed forces which besiege them from all sides. The confinement of the Indian Maoists thus stands out in contrast with the expanse of the Nepalese Maoist fighters who could extend their control over almost two-thirds of the country and surround the capital Kathmandu. While acknowledging that the geographical terrain and the anti-monarchy popular sentiments (different from the Indian situation) favoured the Nepalese Maoists to a large extent, the Indian Maoists can still learn from their comrades in Nepal how to finetune their strategy to the needs and sentiments of the wider segments of the population—the urban poor, the retrenched industrial workers, the disgruntled middle classes and other disaffected sections. More importantly, there is the need to recognize their democratic rights. This latter terrain is where the Maoists have failed everywhere. They have set an atrocious record, whether in China or in Cambodia, or even the few guerrilla zones that they occupy in India today. Painful and heartrending incidents of intolerance in their practice have caused confusion and bewilderment among their sympathizers. They are yet to recognize their mistakes and correct them in direct consultation with the population. All this calls for an imaginative Indian Maoist leadership that can formulate a multilayered strategy and flexible tactics for replacing the present inequitable structure by a socialist system, while at the same time recovering the original moral ideals and renewing the springs of humanitarian impulses at every stage of their struggle.

At the end, however, the Indian Maoists cannot remain alienated from the new trends that are emerging in the world Left movement in response to the challenges posed by the march of globalization by neo-liberal economic forces. It is being felt that the old tools to fight capitalism that were valid and successful in the twentieth century need to be replaced by more modern and sophisticated mechanisms that have to be rooted in a post-Marxian ideology of socialism that is suited for the twenty-first century. An alternative model of economic development from a socialist perspective as opposed to hegemonization by neo-liberal economy is being tried out through various experiments in Venezuela, Bolivia and other Latin American countries, where a combination of both armed struggles and participation in parliamentary elections has paved the way for the emergence of a new generation of socialist leaders. Indian Maoists can contribute to this ongoing struggle for a new socialist alternative by reformulating their strategy and tactics to respond to the needs of the complex Indian reality.

NOTES

1. The Indian communists who led the Telangana struggle were influenced by Mao Zedong's strategy which stressed the role of the peasantry in leading the revolution in agrarian countries—as distinct from the traditional Marxist strategy which allotted that role to the proletariat in the industrial countries. The difference that led to the formulation of the ideological concept of a people's democratic revolution as an intermediate stage (aimed at destroying feudal relations in the countryside) on the way to the final stage of a socialist revolution which would end bourgeois relations, as envisaged in the original Marxist strategy. See P. Sundarayya, *Telengana People's Struggle and Its Lessons* (Calcutta: Communist Party of India [Marxist], 1972).
2. Among the books written on this first phase of the Maoist movement, the

following can be of interest to concerned scholars: S. Banerjee, *In the Wake of Naxalbari: A History of the Naxalite Movement in India* (Calcutta: Subarnrekha, 1980), S. Ghosh, *The Naxalite Movement: A Maoist Experience* (Calcutta: Mukhopadyay, 1974), A. Samanta, *Left-Wing Extremist Movement in West Bengal* (Calcutta: Firma K.L. Mukopadhyay, 1984), R. Ray, *The Naxalites and Their Ideology* (New Delhi: Oxford University Press, 1988) and A.P. Mukherji, *Maoist 'Spring Thunder'* (Calcutta: K.P. Bagchi, 2007).

3. For a fuller account of the causes of the split and the differences in the political agenda of the two parties, see S. Banerjee, *In the Wake of Naxalbari: A History of the Naxalite Movement in India* (Calcutta: Subarnrekha, 1980).
4. Banerjee, *In the Wake of Naxalbari.*
5. K. Mukherji, and R.S. Yadav, *Bhojpur: Naxalism in the Plains of Bihar* (Delhi: Radhakrishnan Press, 1980).
6. For an analytical account of women's role in the Maoist guerrilla zones, see *The Revolutionary Women's Movement in India* (Delhi: New Vistas Publications, 2004) and Vasanth Kannabiran, Volga, and K. Kannabiran, 'Andhra Pradesh: Women's Rights and Naxalite Groups', *Economic and Political Weekly*, vol. 39, no. 45, 6-12 November 2004, pp. 4874-7. (6 November 2004).
7. V. Elwin, *Maria Murder and Suicide* (New Delhi: Oxford University Press, 1950).
8. Kali Kinkar Datta, quoted in Banerjee, *In the Wake of Naxalbari,* 274.
9. In Nepal, I am led to believe from talks with observers there, that the mismatch between the peasants and the middle-class Maoist organizers was less because the latter were students who originally came from the same villages, went to Kathmandu or other cities for studies, got imbued with Maoist ideas, and returned to their villages to organize the peasantry.
10. Such land reforms or official measures to help the agricultural poor have, however, remained incomplete and failed to cover the marginalized segments of rural society—especially the tribal and Dalit (depressed caste) sections. Thus, in the Left Front-ruled state of West Bengal, in the backward tribal belt of Bankura, Midnapur and Purulia districts, the underprivileged communities have been bypassed by the Left Front's land reforms, and they continue to lead a miserable existence. Significantly enough, today it is in this belt, which borders the Maoist dominated areas in Jharkhand, where the Bengal Maoists have become active again. For a fuller discussion on this aspect, see S. Banerjee, 'Beyond Naxalbari', *Economic and Political Weekly*, 22 July 2006, 3159-63. Committee of Concerned Citizens, Third Report 1997-2002 (Hyderabad: Committee of Concerned Citizens, 2002).
11. For detailed accounts of Maoist governance see A. Banerjee, *Inside MCC*

Country (Kolkata: K. Das, 2003) and *New People's War in Dandakaranya* (Kolkata: Biplabi Yug Publication, 2000). For a critique of their activities, see Committee of Concerned Citizens (2002): xix.

12. For a history of efforts to initiate a dialogue between the Maoists and the government in Andhra Pradesh, see S. Banerjee, 'Beyond Naxalbari', *Economic and Political Weekly* (22 July 2006): 3159-63. Committee of Concerned Citizens, 'Third Report 1997-2002' (Hyderabad: Committee of Concerned Citizens) and S. Banerjee, 'All Quiet on the Maoist Front?', *Economic and Political Weekly* (5 February 2005): 500-2.
13. To cite a few recent cases in 2007—(1) a movement against nuclear reactors in Koodankulam in Tamil Nadu; (2) peasant demonstrations demanding land redistribution in Khammam in Andhra Pradesh; (3) agitation against a proposed steel project in Kalinganagar in Orissa; (4) popular resistance against industrial projects in Singur and Nandigram in West Bengal. As evident from the earlier cases, the established parliamentary political parties (whether Left, Centrist or Right in the states that they rule) follow the same neo-liberal model of growth that ends with the marginalization of the rural poor.

CHAPTER 4

Student Memories of the Naxalite Movement in Calcutta

RONOJOY SEN

It was a small item in that day's newspaper. But to Dipanjan Rai Chaudhuri, the news about peasants killing a policeman in Naxalbari in north Bengal on 25 May 1967 literally leapt out of the page. Rai Chaudhuri, then a 23-year-old student at Calcutta University, was part of a growing number of youth in elite colleges who were fired by revolutionary ideology but were increasingly getting disillusioned with mainstream communist parties.

Naxalbari was like a clarion call to Rai Chaudhuri—who retired as head of the department of physics in Presidency College in 2004 and was one of those who featured in V.S. Naipaul's *India: A Million Mutinies Now* (1990)—and many of the best and brightest of his generation. 'I remember clearly reading the news of peasants in Naxalbari resisting police action with bows and arrows, killing police inspector Wangdi in the process. We were elated. We had only read about the armed peasant struggles in China and Vietnam. Now it was actually happening here in our land', says Rai Chaudhuri. Soon posters supporting Naxalbari appeared in College Street and elsewhere. Slogans such as 'China's Chairman is our Chairman' suddenly sprouted on Kolkata walls. The lawns of Presidency College became a meeting ground for students from Calcutta and neighbouring areas, and the informal group came to be known as the Presidency Coalition.

Dipesh Chakrabarty, a Presidency College student of the 1960s who now teaches at the University of Chicago, recalls:

> I came into student politics a year before the insurgency in Naxalbari broke out. But I was very much part of the process that led eventually to the Naxalite movement. There was a three-month long students' strike at Presidency College in the winter of 1966. Many of my friends and I were

involved in that strike and some of the future leaders of the Naxalite movement emerged out of that strike: Ashim Chatterjee, Dipanjan Rai Chaudhuri, Amal Sanyal and others. We were all sympathizers of the Communist Party of India (Marxist) [CPI(M)] that had been formed in 1964. But while the party was not officially Maoist, we were; and there was a degree of mutual unease about the status of Maoism within the party circles. I remember that while singing revolutionary songs in marches organized by the party or its student wing, some people would include in their songs lines glorifying China while some would just choose to remain silent. By the time the historic elections of 1967 were held, there were already whispers of dissension within the party reflecting the global split between China and the Soviet Union.

A large section of students admitted into Calcutta University between 1967 and 1970 became supporters of the movement. Then there were several sympathizers in Jadavpur University, Bengal Engineering College, the four medical colleges in Calcutta and Bankura Medical College. In all these colleges there was a core of activists around which other like-minded students gathered. The movement was also popular in other elite Calcutta institutions such as Scottish Church, Vidyasagar and Bangabasi colleges right from the time of the Naxalbari incident.

By April 1969, a Maoist party—the Communist Party of India (Marxist-Leninist) [CPI(ML)]—had been formed and Naxalite leader Charu Majumdar's call to liberate the countryside was finding ready takers among students. In Majumdar's own words:

> So the first and main duty of the peasant movement today is to destroy the State machinery. . . . What according to us is a liberated area? We shall call that peasant area a liberated area from where we have been able to oust the class enemies. To create this liberated area, the peasants' armed power is necessary. By this armed power we mean the hand-made weapons of the peasants, as well as guns. . . . Where will the peasants get guns? Class enemies have guns and they stay inside villages. Guns should be snatched away from them. . . . For this, the peasant militants will have to be taught all tactics beginning from setting fire to the houses of class enemies. Apart from this, we shall get guns from the armed forces through sudden attacks on them. . . . So to do this, it is necessary to propagate the politics of building up armed struggles extensively among the peasantry. It is further necessary to organize small secret militant groups to carry on the campaign of collecting guns.

In private conversations, Majumdar had outlined the main task to his young recruits: the organizers were to talk to the peasants about people's political power and how winning state power was the prerequisite for any real improvement in the life of exploited people.

The rules as framed by Majumdar—himself a college dropout from Siliguri and a veteran of the Tebhaga movement in north Bengal—for the young organizers were clear: Stay only in the house of a landless or poor peasant; stay secretly right from the first; never expose yourselves. The rural stint did not always go down well with city-bred students. Chakrabarty says, 'Many of the urban youth who went, red-guard style, to liberate villages in the late 1960s came back within weeks with acute bowel problems.'

For those like Rai Chaudhuri, who decided to stay on, life was hard.

> The CPI(ML) had been formed by then, and the line of 'annihilation of class enemies' had taken shape. The idea was that after the killing of a hated landlord in an area, the action would itself act as an 'organizer'. After one or two circuits, I was sent to a new area where there had just been one annihilation. I tried sincerely but could not reap any organisational harvest from that action. But landless and poor peasants, even in the new area, sheltered and protected me. I had come to this new village and spoke about a meeting to a poor peasant, and fixed a date. When I returned at dusk on that date to that household, some other poor peasant was there. As I waited, I immediately explained my politics to him as was our usual practice. He gave me a hearing and then said, 'The watchman has heard of you and is coming to catch you.' In fact a noise and lights were approaching in the distance. I asked my listener for a way out and he showed me a route over the darkening fields and I made my escape.

This was also the time brutal killings became a part of life in Bengal. Indeed one of Majumdar's favourite dictums was: 'One who has not smeared his hands red with the blood of the class enemy is not fit to be called a Communist.' Calcutta, in particular, lived in daily fear of Naxalite violence.

The violent turn to the movement and the subsequent police brutality alienated some of the urban youth. 'While I supported Maoism, I did not have a taste for the cult of violence that Charu Majumdar preached. Also, I did not have the courage to face the prospect of police torture', admits Chakrabarty. The distaste for violence among some students is confirmed by Arun Prosad Mukherjee, who had an intimate knowledge of the psyche of the young activists. As deputy commissioner of police in the special branch from 1969-72, he was in-charge of interrogating arrested Naxalites. Mukherjee, who has written a book on the period called *Maoist Spring Thunder* (2007), believes that the egregious violence propagated by Naxalite leaders deeply unsettled many students from middle-class families.

He cites the case of a Presidency College student who developed 'serious mental aberrations' after committing an act of brutal annihilation.

This was also the time when members of the underworld joined the Naxalite movement—sometimes actively encouraged by the police—leading to an upsurge of violence. There were many students who were shot in cold blood and several more put behind bars. Recalls Rai Chaudhuri:

> Victims have spoken of the inhuman details. I don't want to repeat their almost unbelievable accounts. It was indiscriminate in the sense that the brutality was felt by peasants and workers as well as middle class youth. But the urban youth was specially targeted. There was torture by sadists like Runu Guha Neogy, killing in the guise of 'encounters'; the whole bag of fascist tricks. The terror was planned by the police chief Ranjit Gupta on the request of [chief minister] Siddhartha Shankar Ray, and executed, among others, by detective chief Debi Roy, and certainly condoned, if not directly encouraged, by Arun Mukherjee, chief of political intelligence. No one was charged by the Left Front government when it came to govern the state, even though these butchers had also killed CPI(M) activists. The Left Front government ignored the findings of two enquiry commissions set up by itself.

In end-1971, Rai Chaudhuri—who by then was married and had a daughter—was arrested with another prominent Naxalite leader, Ashim Chatterjee, better known as Kaka, in Deoghar in neighbouring Bihar (now in Jharkhand). After having spent 11 months in jail, Rai Chaudhuri was released on the condition that he and his family leave the country. In August 1972, Rai Chaudhuri was taken straight from jail to Calcutta's Dum Dum airport to board a flight to London where he went on to complete his Ph.D.

Not everyone was as fortunate as Rai Chaudhuri. For some students, their careers were virtually finished. There were, however, many who picked up the pieces of their lives and moved on. There was, for instance, Amal Sanyal who sat for his university exams from prison and later settled down in New Zealand. Chakrabarty joined the Indian Institute of Management, Calcutta, in what he says was a 'peculiar mood that combined elements of self-denial with those of self-affirmation'. Some like Kaka stayed in active politics and even contested elections.

But for most of the youth from elite colleges, who dedicated the best years of their lives to the cause of revolution, the Naxalite movement fundamentally changed their lives. Rai Chaudhuri took to the streets in 2007 to protest the police firing in Nandigram in south Bengal, where farmers were protesting the setting up of a chemical hub on agricultural land. Chakrabarty's involvement with the Subaltern Studies project would never have happened without the Naxalite movement. 'There was a long-term positive academic impact too, and that happened mainly in the field of history. The Naxalite programme of 'beheading', around College Street and elsewhere, statues of some of the stalwarts of the Bengal renaissance led eventually to a healthy debate about the nature of nineteenth-century 'renaissance' in Bengal, and about the nature of the Indian capitalist classes. Without that questioning, Subaltern Studies would not have happened. You have to remember that most historians who were involved in launching the Subaltern Studies project had been part of—or at least sympathizers of—the Naxalite movement', says Chakrabarty. He adds, 'And I do think it affected the people involved for life. Even today I feel a strong sense of bonding with friends with whom I shared my excitement and dreams of those years.'

'Most went back to mainstream life. However, almost all stood out, wherever they worked, by their forthright behaviour, dignity and capability. They retained a strong sense of bonding with the toiling people, proved by their emergence on the streets in protest against the carnage in Nandigram, an army of the grey-haired, outnumbering, perhaps, the young protesters of today', avers Rai Chaudhuri.

On the impact of the Naxalites in villages, Rai Chaudhuri says:

> In the villages, the ideology suffered a setback but never died, waxing and waning in various old and new pockets, in old and new forms, till the early Eighties. It seemed to run out of momentum by that time, most of the old leaders having joined the electoral whirligig. The recent Maoist incursions from the west are well known and all I want to add is that the Maoists are ideologically descended from the same stock, and so, whether we like the Maoists or not, the engagement with Naxalite ideology is by no means over for the students and youth of West Bengal.

While the fires of revolution sparked by Naxalbari have spread and taken on a different character, the events that happened more than 40 years ago still remain a source of inspiration for some from the 1960s generation.

CHAPTER 5

Nepal: The Maoist Insurgency—Origin and Evolution

S.D. MUNI

Violence has played a significant role in Nepal's political history. Both the bloody struggle for power at the apex level and violent resistance against the state at the grassroots level have given decisive turns to Nepali politics. Two of the landmark events smeared in blood at the apex level are: (i) the Kot massacre of 1846 that led to the establishment of the Rana dynasty which ruled Nepal as hereditary prime ministers for more than a 100 years, reducing monarchy into a decorated, paralyzed institution, and (ii) the Narayanhiti (Royal Palace) massacre in June 2001 that changed the character of monarchy and led to its eventual elimination in 2008.

At the grassroots level, there is a long history of peasant revolts in Nepal. They date back to the early 1770s when the Gorkha conquests were still in the process of consolidation. The Rais, the Murmis and the Limbus of the eastern Nepal fought against the Gorkhali forces and later even joined the Chinese in this fight.[1]

Subsequently, the Murmis, Rais, Gurungs, Magars and Kiratis rose in revolt against the Nepali state for over 150 years between 1793 and 1950.[2] In 1951, King Tribhuwan himself led a movement against the autocratic 'Ranacracy', wherein he was supported by the armed revolt of the Nepali Congress and the Communist Party of Nepal. This movement laid down the foundations of a democratic polity under constitutional monarchy in Nepal, but the armed revolts against the state did not come to an end. Soon after the end of the Ranacracy, during 1951-3, the ousted extremist Ranas who had formed the Gorkha Dal revolted against the new government, followed by the group of Nepali Congress militants and peasants who took up arms under the leadership of Dr K.I. Singh and Bhim Dutta Pant.[3]

The experiment to build a constitutional monarchy came to an end in December 1960 when King Mahendra in a coup dismissed an elected Nepali Congress government and the parliament to establish his direct control over the polity. The Nepali Congress took up arms against the king's rule during the early 1960s. This resistance was suppressed, but armed protests by the Nepali Congress continued to erupt as part of their long struggle for democracy until the end of the king-dominated Panchayat system in 1991. In this struggle, the Nepali Congress procured arms through their clandestine sources in India where they also sought refuge and shelter to escape the king's repression, using the open border operating between India and Nepal under the treaty of 1950.

The foundations of the communist movement in Nepal were established in 1947 with the formation of the Communist Party of Nepal. It joined hands with the Nepali Congress in fighting the Ranacracy, but could not build its strength until the beginning of the 1970s. The ideological division in the international communist movement during the 1960s (the Sino-Soviet split) and the polarization of the monarchy *versus* Nepali Congress conflict within Nepal kept the communists divided and fragmented. There were nearly 20 big and small communist groups in Nepal by the 1980s.[4] No major armed struggle was launched by these communist factions except for the Maoists. In a lighter vein, many of these communist groups were termed in Nepal as the king's communists.

RISE OF THE MAOISTS

Maoism in Nepal was inspired by India's Naxalite movement that emerged during the late 1960s in the context of the Cultural Revolution in China. Some of the radical groups among the communists decided to experiment with the Maoist concept of 'people's war' by taking up arms in Nepal's eastern Terai region of Jhapa in May 1971. This is popularly known as the Jhapali revolt in Nepal's political history. The revolt was soon suppressed by ruthless police action. The failure of the revolt, which was followed by the end of the Chinese Cultural Revolution and Mao Zedong's death in 1976, led to serious ideological churning among the radical communists of Nepal, particularly among leaders like Pushpa Lal Shrestha (who had established the Communist Party of Nepal in 1947) and relatively younger leaders like Mohan Bikram Singh and Nirmal Lama. While Pushpa Lal remained committed to the traditional communist line willing to fight against the monarchy through communist unity and in collaboration with other parliamentary parties like Nepali Congress, Singh and Lama remained committed to armed struggle. But they split up in 1983-4 when Lama accepted the line of China's post-Mao leadership (i.e. Deng Xiaoping) while Singh continued to stick to the Maoists' methods. The young radical members of the Mohan Bikram Singh group included Baburam Bhattarai, Mohan Vaidya and Pushpa Kamal Dahal. They are the leaders of the present Communist Party of Nepal (Maoists), as it was named in 1994 after its break from Singh through a series of splits and mergers.[5]

The ideological issues of mass struggle in Nepal were at the root of numerous splits and mergers among the Maoists. They were oscillating between the methods of radical mass movement and Mao's 'people's war'. During both the students' struggle of 1979-80, which led to referendum on the Panchayat system and the first *Jan Andolan* (people's movement) of 1989-90, the Maoists of Nepal joined the Nepali Congress and the parliamentary communist groups to advance the 'mass struggle'. They, however, did not fully endorse the outcome of the first *Jan Andolan* which demolished the Panchayat system and absolute monarchy and restored constitutional monarchy with a multi-party democracy. Their constant ideological emphasis was on securing an elected Constituent Assembly to craft a people's democratic order for Nepal. Accordingly, they decided to pursue a dual strategy of playing the parliamentary game, while also preparing for the 'people's war'.[6] The Maoists fought a fierce people's war for a decade from 1996-2006 that eventually led to the elimination of monarchy, but there has never been a final and lasting ideological resolution among them on the most appropriate strategy for the success of their revolution.

The Maoist insurgency of Nepal has been a product of its socio-economic and political context. Nepal is one of the poorest countries in South Asia. At the end of Ranacracy, 85 per cent of employment and income were dependent on agriculture and less than 25 per cent of the population was literate. The monarchy was using the state for rentier purposes without initiating any development. For 30 years, from the king's takeover in 1960 to the success of the first *Jan Andolan* in 1990, Nepal's gross domestic product grew at an average of 1.5 per cent per annum.[7] Two of its major resources, the hydropower potential and tourism, remained unharnessed for political considerations. Land ownership remained archaic to reinforce feudal dominance. People migrated to India and other countries for livelihood, providing a political cushion to the monarchy.[8] Hope was generated in 1990 with the success of the first *Jan Andolan*. But the dominance of politics without concern for development and the disappointing role of the democratic leadership as well as the monarchy soon frustrated these hopes. Socially, a deep divide exists between the dominant castes (Brahmins, Chetries and Newars) and the marginalized nationalities.[9] Another cleavage between the dominant Paharis (hill people) and the Madeshi/Terians (lower flat-land people) has operated for decades. Madeshi people claim that though they constitute nearly 50 per cent of Nepal's population, their share in administration, army, business and governance is negligible.[10]

The socio-economic and political context of Nepal created conditions for the Maoist insurgency to emerge, but the causal relationship between the two becomes clear only when we look at the anatomy of this insurgency closely. The Maoists' 'people's war' was launched in February 1996 in Nepal's mid-west region compricing Rukum, Rolpa, Jajarkot, Salyan and Gorkha districts of the Rapti Zone. The Maoists also included Sindhuli district in the mid-east region in this launch. The mid-west region is a typical representative of Nepal's socio-economic context where the Maoists established the base of the 'people's war' in Rolpa and Rukum districts. These two districts have been traditional strongholds of the communist since 1950 and have remained one of the most under-developed parts of Nepal. The first road was laid in this region in 2003. Only 10 per cent of the land here is arable. Hashish, which grew in abundance in this area, formed an important source of livelihood, along with migration and recruitment in Indian and British armies. But, in 1976, the government banned 'production, distribution and sale' of hashish leading to considerable economic hardships for the inhabitants.[11]

The objective conditions of economic hardships were fuelled by additional factors to generate a strong sense of deprivation and neglect among the people of this area. Two of the royal princesses, the sisters of King Birendra and Gyanendra, were married to the feudal lords of Rukum and Rolpa. The regional royal families prospered on Kathmandu's patronage and lived in comfortable urban environs without ever paying any attention to the development of this region. A US $50 million Rapti Integrated Development Project run by the United States Agency for International Development (USAID), which otherwise benefitted many in the neighbouring districts, had no impact on Rolpa and Rukum. The development project could not reach these districts due to total absence of transport and communication access.[12] The result was a creeping sense of inequality and discrimination among the people of Rolpa and Rukum. It is this sense of inequality which had more to do with the rise of insurgency than simply the poor level of development.[13] If seen only in terms of the level of development, the far-flung districts of Karnali Zone could be a better theatre for the initial burst of the insurgency. In fact, the people in Rolpa and Rukum had their days of comfortable, if not prosperous living, when they had freedom to grow and sell hashish. The drift in their economic prospects after the ban on this vocation, added to by years of indifference on the part of the Nepali state, stirred among them a resolve to revolt.

The economic deprivation and inequality of the people of mid-west was reinforced by their social marginalization. Most of the inhabitants of the districts were Magars, who constituted 7 per cent of Nepal's population, the largest single minority. Being in a remote and inaccessible part of the kingdom, they were not integrated into the mainstream national life and the state never really governed them. The Magars living here speak Kham, which is distinct from the Magar mainstream language. Even during the creation of modern Nepal by Prithvi Narayan Shah, the Magars did not get fully subjugated, nursing in their subconscious mind an aspiration for autonomy, if not sovereign independence.[14] Rolpa and Rukum also had exposure to Christianity. They believe in their own form of 'animism' and do not quite identify with the Hindu character of Nepal's monarchical state.[15]

These economic and social factors, added to the political isolation and marginalization, facilitated strong communist activities in this part of Nepal. The Maoists had carefully studied the political economy as well as topography of mid-western Nepal while deciding to launch their 'people's war' and make it a base of their 'revolutionary' operations. The party documents adopted at the Third Plenum of the Central Committee in March 1995, describing the 'strategy and tactics of armed struggle in Nepal', clearly took note of the 'conscious peasant class struggle developed in the western hill districts, particularly Rolpa and Rukum. It represents the high level of anti-feudal and anti-imperialist revolutionary struggle. That struggle has given birth to some new tendencies in the Nepali communist movement, which have inspired us to be more serious about the business of armed struggle'.[16] Later in an interview to Li Onesto of *Revolutionary Worker* in 1999, the Maoist chief Prachanda said:

> The west is historically, geographically and culturally the core of the revolution. It is the main starting point for the revolution—the people here are more oppressed by the ruling classes and the government in Kathmandu is very far from here. . . .
>
> . . . masses of the Western region were not so much under the control of the ruling government, and they did not care what the government did or did not do. . .in Western Nepal, there are the Mongoloid ethnic groups. . . . These nationalities are so sincere and such brave fighters—historically they have had this kind of culture. Upper caste chauvinism and feudal ties do not prevail among these nationalities.[17]

BEYOND ROLPA AND RUKUM

The significance of Rukum and Rolpa in the launching of the Maoists' 'people's war' should be seen in the larger context of economic under-development, socio-cultural marginalization and political exclusion of a large number of social groups in the whole of Nepal. Besides Magars who inhabited Rolpa and Rukum, there were a number of other ethnic minorities like Tamangs, Gurungs, Rais, Limbus, Kirats, Tharus and marginalized caste groups like Dalits (untouchables), scattered all over Nepal, in the hills as well as in Terai. The yearnings of these people for a respectable place in the country's social, economic and political system were gaining momentum gradually with the rise of awareness, identity consciousness and aspirations for better life. These excluded groups, including the Madheshis, constituted more than 70 per cent of Nepal's population. They had been asking for their rights over the years, as reflected in the political turbulence and agitation for democracy since the 1930s. It was the failure of the monarchy and of the democratic leadership, which created conditions for the rise of the Maoists as leaders of a new struggle for change. Writing in 2003 on the 'political economy of the People's War', the Maoist leader Baburam Bhattarai said:

> The process of the People's War is a link in a chain of just such a continuous revolution in Nepal to solve its current economic and social problems. The principal objective and rationale of the people's war in Nepal is, thus to develop the social productive forces and create a higher form of society through a continuous revolution of the base and the superstructure by putting 'politics in command'.[18]

Accordingly, the Maoists' agenda for Nepal's socio-economic transformation was not devoid of the goal of assuming power and changing its political structure.

The question may be raised here of the timing of the 'people's war' in 1996, though the Maoist groups have been involved in political processes since the 1970s. The factors that triggered the insurgency may be taken note of. It has been mentioned earlier that the Maoists did not accept the outcome of the 1989-90 *Jan Andolan-I* (people's movement). But they decided to contest the 1991 parliamentary elections and managed to secure a noticeable presence in the democratically elected parliament with nine seats and the status as the third largest party, though way behind the two mainstream parties, i.e. the Nepali Congress and the Communist Party of Nepal (ML) (later renamed as United Marxist Leninist—UML). They mobilized civil servants and other professional groups to agitate for their demands against the government, but these agitations were put down strongly and both the dominant parties got almost united in treating the Maoists shabbily in and outside the parliament.[19] Then came the fall of the government in 1994 and announcement of fresh elections. The Maoist groups got split on the question of elections, with the group led by Prachanda and Baburam being denied recognition by the Election Commission. This group contested its de-recognition and eventually won its case in Nepal courts, but by then elections were over. Having been treated ruthlessly by the state, this faction was not for participating in the election, but the Election Commission's unsustainable denial of recognition added to their alienation from parliamentary politics.

It is true that the Maoists had entered parliament as a part of their 'two line struggle' of working for revolution and simultaneously participating in the parliamentary processes. Their participation in parliament, being a cover for their 'revolutionary' zeal and strategy, was no indication of their lack of commitment to the 'people's war'. But, if the Maoists could be encouraged and accommodated in their parliamentary politics by the other mainstream parties and treated as legitimate partners in political dynamics in the interest of constructive democratic evolution and consolidation in Nepal, their recourse to the 'people's war' in 1996 could have at least been delayed, and in the long run, perhaps gradually weakened. There was a constant debate within the Maoist groups on strategy and tactics as well as also on the timing of the 'people's war'. This debate could have been deepened and the plea for people's struggle within the framework of peaceful parliamentary politics strengthened if the Maoists' agitational politics and mobilization had been spared strong-arm methods. It may not be far off the mark to say that ruthless police operations during 1994-5, particularly the operation code-named as 'Romeo' in 1995, not only reinforced the Maoists' resolve to launch the 'people's war', but also enabled them to swell their ranks by recruiting young cadres and gaining sympathies of large sections of people all over Nepal. The *Human Rights Year Book of Nepal* for 1995 listed the gory details of police oppression.[20] Commenting on 'Operation Romeo' in Rolpa, the Maoist leader Baburam Bhattarai said in a press interview in December 1995:

> Around 1,500 policemen . . . have been deployed to let loose a reign of terror against the poor peasants . . . there has been indiscriminate ransacking and looting of properties of common people by the ruling party hoodlums under the protection of the police force. More than 10,000 rural youth, out of a population of 200,000 for the whole district, have been forced to flee their homes and take shelter in remote jungles.[21]

This repression led the Maoists to submit a charter of 40 demands to the government in February 1996 giving it 10 days to respond. But even before the expiry of the deadline, the 'people's war' was launched. Yet another ruthless police operation on an extended scale covering 18 Maoist-infested districts in 1998, code named 'Kilo Sierra-2', further facilitated the Maoists in getting new recruits and enhanced public support and sympathy. It helped them to spread their 'people's war' into an increasing number of Nepal's districts, reaching 45 out of a total of 75 districts by 2001.

The repression unleashed by the government against the Maoists could have been bloodier if the army had been deployed against them. However, King Birendra did not let this happen. There were a number of considerations in the king's firm resistance to the use of army against the Maoists. Deploying army under the leadership of a political party-led government would have meant a dilution of the king's own power base, as the party could get access to and influence over the Royal Army's command structure. The king was also averse to escalating the civil war which would have resulted from the army's deployment. As the use of the army would have been on a long-term basis, this would also have meant strengthening of the army and incurring more expenses. The escalation of conflict with the ruthlessness of the army would also have resulted in unpopularity of the king among the affected people. King Birendra, known for his comparatively liberal views, emphasized a political approach. He established clandestine contacts with the Maoists through his younger brother Dhirendra and even arranged to have talks with them. The Maoist leader Prachanda disclosed it years later in 2010, when he said: 'Birendra's youngest brother Dhirendra was in touch with us and we were to start direct talks with him within a month with the request to abdicate his throne and become the country's first president. He was killed in this backdrop.'[22] Analysts in Nepal also attribute King Birendra's reluctance to the deployment of army against the Maoists as a reflection of his frustration with the way the political parties were managing the insurgency. The possibility of him making deft use of the Maoist insurgency to weaken and discredit the political parties also cannot be ruled out. The Maoists deeply lamented the assassination of King Birendra and his family and took out public demonstrations to sympathize with him and other victims of the palace massacre. Baburam Bhattarai wrote in an open letter published after the sixth day of the royal massacre:

> Whatever your political ideology might be, one thing every honest Nepali nationalist has to agree with is this: King Birendra's liberal political ideology and his patriotism were seen as his weaknesses and had become a crime in the eyes of the expansionist and imperialist powers . . . his unwillingness to mobilise the army—which has a tradition of loyalty towards the King—to curb the People's revolution taking place under the leadership of the Nepal Communist Party (Maoist) became his biggest crime. . . . Some Marxist pundits, based on this, called us a pro-monarchist party, and we can now say that we—NCP (Maoist) and King Birendra—had similar views on many national issues and this had created in fact an informal alliance between us.[23]

This 'informal alliance' between the king and the Maoists changed into an unmitigated antipathy under the new king Gyanendra. Permission to deploy the Royal Nepal Army (RNA) against the Maoists was granted by the new king in September 2001. Taking advantage of the changed international context after 9/11, where international community supported strong anti-terrorism methods, King Gyanendra resolved to militarily eliminate the Maoists and assume greater powers in the name of fighting terrorism. In this process, he also wanted to sideline the political parties, as since 2002 he increasingly took control of the administration directly into his hands leading eventually to his coup in February 2005.

It was this use of army against the Maoists that made the RNA and the Maoists enemies. There were no indications of hostility between them until the end of King Birendra's regime in 2001. Initially, the RNA fared badly against the Maoists. It had never been exposed to a resolute and well-organized ideological rebellion. In the 23 operations listed between November 2001 and December 2002, the Maoists claimed success against the RNA in all except about four.[24] In these operations, they had destroyed army camps and even taken possession of many of their weapons. The army therefore had to be expanded and heavily equipped. Its strength reached almost 100,000 by April 2006, when the *Jan Andolan-II* eventually brought the Maoist insurgency to an end. But the enhanced strength also did not result in the RNA's victory over the Maoists. At best, it created a stalemate where the army could defend its cantonments only, without stirring out to challenge the Maoists in rural or urban areas. On their part, the Maoists perfected the tactics of paralyzing the movement of goods and people on the main road network of Nepal and creation of chaos in the country. The hostility between the two precipitated the issue of 'civilian supremacy' and equal treatment of the Maoists' People's Liberation Army and the RNA. This issue has vitiated the whole peace process in Nepal and, if not resolved soon, threatens to restart the insurgency as we shall see later.

An important factor in building up the Maoist insurgency and carrying forward their 'people's war' was the nature of leadership. We have noted that the beginning of the Maoist movement in Nepal took place in the early 1970s in the context of the Chinese Cultural Revolution and the rise of Naxal revolt in India. The internal ideological and leadership conflicts kept the Nepal Maoists preoccupied for the first decade. Prachanda admited that by 1985, he and his associates had the clarity that their struggle should be waged on the basis of Marxist-Leninist-Maoist ideas.[25] The present leaders of the Maoist movement stand out distinctly from their predecessors in two areas, namely intellectual sharpness and ideological resilience. The present Maoist leaders, at least the top duo of Prachanda and Baburam Bhattarai, are better educated. While Prachanda completed his graduation in agricultural science, Baburam after obtaining an engineering degree, did his Ph.D. at India's Jawaharlal Nehru University. The intellectual agility and higher educational levels of this leadership have enabled the Maoists to engage with a diversity of contacts and ideas, both within and outside Nepal. This in turn has helped them to broaden their approach and imbibe the lessons learnt from this exposure in carrying their movement forward. It has also enabled them to cast the requirements of their movement to adjust with the prevailing regional and international context within which Nepal is placed, as also the internal socio-economic dynamics that impinges on their political objectives.

The second notable character of the present Maoist leadership is their ideological resilience and strategic pragmatism. Most of their predecessors had remained stuck to the dogmas of Marxist and Leninist thought without relating these thoughts to Nepal's internal and external realities. They also believed in preparing foolproof plans before launching substantial and decisive actions, in turn keeping them static in their proposed struggle. The present leadership analysed the failure of the communist movements and learning from them has tried to evolve a synthesis of the ideal and the real; the praxis of thought and action, in the classical Marxist sense. Explaining his approach to 'people's war', Prachanda said:

> . . . we must also learn war by waging war. The intellectuals' instinctive tendency is that we have to learn all these things, we should read everything, . . . and then we can make war. These kinds of tendencies were there right from the beginning. But we said, no, this is not Maoism. This is not Marxism. This is not dialectical materialism. . . . The issue is of learning war through war itself.[26]

A couple of years later, in 2001, he added: 'In our opinion, the real key to rapid development of the People's War is the fusion between the science of proletarian revolution, on the one hand, and the needs and fighting spirit of the Nepalese people, on the other.'[27]

The ideological resilience and pragmatism is also in the definition of their ideological exposition in the form of *Prachanda Path* (Prachanda Line) that goes beyond Marxist-Leninist-Maoist straitjacket. Prachanda described *Prachanda Path* as 'enrichment of Marxism-Leninism-Maoism' and 'a new example of creative Marxism, opposed to both, the right revisionists and sectarian dogmatists'.[28] Though this amounted to ego projection and bragging on the part of the leader, it nonetheless synergized their Marxist ideology with Nepali nationalism and added a popular flavour and appeal to the movement. The ideological resilience and pragmatism also enabled them to play the Marxists' concept like 'united front' and 'two line struggle' for forging alliances and tactical equations with all sorts of contradictory forces, ranging from monarchy to the multi-party proponents. Consistency has not really been the ideological virtue of the present Maoist leadership. The strength of this approach has been evident in their success in bringing together diverse, marginalized social groups under their struggle and secure support from their known adversaries, howsoever, tactical and short-lived this support might have proved. It moved their movement and political goals ahead. A significant contribution of their pragmatic approach can be seen in the involvement of women in their struggle in a big way. Almost 30 per cent of their cadres have been women and this strengthened the movement in several respects.[29] It has brought gender equality to the forefront of new Nepal's political agenda.

The new Maoist leadership has, however, not been free from internal tensions and rivalries. These tensions have manifested on issues of ideology and tactics, on united front allies and adversaries.[30] A serious ideological and personality cleavage exists between the Maoist supremo Prachanda and his better-educated and ideologically-grounded deputy, Baburam Bhattarai. This cleavage has erupted periodically, at times threatening to split the movement vertically. Some of Prachanda's close associates have also resisted the rise of Baburam Bhattarai within the organization to preserve their own respective places around the party chief. The party has managed to keep the organizational unity largely because Baburam Bhattarai does not seem to have a stronger push for power or personality projection.

THE EXTERNAL DIMENSION

Nepal's Maoist insurgency was considerably helped by the external factor. As noted above, the new Maoist leadership was induced to establish wider contacts and learning from their external exposure. Their first contacts were with the Indian Naxalites in the 1970s, as noted earlier. But the new Maoist leadership has expanded these contacts and there have been reports that Prachanda played a significant role in facilitating the merger of India's Maoist Communist Centre (MCC) and the People's War Group. The Nepal Maoists also established close contacts with the Nepali diaspora (8 to 10 million strong), in pursuance of their political agenda. These contacts with the Naxalites and the Nepali diaspora substantially helped the Maoists in ensuring shelter and 'safe havens', procuring arms, training and mobilizing financial support in India. Way back in 1985, they were among the founding fathers of the Revolutionary International Movement (RIM), which aimed at networking with the radical left movements all over the world. This brought the Nepal Maoists into the contact of Peruvian communists and led them to study and imbibe ideas from the Shining Path. In some ways, the inspiration for evolving its own ideological trademark and naming it as *Prachanda Path* came from the Nepali Maoists' interaction with the Peruvian Communist Party. The Nepal Maoists also took initiative in bringing the South Asian Maoist groups onto one platform by establishing the Coordination Committee of the Maoists Parties of South Asia (CCOMPOSA) in July 2001. There have been annual meetings of CCOMPOSA since then to take a collective position on some of the regional and global issues. Explaining the advantages of all these external contacts and their role in advancing the Maoist movement in Nepal, Prachanda said:

> . . . there was consistent international involvement. First and foremost, there was the RIM (Revolutionary International Movement) Committee. . . . From the RIM Committee, we gained the experience of the PCP (Communist Party of Peru) and of the two line struggle there, and also we shared experience in Turkey, in Iran, in the Philippines. We learned from the experience in Bangladesh and from some of the experience in Sri Lanka. There was a South Asian Conference in which we participated. At the same time we were also having direct and continuous debate with the Indian communists, mainly the People's War (PW) and the Maoist Communist Centre (MCC) groups. All of this helped in one way or another; it helped us to understand the whole process of People's War.[31]

The Nepal Maoists went beyond the communist and Maoist groups in seeking support and establishing linkages in the interest of their struggle. After a careful analysis of the changing international and regional strategic context that had become strongly oriented towards anti-terrorism in the aftermath of 9/11, the Maoists sought to differentiate themselves from the 'terrorist groups'. For this, they wrote letters to various heads of states in the United States, Europe and also to the United Nations Secretary-General. They also tried to reach highest levels in the Government of India to explain their political goals and ensure the Indian government that they would desist from doing anything against India's vital interests.[32] This international mobilization of support was essentially prompted by the fears that King Gyanendra was seeking military support from the

US and the United Kingdom to defeat their 'people's war', invoking the post-9/11 context of counter-terrorism. Support and understanding was secured in India, not only from the government but also political parties, intellectuals and civil society members. This proved critical in fighting against King Gyanendra's autocratic moves and in leading to the success of the *Jan Andolan-II,* launched by the Maoists in alliance with the mainstream political parties of Nepal. The success of the *Jan Andolan-II* in April 2006 marked the culmination, or at least a radical transformation of the 'people's war'.

UNFOLDING OF THE INSURGENCY

Nepal's Maoist insurgency has unfolded gradually in various stages. These stages were influenced by the broader dynamics of Nepali politics and the changing regional and international strategic parameters. The first stage, from the beginning of 1970 to 1985, was of the Jhapali revolt as mentioned earlier, when the Maoists leaders mobilized peasants of Jhapa in eastern Nepal to take up arms. This revolt was an unprepared beginning by romantic Maoists and was quickly suppressed by the Nepali state. This led to an intense debate among the Maoists on the experience of the Jhapali revolt and the strategy to move the struggle forward. By 1985, at least a section of the Maoists had come to the conclusion that Maoism has to be treated as an integrated part of Marxist-Leninist thought and the parameters of the movement have to be cast in the wider context of international experiences. This led to the second stage of further ideological churning and leadership struggle, which ended in 1995 when the present Maoist leadership emerged as a focused group determined to launch the 'people's war'.

The 'people's war' has passed through two major stages. One was from 1996 to 2001, when the Maoists fought with state police forces with rudimentary weapons, expanded their cadres and strengthened their organization, established base areas and developed institutions of governance, including kangaroo courts. According to the Maoists, this stage of the 'people's war' was carried out according to strategic plans namely: decentralized actions within centralized plan and command; balance between political and military offensives against the enemy; political justification of military action; utilization of the contradictions amongst the enemies to isolate the main enemy; organization and mobilization of the masses in the quickest and best possible way.[33] During this stage, the 'main enemy' was the party governments of the Nepali Congress and the Communist Party of Nepal—UML. The king was treated as an ally. Besides attacking police posts, the Maoists also ruthlessly killed many of the political activists of the ruling parties, occupied their properties and distributed their lands to their own cadres.

The second stage of the 'people's war', from 2001 to 2006, began with two major developments: one inside Nepal and another outside. In June 2001, Nepal witnessed the ghastly royal massacre that changed the character of monarchy. The new king Gyanendra followed his father's strategy of acquiring more powers at the cost of representative institutions and popular parties. He dismissed the parliament in 2002 and assumed all executive powers in a coup on 1 February 2005. He also decided to deal with the Maoists strongly, unlike his brother, the slain King Birendra and deployed the army against them. Externally, 9/11 took place unleashing the reactive 'global war on terror' under the US leadership. With this, military assistance started pouring into the RNA, especially from India, the US and the UK. The Maoists' enhanced confidence through their success during the first phase and the deployment of a well-assisted RNA made the 'people's war' dirtier and bloodier. There were brutal killings by both the sides, though independent estimates by a Kathmandu-based NGO—Informal Sector Service Centre (INSEC)—attributed two-thirds of the killings to the RNA and one-third to the Maoists between 13 February 1996 and 24 April 2006.[34] The Maoists expanded their operations, covering more than 80 per cent of all the Nepali districts. The army's responses also gradually improved with greater training and better equipment through external assistance. The brutality of the conflict deepened and reinforced the antagonism between the Maoists and the RNA that subsequently created serious difficulties in the progress of the peace process.

During this second stage of the 'people's war', a realization started dawning on the Maoists that while they may have reached a strategic balance with the RNA by 2002-3, it may not be possible for them to achieve total victory in their struggle. Even if they succeeded in capturing the state through their 'people's war', the international community and India would not let them retain the control of the state for long. They had already activated their political front by exploiting the emerging conflict between King Gyanendra and the political parties, seeking 'united front' with the latter, and also by approaching India and the international community to explain that they were not waging a terrorist war, but a genuine political struggle of socio-economic emancipation for the Nepali people. Between 2001 and 2003, the Maoists had rounds of ceasefires and talks with the king's government and they increasingly interacted with the political parties in search of a 'united front' against the autocratic monarchy. King Gyanendra's coup of 2005 greatly facilitated this search as that move had not only antagonized all the political parties, but also alienated the international community. The result was the 12 Point Understanding signed in November 2005 between the Maoists and the mainstream parliamentary parties of Nepal, who had earlier formed a Seven Party Alliance (SPA). This understanding precipitated a 19-day-long *Jan Andolan-II,* from 6 to 24 April 2006, leading to the collapse of King Gyanendra's autocracy and the eventual elimination of monarchy less than two years later.

Under the 12 Point Understanding and post-*Jan Andolan-II* peace process, the Maoists have abandoned their 'people's war' and committed themselves to peaceful and democratic participation in restructuring a new Nepal. The peace process gave the Maoists a share in power, first as a junior coalition partner under the interim government headed by G.P. Koirala of the Nepali Congress and then as leader of the coalition after the Constituent Assembly elections held in April 2008, in which the Maoists, surprising all their opponents, emerged as the largest block. This Maoist victory seems to have become a source of the undoing of Nepal's fragile peace process.

The vulnerabilities of the peace process arise from serious deviations on the part of both the Maoists and the mainstream political parties in their commitments made under the 12 Point Understanding, as well as the Comprehensive Peace Agreement concluded on 21 November 2006.[35] The Maoists have not returned to the legitimate owners the land and properties that were occupied by them during the insurgency nor have they completely given up their strong-arm methods of coercive political mobilization. This has given rise to doubts about the sincerity of their commitment to democratic functioning, and also because they continue to harp on their radical rhetoric of the 'people's war' period. Possibly, the Maoists accepted the outcome of the *Jan Andolan-II* in the form of the reinstatement of the dissolved parliament and installation of an interim government under G.P. Koirala only as a compromise and yet another stage in their revolutionary struggle. The mainstream political parties on their part have not accepted the Maoists as equal partners in the democratic political process. This was evident during the interim government when no critically important portfolio was given to the Maoist ministers. It became even more evident when a representative government was not installed for three months under the Maoist leadership after the April 2008 elections by the interim Prime Minister Koirala, under one flimsy pretext or the other. Even then, the Nepali Congress decided to stay out of the government and play the role of opposition, contrary to the agreement on consensual politics until the writing of the constitution by the elected Constituent Assembly. The mainstream parties have also been reluctant to integrate the Maoists' armed cadres into Nepal's security forces. It was this issue that precipitated the conflict between the Maoists and the Nepal Army, resulting in the ouster of the Maoist government in May 2009.[36] The mainstream parties united to form an alternative government, keeping the Maoists, the largest single group, in opposition. India and other interested international forces are keeping this fragile government functioning without any real governance or the prospects of the peace process reaching its culmination through the writing of the new constitution, the deadline for which was 27 May 2010.[37]

The hard reality of Nepali politics at this juncture is that Nepal's peace process and constitution writing cannot proceed unless there is a constructive political consensus, at least among the Maoists, the Nepali Congress, the Communist Party of Nepal (UML) and the Terai-based parties. This consensus has actually broken down on the question of power sharing since the installation of the Maoists government in May 2008, when the Nepali Congress as an opposition party created difficulties in carrying the peace process forward. The consensus was further strained on the issue of 'civilian supremacy' over the army raised by the Maoists to secure the sacking of the then army chief General Rukmangad Katawal. The political parties connived with the president to defeat the cabinet decision (with dissent from other coalition partners) of the Maoist-led ministry. The Maoists resigned on this issue and have been demanding redress on the 'civilian supremacy' issue and restoration of a national government under their leadership.

On both these issues, the Maoist position, at least theoretically, is justified because the army cannot defy the civilian authority in a democracy and the largest group in the Constituent Assembly has the legitimate privilege to head the government. However, the deep trust deficit which exists among the main stakeholders in political power is not allowing any way out of the political impasse. It may not be out of place to mention here that while the Maoists have also sufficiently contributed to the prevailing trust deficit, the mainstream parties and the international community can in no way escape blame. They are equally responsible for ensuring the culmination of the Nepali peace process and securing the mainstreaming of the Maoists. The Maoists, at least ostensibly, abandoned their 'people's war' in favour of fair accommodation in democratic politics. Keeping them out is forcing them to consider reviving the 'people's war'. Nepal is certainly not prepared for the 'people's war II', and the Maoists cannot be wished away from the unfolding Nepali politics. Whether an amicable resolution to save Nepal from another round of chaos and anarchy can be engineered remains to be seen.

NOTES

1. M.C. Regmi, *Imperial Gorkha* (New Delhi: Adroit Publications, 1999), p. 11.
2. Harka Gurung, 'Rastriyata re rajniti' (Nationality and Politics), in May des Chene and Pratyoush Onta (eds.), *Nepal ko Sandarbh ma Samaj Shastriya Chintan* (*Social Science Thoughts in the Context of Nepal*) (Lalitpur, Nepal: Himal Books, 2004).
3. For some details see Deepak Thapa, 'Tackling Insurgency: The Nepal Case', in S.D. Muni (ed.), *Responding to Terrorism in South Asia* (New Delhi: Manohar, 2006).
4. Narayan Khadka, 'Factionalism in the Communist Movement in Nepal', *Pacific Affairs*, vol. 68, no. 1 (Spring 1995), pp. 55-76.
5. See S.L. Mikesell, *Class, State and Struggle in Nepal* (New Delhi: Manohar, 1999); Arjun Karki and David Seddon, 'The People's War in Historical Context', in Arjun Karki and David Seddon (eds.), *The People's War in Nepal: Left Perspectives* (New Delhi: Adroit Publishers, 2003).
6. Michael Hutt (ed.), *Himalayan People's War: Nepal Maoist Rebellion* (Bloomington: Indiana University Press, 2004). (Specially see the chapters by Michael Hutt, 'Monarchy, Democracy and Maoism in Nepal', Deepak Thapa, 'Radicalism and Emergence of the Maoists' and Sudheer Sharma, 'The Maoist Movement: An Evolutionary Perspective'. Also see Mahendra Lawoti and Anup Kumar Pahari (eds.), *The Maoist Insurgency in Nepal: Revolution in the Twenty-first Century* (London: Routledge, 2009).
7. Sujeev Shakya, *Unleashing Nepal: Past, Present and Future of the Economy* (New Delhi: Penguin, 2009), p. 50.

8. Dr Baburam Bhattarai, who is now the second-ranking Maoist leader, has been making this argument since the late 1970s. For his analysis of Nepal's developmental dilemma, see Baburam Bhattarai, *The Nature of Underdevelopment and Regional Structure of Nepal: A Marxist Analysis* (New Delhi: Adroit Publishers, 2003).
9. Harka Gurung, op. cit. Also see Pitamber Sharma, *Unravelling the Mosaic: Spatial Aspects of Ethnicity in Nepal* (Kathmandu: Himal Books, 2008).
10. Fredrick H. Gaige, *Regionalism and National Unity in Nepal* (Berkeley: University of California Press, 1975); International Crisis Group, 'Nepal's Troubled Terai Region', *Asia Report #1* (July 2007); Jason Malik, 'Nepal's Terai: Constructing an Ethnic Conflict', *South Asia Briefing Paper #1* (Peace Research Institute of Oslo, 2009).
11. Robert Gersony, 'Western Nepal Conflict Assessment: History & Dynamics of the Maoist Revolt', *Mercy Corps: Be the Change* (September 2003), www.mercycorps.org/sites/default/files/file1137793491.pdf 7 (accessed on 28 July 2010).
12. Ibid.
13. Fran Moore, 'A Spatial Analysis of the Causal Factors of Nepal's Maoist Insurgency', *ES 103-Spatial Analysis of Social and Environmental Systems* (May 2006), www.docstoc.com/docs/2413244/ A-Spatial-Analysis-of-the-Causal-Factots-of-Nepal%EF%BF%BDS-Maoist. Also see M. Mansood Murshid and Scott Gates, 'Spatial-Horizontal Inequality and the Maoist Insurgency in Nepal', *Review of Development Economics,* vol. 9, no.1 (February 2005), pp. 121-34 (accessed on 28 July 2010).
14. Mercy Corps report, op. cit., pp. 26-30.
15. Ibid. Some scholars have also identified alienation of the tribal groups from the Hindu state as a factor in the rise of Maoists in Nepal. Philippe Ramirez, 'Pour une anthropologie religieuse du maoism nepalais' (in French), *Srchieves des sciences sociales des religions,* vol. 42, no. 99 (July-September 1997), pp. 47-68.
16. As cited in Karki and Seddon, op. cit., p. 18.
17. The full text of the interview can be found in www.mcs.net/-rwor/a/v21/1040-049/1043/interv.htm (accessed on 28 July 2010).
18. See his chapter in Karki and Seddon, op. cit., p. 164.
19. Deepak Thapa, 'The Maobadi of Nepal', in K.M. Dixit and S. Ramachandran (eds.), *State of Nepal* (Kathmandu: Himal Books, 2002).
20. Ibid.
21. As quoted in Thapa, ibid.
22. *Hindustan Times* (10 January 2010).
23. *Kantipur* (6 June 2001).
24. *The Worker*, a Maoist organ, has listed these operations. See S.D. Muni, *Maoist Insurgency in Nepal: The Challenge and the Response,* Annexure III (New Delhi: Rupa & Co., 2003), pp. 88-9.

25. Prachanda's interview with Li Onesto, op. cit.
26. Ibid.
27. Interview to *RIM* magazine, 'A World to Win' (28 May 2001). Text in Karki and Seddon, op. cit.
28. Ibid., p. 276.
29. Com. Parvati, *Women's Participation in the People's War*, in Karki and Seddon, op. cit. Also see, Hisila Yami, 'Women's Role in the Nepalese Movement: Making a People's Constitution', *Monthly Review* (8 March 2010), http://mzine.monthlyreview.org/2010/yami080310.html (accessed on 28 July 2010). For the tensions arising from the large women cadres in the movement, see Rita Manchanda, 'Maoist Insurgency in Nepal: Radicalizing Gender Narratives', *Cultural Dynamics*, vol. 16, nos. 2-3 (New Delhi: Sage Publications, 2004), pp. 237-58.
30. For details see, ICG Reports, 'Nepal Maoists: Their Aims, Structure and Strategy', *Asia Report No. 104* (27 October 2005); and 'Nepal's Maoists: Purists or Pragmatists?', *Asia Report No. 132* (18 May 2007).
31. Interview with Li Onesto, op. cit.
32. See S.D. Muni, 'Bringing Maoists Down from the Hill: India's Role', in David Malone et al. (eds.), *Conflict Resolution in Nepal* (forthcoming).
33. Prachanda's interview with *RIM* magazine (May 2001), op. cit.
34. Conflict Study Centre, 'Situation Update VIII: Ratification of International Criminal Court to Just Peace' (15 September 2006), www.nepalresearch.org/coup_2005/paper/csc_060915.pdf (accessed on 28 July 2010).
35. For details see, 'Nepal's Peace Agreement: Making It Work', *Asia Report No. 126* (Brussels: International Crisis Group, December 2006).
36. On the Army-Maoists conflict see S.D. Muni, 'The Civil-Military Crisis in Nepal', *Hindu* (6 May 2009).
37. See the address by B. Lynn Pascoe, the UN Under-Secretary-General for Political Affairs, *Nepal's Peace Process* (Kathmandu: Nepal Institute of Policy Studies, 11 March 2010). Also, W.A. Sunil, 'Political Standoff in Nepal over Constitution', *World Socialist Website* (17 March 2010), www.wsws.org/tools/index.php?page=print&url=http%3A%2F%2Fwww.wsws (accessed on 28 July 2010).

CHAPTER 6

Pakistan: The Rise and Fall of the Maoist Movement

ISHTIAQ AHMED

Pakistan came into being on 14 August 1947 as a result of the failure of extended negotiations mainly between the Indian National Congress (a secular-nationalist party predominantly under modern-educated Hindu leaders) and the Muslim League (an exclusive communal party headed by modern-educated Muslims) to evolve a formula over sharing of power in a united India.[1] The Partition of India was attended by the biggest forced migration in recent history. More than 1 million (current estimates suggest a figure as high as 2 million) Hindus, Muslims and Sikhs lost their lives and some 14-17 million fled their homes in search of safe haven.

In the north-eastern and north-western Muslim-majority zones that were separated from the rest of India and given to Pakistan, there was hardly any industry. Pakistan received only 9.6 per cent of the total number of industrial units (1,414 out of 14,677); 5.3 per cent of the electric capacity (72,700 kW out of a total capacity of 1,375,000 kW); 6.5 per cent of the industrial workers (206,100 out of a total of 3,141,800); and only 10 per cent of the known mineral deposits.[2] Most of the industrial units were small-scale, usually simple home-based production. The economy as a whole was agrarian and in terms of class structure, various categories of peasants and land-owners constituted the bulk of the population.

Radical peasant uprisings had begun to appear in India from the beginning of the twentieth century. Some were inspired by general anti-colonial patriotism while others came increasingly to be associated with the communist movement. The Sikh peasantry in the Punjab was—for a number of cultural, historical and socio-economic reasons—more receptive to radical ideas than Hindus and Muslims and a disproportionately large number of communist activists and militants had emerged from amongst Sikh ranks in the Punjab.[3] It is interesting to note that the Communist Party of India (CPI) had supported the demand for a separate Pakistan, describing it as a popular movement of the Muslim masses for national self-determination.[4] Consequently many Muslim cadres of the CPI had joined the Muslim League and during the election campaign used the public meetings as a platform to propagate the idea of Pakistan as a peasant paradise free from the exploitation of Hindu moneylenders and landlords. At the time of Partition, no formal decision to split the CPI had been taken. However, the annual congress of the CPI at Calcutta in December 1948, which was attended by delegates from Pakistan, decided to split the party. Some prominent communists of Muslim background were instructed to emigrate to Pakistan so as to help organize the Communist Party of Pakistan (CPP).

However, in independent Pakistan, hostility towards communism became a centrepiece of state ideology. In future all sections of Muslim society were to work together rather than confront one another.[5] A popular discourse drawing on notions of an Islamic order and an Islamic state began to be churned out by Muslim *ulama* (clerics) and right-wing newspapers. Quite simply the argument that came to characterize the discussion on the ideological foundations of Pakistan was that it was an Islamic state and, therefore, there was no place for atheistic ideologies in such a polity.

In early March 1951, Prime Minister Liaqat Ali Khan announced that his government had uncovered a plot involving some officers of the armed forces and leading members and sympathizers of the Communist Party to overthrow the government. It was alleged that the conspirators intended to 'create commotion in the country by violent means and to subvert the loyalty of the Pakistan defence forces'.[6] The accused were alleged to have met several times in Rawalpindi to plan the insurgence. Among the civilians arrested was Sajjad Zaheer, the general secretary of the CPP, Faiz Ahmed Faiz, a famous poet and editor of the radical Lahore-based English-language newspaper, the *Pakistan Times*, and Muhammad Husain Ata, a prominent trade union leader. The accused were tried on camera by a special tribunal. The charges could not be proved against them. The court, however, sentenced the civilians to four years in prison and a fine of Rs. 500 each. The military officers received various sentences ranging from three to seven years. The ringleader General Akbar Khan was sentenced to a long exile of 12 years.

In any event, the prevailing policy of imposing restrictions on the activities of the leftists was made even harsher. However, the communists and the pro-communist intellectuals continued to play a part in Pakistani politics through their support to the autonomy movements of the dominated provinces of Baluchistan, East Bengal, North-West Frontier and Sindh. In the provincial elections held in East Bengal in March 1954, a united front constituted by a number of parties opposed to West Pakistani domination won 223 seats out of a total of 237 seats reserved for Muslims. These developments created panic among the ruling Muslim League government. It retaliated by alleging that the united front and the CPP were involved in a conspiracy to undo the unity of Pakistan by supporting secessionist movements. Consequently, a ban was imposed on the CPP in July 1954.[7] Its offices were closed, records and publications impounded and all assets confiscated. A countrywide crackdown on party cadres took place. On the general political, intellectual and cultural fronts, harassment and intimidation of leftists was intensified.

Given the polarization in international politics in the wake of the Cold War, Pakistan's repression of leftists won it considerable acclaim from the United States. Pakistan joined the Southeast Asia Treaty Organization (SEATO) in 1954 and the Baghdad Pact in 1955, and later the Central Treaty Organization (CENTO). In October 1958, the Pakistani armed forces led by the commander-in-chief, General Mohammad Ayub Khan, overthrew the civilian but unelected government of Prime Minister Feroz Khan Noon and imposed martial law.

A view that the military was a major modernizing agent in Third World countries, especially if a country lacked functioning democratic institutions and an autonomous national bourgeoisie, enjoyed significant currency in the conventional development literature produced during the 1960s. Ayub Khan was an apt example of such a developmentalist regime. Operating within an anti-communist ideological framework, his government sought vigorously to promote the industrial sector (on an important substitution basis) and to modernize agriculture. Land reforms with a very high ceiling were introduced: 200 hectares of irrigated and 400 hectares of unirrigated agricultural land in West Pakistan and in East Pakistan the ceiling was raised from 33 to 120 hectares.[8] The objective was clearly to create a strong class of prosperous farmers rather than liquidate landlordism by distributing land among poor peasants.

Pakistan's defence planning has always been based on the assumption that the main threat to its security comes from India. In the 1962 Sino-India war the US had expressed support for India and begun to provide it with armament, which greatly annoyed the Pakistani leaders who argued that a militarily strong India would pose a greater threat to Pakistan. On the other hand, the Chinese government had expressed political support for Pakistan during the India-Pakistan war in 1965. China had even threatened India and supported the Kashmir people's right to self-determination.

Under the circumstances, Ayub Khan's foreign minister, Zulfikar Ali Bhutto, worked out another strategy than dependence only on the US. Pakistan was to develop closer ties with the People's Republic of China.[9] The latter responded warmly to such overtures since its own policy was dictated by an overriding concern to prevent the spread of Soviet influence in regions close to its borders. In turn, the Soviet Union backed India in different manners, including military and economic aid. The US looked upon the Sino-Pakistan courtship with apprehension, but its paramount concern to contain Soviet influence in South Asia suggested that the emerging relation between China and Pakistan could be a useful counterweight.

The 1960s was also a period when the Sino-Soviet political and ideological animosity (which had been brewing for a long time) came to a head. It culminated in an irrevocable split in the international communist movement in the early 1960s. In almost all countries outside the Soviet bloc, the communists split up into pro-Moscow and pro-Beijing parties. While the pro-Moscow parties advocated peaceful strategies for advancing the socialist cause, their pro-Peking counterparts stood for militant armed struggle.[10] Given the exigencies and compulsions of patriotism and nationalism in modern politics, a communist party which looked towards the same ideological centre (either Moscow or Peking) for inspiration as the one with which the state in which it was based had good relations enjoyed the advantage of working more freely than the one associating with a centre with which the state had estranged relations. Thus, while being pro-Soviet in Pakistan was considered unpatriotic, being pro-Chinese was not. In India, the situation was the reverse.

The emerging Sino-Pakistan liaison provided a leeway for a new type of radical politics in Pakistan: one could mix Maoist ideas of peasant revolution with hostility towards the Soviet Union, condemning it as a social-imperialist capitalist restorer, as Mao preached.[11] To it, if one added anti-India rhetoric, then a sufficiently confusing and contradictory theoretical concoction was ready. The authorities were willing to tolerate such developments as long as they remained confined to small groups.

Meanwhile, Zulfikar Ali Bhutto, who had fallen out with Ayub Khan after the 1965 war, entered Pakistani politics as a major contender for power against his former patron. He founded the Pakistan People's Party (PPP) in late 1967. The PPP quickly won a large following among intellectuals, lawyers, journalists, workers, peasants and students. Many Maoists and radical trade unionists also entered the PPP fold. However, many powerful landlords and some smaller industrialists also joined it.[12] The ideology of the PPP was a blend of radical rhetoric borrowed from Maoist jargon, nationalist fervour directed against India, democracy and Islamic socialism. Not surprisingly, the element which distinguished the PPP's ideology from that of the Maoists was the notion of Islamic socialism. It generated controversy and confusion both within the PPP and outside. While the radical wing of the PPP made it its battle-cry for social revolution, the more moderate sections denied that it meant anything more than a concern for social justice in accordance with Islamic traditions. Outside the PPP, the conventional *ulama* and the propertied classes mounted a powerful campaign to damn the notion of Islamic socialism.

Pakistan broke up in December 1971 after the East Pakistan-based Awami League won an absolute majority in the Pakistan parliament in the 1970 general elections—winning 162 seats out of 300. It had a majority to form the government but was overruled by the West Pakistan power elite. Negotiations between the military government, Awami League and the PPP failed. On 25 March 1971, the army struck with all its might against what it perceived was a veritable all-out rebellion. The result was a long civil war which culminated in the intervention of the Indian army on behalf of the Bengali resistance. The Pakistani army was defeated and East Pakistan became the independent state of Bangladesh in December 1971.[13]

In the truncated Pakistan now confined only to West Pakistan, Zulfikar Ali Bhutto came to power. Emboldened by the PPP's coming into power, radical trade union leaders intensified militant activities in 1972. *Gherao* and *kabza* were attempted in many industrial areas of Punjab and Sindh. The workers established their own management committees. In some industrial areas and residential colonies the workers virtually took over the task of administration, including law and order and prompt provision of relief and justice.[14] At the same time, the government ordered stern action against Maoist groups active among the peasants.

From the second half of the 1960s, along with populist left-leaning politics of Z.A. Bhutto and his PPP, many of whose cadres and a few leaders such as Mairaj Muhammad Khan professed Maoist sympathies, more radical revolutionary Maoists established their presence in the trade unions and university campuses. The Pakistan International Airlines trade union was firmly with the Maoists and their student wing, the Nationalist Students Federation (NSF), emerged as a powerful force on the Karachi University Campus. In Punjab, the Nationalist Students Organization (NSO) represented Maoist ideas. Maoists with some presence in the industrial areas and towns formed the Pakistan Socialist Party led by C.R. Aslam and Abid Minto, while those with a peasant-orientation went on to form the Mazdoor-Kissan Party (MKP).

The MKP was founded in 1968. It was a product of the split in the National Awami Party (NAP) into a pro-Moscow, West Pakistan-based wing led by Wali Khan, son of Frontier Gandhi, Abdul Ghaffar Khan, and the East Pakistan-based Maulana Bhashani. In West Pakistan, the Maoists broke away from the National Awami Party (NAP) (Wali Khan) and founded the MKP under the leadership of Afzal Bangash, a Pukhtun like Wali Khan. In 1970 Major (retd) Ishaq Muhammad from the Punjab joined it along with his supporters.[15]

The MKP was able to launch a number of peasant resistance initiatives but the most spectacular was the one in the North-West Frontier Province (NWFP) among the Pukhtuns. The Pukhtuns were the only nationality in Pakistan in which all sections of society bore firearms. As a result, there were militant confrontations between landlords and peasants in the NWFP in the late 1960s and early 1970s. Fighting continued during the military regime of General Yahya, and from 1972 onwards when in the NWFP a coalition government led by NAP (Wali Khan) and an Islamist party, the Jamiyat-Ulama-e-Islam, was in power while Bhutto's PPP ruled at the centre, and in Punjab and Sindh.

The NAP-JU government supported the landlords and banned the MKP. One of the most spectacular clashes between the peasantry and the state took place in July 1971 at Mandani. A heavily-armed force consisting of 1,500 policemen clashed with a smaller force of

MKP cadres, the poor and landless peasants. Another struggle took place when nearly 8,000 police and militia fought MKP fighters and the local peasants. The struggles in the Hashtnagar area of the NWFP liberated an area of approximately 200 sq miles and inspired similar movements all over Pakistan.[16]

In Punjab, the MKP was involved in similar initiative in the western and southern regions where big landlordism was strongly entrenched. However, police repression in such areas proved too strong for the largely unmarked MKP cadres and peasant activists. Many of them were jailed and tortured. Bhutto's fall from government in 1977 brought into power a rabidly right-wing government under General Muhammad Zia-ul-Haq. After Pakistan joined the Afghan jihad in 1979, militant Pukhtuns were absorbed by the campaign to oust the Russians from Afghanistan. In the rest of Pakistan, leftists were also greatly marginalized as the state embarked upon comprehensive Islamization of state and society.

The MKP was an anti-imperialist party open to all progressive individuals. At its core was a hardcore communist leadership consisting of theorists, trade union activists, and peasant leaders and organizers. The MKP allied itself with China and supported its line in international politics as well as on the question of the revolution in Pakistan. The peasantry was declared as the main force of the revolution armed with Marxism-Leninism and Maoism. Major Ishaq wrote a number of articles and plays dealing with the oppression of the people in general, while highlighting in particular, the very sad plight of the indigenous people. The Punjabi faction of the MKP led by Major Ishaq was openly anti-Indian and subscribed to the view that the Soviet Union was a social imperialist superpower. The Afzal Bangash factions, however, were more practice-oriented, less concerned with theoretical fine points, and somewhat wary of taking an open stand against the Soviet Union. However, after the communists captured power in Afghanistan, all factions of the MKP welcomed it and supported it as a progressive revolution. Such developments resulted in repression against the MKP being redoubled by the Zia regime.

The MKP split into different factions in the late 1970s. Major Ishaq and Afzal Bangash became bitter rivals, both accusing each other of betrayal. Following the death of Chairman Mao, China abandoned its revolutionary fervour. That had a profoundly demoralizing effect on the Pakistani Maoists. The Pakistani state did not function even as a formal bourgeois democracy and the few years of Maoism's popular appeal were a product of a regime coming into power under Z.A. Bhutto that was pro-China and also flirted with ideas of socialism. All that became irrelevant in the 1980s.

The Pakistani Maoists survive in several small factions. There are also a number of MKPs. The Maoists continue to pledge commitment to a peasant revolution based on Mao Zedong's ideas. They cooperate with other leftist and democratic forces in the struggle for workers' and peasants' rights. In recent years, they have taken part in some peasant resistance struggles on military farms but Maoism is not an important force in Pakistani politics today.

NOTES

1. I. Ahmed, *State, Nation and Ethnicity in Contemporary South Asia*, (London and New York: Pinter Publishers, 1996).
2. Y.V. Gankovsky and L.R. Gordon-Polonskaya, *A History of Pakistan (1947-1958)* (Lahore: People's Publishing House, 1972), pp. 99-100.
3. B. Josh, 1979, *Communist Movement in Punjab (1926-47)* (Delhi: Anupama Publications, 1979). See also G. Singh, *Communism in Punjab* (Delhi: Ajanta, 1994).
4. G. Adhikari, *Pakistan and National Unity* (Bombay: People's Publishing House, 1944).
5. K. Mahmud, *Pakistan Mein Mazdoor Tehrik* (The Labour Movement in Pakistan) (Lahore: Maktab-e-Fikr-o-Danish, 1987), p. 6.
6. Gankovsky, and Gordon-Polonskaya, *A History of Pakistan*, p. 175.
7. Keith Callard, *Pakistan: A Political Study* (London: George Allen and Unwin Ltd.), pp. 73-4.
8. Mohammad Ayub Khan, *Friends Not Masters* (Karachi: Oxford University Press, 1967).
9. Z.A. Bhutto, *The Myth of Independence* (Karachi: Oxford University Press, 1969), pp. 131-61.
10. S. Banerjee, *India's Simmering Revolution: The Naxalite Uprising* (London: Zed Books, 1984).
11. *Chairman Mao's Theory of the Differentiation of the Three Worlds is a Major Contribution to Marxism-Leninism* (Peking: Foreign Language Press).
12. M. Waseem, *Politics and the State in Pakistan* (Lahore: Progressive Publishers, 1989).
13. Ishtiaq Ahmed, *State, Nation and Ethnicity in Contemporary South Asia* (London and New York: Pinter Publishers, 1998), pp. 222-3.
14. Khalid Mahmud, *Pakistan Mein Mazdoor Tehrik*, pp. 61-4.

15. Ahmad Salim, ***Peasants Lands Rights Movement of Pakistan*** (Islamabad: Sustainable Development Policy Institute (SDPI), 2008), pp. 43-4, www.sdpi.org/research_Programme/human_development/wlr/wlr_Peasants%20Land% 20Rights_final.pdf (accessed on 12 April 2010).
16. ***The Rebel Road, History of the Communist Mazdoor Kisan Party***, http://redtribution.wordpress.com/history-of-the-communist-mazdoor-kissan-party/ (accessed on 12 April 2010).

CHAPTER 7

Bangladesh: Maoism—Past, Present, Future

IFTEKHAR AHMED CHOWDHURY

Bangladesh has had a history of a strong tradition of left politics. During the colonial period, particularly between 1857 and 1947, the region then constituting the eastern portion of Bengal witnessed a number of peasant uprisings. The common population of eastern Bengal comprised mostly Muslims, and the feudal landlords, or *zamindars*, who were mostly Hindus.[1] The umbrage of the peasantry was directed against both the *zamindars* and the British rulers.[2] However, the fact that some of the leaders of the movements were Hindus laid the basis of a secular culture that has been a hallmark of left politics of East Bengal ever since. Two early instances of such uprisings were the 'Indigo Riots' also known as *nilbidraha*, resulting from the coercion of the peasants by British planters to produce the crop at a loss[3] and the 'Pabna Rent Revolt' of 1873, a protest against absentee landlordism. Initially, the British tended to favour the landlords and their legislations facilitated rent-extraction, but eventually they enacted tenancy protection laws aiming at forestalling peasant agitation.[4] An example would be the Bengal Tenancy Act of 1885 that defined the obligations of both *zamindars* and *raiyats* (rent-paying peasants).[5]

The Partition of 1947 divided the subcontinent into the two dominions of India and Pakistan. East Bengal became a part of Pakistan and West Bengal of India. While the struggle for Indian Independence was led by the Congress party and that of Pakistan by the Muslim League, the hardcore communists of both Bengals, all members of the Communist Party of India (CPI) founded in 1920, clung on to the notion that *yeh azadi jhooti hai* (this independence is false). This was because they did not see this as entailing the economic emancipation of the working classes.[6] For now, though, such sentiments were submerged in the waves of euphoria as also the horrendous rioting that accompanied the birth of the two sovereign nations.

LEFT POLITICS IN EAST PAKISTAN

Two developments took the wind out of the sail of left extremism in East Pakistan (called 'East Bengal' till Pakistan became a republic in 1956 when it formally became known as 'East Pakistan'). One was the migration of nearly two-thirds of the total of 20,000 CPI members in East Bengal to India in the aftermath of the 1950 communal riots, since they were Hindus.[7] The second was the adoption of the State Acquisition and Tenancy Act 1950, by which a conservative Muslim League government in East Bengal was able to pass what was seemingly a progressive piece of legislation. This was vastly facilitated by the fact that most of the affected were Hindu landlords or *zamindars*, no constituency of the Muslim League in any case, who had by then already moved to Calcutta.

The East Bengal State Acquisition and Tenancy Act 1950 had a profound impact in creating a more egalitarian society in that province of Pakistan than what was the case in the Punjab, Sindh, Baluchistan or the Frontiers (Pakistan's other provinces—all located in the western wing of the country), mainly due to two reasons. First, by removing the *zamindars* from the scene, the act eliminated what extreme radicals would call *srenishotru* (class-enemy). Second, the state through the District Collector (also known as the District Magistrate) could deliver 'development' or governance goals like law and order more directly to the *raiyats.* Thus being perceived as 'benefactors' rather than 'exploiters', these elements rendered radical slogans much less credible.

For a variety of reasons including the language movement of February 1952, in which the Muslim League was seen to be supporting Urdu as state language as opposed to Bengali, in the provincial elections held in East Bengal in 1954, the government was swept out of office by a combination of parties known as the *Jukto Front* or United Front. The United Front was perceived to be more reflective of the basic urges of the common people, a major player in it being the Awami League, later headed by Sheikh Mujibur Rahman, to shepherd the independence struggle for Bangladesh in 1971.[8] By 1956-7, an Awami Leaguer, H.S. Suhrawardy was the prime minister of Pakistan. It was as a mark of protest against his pro-West foreign policy that the socialist-oriented cleric, Mowlana Abdul Hamid Khan Bhashani, left the Awami League and founded his own National Awami Party (NAP).[9] But while the mainstream socialist politics of Bhashani found empathy with the martial law government of President Mohammed Ayub Khan, soon to become a close ally of China, there was a more radical revolution-oriented party slowly burgeoning as heir to the CPI, the Communist Party of East Pakistan (CPEP).

THE COMMUNISTS AND THE BANGLADESH MOVEMENT

The international communist movement was dichotomized into two separate camps by 1962 on the question of the adoption of the appropriate Marxist techniques. The CPEP was no exception. It was consequently split into the more moderate pro-Moscow and the more radical pro-Peking factions. The pro-Moscow faction led by Comrade Moni Singh, a former Hindu *zamindar* and CPI-member argued for the establishment of socialism through a peaceful parliamentary process, a tactic not very much unlike that of Bhashani (NAP), or that of the pro-Moscow NAP headed by Professor Muzaffar Ahmed. The pro-Peking wing of the CPEP, on the other hand, led by Mohammad Toaha and Sukhendu Dastidar advocated the line of revolutionary class struggle that came to be known as Maoism. Indeed in 1967, a group of young communists under the leadership of Siraj Sikdar founded the Mao-Thought Research Centre in Dhaka.[10] That was the origin of Maoist politics in the region, now Bangladesh. The pro-Peking wing of the CPEP splintered into over a dozen factions during the Bangladesh movement and its aftermath.

The Bangladesh movement in 1971, immensely popular among the masses, threw the CPEP into a theoretical quandary. Apart from Mohammed Toaha, the other person with a significant profile on the issue was Abdul Huq. The break-up of Pakistan generally appeared to them to be giving into the machinations of the Indo-Soviet 'duet' of 'Indian expansionism' and 'Soviet hegemonism'. Abdul Huq was stronger in his view that the disintegration of Pakistan would bring aid and comfort to the Soviet 'hegemonists' and the Indian 'expansionists' than Toaha, who later initiated the concept of a two-way war against the Pakistan Army and the Awami League.[11]

The Huq line appears to have attracted the favour of China. China opposed the break-up of Pakistan, but confined itself to making only 'sympathetic noises' without using any kind of military force to come to Pakistan's rescue.[12] Indeed, Huq's views, along with similar ones held by Ashim Chatterjee of CPI (Marxist-Leninist), were broadcast on 'Radio Peking' and its ally 'Radio Tirana'.[13] The fact that the communists and the ultra-radicals went against the grain of public opinion, which was overwhelmingly supportive on the issue of the independence of Bangladesh was to cost them and their fellow-travellers like the Maoists dearly in political terms later on. Ironically, the same was true of also those on the other extreme in the political spectrum, the Islamists.

SIRAJ SIKDAR AND THE 'SARBAHARAS'

Siraj Sikdar, who headed the splinter group of the young communists who established the Mao-Thought Research Centre in Dhaka in 1967, adopted a line on the Bangladesh struggle that was different from his other pro-Peking comrades. The Sikdar faction opposed both Pakistan and India as colonial powers. Seeking the formation of a Democratic Republic of East Bengal, they set up the *Purbo Bangla* (East Bengal) *Sarbahara* ('Have-nots', literally 'those who have lost everything') Party (PBSP) in June 1971. After Bangladesh's emergence as a sovereign country, the PBSP carried on their militant struggle against the Mujib government. Their intellectual propaganda was a pamphlet called *Lal Jhanda* (Red Flag). Sikdar was killed in January 1975, and thereafter the the PBSP further splintered into various groups, their militancy losing steam. Around this time the extreme left faction of the ruling Awami League, espousing 'scientific socialism' broke off to form the *Jatiya Samajtantri Dal* (JSD, literally, the 'Nationalist Socialist Party', but bearing no resemblance whatsoever to the one with a similar name earlier in Germany!). The JSD also lost momentum in the late 1970s with the execution of Colonel Abu Taher and the strong measures adopted by then strongman, and later president, Ziaur Rahman.[14]

While by the end of the 1970s, the Maoist movement had largely lost its bite in Bangladesh, it still struggled to survive intellectually, drawing nourishment from the burgeoning activities of its counterparts in neighbouring India. Also, as we will see later in the essay, it managed to establish some regional and international linkages. The remnants of the Sikdar-line brought out a pamphlet recently that criticizes 'deviationists' and seeks to project the correct path which according to them is as follows:

> . . . We don't believe in empty theory. [Chairman Mao] has shown that the main law of contradiction is the law of unity of opposites. He has explained the transformation of quantity into quality by the law of the unity of opposites. And he has said that the negation of negation does not exist as a law. What exists is the unity of the opposite of affirmation and negation. [Mao] established monism by discarding the trip list doctrine of development. . . . He, by correcting Engels' formulation regarding freedom showed that freedom is not only understanding necessity but its transformation too. . . .[15]

The problem with this esoteric, heavily-laden philosophical discourse or approach was that it was not possible to use this as a means for generating support among the broad masses. Its appeal could only be confined to a few intellectuals among the universities and the civil society. But without mass support militant Maoism would lack potency in Bangladesh to achieve any of its goals.

EXTERNAL INFLUENCES

Doubtless, there were external influences. Perhaps, the foremost came from next door, Naxalbari of West Bengal in India. There a section led by Charu Majumdar, Kanu Sanyal, and Jangal Santhal had initiated a bloody uprising in 1967.[16] Today, the Naxalites are seen as the forerunners of the wave of Maoist insurgency sweeping across several Indian states. But, in West Bengal, by the 1970s, the government had managed to crush the Naxalite insurgency with an iron hand, just as it was nipped in the bud by the Bangladesh authorities.

The success of the United Communist Party of Nepal (Marxists) would have been something to emulate for the Bangladeshi Maoists, but for several reasons. First, by the time its leader, Pushpa Kamal Dahal, better known as Prachanda or 'the fierce one', had successfully organized the 'people's war' on the basis of the Maoist dictum that 'power flows from the barrel of a gun' from the mid-1990s to 2008 when he assumed power, Maoism was already a spent force in Bangladesh. Secondly, unlike in Nepal, there was no major goal of a constitutional change acceptable to the masses, such as the change from monarchy to a republic. Finally, there were few takers of the *Prachanda Path* in Bangladesh, Dahal's ideology based on his paper 'The Great Leap Forward: An Inevitable Need of History'. So, ironically, even 'the most successful Maoist insurgency in the world in decades', as an analyst described it,[17] had little impact on Bangladesh, which was next door. However, Bangladeshi Maoists interacted with their Nepalese counterparts in regional and international fora, as we shall see.

Developments within China itself were of little assistance to the Bangladeshi Maoists. The horrors of the Cultural Revolution, which were to reveal that Maoism had 'no notion of limits',[18] were of no help in enhancing the attractiveness of 'Mao-thought'. Also, China was always more focused on developing close Beijing-Dhaka ties and had no interest in destabilizing the Bangladesh state, which it was beginning by then to see as an ally, like Pakistan in many ways and unlike India.[19] The reforms introduced in China by Deng Xiaoping obviously did not correspond to what was perceived as 'Mao-thought' by the Bangladeshi Maoists. However, the Chinese reformers, including Deng were careful to stress that the revolutionary side of Maoism was separate from the governance side, leading to the now famous observation that Mao was '70 per cent good and 30 per cent bad'.[20] Some writers saw Maoism as a third way between capitalism and communism, attempting to combine Confucianism with socialism.[21]

There was, however, a school of thought that exerted some influence in shaping the thought-process among the intelligentsia, particularly among the students and scholars of the University of Dhaka, which has always made a major contribution to the politics of the nation. This was the 'dependencia' school of neo-Marxist economists from around the developing world, in particular, Latin America. Its proponents powerfully argued that any relationship involving foreign aid deepens structural dependency, exploits the ex-colonial 'periphery' for the benefit of the former colonial powers, now the metropolitan 'centre', and creates a 'comprador-elite' class to do its bidding. The only path to development was to sever the relationship, better still in all forms, if necessary through a revolution.[22] For an aid-dependent country, which Bangladesh was in the 1970s, and to a certain extent, though far less, is also today, these thoughts were very relevant. These ideas, thus, should have fed radical thinking. However, in Bangladesh, they ran counter to actual experience, for the country was able to use external assistance very effectively, for, among other things alleviating poverty.[23] So these concepts brought no grist to the Maoist mills.

A major factor that has been a cause in the spread of Maoism in India was absent in Bangladesh. This was the large number of Memoranda of Understanding entered into by the government for mining and mineral-based industries, resisted by the masses of the poorer states, mainly tribals, which is the reason the Indian government launched 'Operation Green Hunt' in the jungles.[24] This is a war that the author Arundhati Roy has said that 'India is both proud and shy of'.[25] Another is the disaffection among the tribal population. In India, the Maoist insurgency has a resonance among these people. In Bangladesh, the insurgency among the tribals in the Chittagong Hill Tracts was largely ended by the signing of the 1997 Peace Accord between the then Awami League government and the Parbatta Chattagram Janasanghati Samity (PCJSS), the main political platform of tribal resistance. While there have been complaints about its slow implementation and occasional conflicts between the tribals and settlers from the plains, the government has invested heavily in the area in developmental terms.[26] Overall, it appears that the retractors among the tribals are not making efforts for a common cause with Maoist remnants.[27]

INTERNATIONAL AND REGIONAL LINKAGES

The fledgling Maoists of Bangladesh, however, do maintain international and regional linkages. In 1984, the Revolutionary International Movement (RIM) was created as an international communist organization to uphold the values and principles of Marxism-Leninism-Maoism. Its broad purpose was to try and form a Communist International of a new type. It was to rely on the Maoist strategy of a 'people's war' as being the best method of effecting Marxist revolutions in the developing world. Its membership included several of the Bangladeshi Maoist groups, such as the PBSP, a splinter group formed in 2001 called Purbo Baglar Sarbahara Party (Maoist Bolshevik Reorganization Movement) and the Bangladesh Samyabadi Dal.[28] Again, the last could hardly be said to be revolutionary as its leader, Dilip Barua, sat in the Bangladesh cabinet in 2010.

At a regional level, there exists the Coordination Committee of Maoist Parties and Organisations of South Asia (CCOMPOSA). The various *Sarbahara* factions and the Samyabadi Dal are also its members. The South Asian Maoists meet one another, often in secret gatherings. Some linkages are naturally created at these events, particularly among the Indian Maoists, the Janatha Vimukthi Peramuna (JVP) of Sri Lanka, the Communist Party of Ceylon (Maoist), and the Nepalese Marxists and Maoists. In fact, analysts have observed that it would be ironical if the notion of SAARC cooperation was 'hijacked' by the Maoists of the region before the governments of these countries substantively profit from the concepts of regionalization.[29]

FACTORS IMPEDING MAOISM

The economy of Bangladesh has sometimes been seen as a 'paradox', where despite myriad challenges, a steady growth rate of around 6 per cent has been achieved over the last few years with the benefits more equitably distributed than elsewhere in the region. Contrary to initial pessimism, Bangladesh has come to be regarded as a 'lead performer among the least developed countries and considered as a successful example of graduation of traditional society to modernity at a low level per capita income', with the United Nations Development Programme ranking it as being among the league of countries having achieved 'medium human development'.[30] The absence of abject poverty was a key factor in the prevention of the success of Maoist propaganda.

Another factor is the spread of ideas such as microcredit, for which Professor Mohammed Yunus and his Grameen Bank were awarded the Nobel Peace Prize in 2006, and Sir Fazle Hasan Abed and his Bangladesh Rural Advancement Committee (BRAC) won global plaudits for helping empower women, thereby marginalizing all kinds of extremist thought and action, including Maoism. The fact that Bangladesh is also a preponderantly Muslim society, that too of a syncretic *Sufistic* tradition, is also an impediment to the Maoists, an alien ideology. True, the Muslim peasantry had in the past participated in radical movements, as in the colonial period, but then their 'Muslimness' was also an element in the uprisings directed against the Hindu *zamindars* and British rulers.

Taking all these into account, an analyst has observed: 'The Maoist phase in Bangladesh politics is over. Splintered, and surviving in isolated pockets, those who call themselves Maoists in Bangladesh today are more of a law and order problem than a challenge to mainstream politics.'[31] Interestingly, Bangladesh's famously vibrant civil society has also absorbed many ex-Maoists as NGO leaders. An example is Shafiqul Huq Chowdhury, now heading the Association for Social Advancement, or ASA, an acronym, which translated into Bengali, means 'hope'.[32]

CONCLUSION

A look at any map of South Asia will show that Bangladesh's neighbouring areas are engulfed in ongoing Maoist insurgencies: several states of India to its east and Nepal to the north. Also, Bangladesh historically presented a fertile ground for extreme left politics because of a long tradition of peasant uprisings and the existence of an intelligentsia receptive to external intellectual stimuli. Yet, Maoism (or any other form of extreme radicalism) never took off in a significant way in this country.

Several reasons for this can be extrapolated from this essay. First, even in the pre-Bangladesh East Pakistan period (1947-71), abolition of landlordism, or *zamindaris* and legislations ending the exploitative feudal system robbed such movements of their fodder. Second, the opposition to the independence movement, vastly popular with the masses, cost the extreme left and later the Maoists considerably in terms of public empathy. Third, in the decade after independence, early police action eliminated potential extremists. Fourth, while the excesses of the Cultural Revolution in China during Mao's final years set unattractive examples for Bangladeshis, Beijing also desisted from even appearing to display any kind of solidarity with the Maoists and instead focused on building close ties with all governments in Bangladesh, whom, like those of Pakistan, they considered allies. Fifth, neo-Marxist concepts and ideas like those of the 'dependencia' school, while finding some resonance among scholars and students, were actually belied by the actual experience of equitable growth achieved through appropriate utilization of foreign aid and international linkages. Sixth, initiatives like micro-credit and 'non-formal education' for girls leading to women's empowerment created social conditions unlikely to nurture violent insurrections. Last but not the least, there was little encouragement for extremism in a moderate Muslim society whose basic values were mild and generally shorn of ideological mores. While the state may at times appear weak, its 'collapse or failure', as Naureen Fink argues, 'remains a distant and unlikely outcome because of the many social and political forces which continue to promote a peaceful, democratic and inclusive society'.[33]

All this is not to say threats do not exist. The society, unless vigilant, runs the risk of being destabilized by the Maoists as also by religious extremists. If the Indian Maoists succeed in any major way, the dangers increase. That will also be the case if the other Muslim country in the subcontinent, where Maoism is not an issue but Islamism is, is overrun by Taliban-ite religious extremists, though in this case, the two societies are geographically much further apart (a factor that erodes with globalization). There is also the ever-present danger that Maoists, though weak, may seek to strengthen themselves by linking up with Islamist fundamentalist extremists, and vice versa, creating something like an old-style classical Leninist 'United Front' for tactical gains.

It will, therefore, be in the interest of Bangladesh, as also of its neighbours, mainly India, to cooperate in bilateral, regional and international initiatives to curb the spread of Maoism and other forms of extremism. The visit of the Bangladeshi Prime Minister Sheikh Hasina to India in January 2010 led to a number of agreements designed to fight terror following talks with her counterpart Manmohan Singh. But implementation in letter and spirit will be the key. Also, these agreements are designed to tackle forms of terrorism other than Maoism. There should be regular structured meetings between the home secretaries and the intelligence agencies of the two countries with Maoism also on the agenda. Cooperation is also desirable at the regional level, such as in the South Asian Association for Regional Cooperation (SAARC) and the SAARC Ministerial Declaration on Cooperation in Combating Terrorism signed on 28 February 2009, was a step in the right direction. Support provided by the United Nations (UN) should also be fully and appropriately utilized. Currently, Bangladesh and the UN are negotiating the establishment of a Regional Centre for Capacity Building to fight terrorism, which is a positive step. There should absolutely be no room for complacency, only for eternal vigilance, sober reflection, and good governance.

NOTES

1. Following the advent of Muslim conquerors in Bengal in the thirteenth century, there were large conversions among the inhabitants from Hinduism and Buddhism to Islam. This was partly due to the Hobson's choice before them and partly because of their distaste for 'a rigid system of caste discipline' (E.A. Gait, *Census of India, 1909,* vol.6, part 1, Report, p. 165). This happened largely in the deltaic East Bengal, whereas the western portions, because of better communications and more stable form of

cultivation that contributed to social differentiation, was integrated into the Hindu culture of the Upper Gangetic Plains. See Premen Addy and Ibne Azad, 'Politics and Society in Bengal', in Robin Blackburn (ed.), *Explosion in a Subcontinent* (Penguin, 1975), pp. 80-2.

2. The Permanent Settlement Act of Lord Cornwallis (1793) created the social conditions in East Bengal that were primarily responsible for such sentiments. See Rajat and Ratna Ray, 'Zamindars and Jotdars: A Study of Rural Politics in Bengal', *Modern Asian Studies*, vol. 9, 1975, p. 101.
3. For studies on the two events, see Kalyan Kumar Sengupta, 'The Agrarian League of Pabna, 1873', *The Economic and Social History Review*, vol. 7, no. 2 (June 1970), pp. 253-70; and Chittabrata Palit, *Tensions in Rural Bengal Society: Landlords, Planters, and Colonial Rule, 1830-1860* (Calcutta: Progressive Publishers, 1975), pp. 140-51.The 'Indigo Riots' were the subject of a famous Bengali play called *Nil Durpan* (literally 'Mirror of Indigo') written by Dinabandhu Mitra in 1858-9.
4. Dietmar Rothermund, *Government, Landlord and Peasant in India: Agrarian Relations Under British Rule* (Wiesbaden: Franz Steiner Verlag GMBH, 1978), p. 89.
5. 'Banglapedia: Survey and Settlement Operations', *National Encyclopedia of Bangladesh 2006*, www.banglapedia.org/httpdocs/HT/S_0621.HTM (accessed on 14 May 2010).
6. Saurabh Jyoti Sharma, 'Evaluating Jyoti Basu', *Voice of India Features* (7 February 2010), http://voi.org/07feb2010/saurabhjyotisharma/column-saurabhjyotisharma/evaluatingjyotibasu.html (accessed on 10 May 2010).
7. This fact obtained from Marcus Franda, 'Communism and Regional Politics in East Pakistan', *Asian Survey*, vol. 10, no. 7 (July 1970), pp. 588-606.
8. Iftekhar Ahmed Chowdhury, 'Pre-history of Bangladeshi Nationalism and a Theory of Tripartite Balance', *Asian Affairs*, vol. IV, no. 4, December 1982, pp. 417-18.
9. M. Rashiduzzaman, 'The National Awami Party of Pakistan: Leftist Politics in Crisis', *Pacific Affairs*, vol. XLIII, no. 3 (Fall 1970), p. 395.
10. M. Nurul Amin, 'Maoism in Bangladesh: The Case of the East Bengal Sarbohara Party', *Asian Survey*, vol. 26, no. 7 (July 1986), pp. 759-73.
11. For a study of the positions of the radical Bengali political parties towards the Bangladesh Movement, see Talukdar Maniruzzaman, *Radical Politics and Emergence of Bangladesh* (Dhaka: Bangladesh Books International, 1978), especially pp. 51-2.
12. Stephen Philip Cohen, *The Idea of Pakistan* (Washington DC: Brookings Institution Press, 2004), p. 73.
13. Tariq Ali, 'Pakistan and Bangladesh: Results and Prospects', in Robin Blackburn (ed.), op. cit., p. 318.

14. For an interesting account of this period, see Lawrence Lifsschultz, *Bangladesh: The Unfinished Revolution* (London: Zed Press, 1979).
15. 'Maoist Party in Bangladesh Reorganizes', *Anubad Sahitya Potro* (10th issue). http://southasiarev.wordpress.com/2009/12/13/maoist-party-in-bangladesh-reorganizes/ (accessed on 7 May 2010).
16. See Sankar Ghosh, *The Naxalite Movement: A Maoist Experiment* (Calcutta: Firma KL Mukhopadhyay, 1975).
17. Manish Thapa, 'Evolution of Maoism in Nepal: Understanding Maoist Insurgency from Wider Perspective', *Panorama*, www.tigweb.org/express/panorama/article.html?Content ID=6491 (accessed on 12 May 2010).
18. Dayan Jayatilleka, *Fidel's Ethics of Violence: The Moral Dimension of the Political Thought of Fidel Castro* (London: Pluto Press, 2007), p.168.
19. Iftekhar Ahmed Chowdhury, *A Method in the Dragon's Moods*, ISAS Working Paper, no. 75, p. 12.
20. This assessment of Mao by Deng is reportedly based on Mao's own earlier assessment of Stalin. See, 'Interpreting Mao', *Beijing Review*, no. 40, 5 October 2006, updated 10 December 2006. www.bjreview.com.cn/nation/txt/2006-12/10/content_50364.htm (accessed on 11 May 2010).
21. Martin Cohen, *Political Philosophy from Plato to Mao* (London: Pluto Press, 2001), p. 206.
22. To cite some examples: Andre Gunder Frank, *The Development of Underdevelopment* (Monthly Review Press, 1970); Samir Amin, *Unequal Development: An Essay on the Social Formation of Peripheral Capitalism*, tr. Brian Pearce (New York: Monthly Review Press, 1976); and Gèrard Chiliand, *Revolution in the Third World: Myths and Prospects* (Sussex: The Harvester Press, 1977).
23. See M.A. Muhith: 'Is Foreign Aid Essential for Development in Bangladesh?', Seminar Paper, Department of Economics, University of Dhaka, 10 November 1978. The conclusion of the author, then a senior government official, was affirmative. Muhith has been the finance minister of Bangladesh since January 2009 in the Awami League-led cabinet of Prime Minister Sheikh Hasina.
24. Gautam Navlakha, 'Days and Nights in the Maoist Heartland', *Economic and Political Weekly* (17-23 April 2010), vol. XLV, no. 16, p. 47.
25. Arundhati Roy, 'Walking with the Comrades', *Outlook*, 29 March 2010, www.outlookindia.com/article.aspx?264738 (accessed on 11 May 2010).
26. The author was Adviser (Minister) to the Bangladesh government in charge of Chittagong Hill Tracts Affairs during 2007-8.
27. Ekramul Kabir, 'Terrorism in Bangladesh: How Long the Denial?', *Daily Star*, 19 February 2006.
28. Mohosin Al Abbas, 'Maoism in South Asia: Insurgency or Movement',

Ground Report, www.groundreport.com/opinion/Maoism-in-South-Asia-Insurgency-or-Movement/2865458 (accessed on 7 May 2010).

29. Rajat Kumar Kujur, 'CCOMPOSA: A Mirage or Reality?', Institute of Peace and Conflict Studies, www.ipcs.org/article/Naxalite-violence/ccomposa-a-mirage-or-a-reality-2142.html (accessed on 7 May 2010).
30. Binayek Sen, Mustafa K. Mujeri and Quazi Shahabuddin, 'Operationalizing Pro-poor Growth: Bangladesh as a Case Study', 7 November 2004. http://siteresources.worldbank.org?INTPGI/Resources?342674-1115051237044/oppbangladesh(Nov)pdf (accessed on 11 May 2010).
31. Ekramul Kabir, op. cit.
32. Abhoy, 'From Maoism to Micro-finance–Something to Read for India's Maoists', *Microfinance Business News* (20 April 2009). http://indiamicrofinance.com/blog/microfinance/microfinance-articles/maoism-to-microfinance-maobadi-ban-gaye-microfinance-agents.html (accessed on 7 May 2010).
33. Naureen Chowdhury Fink, *Bombs and Ballots: Terrorism, Political Violence and Governance in Bangladesh* (New York: International Peace Institute, 2010), p. 19.

CHAPTER 8

Sri Lanka: The Maoist Movement

DAYAN JAYATILLEKA

The story of Sri Lankan Maoism is a paradox. Apart from Nepal, Sri Lanka has been the scene of the most efficacious, armed and ideological insurgencies in South Asia. It has seen two such insurrections launched by the same party, the Janatha Vimukthi Peramuna (JVP); the first in April 1971 and the other in 1986-9 which seriously threatened state power. Thus, Sri Lankan Maoism must be viewed against the backdrop of two significant attempts at armed insurrection.

The fact that though the attempts did take place—thereby indicating the availability of a clear space for a revolutionary left—but that they did not spring from a Maoist movement indicates the failure of Sri Lankan Maoism. However, the fact that the JVP, though not itself a Maoist movement, emerged from the bowels of the Maoist movement and its leading cadres were for the most part ex-Maoists, is evidence of the fecundity of Sri Lankan Maoism.

When the Maoists split from the pro-Soviet party in 1964, the new movement was distinguished by the fact that it had been able to carry the main trade unions of the pro-Moscow party with it, which was a rarity in most parts of the world. The Ceylon Trade Union Federation (CTUF) was led by Sanmugathasan, who was the initiator of the breakaway from the pro-Soviet party and took the union federation along with him. The cadre leading the All Lanka Peasants' Congress also went along with Sanmugathasan.

Even more striking was the role played by the Sri Lankan Maoist leader internationally. Sanmugathasan was a well-known ideologue of the national rather than merely the regional or youth sections of the parent communist party, unlike the leaders of most Maoist breakaways the world over. Sanmugathasan's skills with the English language and his knowledge of Marxist-Leninist doctrine made him an ideal instrument for the Communist Party of China in the global polemic with the pro-Moscow parties and splinters. The histories and anthologies of political literature of that period showed the Ceylon Communist Party, as the Maoists were known, the chance to punch above their weight.

The high point of Maoism in Sri Lanka were the meetings that Sanmugathasan had with Chairman Mao and the zenith was clearly the May Day on which he stood by Mao, taking the salute as the sun rose and Mao was hailed by hundreds of thousands of Red Guards in Tiananmen Square.

It was downhill all the way after that. Several key youth and student leaders of the party broke away from it. These included Rohana Wijeweera who went on to form the JVP, launched two insurrections 15 years apart, and died at the hands of the government in November 1989.

When the April 1971 insurrection broke out, Sanmugathasan who had been one of the most acerbic ideological critics of the JVP was jailed along with them by Prime Minister Sirimavo Bandaranaike, to whom they all looked and sounded alike. Sanmugathasan was to suffer a double blow. When he was released from jail, his party had split, with a faction adopting the new foreign policy of China, best exemplified by its line on Sri Lanka and Sudan where it supported governmental suppression of communists and radical leftists it suspected were under the influence of the USSR. This rightward shift in China's foreign policy was the cause and consequence of its new rapprochement with the United States under Richard Nixon.

Sanmugathasan was not entirely and utterly orphaned, though. Having opposed Deng Xiaoping's alleged restoration of capitalism in China and supported Albania (not to mention about obtaining support from the latter), he broke with Deng's policy and guided his vastly diminished party into the Revolutionary International Movement (RIM), which coordinates far left Maoist insurgencies in Asia, including the Naxalites of India.

Preaching Maoist dialectics, Sanmugathasan was fond of emphasizing the primacy of internal over external factors in the development of a phenomenon or process. Using the same methodology, one may say that Sri Lankan Maoism was undone far more by internal rather than external factors, such as the turn in China's foreign policy, though it did play its part. Three factors can be identified:

1. *Ethnicity:* the Maoist leader Sanmugathasan was from the Tamil minority and therefore would be unacceptable to the Sinhala majority—a point made by the most significant of the youth dissidents Rohana Wijeweera (who was to become the founder-leader of the JVP), albeit *sotto voce*, and more hinted at than openly expressed.
2. *Generations and political practice:* Sanmugathasan was an old man, known to have a bad back and an upper-middle-class lifestyle; therefore he was perceived as preaching people's war, but incapable of the practice of armed struggle.
3. *Disconnection between doctrine and socio-political reality:* Maoist formulae were criticized as being irrelevant outside their time and place, namely colonial or semi-colonial societies with backward agrarian structures characterized by large landholdings. Sri Lanka, by contrast, was a modern nation state, capitalist rather than feudal, with capitalist relations or petty commodity production predominant in the countryside. Thus, the 'stage of the revolution' was held to be 'socialist' rather than 'new democratic'.

Of the three reasons listed above, the third seems especially relevant because of the failure of other Maoist organizations, led by younger, educated Sinhalese (which therefore were immune to 1 and 2 above).

However, the fact that the JVP with its unusual admixture of ultra-leftism and Sinhala xenophobia was easily the strongest and most consequential of all anti-systemic or anti-capitalist formations to appear in Sri Lanka, also lends weight to the salience of factor 1.

The Maoist splinters from Sanmugathasan's party, which had followed the rightward shift of Chinese foreign policy and adopted the Theory of the Three Worlds[1] (enunciated by Deng Xiaoping at the United Nations (UN) General Assembly in 1974), joined the mainline Sri Lanka Freedom Party (SLFP) of the Bandaranaikes. Having played a part in the anti-Soviet, anti-Vietnam, anti-Cuba polemics during Sri Lanka's stewardship of the non-aligned movement, these elements dissolved into the SLFP, supporting more populist, Sinhala nationalist and in some cases, anti-Indian policy stances and personalities within and by that party.

The history of Sri Lankan Maoism contains a mystery of a development that never occurred. In the late 1960s, the Jaffna branch of the Maoist party of Sanmugathasan, then in its heyday, had led a violent mass struggle—prefiguring those of today's Naxalites in India—against caste oppression in the mainly Tamil north. Though this struggle was displaced by the emerging Tamil secessionist movement, the left wing of that movement had been influenced by and had considerable respect for the struggle waged by the Maoists. However, despite the invocation of the slogan of a national liberation struggle and the arguable approximation of the conditions in the Tamil areas to those that Asian Maoism took root in, and despite the Tamil ethnicity of the founding father of Lankan Maoism, none of the Tamil Eelam armed movements were Maoist [except for a small, short-lived group called the National Liberation Front of Tamil Eelam (NLFT) which soon spawned a breakaway, the People's Liberation Front of Tamil Eelam (PLFT)].

The lasting residue of the Maoist movement in Sri Lanka then seems to be an ideological gloss and glossary for anti-Indian sentiment that erupts intermittently within the JVP and the Liberation Tigers of Tamil Eelam (LTTE).

The abiding irony of history, though, is the poignant relevance of the essays written by Sanmugathasan in the mid-1980s, reminding the emergent Tamil armed movement of Mao's Rules of Discipline and Points for Attention, cautioning the young militants against terrorism and killing of civilians, and preaching the doctrine of Protracted People's War in which mass organizations form the foundation and politics in command ('all political power flows from the barrel of the gun but the party commands the gun and not the gun the party': Mao). Had Velupillai Prabhakaran heeded this advice of an older Tamil militant leader who once stood alongside Mao, his militia and he may not have been obliterated on the banks of the Nandikadal lagoon in 2009.

NOTE

1. Speech by Deng Xiaoping at the Sixth Special Session of the UN General Assembly, 10 April 1974. *People's Daily*, 11 April 1974, p. 2. 'In 1974, Deng Xiaoping delivered a speech at the Sixth Special Session of the UN General Assembly on behalf of the Chinese government, in which he systematically set forth Mao Zedong's thesis of the three worlds', www.chinadaily.com.cn/english/doc/2004-06/25/content_342508.htm (accessed on 2 June 2010).

‘CAUSES’ AND ‘INDICATORS’

Anyone encountering terms like ‘Maoist violence’ or ‘Maoist inspired’ will puzzle over the circumstances that would lead poor people in remote areas of India or Nepal to rally in the name of a dead Chinese dictator.

The first two essays provide different perspectives on socio-economic reasons for insurgency. Exploitation of vulnerable tribal people is part of the story; the spread of extractive capitalism into remote areas is another; the unintended consequences of forest legislation, yet another. The poor quality of local administrations is often identified as a key element in explaining places where resistance to government finds support and safety. But how do we begin to measure effective local government? One possible measure is to analyse the quality of information and the construction of websites run by government in affected districts. The contrasts between one district and another are striking and point to the need for close-to-the-ground research on the qualities that make some district governments more effective than others.

In accounting for the endurance of Maoist organizations, attractive social reform is one element, notably the prominent role of women that is often commented on and that Maoist leaders proclaim. Though there are charges of sexual exploitation within Maoist organizations, the rhetoric of ‘no revolution without women’ appeals powerfully to a number of young women, as the account in this section and some of the photographs in this book indicate.

CHAPTER 9

Insurgency, Counter-insurgency, and Democracy in Central India

NANDINI SUNDAR

The Naxalite movement began in India in the late 1960s as a peasant struggle (in Naxalbari, West Bengal, hence the name Naxalite). It represented the revolutionary stream of Indian Marxism which did not believe that parliamentary democracy would lead to the requisite systemic change and argued for armed struggle instead. While the Indian state managed to crush the movement in the 1970s, causing an already ideologically fractured movement to splinter further (currently 34 parties by official estimates),[1] in 2004 two of the major parties, the Communist Party of India (CPI) (Marxist-Leninist) People's War (formed out of the merger of the People's War Group with Party Unity) and the Maoist Communist Center (MCC) of India, united to form the Communist Party of India (Maoist).[2] The CPI (Maoist) is currently a significant political force across several states, especially in rural areas where state services have been inadequate or absent.[3]

Since about 2005-6, the Maoists have become the main target of the Indian state, with thousands of paramilitary forces being poured into the areas where they are strong, and the prime minister repeatedly referring to them as India's biggest security threat. As a consequence, armed conflict is occurring across large parts of central India and is taking several hundred lives on an annual basis. In the state of Chhattisgarh, which is the epicentre of the war, sovereignty is contested over large parts of terrain.

COMPETING PERSPECTIVES ON THE MAOIST ISSUE

There are three main perspectives on the Maoist issue. The first, which is the security perspective, equates the Maoists with terrorists.

India's home ministry has put out half-page advertisements in all the national newspapers, proclaiming alongside photos of corpses that 'Naxals are nothing but cold-blooded murderers'. This perspective, which is held by the police-dominated home ministry as well as by many 'security experts', argues that the Maoists no longer have a revolutionary ideology and are a self-seeking group of extortionists out to destabilize the country and impede 'development', by which they mean industrialization. This perspective is blind to the history, ideology, and actual practices of the Maoists.

The second, which is the dominant liberal perspective, epitomized by an expert group constituted by the Indian government's Planning Commission, might be labelled the 'root causes' perspective.[4] According to this view, poverty and lack of 'development' (here meaning employment), and the want of primary services like education, are to blame for pushing people to support the Maoists. This view ignores the absence of a Maoist movement in other poor areas as well as questions of Maoist theory, organizational presence, and local agency. It also ignores the fact that while the bulk of the Maoist cadre are from *adivasi* or dalit communities, middle peasants and upper castes play a significant role, especially in leadership positions.

The third, which is the revolutionary perspective held by the Maoists themselves and their sympathizers, portrays the movement as a product of structural violence. While they describe people as forced into resistance and armed struggle, there is equally an emphasis on active agency and sacrifice, contrary to the root causes perspective that sees people as mainly passive victims. While long-term state capture is an important goal that certainly influences party strategy, in practice, the Maoists also emphasize more concrete economic and social objectives like land distribution, drought relief, farmers debts or caste atrocities. In particular, since 2003-4, they have posited themselves as the only bulwark against mining and land acquisition. This perspective blurs over the history of non-violent but militant struggles elsewhere in India, including against mining, as well as over the contradictions between the long-term demands of a guerrilla struggle aimed at state capture and immediate economic benefits for the people in whose name this struggle is being waged.

A nuanced analysis that seeks to explain the strength of the Naxalite movement in any particular area needs to take into account several factors. These include the specific socio-economic context; the nature of stratification; the specific political history of the area (both in terms of parliamentary parties and social movements); the issues of agency that explain why certain individuals join the Naxalites; Maoist and state ideology; as well as the logics of Maoist and state militarization which create their own momentum. Geographical factors—e.g. the suitability of territory for guerrilla struggle—also matter. But above all, it is questions of injustice and impunity which best explain the overall trajectory of the Maoist movement in India.

OVERALL CONTEXT FOR THE CURRENT CIVIL WAR

The driving forces for the current civil war are sharpening inequality, the creation of the new states of Chhattisgarh and Jharkhand in 2001 which strengthened rent seeking among the local bourgeoisie and political actors, a liberalized national mining policy in 2003, and a growing emphasis on industrialization, as well as Maoist unification in 2004. Faced with growing resistance to land acquisition, militarism has become the preferred state option to ensure rapid industrialization.

POVERTY

Since India started liberalizing in the early 1990s, inequality has grown. Depending on the formula, anywhere between 28-80 per cent of Indians were below the 'poverty line' in 2010,[5] and the latest UNDP figures reveal acute poverty in eight states, all of which (except for Rajasthan and Uttar Pradesh) have a strong Naxalite presence.[6] While the size of the Indian middle class is debated, it is commonly estimated to account for merely some 300 million people. Meanwhile, national newspapers report on the globally acquisitive abilities of Indian companies,[7] and the fact that India has the highest number of billionaires in Asia.[8]

However, it is fallacious to argue that it is inequality, poverty, or lack of development *per se* that leads to people joining the ranks of the Naxalites (the root causes argument), or conversely, that it is Naxalites who are impeding development (the security perspective). While there is no doubt a strong correlation between areas of high poverty and Naxalism, a causal link or direction has not been established. For instance, Jhabua, in western Madhya Pradesh, has roughly similar socio-economic and demographic indicators as

Dantewada in Chhattisgarh. According to the 2001 census, the population in Jhabua is 85 per cent tribal, with 47 per cent of the population living below the poverty line and only 36.87 per cent literate (2001 census). But unlike Dantewada, which is the heartland of the Maoist movement, Jhabua has been the site of a remarkable non-violent movement for many decades now (the Narmada Bachao Andolan), apart from other local struggles over land and forests. Similarly, the region of Bundelkhand in central India is one of the poorest areas of the country, and while there is a high degree of stratification, there are no Naxalites. Furthermore, in order for people to support the Naxalites (or any other social formation), they have to be present, and historically, the Naxalites have not made much headway in western India, despite the presence of a sizeable *adivasi* or Scheduled Tribe population in Gujarat, Rajasthan, and western Madhya Pradesh.[9]

It is also important to remember that in each of the states where the Naxalites are present, the local configuration of power as well as Naxalite demands vary. In states like Andhra Pradesh or Bihar, a feudal set-up and sharp social stratification (in terms of both caste and class) have meant that the Naxalites have been pitted against local landlords in their defense of the poor. Meanwhile, in the *adivasi*-dominated tracts of Chhattisgarh, Jharkhand, and Orissa, the main concerns of the people have been exploitation by the government's police and forest departments, pitting the Maoists directly against the state.

Security experts claim that 'development' is possible only once an area is within government control, and hence 'area domination' through military measures is necessary before people's rights can be recognized. However, high-poverty areas like Jhabua and Bundelkhand have always been within government control and nobody has prevented the government from implanting whatever welfare schemes it wishes. On the contrary, one often sees more welfare services being implemented in areas under Maoist influence, if only because of their purported usefulness in low-intensity counterinsurgency. The large financial packages sanctioned to insurgency-affected areas by the Planning Commission (which allocates funds between government departments and states) may as well be seen as the success rather than the failure of a model of armed struggle in terms of getting benefits for people. The passage and implementation of the Scheduled Tribes and Other Traditional Forest Dwellers (Recognition of Forest Rights)

Act of 2006, which aims to provide secure land tenure to *adivasis*, is officially conceded as arising out of the need to undercut the core constituency of the Maoists.

Industrialization

If poverty is the context rather than the direct cause for the growing strength of the Naxalite movement, then the same must be said about India's industrialization regime, which is threatening to displace large numbers of people without providing commensurate employment. Industrialization provides the background not so much for understanding why the Naxalites are active—after all, the major struggles against land acquisition are led by non-Maoist local campaigns, and the Maoist's own roots lie in land reform—but instead as a reason for why the government is interested in finishing off the Naxalites.

The formation of the CPI (Maoist) in 2004 coincided with the liberalization of India's mining policy in 2003, and with the SEZ Act in 2005, which set-up SEZs. In 2001, the formation of the states of Chhattisgarh, Jharkhand, and Uttarakhand also provided an incentive for the ruling parties in these states to intervene more actively in areas which had hitherto been relatively neglected in the larger parent states of Madhya Pradesh, Bihar and Uttar Pradesh. Both Chhattisgarh and Jharkhand, states with large mineral and forest areas predominantly inhabited by Scheduled Tribes, explicitly set out to promote industrialization, signing a number of Memorandums of Understanding (MOUs) with industrial houses. Several of these MOUs are suspect, with local politicians and industrialists colluding to make quick money.[10] Occasionally, the loot becomes so glaring that face-saving legal action is required for state legitimacy—leading, for example, to a former chief minister of Jharkhand, Madhu Koda, being charged by the Central Bureau of Investigation for corruption. The emphasis on mining has made it important to vacate the areas of Maoists, whose *de facto* control over the region constitutes an obstacle to rapid industrialization and land acquisition.[11] Industry associations have explicitly supported the government's offensive against the Naxalites, and have called for the involvement of the private sector in this effort.[12] Predictably, these associations have also opposed a government proposal to give tribals a 25 per cent share in mining profits, on the grounds that a lower profit margin would adversely affect investment.[13] Ironically, however, while industry is opposed to any government regulation, it is happy to have the government acquire land on its behalf.

Government Repression

Forcible land acquisition has been an ongoing irritant in the Indian government's relations with village communities, leading to often-violent clashes in which villagers are killed by the police, who act almost as private agents for companies.[14] While these struggles are not led by the Maoists, and are usually local campaigns with activists taking care to keep their distance from any armed action, the repression against the Maoists provides an occasion to arrest and harass the activists in all these campaigns. The charge of being a Maoist sympathizer is easily levelled, and once arrested, even without the application of extraordinary law, legal redress takes time, effort, and money. The protests against land acquisition have also encouraged the Maoists to believe the situation is sufficiently ripe for them to expand, and to exploit in order to gain support. This belief is only strengthened when the government uses force against peaceful protestors—even at a time when it is exhorting the Maoists to come to dialogue.[15]

Above all, Maoists owe their growing support to the form and brutality of the government counter-insurgency campaign. This has effectively elevated a movement with local roots into one with a national presence. In West Bengal, the People's Committee against Police Atrocity (PCPA), which is widely seen as close to the Maoists, originated as a reaction to police repression after a Maoist attempt in November 2008 on the life of the state's chief minister. In Chhattisgarh, government responses have taken the form of state-sponsored vigilantism and between 2005-7, strategic hamletting. In this phenomenon known as Salwa Judum (purification hunt) which has carried on till 2011, the security forces and special police officers, who are locally recruited youth, together go and burn houses, loot property and kill people, initially in an effort to drive them into camps, and later, simply to keep up pressure on the Maoists through their base. Officially over 600 villages are affected. When this boomeranged by increasing civilian support for the Maoists, New Delhi started Operation Green Hunt in 2009. The controversial nature of this operation—a very visible one, spread across several states—has turned some sections of Indian civil society against the government.

Security experts often concede that state response is a critical factor in explaining Maoist activity; indeed they place all their faith in a military response wiping out the Maoists. But their narrative usually centres around the so-called success story of Andhra Pradesh, which has used a mixture of local development and a no-holds-barred police response in which several Maoists have been killed in extra-judicial 'encounters' by a specially trained force called the Greyhounds. In Bihar, on the other hand, before the crisis of September 2010 in which the Maoists held four policemen hostage in exchange for eight of their comrades, the trajectory has been quite different. Bihar used to have a high incidence of Maoist-state-vigilante conflict, but during the Rashtriya Janata Dal regime, relative quiet was bought through a tacit understanding between the Maoists and the RJD.[16] In either state, however, agrarian crises continue to be a problem showing, once again, both that 'objective conditions' do not necessarily find expression in Maoist politics; and conversely, that it is not Maoist presence which is impeding welfare, but the state's own indifference.

It is also important to note that the Maoists are not internally homogeneous. Differences between the Maoist Communist Centre (MCC) and People's War Group (PWG) persist even though they have merged and cadre are transferred between states. For example, the MCC is widely considered more militarist and doctrinaire than the former PWG. In Jharkhand, police have been successful in encouraging breakaway Maoist groups like the Jharkhand Liberation Tigers, as compared to Chhattisgarh, where not only is there a larger and more homogeneous tribal base in the party, but the party has established much stronger roots through its mass struggles for land and remunerative prices for forest produce. The balance between militarization and mass politics has a variety of spin-off effects in terms of which demands get taken up and how.

THE BATTLE OVER PUBLIC PERCEPTION

For both the government and the Maoists, proving local support is critical. For the government, this is because its claim to being a democracy rests on a version of social contract theory, which in turn presumes legitimacy among the public at large. For the Maoists, local support is necessary for a movement that claims to be fighting for the people.

But it is precisely in such situations of civil war and conflict that support can never be gauged accurately. Indeed, apart from the perils of voicing an opinion in times of conflict and the safety-driven impulse to under-report support for the Maoists, people themselves often do not know what they want, because the present is so bad, and the alternative so dim. But even taken at face value, what emerges from media polls is a strong preference for developmental solutions over military ones, for unconditional dialogue, and for reform of the existing political process.[17]

This is especially remarkable given how hard the government has tried to securitize the problem. Until recently, official pronouncements on the Naxalites located the movement largely in a 'socio-economic' context, as not 'merely' a law-and-order problem, but one born out of a development deficit.[18] In the last three or four years, however, in what Huysmans calls the performative function of security labelling, noting that 'the signifier "security" does not describe social relations but changes them into security relations',[19] the Indian government has converted the Naxalite 'problem' almost exclusively into a security issue, with an 'effective police response' overriding all other solutions.[20] Even normal development and administrative processes are 'securitized'— as seen in the use of the Border Roads Organization traditionally deployed in frontier areas to build roads in the heart of India, and in the proliferation of smaller administrative and police units.[21]

Much of the discourse around Naxalism in India today is akin to what Stuart Hall identified as the creation of a 'moral panic' around mugging in 1970s' Britain:

> When the official reaction to a person, group of persons or series of events is out of all proportion to the actual threat offered, when 'experts' in the form of police chiefs, the judiciary, politicians and editors perceive the threat in all but identical terms, and appear to talk 'with one voice' of rates, diagnoses, prognoses and solutions, when the media representations universally stress 'sudden and dramatic' increases (in numbers involved or events) and 'novelty' above and beyond that which a realistic approach would sustain, then we believe it is appropriate to speak of the beginnings of a *moral panic*.[22]

This moral panic, created by the government's response and its amplification by the media, is primarily responsible for giving the Maoists a visibility they did not possess earlier.

What is then at stake is the government's image of being firm and taking action; action which may have no direct relevance or efficiency in tackling the problem at hand. The 'Naxalite problem' is not so much about violence in absolute terms, as it is a reflection of the threat posed by Naxalites to the *status quo*. It is also a function of the security establishment's need to project a 'threat' that justifies more—often unaccountable—funding and forces. In fact, states are compensated by the federal government for any anti-Naxalite expenses, including those expended on 'local resistance groups'. This gives many cash-strapped states an incentive to project a greater threat from Naxalites than they actually pose.[23]

This is not to say, however, that the Maoists do not see armed challenge as the only serious alternative to the state.[24] The Maoist fetishization of militarism is connected to their goal of capturing state power through armed struggle, and establishing, in a slogan commonly attributed to them, *Lal Qile par Lal Jhanda* (Red flag on the Red Fort).[25] The combination of Maoist self-projection as a significant military force and government projections of them as a military threat makes it difficult for independent observers to insist that both sides go beyond the logic of war. While the government brands any critic of its counterinsurgency policies as pro-Maoist, the Maoists have declared that those who criticize their acts of violence are ultimately 'apologists for the oppressors, in spite of their good intentions and sincere attitude'.[26]

MAOIST ORGANIZATION, MILITARIZATION AND FINANCING

The Communist Party of India (Maoist) is organized like every other communist party, with a politburo and central committee, which oversees various state committees or special zonal committees. These state/zonal committees straddle existing state boundaries. For instance, the Dandakaranya Special Zonal Committee has seven divisions under it, which include Bastar in Chhattisgarh and Gadchiroli in Maharashtra. Below this are regional, divisional, or district committees, area committees, and so on down to local cells in villages or factories.

There are also various mass organizations that have units in villages. In the Dandakaranya region, these are known as *sanghams* or collectives—like the women's organization, the seed-sowing cooperatives, and the village defense committee. These collectives are supervised by a visiting squad or *dalam* comprising some 10 to 15 people, which carries arms but is not primarily involved in military action. There is a separate military wing, the People's Liberation Guerrilla Army, which is assisted by people's militias (made up of village defense committees) for specific actions.

The Maoists are estimated to have 7,300 weapons for 10,500 armed cadres nationwide, a 25,000-strong people's militia, and 50,000 members in village-level units.[27] According to police sources, they also have 'AK-series assault rifles, carbines, 7.62 [millimeter] self-loading rifles, grenade launchers, mines, improvised explosive devices and mortars', and are manufacturing their own weapons.[28] Despite occasional police claims that Maoists get their weapons from China or Sri Lanka, in its saner moments the security establishment recognizes that most of this weaponry is looted from the police themselves or from raids on government armories. The Maoists have engaged in some major military actions—breaking open jails, as in Dantewada and Jehanabad; looting ammunition depots and explosives from the National Mineral Development Corporation warehouses in Dantewada; blasting transformers; and attempting assassinations of prominent politicians. In 2008, they ambushed and killed 38 members of the elite Greyhound forces on the Balimela reservoir in Orissa, while in April 2010 they killed 74 personnel of the Central Reserve Police Force (CRPF) in the Dantewada district of Chhattisgarh. These deaths were memorialized by the state in ways similar to those who died in the Kargil war between India and Pakistan, with at least one television commentator calling for a war between 'India' and the Maoists.

The actual violence by the Naxalites belies the threat they supposedly pose in military terms. Even in Chhattisgarh, the state affected the most by government-Naxalite conflict figures prior to the current counter-insurgency offensive suggest no need for the 16 companies of special armed police that were sent there in 1998, or for the 10 battalions of paramilitary forces that are currently posted there. While Naxalite killings have certainly gone up since 2005, and especially in Chhattisgarh, this spike is seen by both sides as an expression of retaliation against the Salwa Judum militia, and hence cannot be used as a causal justification for counter-insurgency. According to the Ministry of Home Affairs, there were 908 Naxalite-related deaths in the country as a whole in 2009.[29] However, much of this data, as well as data published by the South Asia Terrorism Portal (SATP), which are drawn from open-access sources like news reports and are widely cited, are inaccurate and misleading. For instance, the SATP lists 518 civilians, 608 security forces, and 491 'terrorists' killed in Chhattisgarh between 2005 and 2010, coming to a total of 1,617.[30] However, during the initial two years of Salwa Judum, there were also a number of people killed by security forces and vigilantes whose deaths were simply not recorded, or they were recorded as killed by Naxalites since state compensation is available only to those killed by Naxalites.[31] In later years, due to public pressure, these extrajudicial killings have been recorded as 'encounters'.

The overwhelming establishment focus on Naxalite violence also casts into stark relief the double standards espoused by India's ruling parties. The Congress and the BJP have each been responsible for the deaths of thousands of citizens.[32] The BJP, especially, but not uniquely, has several fronts which are openly engaged in vigilante violence against the vulnerable, including artists, filmmakers, and authors whose views are deemed unpalatable, as well as Christians, Muslims, and others.[33] The BJP's mother organization, the Rashtriya Swayamsevak Sangh (RSS), openly disavows India's secular constitution. Violence or killings alone, therefore, cannot account for the government's anxiety about Naxalism. What frightens New Delhi is the fact that the violence is primarily directed against security forces and those in power, rather than against the poor, who are already daily objects of violence in India.

The Maoists finance their operations through what they call levies on industries and forest contractors, enabling the rise of dynamics of corruption, patronage, and protection. Indeed, industrialists often work out private bargains with the Maoists. For instance, this author was told by a surrendered Maoist from Orissa that a senior official of the Essar Group appealed to him to allow a pipeline to pass through his territory. This pipeline is meant to pump iron ore from mines at Bailadilla in Chhattisgarh to Vishakhapatnam port. The Essar official said: 'Since you are the local government here we will pay you the same rate of royalty we pay the government.' Given that this rate is abysmally low (considerably less than US $1, or Rs. 27 per ton), and given that the market rate for iron ore is US $120 (about Rs. 5,600) per ton,[34] this did not constitute much hardship for the Essar Group. The Maoists decided to divide the Rs. 2.8 crore they got annually between party funds and local development, but in the first year they spent it all on roofing tiles for 60 villages. The following year, however, the Chhattisgarh state unit of the Maoists objected to the mining by

Essar on the grounds that it devastated the local environment and provided no benefit to the people of Chhattisgarh. Consequently, the Maoist Central Committee called off the deal with Essar, and ordered the Orissa committee to break the pipeline. The Maoists repeatedly claim that their deals with companies and contractors do not come at the expense of their own constituency, e.g. even when they have a deal with a contractor, they insist on minimum wages. However, this scarcely enables transparent alternatives to the system of industrial capitalism.

Maoist levies (the government calls these 'extortion' schemes) must, however, be placed alongside other parallel systems of informal taxation that routinely operate without government censure. Regular levies extracted by forest and police staff to facilitate illegal tree-felling or tin mining are routine in mineral-rich and forested states like Chhattisgarh. State facilitation of private accumulation is extensive, ranging from 'sweetheart deals' between politicians and corporates over disinvested public sector enterprises, or the licensing of scarce natural resources and government contracts to government doctors and teachers who, because of their failure to work, push people toward private health care or tuition.[35]

DEMOCRACY AT WAR: INSTITUTIONAL RESPONSES TO THE MAOIST CHALLENGE

Almost as remarkable as the coming to centrestage of the Maoists between 2005 and 2010 has been the timidity of India's democratic institutions when faced with what is termed a 'national security' issue. This is of course hardly unique to India, as demonstrated by the failure of statutory checks on excesses committed during the US-led 'war on terror' worldwide. While the main ruling parties, the Congress and the BJP, colluded in sponsoring the Salwa Judum in Chhattisgarh, the Communist Party of India (Marxist), which ruled West Bengal, conducted a war there through its own armed gangs, locally called the Harmad Vahini. Parliament has thus offered little protection for the people. While *adivasi* legislators have been generally opposed to a militaristic solution, they are dependent on their parties for tickets and funding and have been unable to provide an alternative voice.

Independent statutory commissions have also failed the victims of vigilante and state violence. The National Human Rights Commission did not respond to repeated pleas from victims in Chhattisgarh, and when directed by the Supreme Court in 2008 to undertake an inquiry, sent a team of 16 police personnel who went to villages in armoured tanks, accompanied by some of the very SPOs who had been responsible for the violence. The National Commission for Women has not taken up the cases of rape victims, while the National Commission for Scheduled Tribes has been silent. The only commission which has displayed any enthusiasm or integrity is the National Commission for the Protection of Child Rights, but it is relatively new and powerless.

Within the government, the Home Ministry calls the shots on this issue, with the Ministry of Tribal Affairs completely irrelevant. The Home Ministry Naxal Management Cell is dominated by policemen or 'security experts', and the home minister himself, P. Chidambaram, has made the war against the Maoists his own. While elements in the Congress party have been uncomfortable with this approach, with party colleagues calling the home minister 'intellectually arrogant' and his ministry 'paranoid', the Congress party leader, Sonia Gandhi, has acquiesced in the war on *adivasis.*

The Supreme Court has been the only institution to uphold its mandate of protecting the rule of law, but court processes are tortuous and the writ petitions against vigilante violence and abuses of human rights have already lasted three years. In any case, repeated judicial directions to the state of Chhattisgarh to carry out elementary tasks, like registering First Information Reports (FIRs) or rehabilitating those whose houses were burned, have been met with outright refusals to act.

In the initial years of Salwa Judum (2005-8), the media were largely quiet, especially in Chhattisgarh. This was enabled through a combination of government censorship and threats against the media; the enactment of the Chhattisgarh Special Public Security Act 2005, which penalized anything that could be construed as support for the Maoists; and a language and reality disconnect between journalists and *adivasis.* The strategy of arresting the secretary of the People's Union for Civil Liberties, Dr. Binayak Sen, had a mixed effect. On the one hand, his release became a cause célèbre, bringing some media attention to the issue. On the other hand, it focused all civil society attention on his person, at the expense of the wider issues involved. In West Bengal, a much stronger democratic tradition; an active opposition party, the Trinamool Congress, intent on winning elections (which it did); and the national media's virulent anti-communism ensured that the ruling CPI (Marxist)'s handling of the Maoist issue got sufficient coverage. Since Operation Green Hunt started, Maoist attacks escalated, and with prize-winning authors like Arundhati Roy having adopted the Maoist cause, the issue has finally become front-page news.

Despite repeated exhortations to the Maoists to agree to peace talks, the central and state governments are clearly unwilling to engage with them in practice, on the grounds that Naxalites' willingness to talk is merely a ploy to buy time. The nadir was the police arrest and killing of the Maoist leader Cherukuri Rajkumar, aka Azad, in June 2010, precisely at a time when he was about to confirm dates for peace talks to begin. In early 2011, the high-profile kidnapping of a collector in Malkangiri district of Orissa led to mediators negotiating a number of demands, including that ordinary villagers accused of Maoist crimes be released, and festering land issues in Koraput be addressed, but after the release of the collector, the government appears to be reneging on all its agreements.

The latest in the saga is the proposal to flood Maoist areas with funds, largely for the building of roads, but also for 'basic social infrastructure'. Despite reservations by the Planning Commission which allocates money between schemes and states, and which originally drafted an 'Integrated Action Plan' for 'Left wing-extremist-affected' districts, the Home Ministry pushed through a scheme which allocates Rs. 55 crore per district for two years to a committee comprising the collector, the superintendent of police and district forest officer. But it is unlikely that this money will yield much that is useful, given the basic structure of exploitation in which the local administration in collusion with industrialists, traders, and contractors makes all decisions, without consulting the villagers. And compared to the Rs. 800 crore that the Chhattisgarh government has spent on housing and feeding the paramilitaries to repress people in the past few years, the idea that hearts and minds will be won with Rs. 55 crore is laughable.[36]

Above all, there is no appreciation for *adivasi* lifestyles or any attempt to build upon existing strengths, and tired versions of modernization theory continue to be espoused by India's ruling politicians. Such stale rhetoric is clearly apparent in this reportage from the *Hindu*, citing comments made by the Home Minister P. Chidambaram: 'The Minister indicated that while implementation of laws such as PESA and FRA might give rights to forest dwellers, the long-term solution lay in the basic development which would bring them out of the forests.'[37]

What I.F. Stone wrote decades ago about Vietnam rings as true today of India's blinkered political classes:

> In reading the military literature on guerrilla warfare now so fashionable at the Pentagon, one feels that these writers are like men watching a dance from outside through heavy plate-glass windows. They see the motions but they can't hear the music. They put the mechanical gestures down on paper with pedantic fidelity. But what rarely comes through to them are the injured racial feelings, the misery, the rankling slights, the hatred, the devotion, the inspiration and the desperation. So they do not really understand what leads men to abandon wife, children, home, career, friends; to take to the bush and live gun in hand like a hunted animal; to challenge overwhelming military odds rather than acquiesce any longer in humiliation, injustice or poverty.[38]

Justice. Political overtures instead of mere economic packages. Development to benefit citizens, not corporates. Apologies for the past rather than homilies for the future. These would all go a long way toward negotiating peace.

NOTES

1. Subhashis Mitra, 'Terror Tentacles', *Force*, August 2007, p. 38.
2. For the first phase of the Naxalite movement, see Manorajan Mohanty, *Revolutionary Violence: A Study of the Maoist Movement in India* (New Delhi: Sterling 1977); Sumanta Banerjee, *India's Simmering Revolution: The Naxalite Uprising* (New Delhi: Select Book Service Syndicate, 1984); for the more recent phase in Andhra Pradesh, see Committee of Concerned Citizens (CCC), *Third Report: A Detailed Account of the Committee During the Five Years to Intervene in the Climate of Turmoil and Social Violence in Rural Andhra Pradesh* (Hyderabad: CCC, 2002); CCC, *Negotiating Peace* (Hyderabad, 2006); Bela Bhatia, 'The Naxalite Movement in Central Bihar', *Economic and Political Weekly* (henceforth *EPW*), 9 April 2005. See also articles in the special section on the 'Maoist Movement in India', *EPW*, 22-8 July 2006, and response by Azad, 'Maoists in India: A Rejoinder', *EPW*, 14 October 2006.
3. In the rest of this article, while I generally use the term Maoist, I occasionally use the term Naxalite, especially if a generic use is called for.
4. See the report of the Expert Group to the Planning Commission, *Development Challenges in Extremist Affected Areas* (New Delhi: Planning Commission, 2008).

5. The economist Jean Dreze writes: 'At least four alternative figures are available: 28 per cent from the Planning Commission, 50 per cent from the N.C. Saxena Committee report, 42 per cent from the Tendulkar Committee report, and 80 per cent or so from the National Commission for Enterprises in the Unorganised Sector (NCEUS). Jean Dreze, 'Poverty Estimates vs. Food Entitlements', *The Hindu*, 24 February 2010, http://www.hindu.com/2010/02/24/stories/2010022456271200.htm (accessed on 24 February 2010).
6. 'There are more MPI [Multidimensional Poverty Index] poor people in eight Indian states alone (421 million in Bihar, Chhattisgarh, Jharkhand, Madhya Pradesh, Orissa, Rajasthan, Uttar Pradesh, and West Bengal) than in the 26 poorest African countries combined (410 million).' 'Oxford and UNDP Launch a Better Way to Measure Poverty', Oxford Poverty and Human Development Initiative and United Nations Development Program, 14 July 2010, http://hdr.undp.org/en/mediacentre/announcements/title,20523,en.html (accessed on 14 July 2010).
7. In 2007, Tata Steel of the Tata group bought British steelmaker Corus for $12 billion, Hindalco of the Aditya Birla group bought US aluminium sheetmaker Novelis for $6 billion, and Jindal Steel acquired the development rights for the El Mutun mine in Bolivia for $2.3 billion. 'The value of takeovers by Indian firms has risen sharply, from less than $1 billion in 2000 to an estimated $8 billion in 2006. Acquisitions in the first six weeks of 2007 added up to more than $18 billion.' See 'Indian Companies Become Major Players in Overseas Acquisitions', HULIQ, 19 February 2010, http://www.huliq.com/11617/indian-companies-become-major-players-in-overseas-acquisitions (accessed on 19 February 2010).
8. Narayanan Madhavan, 'India's Band of Billionaires Biggest in Asia', *Hindustan Times*, 10 March 2007, http://www.hindustantimes.com/India-s-band-of-billionaires-is-the-biggest-in-Asia/Article1-209306.aspx (accessed on 19 February 2010).
9. There are several reasons for this. They include the origins of the Maoist movement in Andhra Pradesh and Bengal, from where they spread to neighbouring states, as well as the dominance of Hindu reform movements in *adivasi* areas in western India. In Gujarat, the Rashtriya Swayamsevak Sangh has recently appropriated these populations for a Hindu chauvinist agenda, although *adivasi* movements fighting for land and forest resources continue to be active.
10. Supriya Sharma, 'Iron Ore Mines Going for Rs 1 Lakh in Chhattisgarh?' TNN, 2 August 2010, http://timesofindia.indiatimes.com/india/Iron-ore-mines-going-for-Rs-1-lakh-in-Chhattisgarh/articleshow/6245781.cms (accessed on 2 August 2010).
11. However, contrary to much activist hype, there is no direct co-relation between two proposed steel plants for mining in Dantewada and the

forcible evacuation of villages under the state-sponsored vigilante movement called Salwa Judum. Salwa Judum specifically targeted Maoist strongholds, not villages which are situated in mining areas. This is clear if one maps the progress of Salwa Judum.

12. 'The growing Maoist insurgency over large swathes of the mineral-rich countryside could soon hurt some industrial investment plans. Just when India needs to ramp up its industrial machine to lock in growth and when foreign companies are joining the party—Naxalites are clashing with mining and steel companies essential to India's long-term success.' *FICCI (Federation of Indian Chambers of Commerce & Industry) Task Force Report on National Security and Terrorism* (New Delhi: FICCI, 2009), http://www.ficci.com/SPdocument/20032/terrorism-report.pdf (accessed on 25 July 2010). This report also calls for private security agencies to be given arms licenses, which is dangerous given that hired goons are already being used against villagers.
13. 'FICCI Opposes Mining Bill, Debunks Tribal Compensation Scheme', *Economic Times*, 25 July 2010, http://economictimes.indiatimes.com/news/economy/policy/FICCI-opposes-mining-bill-debunks-tribal-compensation-scheme/articleshow/6214184.cms (accessed on 25 July 2010).
14. See, for instance, police firings at Maikanch village in Rayagada district, Orissa, where three people were killed while protesting against land acquisitions for bauxite mining (2001); at Tapkara in Ranchi district, Jharkhand, where nine were killed while protesting against the Koel Karo dam (2001); at the Khuga dam site in Churachandpur district, Manipur, where three were killed (2005); at Kalinganagar in Orissa, where 12 were killed while protesting against a Tata Steel plant (2006); at Nandigram in West Bengal in 2007, where 15 were killed while protesting against land acquisitions for a special economic zone. This is by no means an exhaustive list of recent police firings related to land acquisitions. The police usually claim that they were attacked first and were forced to maintain law and order; this is contested by the human rights groups that have conducted independent investigations into the incidents.
15. On 15 May 2010, the police fired upon and injured protestors peacefully demonstrating against a proposed POSCO steel plant in Orissa. On 12 May 2010 they killed one protestor at the Kalinganagar industrial complex.
16. Arindam Sen, 'Anarchism or Revolutionary Marxism', prepared for 'Resurgence', a symposium on the Naxal/Marxist challenge to the state, March 2010, http://www.india-seminar.com/2010/607/607_arindam_sen.htm (accessed on 25 July 2010).
17. An August 2010 survey by an academic agency and two media houses (*The Week*-CNN-IBN-CSDS) across the 'red belt' claimed that 49 per cent support the government, and 60 per cent have faith in the democratic

process, although 76 per cent want the political system to be reformed. A month later, according to a *Times of India* poll in the five districts of Telengana in Andhra Pradesh from where the Maoists have reportedly been wiped out, 58 per cent said Naxalism was good. (Rupashree Nanda, 'State of the Nation: Government Preferred Over Naxals,' IBN Live, 9 August 2010, http://ibnlive.in.com/news/people-in-Naxalhit-areas-prefer-govt-poll/128447-37-64.html?from=tn; http://articles.timesofindia.indiatimes.com/2010-09-28/india/28244131_1_toi-poll-Naxalism-maoists) (accessed 13 April 2011).

18. 'Naxalites operate in a vacuum created by inadequacy of administrative and political institutions, espouse local demands and take advantage of the prevalent disaffection and injustice among the exploited segments of the population and seek to offer an alternative system of governance which promises emancipation of these segments', Ministry of Home Affairs, Internal Security Division, 'Status Paper on the Naxal Problem', 18 May 2006.
19. J. Huysmans, 'Security! What do You mean? From Concept to Thick Signifier', *European Journal of International Relations*, 1998, 4(2), 226-55, p. 232.
20. For the police, 'effectiveness' means huge expenditure, for instance, on mine-protected vehicles, helicopters, the fortification of police stations, etc., rather than simply greater professionalism and courteous treatment of the public. This, despite the fact that police behaviour and contempt for villagers is a major cause of support for Naxalism.
21. On 13 July 2010, the Government of India proposed a Unified Command to carry out anti-Naxal operations. 'The Centre also offered more helicopters, logistical support and intelligence sharing to the States to fight the Maoist menace. It sanctioned about 16,000 additional Special Police Officers, taking the total number of such posts to about 30,000. It also decided to fund the establishment or strengthening of 400 police stations in the affected districts at the rate of Rs. 2 crore a police station on 80:20 basis over two years. The States were asked to set up an empowered group, chaired by Member-Secretary, Planning Commission, to modify the norms and guidelines to implement development schemes having regard to the local needs and conditions in the affected districts. It was decided to improve road connectivity in 34 worst affected districts. A number of roads and bridges are proposed to be included at a cost of Rs. 950 crore by the Road Transport and Highways Ministry. The Chief Ministers were told that the Planning Commission was considering a Special Development Plan for the affected districts with focus on primary education, health care, drinking water and road connectivity.' Vinay Kumar, 'Centre Proposes Unified Command to Fight Naxals', *The Hindu*, 15 July 2010, http://www.hindu.com/2010/07/15/stories/2010071557350100.htm (accessed on 15 July 2010).

22. Stuart Hall et al., *Policing the Crises: Mugging, the State and Law and Order* (New York: HM Publishers, 1978), p. 16.
23. Author's interview with Shivraj Patil, India's home minister, February 2007.
24. In a reply to an open letter written by the Independent Citizens Initiative (a six-member group that visited Dantewada to carry out an investigation into the Salwa Judum, and of which this author was a member), Ganapathi, the Maoist General Secretary, asks: 'Can you show us one instance from the pages of Indian history where the rights of *adivasis* were ensured through non-violent and open means? And not just in India, but anywhere else in the world for that matter?' Ganapathi, 'Open Reply to Independent Citizen's Initiative on Dantewada', *Economic and Political Weekly*, 6 January 2007.
25. The Red Fort in Delhi has been the symbolic seat of India's power from Mughal times onwards.
26. Ganapathi, 'Open Reply'.
27. Gautam Navlakha, 'Maoists in India', *Economic and Political Weekly*, 3 June 2006, p. 2187.
28. Rahul Bedi, 'Maoist Insurgency Spreads in India', *Jane's Intelligence Review*, 1 July 2006, pp. 21-5.
29. Ministry of Home Affairs, Government of India, *Annual Report 2009-10*, http://www.mha.nic.in/pdfs/AR%28E%290910.pdf (accessed on 15 July 2010).
30. 'South Asia Terrorism Portal (SATP) Fatalities in Left wing Extremist Violence, Chhattisgarh 2005-2010', http://www.satp.org/satporgtp/countries/india/maoist/data_sheets/annualcasualtieschhatisgarh.asp (accessed on 15 July 2010).
31. Nandini Sundar, 'Pleading for Justice', prepared for 'Resurgence', a symposium on the Naxal/Marxist challenge to the state, March 2010, http://www.india-seminar.com/2010/607/607_nandini_sundar.htm (accessed on 15 July 2010).
32. Two thousand seven hundred thirty-three people officially died in Delhi in the anti-Sikh pogroms of 1984 (see www.carnage84.com/official/ahooja/ahooja.htm), and 1,254 in the anti-Muslim pogroms of Gujarat in 2002 (answer in Parliament, provided by Minister of State for Home Affairs, August 2005).
33. Nandini Sundar, 'Vigilantism, Culpability, and Moral Dilemmas', *Critique of Anthropology*, 30 (March 2010), pp. 1-9.
34. 'Should India Ban Iron Ore Export?' Zeebiz.com, 30 July 2010, http://biz.zeenews.com/interviews/story.aspx?newsid=109 (accessed on 25 July 2010).
35. In late 2010, four major scandals surfaced showing the collusion between ministers and corporates: the allocation of mobile telephone spectrum to cherry-picked companies for an estimated loss of $40 billion to the

treasury, overpriced contracts for the Commonwealth games favouring associates of the chairman of the organizing committee, the illegal diversion of government land to the Karnataka chief minister's sons, which was then resold for a huge profit, and the Adarsh housing society scam in Mumbai in which flats meant for war widows were given to influential politicians and senior members of the armed forces.

36. Chhattisgarh Seeks Waiver on Anti-Maoist Forces Expenditure', Zee News, 19 January 2011, http://www.zeenews.com/news681662.html (accessed 14 April 2011).
37. Ibid.
38. I.F. Stone, *In a Time of Torment, 1961-1967* (New York: Little Brown & Co, 1967), p. 173.

CHAPTER 10

Socio-economic Roots of Maoism Post-1980

S. NARAYAN

With heightened concerns about security and terrorism, there has been an active debate about the measures required to combat it. Faced with insurgency in the north-east, militant Maoists in several states and bomb blasts in public places, India's state governments have been rethinking the security paradigm and redefining the roles of different agencies and institutions. Several states have passed anti-terrorist laws that provide for preventive custody. Recently, the Chief Justice of the Supreme Court of India, Justice K.G. Balakrishnan, warned the country about the dangers of lawmakers in several states introducing such legislation and using it in a high-handed manner. There have been instances where these laws have been used against those who have opposed industrialization programmes of the state by highlighting the interests of the poor. There have also been instances, much debated in the media, about arrests on flimsy grounds of waging war against the state. The approach of picking up people for questioning, holding them without charges and bringing the cases to trial constitutes a major violation of human rights. Media and intellectuals have repeatedly been highlighting these issues before the public, yet the jails are full of inmates that have been held on flimsy evidence and have spent years without being charged. With increasing security concerns, the public is merely told that a suspect has been picked up and little is heard of the trial or conviction. That these laws are used to settle political scores and that they invariably work against the interests of the poor has been established again and again in specific instances covered by media. There is adequate evidence that the population of these tribal areas feels that economic development has marginalized their livelihood patterns.

Two important developments took place in the 1980s that could have some relevance to the increased alienation of the tribal populations from the mainstream of development. When Prime Minister Indira Gandhi came back to power in 1980, the country was facing severe shortages in power generation and infrastructure. Existing power stations were not getting adequate coal and the shortages were quite severe in northern India and Punjab. The new government decided to invest heavily in opening up new coal mines and establishing power stations based on coal. The activity was taken up entirely in the public sector, with Coal India, the National Thermal Power Corporations, and other governmental agencies nominated as executing agencies. The large-scale mining operations taken up during 1980-4 involved the resettlement and rehabilitation of millions of people in Chhattisgarh, Jharkhand (then Bihar), Madhya Pradesh and southern Uttar Pradesh. The Singarauli and Pench coal fields were opened up during that time along with the Talcher and IB Valley fields in Orissa. Close to 100 million tonnes of coal per annum was targetted from these fields and there was a frenetic pace of project execution. These were also the places in which there was a high density of tribal population—economically marginalized people who, depending on traditional activities, were dislodged from their centuries-old traditions and moved from mine sites. This was perhaps the largest movement of the impoverished that development programmes of the government had mandated and the signs of resentment can well be traced back to this period.

A second development that took place was the enactment of the Forest (Conservation) Act in 1980. This legislation was an attempt to protect flora from being exploited in the name of projects and commerce. The Forest Act followed the Wildlife (Protection) Act of 1972, which attempted to protect biodiversity in the country. This was also the time when the proposed Silent Valley project in Kerala was being criticized for damaging eco-diversity. Rachel Carson's *Silent Spring* (1962) was still influential, and suddenly the importance of nature had dawned on everyone. The 1980 Forest Act was, in some senses, a strong piece of legislation; it gave enormous powers to the forest officials to prevent encroachments, and indeed habitations within declared forest areas. As areas were delineated as reserve forests, traditional occupations of even gathering twigs ('lops and tops' in the forester's language) was forbidden. People who earned their livelihood through access to forest resources in a sustainable manner suddenly found themselves outside the law. Further, this Act did not distinguish between habitations that existed within the forests for generations; the habitants suddenly found themselves to be encroachers on their own traditional land. For the Forest Department, it was inconceivable to allow tenancy rights within the reserve forests after the 1980 Act. This has perhaps been a major contributor to the disenchantment of the tribal populations living in forests with the entire development process. At the same time, encroachments on the fringes continued, with the rich and powerful eating into forest areas on expanding plantations. It was only in 2008, nearly three decades after the damage of the 1980 Act, that a revised legislation—one that recognized traditional dwellers' rights within forest areas—was enacted. This legislation, though somewhat flawed, sought to provide some protection for traditional dwellers and their rights.

It is argued by those working with indigenous people in Jharkhand, Orissa and Chhattisgarh that want of resources—due to a lack of access to traditional means of livelihood and total neglect by the state—has been at the bottom of the total disenchantment of the people of this region. This is perhaps the reason for the growing lawlessness in these regions.

In short, the public appears to be alienated from the state in the maintenance of law and order, and views state agencies as enemies and not as allies. There is considerable evidence that this has led to the rise of local strongmen that administer peace in their domain. The larger manifestation is the Maoists; where the Maoists operate, they are the law and not the state. At the same time, it is important that the state exercises administrative control and steps are being taken now to bring the rule of law into these disturbed areas, which is a step in the right direction. However, development must follow immediately. It is necessary that state governments quickly plan programmes that will be directed towards the economic improvement of these areas to prevent the people from slipping back into anarchy. The good news is that we have encountered such situations in the past and have some experience in dealing with them.

State agencies, on the other hand, plead institutional helplessness. The lawbreakers are often better armed and trained; they have political access and support, and the legal system poses innumerable hurdles to speedy conclusion of trials. Most importantly, the law enforcement agencies no longer command the respect and affection of the people. Therefore, the state is no longer privy to information or intelligence, and hence unable to come to grips with crime or terrorism. The only way they can enforce obedience is through 'state terror'—picking up suspects, holding them under draconian laws, lumping the innocent and the guilty together, and ensuring that things do not get out of hand. Little do they realize that this further alienates the public.

The recent encounters at Lalgarh in West Bengal, seen so vividly on television, are a stark reminder of the problems that are being faced in several states. From the media, it appears as though the writ of the state does not run in a large number of districts and that there is a willing and ready supply of fighters for the rebel cause. This is indeed worrying.

Several questions arise. How do the Maoist extremists sustain themselves—who gives them money and arms? Secondly, where do they get their rhetoric and ideology from, for they all appear to be rural peasants of fairly limited educational attainments? And thirdly, what do they really want—what are their demands and aspirations?

Answers to these questions are not easy to find, nor are they satisfying. Recent aerial photography of areas where the Maoists have their pockets of influence has shown a substantial increase in the cultivation of poppy. No factories that process opium have yet been found, but this is a small garage venture, and it is possible that opium in its raw form constitutes a stable source of revenue. Of course, this also means that they have access to trade channels that are entrenched in drug trafficking, though this may not be their only source of funds. It is also clear that they have access to those who supply arms, and that the intelligence of the state has not been able to bring any of these suppliers to book. The famous air dropping of arms in Purulia comes to mind, but we know very little about the threads that it led to. There is also evidence of extortion and forced collection of revenue from the peasants which would be yet another source of funds.

In terms of ideology, the answers are somewhat easier—there are a number of intellectuals, including academics and teachers, who have espoused their cause. Dr Binayak Sen,[1] who was held by the police for a long time, suspect to espousing this radical cause, is an example; and there are many others, notably from Andhra Pradesh. It is interesting that this state, which has brought forth so many entrepreneurs in the last decade, is one where the differences between the rich and the poor, the urban and the rural, and the feudal nature of the society make it a natural breeding ground for dissent against the prevalent structure of the society.

The third question, even more difficult to answer, is what exactly do they want. Earlier peasant movements including the Naxalbari movement of the 1960s sought to overthrow landlords and restore the tillers' rights to lands and the produce. Today, ownership of land is no longer the sure way to wealth and prosperity, not even of sustained livelihood. It is also clear that the form of governance practised in Maoist-held areas is largely focused on redistribution of agricultural land and solving of village-level disputes through an ad hoc judgement mechanism. What is next and what they really want are questions difficult to answer. In Nepal, after the Maoists had won their armed struggle against the monarchy, they were content to mainstream their activities through the democratic system. If this is the aspiration in India, the solutions are not difficult. But, if like the Liberation Tigers of Tamil Eelam (LTTE), the attempt is to destabilize the state and to bleed it endlessly, then there is no solution to the problem other than to engage them.

If we add to the above the concerns of deteriorating law and order in the major cities and the increase in crime and accidents, there is a fear that matters are slipping out of control. These threats manifest internally, with some overtones of external influences, and are likely to hinder development, growth and stability.

There is still the threat of external terrorism that seeks to inculcate its ideology into the misguided youth in India. This can be handled only through better intelligence and preparedness. State police and intelligence agencies need to be better armed and protected, intelligence gathering should be digital not person-dependent, and greater surveillance over borders and coasts is necessary. This needs to be done quickly so that an effective deterrent internal security force is available. The introduction of the Unique Identification Number will help, and this programme should be implemented quickly, ensuring that infiltrators are properly screened before the cards are given out.

Finally, there is the issue of governance, especially in the urban areas. The average citizen has little faith in the police or the law and order machinery, and media continue to highlight the failings of the state. Unless citizens have confidence in the authorities, they will not trust them. The first step towards building trust is to establish an effective grievance redressal mechanism. If those who govern are seen as oppressors that have to be appeased or fought, there is little hope for security or peace.

Why have we come to this? Thirty years ago, a collector in a crime-prone district used to get information about every crime committed the same day, and the name of the perpetrator within 48 hours. It was not an intelligence system that was operating—just a fair administrative system that ensured that grievances were given due attention. In return, the villages cooperated and felt that they were part of the state. The important lesson was that the state was their friend and ally.

The state and its institutions are in decay, notwithstanding the rising Sensex and the mighty conclaves of the government and the rich. They are in decay because the institutions that deal with the public have become exploitative and whimsical—seeking to deal with all dissent with a heavy hand and meting out unfair laws to a mute populace.

There is also the worry that politicians are using Maoists as a vote bank with whom electoral or commercial adjustments can be made. They are even prepared to take a soft line with the Maoists. 'For a significant proportion of our politicians, democracy is just a career path, a road to power and affluence.'[2] If the Maoists are able to command a proportion of votes that would get them elected, then for the politicians they become a legitimate constituency.

For long-term growth and stability, institutional and governance issues are very important to address concerns of internal security.

NOTES

1. Dr Binayak Sen, the national vice-president of the Peoples' Union for Civil Liberties (PUCL) in India, was arrested in May 2007. He was granted bail by the Supreme Court in May 2009 (accessed on 24 November 2010).
2. See K. Subrahmanyam, *Business Standard* (9 May 2010), 'The Dangers of Playing Footsie with Maoists', http://www.business-standard.com/india/news/k-subrahmanyamdangersplaying-footsiemaoists/394207/ (accessed on 24 November 2010).

CHAPTER 11

PESA: Legislation as Myth

AJAY DANDEKAR
CHITRANGADA CHOUDHURY

In 1996, the Indian parliament passed the Panchayats (Extension to Scheduled Areas) Act or PESA, acknowledging the need to protect the rights and resources of the communities in Schedule V areas by recognizing and upholding their right to self-governance. Schedule V refers to the fifth appendix of the Indian constitution which outlines special provisions for areas inhabited by tribal people. The law of 1996, according to Dileep Singh Bhuria, the chairman of the committee that worked on it, was intended to 'mark the beginning of a new era in the history of tribal people. . . .'

Tribal communities—more than 8 per cent of India's population—have had a long experience of violation of their land and forest rights, sometimes leading to complete displacement or dispossession. They have also experienced exploitative economic relations with the world at large and the erosion of their cultural practices. The passage of PESA in 1996 was an admission of the need for greater protection for these communities. How was this law meant to operate?

PESA recognized the Gram Sabha as having the right to be consulted on matters of land acquisition and of being competent to act on a range of powers, including the powers to:

- prevent alienation of land in the Scheduled areas and to take appropriate action to restore any unlawfully alienated land of a Scheduled Tribe.
- own minor forest produce.
- enforce prohibition, or to regulate or restrict the sale and consumption of any intoxicant.
- control money-lending to the Scheduled Tribes.
- control institutions and functionaries in all social sectors.

- control local plans, and resources for such plans, including tribal sub-plans.
- recommend or reject the granting of prospecting licenses or mining leases for minor minerals as well as for the grant of concessions for the exploitation of minor minerals by auction.
- issue utilization certificates for government works undertaken in their village.

PESA constructed tribal self-governance around certain key features. The first feature through Section 4(b) affirmed that an organic self-governing community rather than an administrative unit is the basic unit of self-governance. It recognized that a habitation was a natural unit of the community, whose adult members constituted the Gram Sabha. Communities were declared competent to safeguard and preserve their culture and tradition, exercise command over natural resources, enjoy ownership of minor forest produce and adjudicate their disputes (Section 4 [d] and 4 [m] [ii]). The village assembly was empowered to monitor all state institutions within its jurisdiction, such as schools and health centres, with the functionaries placed under its control (Section 4 [i], [j], [k] and [l]).

PESA thus marked a departure from colonial laws like the Land Acquisition Act, or the Forest and Mining Acts. It ordained that communities must be consulted on acquisition of, or access to, land and land-based resources. It affirmed that the tribal community had the capability and competence to adjudicate on, and put an end to, exploitative relations including land alienation, money lending, market relations and the alcohol trade. In the words of a key figure involved in the grassroots movement for the passing of the legislation, 'PESA moved from development delivery to empowerment; from implementation to planning; from circumscribed involvement to conscious participation'.[1]

Thus PESA envisaged a radical shift in the balance of power—from the state apparatus and economic and political elites to the community. However, in the decade and a half after it was passed, the experience of PESA was tragically stilted. When passed by the Indian parliament in 1996, the law envisaged that the states with Schedule V areas within their boundaries would enact legislation devolving power to their tribal communities and amend pre-existing laws to harmonize them with PESA. This was intended to happen within a year. The legislative and executive work, which was meant to be undertaken by state governments, remains incomplete. As Table 11.1 selectively

TABLE 11.1: PESA IN SELECT STATES

The Central PESA Act's provisions	Andhra Pradesh	Chhattisgarh	Jharkhand	Gujarat	Madhya Pradesh	Orissa
Section 4 (i): The Gram Sabha or the Panchayats at the appropriate level shall be consulted before acquiring land in the Scheduled Areas for development projects and before resettling or rehabilitating persons affected by such projects in Scheduled Areas.	The AP Act has made provisions to consult the Mandal (Block) Parishad before acquiring land in Scheduled Areas. However, planning and implementation of such projects will be coordinated at the level of the state government.	The Chhattisgarh Act has made provisions that before acquiring land for development projects, the Gram Sabha will be consulted.	The Jharkhand Act has no provision in this regard.	The Gujarat Act has assigned this responsibility to Intermediate Panchayat bodies.	The MP Act has made provisions that before acquiring land for development projects, the Gram Sabha will be consulted.	The Orissa Act said the District Panchayat shall be consulted before acquiring land. The revenue department has issued instructions to collectors to obtain the Gram Sabha's recommendation during land acquisition. The law also ensures bureaucratic control over the Gram: 'The Collector or such other officer or person specially authorised on

(*Contd.*)

TABLE 11.1 Contd.

The Central PESA Act's provisions	Andhra Pradesh	Chhattisgarh	Jharkhand	Gujarat	Madhya Pradesh	Orissa
						the behalf of the State Government shall exercise general powers of inspection, supervision and control over the exercise of powers, discharge of duties and performance of functions by the Gram Panchayat
Section 4 (j): Planning & management of minor water bodies in the Scheduled Areas shall be entrusted to Panchayats at the appropriate level.	The AP Act has assigned this power to either of the three tiers of Panchayats as the case may be.	The Chhattisgarh Act has assigned powers to the Gram Sabha. Intermediate and District Panchayats also have powers to plan, own and manage minor water bodies	The Jharkhand Act has assigned this power to the Gram Panchayat.	The Gujarat Act entrusts this power to the Gram Panchayat.	The MP Act has assigned functions to the Gram Sabha to plan, own and manage minor water bodies situated within its territorial jurisdiction.	The Orissa Act has assigned this power to the District Panchayats.

Section 4 (k): The recommendations of the Gram Sabha or the Panchayats at the appropriate level shall be made mandatory prior to grant of prospecting licence or mining lease for minor minerals by auction.	Recommendations of the Gram Panchayat shall be considered prior to grant of prospecting licenses.	Prior recommendation of the Gram Sabha is mandatory.	No provision made in this regard.	The Gujarat Mines & Minerals (Regulation & Development) Act provides that prior to granting the quarry lease and quarry permit, recommendations of the Gram Panchayat shall be obtained.	Prior recommendation of the Gram Sabha is mandatory.	The Orissa Act has assigned this power to the District Panchayat.
Section 4 (l): The prior recommendation of the Gram Sabha or the Panchayats at the appropriate level shall be made mandatory for grant of concession for the exploitation of minor minerals by auction.	The AP Act has provided that prior recommendations of Gram Panchayat shall be considered.	The Chhattisgarh Act has no provision in this regard.	The Jharkhand Act has no provision in this regard.	The Gujarat Mines & Minerals Act provides that prior to granting the quarry lease and quarry permit, recommendations of the Gram Panchayat shall be obtained	Prior recommendation of the Gram Sabha is mandatory.	The Orissa Act has assigned this power to the District Panchayat.

(Contd.)

TABLE 11.1 Contd.

The Central PESA Act's provisions	Andhra Pradesh	Chhattisgarh	Jharkhand	Gujarat	Madhya Pradesh	Orissa
Section 4 (m)(i): The power to enforce prohibition or to regulate or restrict the sale and consumption of any intoxicant.	The AP Act has assigned this function either to the Gram Panchayat or the Gram Sabha as the case may be.	The Chhattisgarh Act has assigned this power to the Gram Sabha.	The Jharkhand Act has assigned this power to the Gram Panchayat.	The Gujarat Act has no provision as prohibition extends to the whole state.	The MP Act said the Gram Sabha has the requisite powers.	The Orissa Act has assigned powers to the Gram Panchayat to be exercised under the direct supervision of the Gram Sabha.
Section 4 (m)(ii): The ownership of Minor Forest Produce.	The AP Act said that Gram Panchayat or Gram Sabha as the case may be, shall exercise powers in this matter, as may be prescribed.	The Chhattisgarh Act has no provision in this regard.	The Jharkhand Act has assigned these powers to three tiers of Panchayat.	The Gujarat Act has given the right to ownership of MFP to Gram Panchayat. Sale proceeds shall be paid into and form part of the village fund.	The '*Madhya Pradesh Laghu Van Upaj (Gram Sabha Ko Swamitwa Ka Sandan) Vidheyak 2000*' submitted by the Forest Department of MP is under revision to include issues like 'Ownership of Minor Forest Produce', 'Jurisdictional Issues', etc.	The Orissa Act has assigned powers to the Gram Panchayat to be exercised under the direct supervision of the Gram Sabha.

Section 4 (m)(iii): The power to prevent alienation of land in the Scheduled Areas and to take appropriate action to restore any unlawfully alienated land of a Scheduled Tribe.	The AP Act said that either the Gram Panchayat or the Gram Sabha shall perform such functions.	The Chhattisgarh Act has no provision in this regard.	The Jharkhand Act has assigned this power to District Panchayats.	The Gujarat Act has assigned this power to the District Panchayat.	The Gram Sabha is endowed with such powers.	The Orissa Act has assigned powers to the Gram Panchayat to be exercised under the direct supervision of the Gram Sabha.
Section 4 (m)(iv): The power to manage village markets by whatever name called.	The AP Act has assigned powers to the Gram Panchayat or the Gram Sabha as the case may be.	The Chhattisgarh Act provides that the Gram Sabha shall have powers to manage village markets and *melas* through the Gram Panchayat	The Jharkhand Act has assigned this power to all three tiers of Panchayat.	The Gujarat Act has assigned this power to Gram Panchayats.	The MP Act provides that the Gram Sabha shall have powers to manage village markets and *melas* through the Gram Panchayat	The Orissa Act has assigned powers to the Gram Panchayat to be exercised under the direct supervision of the Gram Sabha.
Section 4 (m)(v): The power to exercise control over money-lending to the Scheduled Tribes.	The AP Act states that either the Gram Panchayat or the Gram Sabha shall perform such functions	The Chhattisgarh Act has amended its laws, giving such powers to the Gram Sabha.	The Jharkhand Act has assigned this power to the District Panchayat.	The Gujarat Act has assigned this power to the Gram Panchayat.	The Gram Sabha is endowed with such powers.	The Orissa Act has assigned powers to the Gram Panchayat to be exercised under the direct supervision of the Gram Sabha.

outlines, the legislative issues are yet to be harmonized across all the nine states where PESA is supposed to be in operation (Table 11.1 covers only states with a Maoist presence).

To begin with, PESA is founded on a 'self-governed village community'. It is therefore paramount that the unit of self-governance is such a community and not an artificial administrative construction. The second component, participatory democracy, is integral to the regular working of a face-to-face, self-governing community. While some states have redefined 'a village' in their Panchayat legislations, administrations at the grassroots often continue to work with their earlier revenue definitions of 'a village'. In such definitions, 'a village' consists not just of 10-12 scattered hamlets. Rather, several revenue villages are clubbed together to form a Gram Panchayat. This effectively precludes the functioning of a 'face-to-face' community as envisaged in the act of the central government and reduces the likelihood of a functioning Gram Sabha, in which people assert their rights and fulfil responsibilities.

In many instances, state legislation has diluted PESA's power. Barring Madhya Pradesh and Chhattisgarh, most state laws have given the bulk of powers to the Gram Panchayat and not the Gram Sabha. This runs contrary to Section 4 (n) of PESA. Moreover, neither the state laws nor the rules for their implementation adequately address questions about how communities might exercise their powers over issues such as land, displacement, liquor, and so on. They have also failed to create redressal mechanisms that communities can use when their powers are violated.

Some state acts in fact put barriers to a Gram Sabha's powers under PESA. For example, subsection 10.8 of the Jharkhand 2001 Gram Panchayat Act says that the powers of the Gram Sabha defined in section 10(1.a) (formulating schemes for economic development) and section 10(5) (powers of the Gram Sabhas in Scheduled Areas) will not affect the rules and jurisdiction of the government. The state government therefore retains the power to override the Gram Sabhas whenever it wishes.

Critical areas with regard to the unfinished legislative agenda relate to resources and land.

In the case of resources, a crucial question is: what is the status of the various laws passed by central and state governments relating to community resources? Which laws take precedence? States have dealt with this in different ways. Madhya Pradesh has proceeded with accepting the provisions of PESA unequivocally as constitutional provisions. Accordingly, the management of natural resources, under Section 129c(iii) of the Madhya Pradesh Panchayat and Gram Swaraj Act is envisaged to be 'in accordance with its tradition and in harmony with the provisions of the constitution'. Thus nothing in the tradition of the community can be invoked that may be against the basic tenets of the constitution. In so far as the ordinary laws on the subject are concerned, this provision of the Madhya Pradesh Act envisages 'due regard to the spirit of other relevant laws for the time being in force'. Chhattisgarh has also followed this approach. Jharkhand has followed the same precedent. But the tenor in Orissa's law is different. The competence of the *grama sasan* (village assembly) under Section 5(6) of the Orissa Gram Panchayat Act is qualified by the clause 'consistent with the relevant laws in force and in harmony with basic tenets of the constitution'. A plain reading of this clause suggests that the relevant laws are superior and accordingly PESA should be adapted suitably.

In most states, the enabling rules are not yet in place for the Gram Sabha's control over prospecting for minor minerals, planning and management of water bodies, control and management of Minor Forest Produce (MFP) and dissent from land acquisition. This suggests reluctance by the state governments to honour the mandate of PESA. In states like Andhra Pradesh and Gujarat, the rules are yet to be framed for PESA because of bureaucratic inaction. For example, in Andhra Pradesh, draft rules were prepared in 2007, but they had not been notified by 2011 because they had to be put for approval before the state Tribal Advisory Council. Without the rules, the operation of PESA on the ground becomes null and void.

In the case of land, alienation and land acquisition are the most critical issues in the tribal areas. PESA unequivocally recognized the crucial importance of this issue. Thus the power envisaged for the Gram Sabha in respect of 'prevention of land alienation as also restoration of illegally alienated land' is unequivocal. A unique feature of this law is the provision that if the Gram Sabha is unable to restore such lands, it is empowered to direct the sub-divisional officer to restore possession within three months:

> if a gram sabha in the scheduled area . . . finds that any person, other than a member of an aboriginal tribe, is in possession of any land of a bhumiswami belonging to an aboriginal tribe, without any lawful authority, it shall restore the possession of such land to that person to whom it originally belonged

> . . . provided that if the gram sabha fails to restore the possession of such land, it shall refer the matter to the sub-divisional officer, who shall restore the possession of such land within three months from the date of receipt of the reference (170-b [2a]).

This radical provision has remained virtually unimplemented in all the states.

Most states have not formalized the process of consultation before acquisition of land, as envisaged under Section 4(i) of PESA. An exception is Madhya Pradesh (then including Chhattisgarh) where the state government made elaborate rules in the year 2000 about consultation with concerned Gram Sabhas before acquisition of land. These rules envisaged 'consultation with gram sabha before issuing notification under Section 4 of the Land Acquisition Act'. A detailed procedure was prescribed so that consultation would be transparent and informed. The objective was to enable the people to come to a rational decision based on facts. The collector and a representative of the company were mandated under rule 3(vi) to attend the final meeting of the Gram Sabha before it formally adopted a resolution for or against the acquisition. Thus, in theory, there is a paradigm shift in favour of the people in a crucial aspect of governance concerning acquisition of land. The open assembly of the Gram Sabha precedes the deliberations involving the collector. The collector is expected to satisfy the people in the familiar setting of the Gram Sabha, where the people feel empowered, before starting the formal process of land acquisition.

Regrettably, these rules are not followed in their true spirit. There are cases where the formal resolutions of a Gram Sabha expressing dissent have been destroyed and substituted by forged documents. Even in the states which have done extensive work on their legislation, the Gram Sabhas are only given the power of consultation and not consent, thus diluting the principle of self-governance. Nor have state governments outlined ways of recognizing and abiding by a negative response from a community when it is opposed to proposed acquisition of their land.

It is tragic that in none of the states, the governor, who is accorded limitless powers by the constitution to ensure the upholding of PESA, has monitored or intervened. As required by Paragraph 3 of Schedule V, governors are required to submit a report annually, which is their independent assessment of the quality of governance in PESA areas. An analysis of annual reports submitted by the governors to the centre in the past eight years shows that these are not objective assessments as required by law, but largely a laundry list of physical targets and financial allocations under various schemes reported by the state government's departments. None of the reports analysed or touched on the themes of displacement, alienation, poor governance and insurgency, which are the dominant facts of life in many PESA areas. In some cases, reports of successive years have reproduced exactly the same paragraphs, suggesting how the exercise has become one of going through the motions.

The challenges to a tribal community's way of life have severely intensified in the twenty-first century as a liberalizing economy woos private capital and rushes for natural resources, particularly minerals and farmland. Communities bear the brunt of this violent mining and industrialization. Their experience also testifies to the fact that the immense profitability of the exercise skews the political and administrative agenda in favour of industry and away from protective laws like PESA. Left-wing insurgencies, nourished by people's problems and experiences of violation, are one result. In these circumstances, the neglect of PESA has had particularly tragic and violent implications.

For PESA to work effectively, it would require that economic and political elites respect the law and honour their part of the constitutional and legal contract. This has not happened, and there is a crisis in various PESA areas of the country—a damaging mix of misgovernment, alienation, violent insurgency, and counter-violence by the state as well as non-state actors. In the words of one analyst, 'some tribal communities, such as those in Bastar, are probably witnessing the most severe crisis since their existence'.[1] While every state has its own specificities, our fieldwork suggests that the crisis has broad and interlinked dimensions across central India. Together, they are rendering PESA weak, even meaningless, on the ground.

NOTE

1. Unpublished proceedings of Institute of Rural Management Anand (IRMA) conference on PESA, February 2010.

CHAPTER 12

The 'Affected Districts' Database

PRATIMA SINGH

The Ministry of Home Affairs of the Government of India by 2011 had listed 83 Left Wing Extremist (LWE) affected districts spread across 9 states of the country. It highlighted 35 'focus districts' as the worst affected and marked them out for intensive development under a 'control, hold and build' strategy.

This article focuses on those 35 districts. It offers a cursory, though revealing, analysis of the websites of these districts. Such analysis suggests levels of detailed knowledge of the districts and of the capacity of district administrators to produce useful resources for their citizens, while extracting rudimentary data for each of the districts helps us to gain a basic understanding of their levels of development. The quality and detail of the websites vary considerably, and from such differences, we may begin to ask which districts are more electronically present than others—and why. Websites alone do not equate to effective administration; but a poorly developed website may suggest that a district has limited capacity. Further research into such districts would be revealing. When analysts seek reasons for the spread of Maoist influence, inept or deficient local administration is often seen as an important cause.

I list five statistics for each of the districts:

- total population,
- percentage of tribal population,
- number of primary schools,
- number of primary health centres, and
- length of metalled roads.

The first two variables are demographic while the latter three indicate levels of development in the district. They thereby tie this argument with the hypothesis that lack of development is a main cause of left wing extremist influence. Since the Maoist insurgency is said to have gained momentum by aligning its interests with small-scale tribal uprisings and by tapping into the dissatisfaction of tribal populations, we can see the movement having more of a presence in districts where Scheduled Tribes (STs) are a significant percentage of the population. Our database shows that only 24 of the 35 LWE worst affected districts have information on the percentage of STs on their websites. Out of these 24 districts, 14, situated in the states of Chhattisgarh, Jharkhand, Maharashtra and Orissa, have STs comprising more than a quarter of their total district population.

Table 12.1 shows that four of Orissa's five worst-affected districts, four of Chhattisgarh's seven, four of Jharkhand's eleven and both of Maharashtra's worst-affected districts have STs comprising more than 25 per cent of their population. Forty per cent of the 35 worst-affected districts, therefore, have more than a quarter tribal populations.

Eleven districts had no data on STs on their websites in 2011. However, if we go to the 2001 Census of India, we find that three worst-affected districts have a negligible ST population (Aurangabad and Gaya in Bihar and Sonbhadra in Uttar Pradesh). However, Scheduled Tribes comprise 66.31 per cent of the population of Bastar district in Chhattisgarh, Malkangiri district in Orissa and Lohardaga district in Jharkhand have more than half tribal populations. Despite this high ST population none of their websites display the per cent of ST population.

The other three variables—the number of primary schools, primary health centres, and the length of metalled roads—suggest levels of development in these districts. The number of primary schools in a district is, by itself, not particularly revealing. But such numbers do begin to paint a picture when presented as a ratio of the number of

TABLE 12.1: DISTRICTS WITH > 25% ST POPULATION

	Total 'worst-affected' districts	'Worst-affected' districts with > 25% ST population
Chhattisgarh	7	4
Jharkhand	11	4
Maharashtra	2	2
Orissa	5	4
TOTAL	25	14

Source: The official websites of each of the districts.

people to one primary school. The *national* average for this ratio is 1,800 people to one primary school[1] and so anything above this means the district education system is performing more poorly than the national system because more than 1,800 people are served by one primary school. Data on primary schools are hard to find—again, an indication of the level of administrative capacity in a district—with only 18 of the 35 districts having them on their websites. Table 12.2 shows that 11 of these 18 districts have a ratio less than 1,800:1 for primary schools. This means that 11 districts have ratios better than the national average. The other seven districts perform worse than the national system—three of Bihar's six districts and four of Jharkhand's eleven. This may come as a surprise, since the majority of the districts have a better education system than its national counterpart, but given that 17 districts don't even give us a number for primary schools we cannot make any conclusions. It could also be that the more backward districts (those with more than 1,800 people to one primary school) don't put up the information on their websites, thereby giving us a skewed impression of the situation. But if we assume, based on our sample, that the majority of the districts have a better primary education system than the national system,

TABLE 12.2: DISTRICT DEVELOPMENT VARIABLES IN COMPARISON WITH THE NATIONAL AVERAGE

Variable	National Average	Number of districts better off (ratio < national average)	Number of districts worse off (ratio > national average)
Number of primary schools	1,800 : 1	11 (Khammam, Jamui, Bastar, Dantewada, Lohardaga, Balaghat, Gadchiroli, Deogarh, Rayagada, Sambalpur, Medinipur West)	7 (Arwal, Jehanabad, Rohtas, Bokaro, Garhwa, Palamu, Ramgarh)
Number of primary health centres	5,2000 : 1	15 (Khammam, Arwal, Bastar, Dantewada, Latehar, Lohardaga, Balaghat, Gadchiroli, Gondia, Deogarh, Gajapati, Rayagada, Sambalpur, Sonbhadra, Medinipur West)	6 (Jamui, Jehanabad, East Singhbhum, Palamu, West Singhbhum, Ramgarh)

Source: The official websites of each of the districts.

further research must be undertaken to study the causes behind why, despite government investment, the benefits of education are not realized in these districts.

Data on the number of primary health centres are available for 21 of the 35 districts. Again we put this in a population-to-primary-health-centre ratio, which is more useful for our analysis. As shown in Table 12.2, the national average of this ratio is 52,000 people to one primary health centre;[2] 15 of the 21 districts have ratios lower than this national average making their health care performance better than the national average. The other six districts—two of Bihar and four of Jharkhand—have ratios higher than 52,000 to one. This means that their district health care system is performing more poorly than the national system since more than 52,000 people are served by one primary health centre. Again, it's a surprise that 42 per cent of the 35 'worst-affected' districts have better primary healthcare than the national average but there are still 14 districts that don't provide any information on health care, giving us a one-sided story.

Finally, the data for the last variable, the length of metalled roads, is available for 16 of the 35 districts but in inconsistent units and categorized incomparably. It is clear from the above analyses that most of the LWE worst-affected districts have a sizable proportion of Scheduled Tribes in their district population. It is also safe to say that primary schools and health centres are lacking given the population size in these districts leading to a dearth of education and health care. The data thus reinforces an argument that districts with certain demographic and development attributes are more open to Maoist influence than others.

The above analysis was carried out only for those districts that had data for these variables on their websites. From this analysis of the websites, it is worth pointing out that in an era when efficient e-governance is believed to have far-reaching benefits (evidenced in states like Tamil Nadu, Himachal Pradesh and Haryana), a number of districts still do not have even basic information on their websites. This leads to an analysis of what the missing numbers indicate.

Bijapur district and Narayanpur district of Chhattisgarh were carved out of Dantewada and Bastar districts respectively in 2007. Despite it being four years since they were formed, neither district has a website yet. Almost all other district websites have the 2001 census population figure, except Aurangabad in Bihar which has very little information, and in April 2011 the site had not been updated since

November 2010. It has figures only for population but it is organized messily and divided into blocks, villages and other smaller categories without any total population figure.

Scheduled Tribes data as a percentage of the total population are available for 24 of the 35 LWE worst-affected districts. Eight more districts, excluding the three mentioned above, have no data on Scheduled Tribes. These include Bastar district of Chhattisgarh, which has one of the highest proportions of Scheduled Tribes in their population; Gaya district, Bihar, which only has general information but no useful data; Lohardaga and Palamu in Jharkhand, Balaghat district, Madhya Pradesh, Sonbhadra district in Uttar Pradesh, Malkangiri district, Orissa; and Medinipur West district, West Bengal. Data for primary schools, primary health care centres and metalled roads are readily available for some districts, while absent for others. As shown in Table 12.3, Khammam district, Andhra Pradesh; Arwal, Jamui and Jehanabad districts of Bihar; Dantewada district, Chhattisgarh; Gadchiroli, Maharashtra; and Deogarh and Rayagada districts of Orissa are the only eight districts with data for all five criteria.

In this analysis, we are simply using the sophistication and extent of a website as a possible measure of the efficacy of a district's

TABLE 12.3: DISTRICT WEBSITES CATEGORIZED BY AMOUNT OF INFORMATION AVAILABLE

Data on all 5 criteria	Data on 4 criteria	Data on 3 criteria	Data on 2 criteria	Data on only 1 criterion	No data
8 districts (Khammam, Arwal, Jamui, Jehanabad, Dantewada, Gadchiroli, Deogarh, Rayagada)	8 districts (Rohtas, Garhwa, West Singh-bhum, Ramgarh, Balaghat, Gondia, Sambalpur, Medinipur West)	10 districts (Bastar, Kanker, Bokaro, Chatra, East Singh-bhum, Latehar, Lohardaga, Palamu, Gajapati, Sonbhadra)	4 districts (Rajnand-gaon, Surguja, Gumla, Hazaribagh)	2 districts (Gaya, Malkangiri)	3 districts (Aurangabad, Bijapur, Narayanpur)

Source: The official websites of each of the districts.

administration. If a district has a good website, the administration of the district is perceived as energetic and thereby perhaps capable of imparting better governance. This is a rough-and-ready tool, but it is obvious that a district website that makes important announcements, makes data easily available and has forms and information online that helps both the people and the administration to run smoothly.

The *quality* of information, and not merely data alone, can help gauge the extent of an administration's experiments with e-governance and even its ability to provide basic information to officials. The state of Bihar stands out in this instance. Five of the six districts of Bihar, with the exclusion of Aurangabad, have an SMS Monitoring System online which helps track the status of 10 development schemes at the district and block levels. The system has helped improve the performance of the administration and enhanced accountability in the state. Chhattisgarh and Jharkhand, two of the states most troubled by Maoist influence, had average websites with mostly general information that was not updated regularly. Gadchiroli district, Maharashtra, and Gajapati district, Orissa, started e-governance initiatives in 2011 reporting important news and events in the district. Another Orissa district, Rayagada, has a blog (http://rayagadainfo.blogspot.com/) which serves as a news and event announcement system as well as a public grievance portal. All of these measures help citizens by empowering them with more than just information. It serves as a feedback mechanism, giving citizens a chance to use the websites to make the government work better, thereby making it more participatory. All this also depends, to some extent, on the zeal of the district collector, and this is one of the main reasons why large intra-state differences become apparent as is in the case of Chhattisgarh. In April 2011, Dantewada district was the only district to report at once the basic population data from the 2011 census of India which had been released less than a week before.[3] Contrast this with many other districts that did not carry even basic ST population figures, though they have significant ST populations.

In this description and analysis of websites of Maoist-affected districts, one observation becomes startlingly clear: there are a lot of blank spaces and missing numbers in the database tables. This suggests a lot of potential to develop e-governance. Governments and administrators can use digital technology to empower people, as appears to be happening in Bihar. Some governments use websites to make basic administration easier by uploading current information, making announcements, and so on. A more important step lies in using websites to involve citizens in a more participatory and responsive system of governance, which might make the entire system work more efficiently.

S. No.	State	District
1.1	Andhra Pradesh	Khammam
2.1	Bihar	Arwal
2.2		Aurangabad
2.3		Gaya
2.4		Jamui
2.5		Jehanabad
2.6		Rohtas
3.1	Chhattisgarh	Bastar
3.2		Bijapur
3.3		Dantewada
3.4		Kanker
3.5		Narayanpur
3.6		Rajnandgaon
3.7		Surguja
4.1	Jharkhand	Bokaro
4.2		Chatra
4.3		East Singhbhum
4.4		Garhwa
4.5		Gumla
4.6		Hazaribagh
4.7		Latehar
4.8		Lohardaga
4.9		Palamu
4.10		West Singhbhum
4.11		Ramgarh
5.1	Madhya Pradesh	Balaghat
6.1	Maharashtra	Gadchiroli
6.2		Gondia
7.1	Orissa	Deogarh
7.2		Gajapati
7.3		Malkangiri
7.4		Rayagada
7.5		Sambalpur
8.1	Uttar Pradesh	Sonbhadra
9.1	West Bengal	Medinipur West

1.1 ANDHRA PRADESH: KHAMMAM DISTRICT
(http://khammam.nic.in/)

Total Population	25,62,412
Percentage of Tribal Population	21.81%
Number of Primary Schools	2,622
Number of Primary Health Centres	56
Metalled Roads	480 km

2.1 BIHAR: ARWAL DISTRICT
(http://arwal.bih.nic.in/)

Total Population	5,89,476
Percentage of Tribal Population	0.05%
Number of Primary Schools	282
Number of Primary Health Centres	22
Metalled Roads	(a) NH-110 Arwal to Jehanabad (b) NH-98 Arwal-Aurangabad-Patna

2.2 BIHAR: AURANGABAD DISTRICT
(http://aurangabad.bih.nic.in/)

Total Population	20,13,055*
Percentage of Tribal Population	0.08%*
Number of Primary Schools	
Number of Primary Health Centres	
Metalled Roads	

2.3 BIHAR: GAYA DISTRICT
(http://gaya.bih.nic.in/)

Total Population	34,73,428
Percentage of Tribal Population	0.08%*
Number of Primary Schools	
Number of Primary Health Centres	
Metalled Roads	

2.4 BIHAR: JAMUI DISTRICT
(http://jamui.bih.nic.in/)

Total Population	13,98,796
Percentage of Tribal Population 1991 census abstract	4.80%
Number of Primary Schools	940
Number of Primary Health Centres	10
Metalled Roads	PWD: 320 km District board rd: 493.95 km REO rd: 389.90 km

2.5 BIHAR: JEHANABAD DISTRICT
(http://jehanabad.bih.nic.in/)

Total Population	9,24,839
Percentage of Tribal Population	0.11%
Number of Primary Schools	484
Number of Primary Health Centres	7
Metalled Roads	Road distance from Patna is 70 km and from Gaya is 45 km

2.6 BIHAR: ROHTAS DISTRICT
(http://rohtas.bih.nic.in/)

Total Population	24,50,748
Percentage of Tribal Population	1.05%
Number of Primary Schools	1,169
Number of Primary Health Centres	
Metalled Roads	GT road

3.1 CHHATTISGARH: BASTAR DISTRICT
(http://bastar.nic.in/)

Total Population	13,02,253
Percentage of Tribal Population	66.31%*
Number of Primary Schools	1,473
Number of Primary Health Centres	64
Metalled Roads	

3.2. CHHATTISGARH: BIJAPUR DISTRICT

Total Population	Didn't exist in 2001
Percentage of Tribal Population	
Number of Primary Schools	
Number of Primary Health Centres	
Metalled Roads	

3.3 CHHATTISGARH: DANTEWADA DISTRICT
(http://dantewada.nic.in/)

Total Population	4,78,314
Percentage of Tribal Population	77.07%
Number of Primary Schools	1,236
Number of Primary Health Centres	24
Metalled Roads	Major district rd: 110.40 km Other district rd: 273.25 km

3.4 CHHATTISGARH: KANKER DISTRICT
(http://kanker.nic.in/)

Total Population	6,51,333
Percentage of Tribal Population	56.08%
Number of Primary Schools	
Number of Primary Health Centres	
Metalled Roads	NH-43 Raipur (139 km) and Jagdalpur (160 km)

3.5 CHHATTISGARH: NARAYANPUR DISTRICT

Total Population	Didn't exist in 2001
Percentage of Tribal Population	
Number of Primary Schools	
Number of Primary Health Centres	
Metalled Roads	

3.6 CHHATTISGARH: RAJNANDGAON DISTRICT
(http://rajnandgaon.nic.in/)

Total Population	12,83,224
Percentage of Tribal Population	26.63%
Number of Primary Schools	
Number of Primary Health Centres	
Metalled Roads	

3.7 CHHATTISGARH: SURGUJA DISTRICT
(http://surguja.nic.in/)

Total Population	19,72,094
Percentage of Tribal Population	54.6%
Number of Primary Schools	
Number of Primary Health Centres	
Metalled Roads	

4.1 JHARKHAND: BOKARO DISTRICT
(http://bokaro.nic.in/)

Total Population	17,77,662
Percentage of Tribal Population	12.3%
Number of Primary Schools	702
Number of Primary Health Centres	
Metalled Roads	

4.2 JHARKHAND: CHATRA DISTRICT
(http://chatra.nic.in/)

Total Population	7,90,680
Percentage of Tribal Population	3.74%
Number of Primary Schools	
Number of Primary Health Centres	
Metalled Roads	PWD: 134.5 km; REO: 219.89 km Chatra district has a good number of metalled roads and almost all the block headquarters are connected by such roads.

4.3 JHARKHAND: EAST SINGHBHUM DISTRICT
(http://jamshedpur.nic.in/)

Total Population	19,82,988
Percentage of Tribal Population	27.85%
Number of Primary Schools	
Number of Primary Health Centres	10
Metalled Roads	

4.4 JHARKHAND: GARHWA DISTRICT
(http://garhwa.nic.in/)

Total Population	10,34,151
Percentage of Tribal Population	19.91%
Number of Primary Schools	476
Number of Primary Health Centres	
Metalled Roads	There are no National Highways in this district. There is 210 km of State Highway and 96.95 km of district roads. Link roads and corridors add up to 190 km.

4.5 JHARKHAND: GUMLA DISTRICT
(http://gumla.nic.in/)

Total Population	7,92,686
Percentage of Tribal Population	69.1%
Number of Primary Schools	
Number of Primary Health Centres	
Metalled Roads	

4.6 JHARKHAND: HAZARIBAGH DISTRICT
(http://hazaribag.nic.in/)

Total Population	22,77,108
Percentage of Tribal Population	12.2%
Number of Primary Schools	
Number of Primary Health Centres	
Metalled Roads	

4.7 JHARKHAND: LATEHAR DISTRICT
(http://latehar.nic.in/)

Total Population	5,58,831
Percentage of Tribal Population	45.17%
Number of Primary Schools	
Number of Primary Health Centres	101
Metalled Roads	

4.8 JHARKHAND: LOHARDAGA DISTRICT
(http://lohardaga.nic.in/)

Total Population	3,18,325
Percentage of Tribal Population	55.7%*
Number of Primary Schools	213
Number of Primary Health Centres	15
Metalled Roads	

4.9 HARKHAND: PALAMU DISTRICT
(http://palamu.nic.in/)

Total Population	15,33,173
Percentage of Tribal Population	18.7%*
Number of Primary Schools	821
Number of Primary Health Centres	10
Metalled Roads	

4.10 JHARKHAND: WEST SINGHBHUM DISTRICT
(http://chaibasa.nic.in/)

Total Population	12,33,945
Percentage of Tribal Population	65.36%
Number of Primary Schools	
Number of Primary Health Centres	15
Metalled Roads	4 state highways, 6 zilla parishad roads and 3 forest roads

4.11 JHARKHAND: RAMGARH DISTRICT (http://www.ramgarh.nic.in/)

Total Population	8,39,482
Percentage of Tribal Population	2.3%
Number of Primary Schools	181
Number of Primary Health Centres	4
Metalled Roads	

5.1 MADHYA PRADESH: BALAGHAT DISTRICT (http://balaghat.nic.in/)

Total Population	14,97,968
Percentage of Tribal Population	21.8%*
Number of Primary Schools	1844
Number of Primary Health Centres	345
Metalled Roads	2,059 km

6.1 MAHARASHTRA: GADCHIROLI DISTRICT (http://gadchiroli.nic.in/)

Total Population	9,70,294
Percentage of Tribal Population	38.31%
Number of Primary Schools	1,618
Number of Primary Health Centres	45
Metalled Roads	Major district rd: 1,941 km Other district rd: 1,744 km

6.2 MAHARASHTRA: GONDIA DISTRICT (http://gondia.gov.in/)

Total Population	12,00,151
Percentage of Tribal Population	25.82%
Number of Primary Schools	
Number of Primary Health Centres	39
Metalled Roads	Major district rd: 678.86 km Other district rd: 76.88 km

7.1 ORISSA: DEOGARH DISTRICT (http://deogarh.nic.in/)

Total Population	2,74,095
Percentage of Tribal Population	27.07%
Number of Primary Schools	350
Number of Primary Health Centres	9
Metalled Roads	Major district rd: 6 km

7.2 ORISSA: GAJAPATI DISTRICT
(http://gajapati.nic.in/)

Total Population	5,18,837
Percentage of Tribal Population	50.78%
Number of Primary Schools	
Number of Primary Health Centres	20
Metalled Roads	

7.3 ORISSA: MALKANGIRI DISTRICT
(http://malkangiri.nic.in/)

Total Population	5,14,836
Percentage of Tribal Population	57.43%*
Number of Primary Schools	
Number of Primary Health Centres	
Metalled Roads	

7.4 ORISSA: RAYAGADA DISTRICT
(http://rayagada.nic.in/)

Total Population	8,23,000
Percentage of Tribal Population	56.04%
Number of Primary Schools	1,482
Number of Primary Health Centres	34
Metalled Roads	Major district rd: 130 km Other district rd: 69 km

7.5 ORISSA: SAMBALPUR DISTRICT
(http://sambalpur.nic.in/)

Total Population	9,35,613
Percentage of Tribal Population	34.5%
Number of Primary Schools	913
Number of Primary Health Centres	28
Metalled Roads	

8.1 UTTAR PRADESH: SONBHADRA DISTRICT
(http://sonbhadra.nic.in/)

Total Population	14,63,468
Percentage of Tribal Population	0.03%*
Number of Primary Schools	
Number of Primary Health Centres	31
Metalled Roads	Well connected to Lucknow, Allahabad, Varanasi, Mirzapur by road

9.1 WEST BENGAL: MEDINIPUR WEST DISTRICT
(http://paschimmedinipur.gov.in/)

Total Population	51,93,411
Percentage of Tribal Population	8.31%*
Number of Primary Schools	4,668
Number of Hospitals and Health Centres	244
Metalled Roads	9,716

*Indicates statistics taken from the census 2011 website which are not available on the official district website.

NOTES

1. Ratio calculated from data for the year 2001 to maintain consistency.
2. Ibid.
3. Further research on comparing the census 2011 district statistics with the census 2001 data in this paper could be undertaken.

CHAPTER 13

No Revolution without Women, No Liberation without Revolution: Women in India's Maoist Insurgency

AKANKSHA MEHTA

It is estimated that women currently constitute approximately 40 per cent of the cadre force of the Communist Party of India (Maoist). Assuming a wide range of roles from fully-fledged guerrilla fighters, organizers, messengers to nurses and cooks, thousands of women have been actively involved in the organization since its inception in 2004.[1] Journalists covering the movement in Maoist strongholds have often brought back images of women carrying weapons and dressed in combat fatigues. Moreover, it has been reported that women Maoists have been actively involved in encounters and recent attacks against Indian security forces. For instance, Jagari Baskey, a female commander, led around a hundred cadres in the 15 February 2010 ambush on an Eastern Frontier Rifles camp in Silda, West Bengal (killing 24 paramilitary personnel).[2]

Maoist leaders have repeatedly asserted (both in oral and print discourse) that the 'people's war' against state oppression also aims to obliterate patriarchy and the subjugation of women. Party discourse on women is largely built on narratives of 'victimhood' of women brought about by state atrocities. For instance, the party's Resolution on State Violence Against Women mentions that 'the Unity Congress-9th calls upon all sections of women and democrats to oppose the violence being perpetrated by the state forces and vigilante forces on women.'[3] On the other hand, the state's counter-insurgency discourse views Maoist women as 'victims' of male cadres who have not only instrumentalized women into their cause, but also routinely 'victimize' women cadres with sexual violence and aggression. Both these discourses revolve around 'victimhood' and not agency. Furthermore, feminist analysis of militant women often ignores their agency, viewing violent women as lacking empowerment as violence is seen as a 'masculine' domain with patriarchal goals.[4]

While I acknowledge that few women cadres have risen to higher ranks within the organization, in this article I elaborate on the agency and role of women in India's Maoist insurgency. Although narratives of 'victimhood' are crucial to capturing the role of women in political violence, I argue that the aforementioned narratives neglect agency and activism of violent and militant women. Therefore, I emphasize that a revised feminist security perspective remains necessary to understand the role of women in the current Maoist movement and the agency of militant women worldwide.

POLITICAL VIOLENCE, INSURGENCY AND GENDER

Early literature on political violence and insurgency simply overlooked and omitted women's participation. As Enloe points out, political violence, insurgency, and armed conflict were all seen as completely 'masculine' domains.[5] Later analysis argued that women were less likely to engage in violence than men as they were more accepting of non-violent means (negotiation, compromise, etc.) of settling disputes.[6] This notion of women being 'intrinsically' more passive and peace loving than men created a dichotomy between 'men's violence' and 'women's peace'.[7] As York elaborates, two problematic arguments based on conceptions of 'womanhood' have been used to create and further this dichotomy. Firstly, women are nurturers and mothers and are hence considered 'biologically' opposed to violence. Secondly, cooperation, caring, and nurturing are all identified as 'feminine' traits, while dominance and violence as 'masculine' traits.[8]

This biological determinism has been used to assert that aggression and violence are 'inherently' masculine, and women who are violent are either irrational (incapable of rational choice) or a 'victim' of a larger masculine (patriarchal) plan.[9] Furthermore, narratives of women in political violence and insurgent action have been largely embroiled in the 'victimhood' of the woman, wherein women are seen as victims of violence (and sexual abuse linked to it) and men as the perpetrators.[10] This exclusion of their roles beyond victimhood results in insufficient recognition of their involvement and participation in violence and conflict, delinking them from their agency.[11]

While there has been a gradual shift in analysis towards the inclusion of female agency in debates on political violence, as Sylvester highlights, militant women who use political violence are still seen as deviant by other feminists with harsh judgments issued on them.[12] Emphasizing that violence (both left and right wing) remains patriarchal, it has been argued that women's emancipation and empowerment remains limited even if they exercise agency and activism within a violent movement. Some feminist analysis of violence has also asserted that while militant women do challenge gender norms, their new gender roles and they themselves are forgotten in the aftermath of the conflict[13] (as militant structures remain inherently patriarchal and subordinating). Participation of women in insurgent and politically violent movements (like the Maoist insurgency in India) have, therefore, often been referred to as 'accidental activism', wherein women are seen as instrumentalized participants serving 'masculine' (patriarchal) goals.[14]

WOMEN OF THE RED TIDE: NARRATIVES OF WOMEN MAOIST INSURGENTS IN INDIA

Point 22 of the Party Programme of the Communist Party of India (Maoist) asserts that the party must pay special attention to the mobilization of women. It says that the party must assist women in coming forward to join the People's War and in nurturing them [women] to become staunch communist leaders.[15] The programme also states that women are victims of social, economic, and political patriarchal systems (caste, property, family, feudal oppression, workplace harassment, globalization, etc.) and rape and abuse of women has often been used as weapons of oppression. In a video interview, Roy opines that prior to her engagement with women Maoist cadres, she believed that women cadres were largely 'victims'. However, during her visits to Maoist strongholds, she realized that indeed 40-50 per cent of the cadre strength was women. Additionally, women's organizations linked to the insurgency such as the Krantikari Adivasi Mahila Sangathan (Revolutionary Indigenous Women's Association), have a membership of almost 90,000. Roy asserts that women have taken up arms and joined these organizations to 'fight and escape the patriarchal systems that surround them'.[16]

Other researchers and journalists who have engaged with women cadres have also elaborated on the reasons behind the active involvement of women in the movement. Several narratives of oppression of the *adivasis* (indigenous/tribal people) and direct and indirect violence against them (especially the tribal women) have emerged from these elaborations. In this context, direct violence refers to acts of physical aggression and sexual violence against tribal women. Meanwhile, indirect violence refers to the various manifestations of routine structural violence against the tribal communities (and tribal women in particular). This encompasses both routine exploitation (monetary, physical, and sexual) and oppression by people of authority as well as exploitation of women via patriarchal systems of caste, family, marriage, property ownership, etc.

In his piece '100lb Guerrillas', Pandita elaborates that in 1980, exploitation of tribals in Maharashtra's Gadchiroli district was at its peak (Maoist rebels entered the district in the same year). Forest officers, big-town businessmen, and contractors routinely exploited the *adivasis* and even collected large amounts of money from the poverty-stricken community merely in lieu of allowing them to stay in the jungle and collect firewood. Additionally, there was routine sexual abuse and exploitation of tribal girls. Pandita highlights that these injustices prompted female cadre, Tarakka, to approach the Maoist camp in the area and join the armed Maoist movement.[17] Chandra, a female cadre who was active for 18 years in south Gadchiroli (before surrendering in 2008), affirms that the reason many women take up arms and join the insurgency is because 'they want to fight the physical and sexual exploitation by outsiders and police'.[18] Furthermore, in the aftermath of Salwa Judum, a state-sponsored counter-Maoist campaign wherein hundreds of villages were burnt and destroyed, recruitment (including women's recruitment) into the insurgency increased significantly.

In addition to what the CPI (Maoist) refers to as 'Brahminical and upper caste' brutalities against tribal women,[19] there also exist grave inadequacies and vacuums of state polity and judiciary that prompt women to take up the Maoist cause and join the insurgency. In tribal areas where the state's systems remain absent or corrupt, Maoist rebels establish camps and people's courts, and distribute pamphlets that speak of justice and equality for women. As Chandra, the aforementioned cadre, elaborates, 'The poor *adivasis* can't approach any system—political or judicial—where they can plead their plight or seek redress against injustice. Maoists have that system, so the villagers naturally support them.'[20]

Pandita also highlights that 'the CPI (Maoist) has an open policy about relationships. A man can marry a woman comrade with mutual consent.'[21] This is an interesting point because it has been reported that in some cases women have joined the insurgency to escape from forced marriages, or conversely to marry someone against their family's consent (outside of their caste, etc.).[22] Furthermore, some women cadres join the insurgency to follow in the footsteps of their husbands, fathers, brothers or other close family members.[23] While most female cadres are rural, agrarian women, there have been a few women cadres, commanders, and leaders who are urban, middle class, educated ideologues and activists, joining the movement not to escape or fight personal exploitation, but out of an elevated recognition of imperialist class oppression in the nation. Among these, the most prominent remains Anuradha Ghandy, the late wife of now arrested Maoist leader Khobad Ghandy, and the only woman who has been in the Central Committee of the party. Others include Rajitha, a state committee member, and Padma, Suguna, and Aruna, all three being on their way to be state level leaders at the time of their death.[24]

MEN COOK, WOMEN PATROL: ROLES OF WOMEN MAOISTS

'By the way, did you try that *karela* [bitter gourd] *chutney*? I made it, she adds, as she fits the magazine to her gun. It goes in with a distinct click.'[25]

The above-mentioned exchange from Pandita's article captures the evolution of normative gender roles in the Maoist insurgency. Pandita elaborates that in the Maoist camp, men help with the cooking and women go around with axes to chop wood. He also mentions that while women cadres go about carrying out mundane tasks like boiling water, reading, listening to music, and combing their hair, the gun always remains next to them. Furthermore, while some cadres relax, others rehearse for a cultural performance; simultaneously some attend a class on military strategy.[26] This elaboration not only highlights the fluidity (and even reversal) of normative gender duties in the camp, but more importantly also juxtaposes the imagery of women carrying out 'feminine' everyday tasks and armed female militants who have been trained in strategic and military combat.

As mentioned earlier, several female cadres have engaged in violent encounters and deadly attacks. Many have even led brutal attacks and are feared and admired for their bravery and fearlessness. Almost all major attacks against security forces in the last few years have involved women militants, with some being led by women as well. Maoist leaders have even stated that there is no difference between the training, exercises, and diet of men and women cadres. However, while women have been actively engaging in violence and combat, few have risen up the organizational and ideological ranks of the party. Several women serve as squad commanders, however, few have risen above that level. As mentioned earlier, Anuradha Ghandy was the only woman to be on the Central Committee of the party. She led the Central Committee's *mahila* (women) sub-committee, actively engaging in feminist critique of the party's policies and actions. She also educated other women cadres on feminism and gender issues, held workshops on the subject, and researched and wrote academic papers.[27]

While equality between the sexes is preached and considerably practised within the CPI (Maoist) the lack of women in decision-making roles is troubling. Maoist leaders often see women as 'followers', not leaders.[28] Furthermore, there have been a few reported cases of sexual harassment and abuse of women cadres within the movement. Shobha Mandi *alias* Uma, the Jhargram area commander, surrendered in August 2010 in the West Midnapore district and revealed that she had been assaulted and raped by senior leaders of the outfit in West Bengal.[29] In the case of Lanka Papi Reddy, a Central Committee member who surrendered in 2008, Maoist leaders took strict action against his misbehaviour with women cadres. He was demoted and shifted out of his area of operation and later surrendered to the police.[30]

IN CONTINUATION OF A REVOLUTIONARY PAST: CONSTRUCTING A 'FEMALE' MAOIST DISCOURSE

> Mother Goddesses are worshipped
> Mythical heroines remembered
> Jhansi Lakshmibai is given tearful tributes
> Sarojini Devi gets garlands and praises
> Yet, the name of Panchadi Nirmala gives them tremors[31]

These lines speak of Comrade Panchadi Nirmala, who was a part of the Naxalbari revolution and was killed by security forces in 1969. In 2010, the Communist Party of India (Maoist) released a detailed and elaborate document titled 'Women Martyrs of the Indian

Revolution (Naxalbari to 2010)'. The document had narratives on the roles and lives of hundreds of women who were part of the Maoist insurgency and were killed by security forces. The aforementioned lines are from the leading narrative about Naxalbari's most historic woman martyr. The document states that the purpose of capturing these narratives is to firstly highlight the participation of women in the movement, secondly offer insight into how these women fight patriarchy and balance their roles as mothers and cadres, and thirdly elaborate on how the movement undergoes feminist critique from within that allows it to become more and more egalitarian.[32]

It is significant to note that while the party's leadership might be publishing this document for the aforementioned reasons, for the women these narratives provide a means of placement and continuation in an 'imagined community'.[33] Women in other nationalist movements such as the Hindu nationalist movement in India have often used mother goddesses, mythological figures, and historical figures (like Rani of Jhansi, Sarojini Naidu, etc.) to create the identity of the fearless, warrior woman.[34] Similarly, narratives that speak of revolutionary heroes (that in the aforementioned case surpass mythological, historical figures) allow women Maoist cadres to create a 'female' discourse within the larger movement, wherein they see themselves as embodiments of these martyrs.

The narratives mentioned in the document specifically outline how and why these women joined the 'revolution', the atrocities that were committed against them or the ones around them, the hardship they faced in the jungles, and their 'brutal murders' in encounters with security forces. Additionally, the motif of the 'brave warrior woman', who was both a mother and a 'revolutionary', runs through the narratives. In Comrade Nirmala's story, it is mentioned that she joined the struggle with her baby strapped to her. However, one day, the baby began to cry and the police almost located the camp because of the noise. A male leader explained to her that she had to let go of the child to be a 'revolutionary', and that women in Vietnam had done the same. She, therefore, sent the child back to her parents and continued her life in the struggle.[35] These narratives allow thousands of women cadres who have made similar choices and been in similar situations to identify with 'martyred' women cadres and continue the revolution. Furthermore, narratives of the arrests of women cadres and leaders and their condition in police cells are also used to mobilize other women cadres. All these narratives intertwine stories of 'victimhood and suffering' with stories of 'resistance and doing', placing 'everyday' lives of women Maoist cadres in a larger discourse on 'heroic, brave, and martyred women Maoists'.

AGENCY NOT 'VICTIMHOOD'

'I knew the consequences of participating in such movements. They never deterred me. I was not disappointed by the failed attack, as I never lost sight of the ultimate goal of a changed world. . . . Why should anyone be surprised by women taking up arms? During the Vietnam War, and in all guerrilla warfare movements the world over, women have been very active', says Ajitha Kummikal, Kerala's first female Maoist cadre.[36]

The defining agency here is the ability to make individual, autonomous choices; as mentioned earlier, militant women are often seen as devoid of agency as violent movements are seen as patriarchal domains. Analysing gender in the Sri Lankan conflict, Mel (2001) therefore puts forward the two key questions on female agency in militant movements. She asks, 'Do women who participate in militant armed struggle enjoy full agency? . . . How radically have women militants been able to transform societies to ensure greater social justice and gender equality?'[37]

In the case of the Maoist insurgency in India, it has been hinted that as women mainly constitute the lower rungs of the movement, they remain 'victims' and do not achieve any notable or significant empowerment through the Maoist cause. While it is true that not many women have risen up the organization's leadership, Maoist women are reportedly significantly more active and independent than the average rural women. They are able to get on with life more efficiently than the ordinary rural women.[38] Thousands of women have joined the movement independent of their husbands and other male members of their family. Moreover, gender roles are significantly altered in Maoist camps, and insurgent women give up roles of motherhood and nurture to take up arms, problematizing if not questioning the dichotomy between 'women as peaceful mothers', and 'men as violent warriors'. The creation of a discourse based on female narratives, addressing the 'everyday' female experience and creating continuity with a revolutionary past, is also illustrative of women cadres carving out an independent space within the larger movement. All the above-mentioned are manifestations and expressions of activism and agency.

While there still remains the question (as put forth by Mel) of if and how women militants will be able to transform societies, viewing the role of women in militant movements from a lens of 'victimhood' and 'larger empowerment' neglects the 'everyday experiences' of women cadres and how they shape and reshape the larger movement, transforming 'everyday' insurgent spaces. This neglect denies them any agency and sidelines their action and activism. While the discourse of insurgency and counter-insurgency will continue to focus on narratives of 'victimhood', feminist analysis of militancy needs to move beyond 'victimhood' and analyse everyday agency of female militants. As Manchanda asserts, there is thus a need to 'feminize' conflict and security, as women's voices and experiences are vital to the understanding of the very meaning and understanding of human security, political violence, and conflict.[39]

In 2004, feminist groups in Andhra Pradesh conducted a number of meetings with the Communist Party of India (Maoist), critiquing the party's positions and actions linked to women members. The exchange that followed vocalized female voices and experiences within the party and criticized constructively the shortcomings of Maoist goals on women's equality.[40] For understanding the current phase of the Maoist insurgency and the role of women militants in conflict, such critique is absolutely necessary, as it includes experiences and voices that are often excluded yet significant. The Communist Party of India (Maoist) has stated, 'Women represent half the sky. Without unleashing the pent-up fury of women as a mighty force of revolution, victory in revolution is impossible.'[41] It is similarly pertinent that analysis of political violence and insurgency includes this half of the movement.

NOTES

1. In September 2004, People's War Group (PWG) and Maoist Communist Center of India (MCCI) merged to form the Communist Party of India-Maoist.
2. Dan Nelson, 'Maoist Attack on Indian Troops "led by Female with Mesmerizing Cobra Eyes"', *The Telegraph,* 18 February 2010, http://www.telegraph.co.uk/news/worldnews/asia/india/7259130/Maoist-attack-on-Indian-troops-led-by-female-with-mesmerising-cobra-eyes.html (accessed on 30 January 2011).
3. CPI (Maoist): 9th Congress, *Resolution on State Violence against Women,* Paragraph 9. http://www.bannedthought.net/india/CPI-Maoist-Docs/index.htm (document accessed on 25 January 2011).

4. Sara Ruddick, 'Women of Peace: A Feminist Construction', in Lois A. Lorentzen and Jenifer Turpin (eds.), *The Women War Reader* (New York: New York University Press, 1998).
5. Cynthia Enloe, *The Morning After: Sexual Politics at the End of the Cold War* (Berkeley, Los Angeles, London: University of California Press, 1993).
6. Simona Sharoni, *Gender and the Israeli-Palestinian Accord: The Politics of Women's Resistance* (New York: Syracuse University Press, 1995); Betty Reardon, 'Women and Weapons: The Militarist Sexist Symbiosis', in Ingeborg Breines et al. (eds.), *Towards a Women's Agenda for a Culture of Peace* (Paris: UNESCO, 1999); Sara Ruddick, 'Women of Peace: A Feminist Construction', in Lois A. Lorentzen and Jenifer Turpin (eds.), *The Women War Reader* (New York: New York University Press, 1998).
7. Anuradha Chenoy, *Towards a New Politics: Agenda for a Third Force* (New Delhi: Sangam, 1996).
8. Jodi York, 'The Truth about Women and Peace', in *The Women War Reader.*
9. Caron E. Gentry and Laura Sjoberg, *Mothers, Monsters, Whores: Women's Violence in Global Politics* (London and New York: Zed Book, 2007).
10. L. Kelly, 'Wars against Women: Sexual Violence, Sexual Politics, and the Militarized State', in S. Jacobs, R. Jacobson, and J. Marchbank (eds.), *States of Conflict: Gender, Violence and Resistance* (London and New York: Zed Book, 2000); Yuval-Davis, *Gender and Nation* (London: Sage Publications, New Delhi: Thousand Oaks, 1997).

    Also, it is to be noted that even when men were victims in war and violence, they were represented and portrayed as 'masculine' heroes, the discourse of victimhood focused on the women (in this case their widows and mothers). For more on this, see C.O.N. Moser and F.C. Clark, 'Introduction', in C.O.N. Moser et al. (eds.), *Victims, Perpetrators or Actors?: Gender, Armed Conflict and Political Violence* (New Delhi: Kali for Women, 2001).
11. C.O.N. Moser and F.C. Clark, 'Introduction', in *Victims, Perpetrators or Actors?: Gender, Armed Conflict and Political Violence.*
12. Christine Sylvester, 'Tensions in Feminist Security Studies', *Security Dialogue*, vol. 41, issue 6, 2010, pp. 607-14.
13. Yuval-Davis, *Gender and Nation.*
14. R. Manchanda, 'Where are the Women in South Asian Conflicts?', in R. Manchanda (ed.), *Women, War and Peace in South Asia: Beyond Victimhood to Agency* (New Delhi: Sage, 2001); S. Emmanuel, 'Re-Examining Feminist Discourses on Female Militancy: A Critical Analysis of Writings on the Women of the Liberation Tigers of Tamil Eelam', M.A. thesis, Institute of Social Studies (ISS), The Hague, Netherlands, 2004.

15. Communist Party of India (Maoist) *Party Programme*, Point 22, http://www.bannedthought.net/india/CPI-Maoist-Docs/index.htm (accessed on 25 January 2011).
16. Arundhati Roy, Video Interview with Laura Flanders, *GRITtv*, http://www.dailymotion.com/video/xcq2le_grittv-arundhati-roy-women-revoluti_news (accessed on 12 February 2011).
17. Rahul Pandita, '100lb Guerillas', *Open Magazine*, September 2010, http://www.openthemagazine.com/article/nation/100lb-guerillas
18. Jaideep Hardikar, 'Daughters of Mao', *Daily News and Analysis*, 1 November 2009.
19. CPI (Maoist): 9th Congress, *Resolution on State Violence against Women*, Paragraph 9. http://www.bannedthought.net/india/CPI-Maoist-Docs/index.htm (accessed on 25 January 2011).
20. Jaideep Hardikar, 'Daughters of Mao'.
21. Rahul Pandita, '100lb Guerrillas'.
22. P.V. Ramana, 'Pretty Ones are Married Off to Senior Leaders', *Daily News and Analysis*, 1 November 2009, Mumbai.
23. Ibid.
24. Communist Party of India (Maoist), *Women Martyrs of the Indian Revolution (Naxalbari to 2010)*, http://www.bannedthought.net/india/CPI-Maoist-Docs/index.htm (accessed on 30 January 2011).
25. Rahul Pandita, '100lb Guerrillas'.
26. Ibid.
27. Communist Party of India (Maoist), *Women Martyrs of the Indian Revolution (Naxalbari to 2010)*.
28. Discussion with Dr. P.V. Ramana, Institute of Defense Studies and Analyses (IDSA), New Delhi, August 2009 and January 2011.
29. Mohan Fakir Pradhan, 'Maoists: Women in the Camp', *South Asia Intelligence Review*, 25 October 2010.
30. Srinivas K. Reddy, 'Papi Reddy a Renegade: Maoists', *The Hindu*, 10 February 2008, http://www.hindu.com/2008/02/10/stories/2008021058930400.htm (accessed on 30 January 2011).
31. Communist Party of India (Maoist) (2010), *Women Martyrs of the Indian Revolution (Naxalbari to 2010)*, p. 24 http://www.bannedthought.net/india/CPI-Maoist-Docs/index.htm (accessed on 30 January 2011).
32. Ibid.
33. Benedict Anderson, *Imagined Communities: Reflections on the Origin and Spread of Nationalism*, (New York and London: Verso, 1983).
34. Akanksha Mehta, 'From "Nurturing Mothers" to "Aggressive Protectors": Identity and Agency of Hindu Right Wing Women in India', unpublished dissertation, S. Rajaratnam School of International Studies, Singapore.
35. Communist Party of India (Maoist) (2010), *Women Martyrs of the Indian Revolution (Naxalbari to 2010)*, p. 24.

36. Ajitha Kummikal, 'Women have Always Fought in Guerrilla Movements', *Daily News and Analysis*, 1 November 2009, Mumbai.
37. N.D. Mel, *Women & the Nation's Narrative: Gender and Nationalism in Twentieth Century Sri Lanka*, Social Scientists' Association, Sri Lanka.
38. Discussion with Dr. P.V. Ramana, Institute of Defense Studies and Analyses (IDSA), New Delhi, August 2009 and January 2011.
39. CPI (Maoist): 9th Congress, *Resolution on State Violence against Women*, Paragraph 9. http://www.bannedthought.net/india/CPI-Maoist-Docs/index.htm (document accessed on 25 January 2011).
40. Vasanth Kannabiran, Volga, Kalpana Kannabiran, 'Andhra Pradesh: Women's Rights and Naxalite Groups', *Economic and Political Weekly*, vol. 39, no. 45, 6-12 November 2004, pp. 4874-7.
41. Rita Manchanda, 'Redefining and Feminising Security', *Economic and Political Weekly*, vol. 36, no. 22, 2-8 June 2001, pp. 1956-63.

CHAPTER 14

The Experience of Negotiations with Maoists in Andhra Pradesh

OM PRAKASH

From about 2006, Maoism has become a buzzword in Indian politics. From breaking news on 24-hour television news channels to debates in print media, this issue has raised serious intellectual concerns on the one hand and untamed, frenzied passion on the other. Depending on one's political discourse, Maoism or 'left wing extremism' is perceived as either a response to India's neglect of the most deprived sections of society or the conspiracies of a gang of criminals and terrorists. Another segment of civil society perceives Maoism as the leading credible political force that stands against the undemocratic and violent assault of capitalist development on people and their resources that has surged in recent times. Yet others see Maoists as one amongst several oppositional forces in Indian democracy. This section of civil society seeks explanation from the Maoists regarding democratic norms that they follow within their own organization as well as towards other political formations involved in anti-capitalist struggles. However, what has brought the greatest attention to the Maoist movement in India is a statement by the Indian prime minister in 2006, which described the movement as the greatest internal security threat that the country faces. Whether by accident of history or by design and political endurance of over 40 years from 1967, Maoists have come to occupy a central political space at the beginning of the twenty-first century.

Various efforts and experiments have been undertaken to try to redress underlying grievances and counter the politico-military challenge that the Maoists posed to the state. Some like the Mahatma Gandhi National Rural Employment Guarantee Act or the Planning Commission's assessment in 2008, *Development Challenge in the Extremist Affected Areas*,[1] may be classified as the democratic responses. Others, like the 'Area Domination' exercise or what goes by the name of Operation Green Hunt, can be classified as a militaristic response. This paper elucidates yet another approach: engagement between the state and the CPI (Maoist)/Naxalites/CPI (Marxist-Leninist) groups[2] in India—a 'deliberative approach'. It is based on the experience of Andhra Pradesh in 2004 and provides a landmark in the history of attempts of the Indian state to cope with Maoist-inspired challenges.

This essay analyses the working of the deliberative processes against the background of deep ideological and political divides. It seeks to understand whether deliberation can transform the vicious cycle of violence and counter-violence into political oppositional form. In other words, can deliberations reorder conflict in a manner that debate over substantive socio-economic issues is foregrounded?

CONTEXT

Andhra Pradesh (AP), a state in southern India, witnessed intense political mobilization even as India stood at the threshold of independence. It has been an epicentre of a wide variety of radical political struggles along class, caste and gender lines. Experiences from the battlefields of the Telengana region of the state in the course of the historic peasant revolt against the feudal forms of power locally and the coercive might of the Indian state eventually served twin purposes. It played a key role in shaping and adjusting the overall strategy of the communist movement in India. It also gave insight into the policy of engagement that the Indian state was to adopt when pressed with revolt.[3]

The lessons from the Telangana peasant revolt forced the national leaders of the Communist Party of India (henceforth CPI) to relinquish revolutionary socialism for the immediate future. They instead probed the avenues of parliamentary democracy within the constitutional framework to advance socialist goals. The local leadership from Andhra and Telangana regions, however, refused to relent. It is therefore hardly surprising that the echo of Mao Zedong's 'New Democratic Revolution' was first heard from the Andhra leadership and came to be known as the 'Andhra thesis'. The Andhra thesis drew parallel between the Chinese revolution and the revolutionary situation in India. It called upon the peasantry to be the mainstay of the democratic revolutionary alliance in India. Besides, it also outlined prolonged civil war and guerrilla warfare as the backbone of revolutionary strategy.[4]

CIVIL SOCIETY AND THE NAXALITES

One can identify broadly three distinct phases in the evolution of the Naxalite movement in Andhra Pradesh. In the first phase, the movement was generally concentrated in coastal Srikakulam district. The rise and fall of this phase was coterminous with the rise and fall of the Charu Mazumdar-led movement in other parts of India by 1975. The second phase can be termed as the phase of mass mobilization in between 1977-80. This period saw the geographical spread of the movement to north Telengana districts of Karimnagar, Warangal and Khammam. During this phase, the emphasis was on mass mobilization and popular forms of protest around the issues of landlord oppression and coercion, the practice of *vetti* (bonded labour), land to the landless, usury, etc. It is during this phase that the CPI(ML) People's War group (henceforth PW) formed various mass organizations like the *Ryot Coolie Sangham* (Agricultural Labourer Association), Radical Youth League (students union wing), *Viarasam* (Revolutionary Writer's Association), *Jana Natya Mandali* (cultural wing), etc. The formation of these mass organizations to propagate radical ideas and the CPI(ML) ideology was specific to this period, as earlier the considerations for politics of this kind were accounted for as 'revisionism' within the CPI(ML).[5] The third phase of Naxalite movement since 1980 onwards leading up to the historically significant unification of the PW and the All India Maoist Communist Centre of India (MCCI) to form the CPI (Maoist) in 2004 and thereafter saw greater reliance on a militarization strategy. Emphasis of the movement in this phase was on carving out stable political and military bases amongst the people, termed in Maoist vocabulary as Guerrilla Zones and Liberated Zones.

There were varied and layered responses by state agencies and governments towards the Naxalite movement in AP. Leaders of dominant political parties in the state, the Congress and Telugu Desam Party, praised their contribution to win the votes of depressed classes that lived predominantly in rural areas. Judges from the AP High Court, while delivering specific judgements have honoured and appreciated the contribution of the movement. The movement has been credited with bringing the focus back to issues of life and livelihood of the most depressed and ignored sections of society.[6] Undoubtedly certain policy shifts related to land relations, particularly concerning the *adivasi* (tribal), have been brought about to ameliorate the Naxalite appeal. Yet, a blanket response of the state towards the Naxalite movement has been that of repression. Quite frequently, such measures have transgressed the normative constitutional vision of right to life. This particularly in the case of staged 'encounters', for which the AP police became notoriously famous.[7] Encounters were only an extreme manifestation of state's response to the Naxalite challenge. Conspiracy cases, intimidation, detention without trail for prolonged periods and carving spaces of legal impunity for the police by enforcing draconian laws like the Madras Suppression of Disturbances Act 1948 and the AP Public Safety Act were other measures used to contain the rapidly advancing political ideology and influence of the rebels. In due course, commented K. Balagopal, a prominent human rights activist and lawyer from AP, the Naxalite response to such measures became equally retributive. While the state went after whoever it suspected to be a Naxalite leader, cadre or even sympathizer, the Naxalites started identifying suspected police informers amongst people and handing out physical punishments and quite often killing them in cold blood. It is in this context that the role of the civil society became quite significant.

AP has a long history of civil society activism. The Andhra Pradesh Civil Liberty Committee and Human Rights Forum are two prominent organizations that gained momentum alongside the Naxalite movement. Many in this movement have reasonable ideological sympathy as well as critical attitude towards the Naxalite strategy. However, an event of remarkable significance took place in 1997. Some members of AP's vibrant civil society came up with the idea of halting the cycle of violence and counter-violence between the Naxalites and the state. These were people from different professional shades in AP ranging from high bureaucracy to journalism, prominent legal experts to academics. They called themselves the Committee of Concerned Citizens (henceforth CCC).

THE COMMITTEE OF CONCERNED CITIZENS AND ITS PEACE EXPERIMENT

The CCC comprised 15 members and was headed by a retired Indian Administrative Services officer S.R. Sankaran, who held the post of

Principal Secretary of Social Welfare in the Government of Andhra Pradesh. Besides Sankaran there were other civil-liberty activists, lawyers, Dalit rights activists, journalists, academics and political leaders.

The first report of the CCC published in 1998 was titled 'In Search of Democratic Space'. The title perhaps reflects the socio-political conditions that came to characterize rural AP in the context of the CPI(ML) movement and the state response to it, in which, according to the CCC, the people have become 'mute spectators'.[8] At the outset, the CCC addressed the problem of violence committed by both the state agencies and the Naxalites. It questioned the state practice of 'violation of the rule of law' in dealing with a political movement that has a 'distinct social and economic base'. Strict adherence to the rule of law, claimed the CCC, was the only 'moral authority for the state to rule' and that in no circumstance can the state transgress the rule of law, not even in the name of 'maintaining the law and order'.[9] On the other hand, the CCC blamed the Naxalite groups for indulging in 'irresponsible violence'. It contended that the 'political mobilization by the Naxalites has been over taken by indiscriminate use of armed power'.[10]

The CCC adopted a fourfold objective:

1. Arriving at a vantage point to understand the Naxalite movement with the focus on people's aspiration.
2. Intervening to solve some of the persistent problems.
3. Effecting policy shift.
4. Halting killing and preventing further brutalization of society.[11]

At the commencement of its work in 1997 the CCC visited some of the villages in the north Telangana districts of Adilabad, Karimnagar and Warangal, meeting local body representatives, people and the district administrative officers. In tune with the information gathered through these meetings the CCC issued recommendations to both the government and the Naxalite parties.[12] The CCC's recommendations to both the government and the Naxalites were to end arbitrary violence and allow people and their elected representatives to participate in a debate on the issues pertaining to 'rights', 'equity' and 'justice'.[13] The CCC suggested that the first round of its consultations in the villages reinforced the fact that the present state of violent conflict in AP was centrally woven around the 'key issue of land'. It asserted:

> The Naxalite movement is not a new phenomenon in Andhra Pradesh. Land-based struggle of poor peasants and tribals have taken place several times in its history. These struggles are political in nature and have a socio-economic base. Attempts to crush them with force may drive them underground and render their course more brutal. . .the committee would therefore take such studies beginning with land relation and unemployment situation.[14]

The second report of the CCC therefore focused on analysing the land relations in the districts of the Telangana region. Land rights being part of the normative agenda for equity, justice and livelihood of the Indian state, the CCC emphasized that successive governments in AP had failed to implement land reform legislations in the true spirit. It is on the terrain laid out by the failure of the 'state sponsored' land reforms and Land Transfer Regulation (LTR) Acts that the CPI(ML) movements resurrected themselves in the 1970s against landlordism and 'oppressive social order'.[15] The CCC claimed that the revolt of the poor peasantry under the leadership of the CPI(ML) groups against socio-economic and political dominance of the landlords had become the 'bone of contention' between the state and the Marxist-Leninist parties. While the state claimed the seizing of land from the control of the landlords and its redistribution under the leadership of the CPI(ML) parties to be illegal, the latter insisted it was a 'legitimate' measure. The situation, pointed out the CCC, got further complicated by inadequate functioning of the government machinery like the *girijan* (tribal) cooperatives, lack of assets, institutional credit and irrigation facilities which consolidate the power and control of the moneylenders over the rural poor and their livelihood assets.[16]

The initial reports of the CCC therefore contextualized the debate over 'violence' in rural AP. Through its investigations in the rural areas, the CCC clearly laid out that 'inequitable land relations are central to any debate on violence in rural areas. Any attempt to mitigate the degree of violence is unlikely to yield results unless the land question is fully addressed'.[17]

In course of the debate, the CCC outlined its own role as the 'facilitator' of the concerns of all sections of society including the local body representatives and the NGOs who wanted to participate in the debate over the CPI(ML) movement and the state's response to it. Both the state government and the CPI(ML) parties responded to the reports prepared by the CCC on the basis of the investigations made by the latter in the villages of the north Telangana districts. The then CM of AP Chandrababu Naidu 'appreciated' the initiative of the CCC and expressed the desire to find a permanent solution to the 'problem'. In a brief response to the CCC's report, the CM expressed the desire to establish peace for ensuring 'expeditious development process'.[18] The PW, in contrast, gave a more detailed written response to the CCC reports and engaged with specific recommendations of the CCC from their own perspective.

THE CCC REPORTS

The CCC published two reports in 1997 in which it listed the concerns expressed by several individuals, groups and representatives of the local body. Besides contextualizing the conflict in the political economy of rural AP, the CCC's report generated a 'perspective on violence in rural AP'. The local experience generated through the CCC reports questioned the violations of the rule of law and the right to life by the state administrations, particularly the police and the anti-insurgency forces in pursuit of containing the Naxalite parties.[19] At one instance the report revealed 'A disturbing trend has been reported from Karimnagar district, where even the elected representatives of *local body institutions*, can be locked up and beaten up for protesting against fake encounters or for demanding to know the whereabouts of the arrested persons.'[20]

Similarly, the CCC's report also highlighted the local experience of coercion and violence perpetrated by the CPI(ML) groups. It reported the coercion of the local body representatives in Medak and Mehboobnagar districts by the Naxalites which led to resignation of elected representatives under duress from the Naxalites.[21] It also highlighted cases brought forth to its notice in the villages where inadequate handling of community disputes in the villages by the PW had created chronic disputes amongst largely subordinate communities and the Dalits.[22]

The whole issue of violence and counter-violence; anti-extremist measures by the state and violence committed by the Naxalites in pursuit of the realization of social transformation was thus 'brought forth for debate' through these reports which highlighted the experiences of the villages. The questions that the CCC reports asked pertained to the impunity of the state from the rule of law and other constitutional obligations like the right to life and livelihood, freedom of speech and expressions, etc., in pursuit of maintaining the law and order and apprehending extremists. On the other hand, the methods of the CPI(ML) groups were also questioned, particularly their intolerance towards those who differed from them on key socio-economic issues in the villages, including the elected representatives, and the scant respect for the right to life in the broader traditions of the human rights framework.[23]

THE RESPONSE TO THE CCC

The 'composition of the CCC' and the response from the people in the villages and from all over the state including the press, writes Balagopal, made it imperative for both the government and the CPI (ML) groups to engage in the debate around the reports placed by the CCC.[24] The CCC comprised members upon whom both the Naxalites and the state had relied at crucial junctures to tide over crisis situations that precipitated from mutual hostility in more than three decades of conflict in AP. It is not clear whether such crises emanated from the kidnap of public representatives and bureaucrats by the PW or when the PW cadres and leaders had to seek legal protection of their rights as prisoners and convicts or even while seeking investigations into encounter deaths of the Naxalites.[25] Largely, however, the effort of the CCC came under appreciation from all sections of the Andhra society including the leaders of the parties in opposition like the Congress, CPI, CPI(M) and the Bharatiya Janata Party. Moreover, the response that the CCC generated from the villagers while highlighting the severity faced by them augmented the urgency for both the state and the CPI(ML) groups to respond to the issues raised by the CCC from time to time.[26]

There was, however, a detectable difference in the approach of the PW and the Government of AP while responding to the concerns raised by the CCC. The Government of AP and its CM's response to CCC's pointers to specific problems were generally wavering. For example, the minutes of one such meeting with the CM of AP on the issue of encounter and rule of law, recorded by the CCC members, suggests that the CM agreed to the CCC's finding that the police was not handling the issue correctly. The CM further assured the CCC members that there would be no fake encounters in future. In one case of molestation of a surrendered woman Naxalite, the chief minster said that he felt 'personally humiliated by this occurrence' as the said Naxalite had surrendered before him.[27] CM Chandrababu Naidu also assured the CCC that he would look into the socio-economic problems including the issue of land relations, and highlighted the schemes already in progress in the state under *Janmabhoomi*[28] and other initiatives with the aid of World Bank. Yet there was no forthcoming response from either the government or the CM of the follow-up on the concerns raised in the meetings with the CCC.

The PW's, responses to the CCC reports were prompt and well documented. The PW specifically responded to both the reports of the CCC published in 1997. There was also one integrated response from the Central Committee of the PW to the questions raised by the CCC in its two reports. The Central Committee of the PW stated:

> The loss of life and property and suffering of the people in the war between repression and resistance has been causing anxiety to the democratically minded people. A section of such democrats have already come forward to protect civil liberties. . . . They too have been laying down lives. But a new section, which has been completely away from the movement and is essentially liberal in character, has begun to come forward to join this struggle. Such people recently formed the Committee of Concerned Citizens to make an effort to reduce the 'violent struggle' between the Government and the Naxalites (read people) . . . we have to take them along with us, however vacillating these friends may seem to be. . . . *They have pointed out several mistakes that have occurred in our practice* . . . we have to take note of the mistakes pointed out by the democrats and correct ourselves to further revolutionary movement by taking majority of people with us.[29]

The Central Committee of the PW then went on to extensively appraise several of its practices in the light of the recommendations made by the CCC.

DOING VIOLENCE, TALKING PEACE

Even after the assurance from the state CM and Central Committee of the PW, both parties did not refrain from violence. The CCC petitioned the NHRC several times and directed its attention towards gross violations of human rights in AP by state institutions, particularly the police.[30] It urged the NHRC to intervene and hold the state accountable in the light of its earlier directives in 1997 on the encounter issue. Meetings of political parties were called on several occasions to reinforce the appeal for letting down of violence from both the state and the CPI(ML) groups and putting the questions beyond simply a 'law and order problem'. Most pertinently, however, the CCC used the assurances given by the CM and the PW, in the background of the two reports of the CCC, to assert moral pressure by pointing out specific deviations in the practices of both the government and the PW.

On many occasions the deviations of the CPI(ML) groups and the state from the assurances given by them to the CCC were widely publicized through the press statements of the CCC and publications in newspapers. The purpose of widely publicizing these issues, according to the CCC, was to initiate a 'public debate' and make both the government and the PW accountable to the people.[31] Many eminent journalists of the state complimented the effort of the CCC and urged the cessation of violence from the state and CPI(ML) groups and called on them to address the issue 'politically'. This was possible, added the editors, only if there was de-escalation of 'armed activity' by the state and the CPI(ML) groups. This would allow the government personnel including the police to go into the villages and in turn also allow the 'unarmed' CPI(ML) groups to interact freely with the people.[32] The editors insisted that the ensuing peace after the cessation of armed activity should be followed by a 'meaningful dialogue between the government on one side and the revolutionary groups on the other'.[33]

Even as the appeals for cessation of armed activity on the part of the government and the CPI(ML) groups were being made by various political parties, journalists and the CCC, the central government on the advice of the AP chief minister, contemplated an all-India ban on the Naxalites. The proposal for a ban was mooted in a meeting of the CMs of AP, Maharashtra, Madhya Pradesh and Orissa to set up 'joint operational centres to direct and monitor anti-Naxalite operations in these states'.[34] Around this period the CCC met the Andhra CM, the state home minister and other officials including the director general of police. The CCC directed the attention of the CM towards unrelenting violence and killings by the state in spite of the assurance of the CM to the contrary in earlier meeting in 1998.[35] It also pointed out the socio-economic neglect of the Telangana region and sanctions imposed by the state on political activities like organizing meetings and protests.

Denying that there was any linkage between socio-economic

problems and Naxalism, the CM suggested that the government had to focus on maintaining 'law and order' to ensure development. He further added that the 'Naxalites are coming in the way' of developmental programmes aimed at empowering people.[36] During this period the PW also indulged in the high-profile killing of the ex-home minister of AP, Madhava Reddy, then serving as the minister of Panchayati Raj.[37]

Evidently there was hardly any fundamental shift in the approach towards political conflict and its resolution in AP either from the side of the state or the PW. The relentless campaign of the CCC escalated the pressure on both the government and the PW to give up violence and resolve politically contentious problems through a dialogue.

A significant breakthrough was achieved in December 2001 when the AP Congress Committee (henceforth APCC) president M. Satyanarayan Rao wrote to the CM calling for initiating 'unconditional dialogue' without delay with the People's War Group.[38] This was followed by an announcement by the home minister of AP in the state assembly that the state government was prepared to hold talks with the CPI-ML-People's War Group.[39]

Analysing the attempts by the CCC, Balagopal writes that in the process of its effort the CCC mobilized 'public opinion' in the state in cooperation with the press. As a result of this, according to Balagopal, the space dividing the 'extreme view points' was bridged as public opinion directed the two sides to initiate dialogue.[40] The extreme viewpoint generally expressed by the police establishment in AP and some of the more 'militant' cadres and sympathizers of the PW argued that there could be no meaningful dialogue between the state and the CPI(ML) groups. The only relationship possible between two such antagonistic adversaries was a 'strategic relationship', including violence, to outwit each other. Statements of senior police officers in the state contended that the PW, already demoralized by the state offensive, entered into peace talks to consolidate their mass base by reaching out to the people.[41]

DIALOGUE BETWEEN THE STATE AND PEOPLE'S WAR

The expectations arising from dialogue between the Government of AP and the PW started to mount with PW making an 'unconditional' offer for such a dialogue. However, it urged the government to create a 'conducive atmosphere' by stopping 'police encounters and raids for a couple of months'.[42] The Government of AP remained circumspect in its reaction to the PW's offer. The CM suggested that he wanted to probe 'legality' and constitutional limitations in going for dialogue with an 'illegal' outfit. Perhaps to intimidate the PW, the CM questioned the integrity of the PW suggesting that it has no 'ideological' and 'philosophical' vision.[43] It was only after the All Party meeting on 13 February 2002 in which there emerged 'unanimity' for holding talks with the PW that the government accepted the offer for dialogue extended by the PW.[44] Incidentally, the police department of AP resolutely maintained a distinction between the 'political initiative' of dialogue and its own administrative responsibility of maintaining 'law and order'. The 'normal' course of 'policing' in AP therefore was to continue as far as the CPI(ML) groups and their activities were concerned.[45] In the meanwhile, the PW, in the backdrop of the appeal made by the CCC to abjure violence for a stated period of three months, declared a 'ceasefire' towards the government of AP.[46]

A major setback to the expectations of 'dialogue' between the PW and the Government of AP came with the 11 March 2002 'encounter' at Tupakulagudem in Warangal district of AP in which six PW cadres were killed.[47] The 'encounter' was the result of the 'combing' operation carried out by the police assisted by the Greyhounds, the specialized anti-naxal force created by the Government of AP.[48] The Tupakulagudem 'encounter' led to the PW's calling off of the 'ceasefire', which had been in effect from the second week of February. It suggested that the AP government did not sincerely want to probe the option of dialogue and wanted to tackle the CPI(ML) groups through 'repression'.[49]

However, the deteriorating environment in the wake of the withdrawal of the 'ceasefire' by the PW was arrested with the AP government's announcement that it would hold 'direct talks' with the PW following the all-party meeting on 22 March 2002.[50] In the all-party meeting there emerged a broad consensus that the government should take 'initiative' for talks, the talks should be held between the government representatives and the PW leadership, conditions laid down by the PW should be discussed during the talks and all concerned should work towards a 'peaceful atmosphere' for talks.[51]

The process of 'dialogue' between the Government of AP and the PW was initiated on 5 June 2002.[52] The PW's representatives for the dialogue were Varavara Rao and Gummadi Vittal Rao alias Gaddar, long associates of the literary and cultural wing of the peasant movement in AP. The Government of AP nominated Minister for Commercial Taxes, K. Vijayarama Rao, and the Minister for Excise, Thammineni Seetaram. K. Vijayrama Rao was formerly an Indian Police Service officer with experience handling Naxalite issues in AP, and Thammineni Seetaram represented an assembly constituency in Srikakulam district where the Naxalite movement in the state began.

Three rounds of dialogue were held between the emissaries of the PW and the government between 5 and 20 June 2002.[53] These negotiations confined themselves to discussing modalities for the creation of a 'conducive atmosphere' to facilitate dialogue between the Government of AP and the leadership of the PW.[54]

At the third round of negotiation between the emissaries of the PW and the government on 20 June 2002, an agreement was drawn up bringing about 'direct' talks between the leaders of the PW and the government representatives, with the latter agreeing to create conditions for such engagement.[55] However, the expectations for such 'direct' engagement were soon clouded with the government engaging in a series of 'encounters' in which senior leaders of the PW were killed.[56]

After one such encounter on 2 July 2002 in which a senior leader of the PW, Padmakka, *alias* Nelakonda Rajitha, was killed along with several other cadres, the PW emissaries withdrew from the dialogue in protest.[57]

The final blow to the dialogue between the PW and government of AP came when the government decided to extend the 'ban' imposed on the PW under the AP Public Security Act on 15 July 2002. The PW finally called off its participation in 'dialogue' on 19 July 2002.

Political life in rural AP reverted to violence and counter-violence.[58] The CM of AP made a statement that any dialogue with the Naxalites was possible only if the latter laid down weapons.[59] The fresh round of hostility culminated in a near-fatal attack on the CM on 1 October 2003.[60]

ELECTIONS AND THE PEACE PROCESS

The CM of AP in the aftermath of the attack on his life advanced the elections to the legislative assembly in a bid to cash in on the 'sympathy wave' ensuing from the close escape he had from the landmine triggered by the PW. The political resolution moved by the home minister of AP emphasized the party's intention to go to the people on the plank of meeting the Naxalite challenge 'with fresh support from the people'. Blaming the opposition parties for turning a blind eye to the 'problem' of Naxalism, the resolution claimed that the government had a moral responsibility to 'combat' 'anarchic' forces.[61] The CM asserted that 'extremism poses serious threat to state's development', and therefore to counter extremism in a 'decisive' and effective manner he wished to seek a clear mandate from the people.[62] The CM contrasted his decisive stand against the extremists with the 'opportunistic approach' of the opposition who urged talks with the extremists.[63]

The election manifesto of the Congress party for the 2004 state elections highlighted the economic neglect of rural AP by the Telugu Desam Party which, the Congress claimed, had contributed to the rise in extremist activities. The manifesto proposed to look at the extremist 'movement' from a socio-economic perspective and address it through 'dialogue and consultation'.[64]

The approach of political parties towards Naxalism therefore became one of the important issues on which elections were contested. Indirectly allied to this issue was the debate on the pattern of development followed by Chandrababu Naidu's government. The Congress party pledged to focus on agricultural and rural development and to engage the Naxalites in a dialogue. The PW's strategy of an election boycott was enmeshed with selective targeting of the TDP and the Bharatiya Janata Party campaign.[65] Gaddar, a longtime associate of the PW who participated in negotiations with the Chandrababu Naidu government, explained that though he believed that elections were a 'farce', he urged people to defeat the TDP government.[66]

In what was seen as an attempt at 'derailing' the democratic process, Vidyasagar Rao, a minister of state in the central government, urged the media in AP to show 'restraint' while reporting on issues pertaining to PW activities on the grounds that excessive reporting gave 'credibility' to a banned organization.[67] The AP Director-General of Police (henceforth DGP), S.R. Sukumara, reinforced this appeal by suggesting that provisions of the AP Public Security Act 1992 and POTA (Prevention of Terrorist Activities Act) might be used against reporters found guilty of reporting PW activities in ways contrary to these laws.[68] The DGP suggested that the 'Election Commission of India has also voiced similar opinion'.[69]

The Congress party and its allies won a comfortable majority.[70] One of the first things that the Congress government led by the Y. Rajasekhar Reddy did was to call upon the police to end 'fake encounters' and indicated a possible lifting of the ban on the PW.[71] Gradually, between May and July 2004, some crucial decisions were taken by the state government to facilitate dialogue between the state and the PW. It started with the new CM's offer to withhold a 'ceasefire' in order to create a peaceful atmosphere to facilitate dialogue. Rajasekhar Reddy said, 'We have expressed our willingness to hold talks with the People's War. It should respect our initiative for a ceasefire. In fact, both sides should maintain utmost restraint with the decks having been cleared for an open dialogue.'[72] Some key anti-Naxal policies of the Chandrababu Naidu government—for example, giving cash rewards to the police for killing a Naxalite leader and combing operations by the police—were halted.[73] The ban on the PW under AP Public Security Act that was to be reviewed by July 2004 was allowed to lapse. The PW was permitted to carry out its activities without being deemed to cause a 'breach of law and order'.[74] Significantly the AP government's endeavour also found support from the central government. The Common Minimum Programme of the United Progressive Alliance government that came to power at the centre in 2004 stressed upon ending 'fake encounters'.[75] The PW also reciprocated the government's offer for a ceasefire and dialogue.[76]

LAYING DOWN RULES OF ENGAGEMENT

One of the major challenges for the proposed peace talks was arriving at consensus on the 'code of conduct' to be followed by the PW and the state. The code of conduct referred to as a 'cease-fire' agreement by the PW and 'ground rules' for dialogue by the government aroused a deep disagreement on certain issues including the 'concept' itself—that is whether to call it a 'cease-fire' agreement or 'ground rules for dialogue'.[77] More substantially, however, the issues to be resolved were the nature of political freedom accorded to the PW to carry out its political programmes. Should a party that was hitherto under ban be allowed to freely mix up with people? What kinds of restrains should be imposed upon the police in dealing with the members of organization that mostly had an 'underground' and 'illegal' life? Who should decide on violations of the code of conduct?

A general agreement between the PW and the government laid down that both sides would avoid the loss of life and harassment of people. Both sides were expected not to use fire arms against each other. The PW was to desist from attacking the police and political leaders and avoid violent protest leading to loss of government or private property. In turn the police was expected to stop 'combing operations' for PW cadres and sympathizers and not to 'obstruct', 'harass' or arrest anybody who came to meet PW leaders.[78] An independent monitoring committee comprising 'intellectuals having clear understanding on the issue' was to be set up to oversee the violations of the code of conduct during the period of dialogue.[79]

Two of the clauses of the initial 'ground rules' for dialogue that aroused deep disagreements between the parties were Clause (7): '. . . police should not obstruct the political campaign taken up by the PW, *without arms*'; and Clause (9), which laid down that the 'PW should not do recruitments in order to increase their strength . . .'.[80] While Clause (9) was finally dropped by the state, Clause (7) threatened to derail the peace talks with both the PW and the government sticking to their positions. The PW maintained that its weapons were only for 'self defence' against the 'enemies' it had made in the villages in the course of its anti-landlord and anti-feudal struggle against 'vigilante' groups. The government insisted that no 'political group' shall be allowed to move with arms as doing so would create a law and order problem. Clause (7) was finally retained even as disagreement on it persisted.

The state police accused the PW of a series of violations of the code of conduct during the period of peace talks. Cases were lodged against the PW representatives for delivering 'provocative' speeches at public meetings.[81] PW leaders were told not to raise issues about the pay scale and 'service conditions' of the police officers.[82] The state administration declined permission for holding meetings to the PW leaders in response to the 'alleged violations', for using 'provocative language' and inciting people to take up 'armed struggle' against the state.[83]

In the course of finalizing the modalities of dialogue, the CPI (ML), PW, and the All-India Maoist Communist Centre of India (MCCI) merged to become CPI (Maoist) on 14 October 2004. The talks between the government representatives and the CPI (Maoist) and the CPI(ML) Janashakti took place from 15 to 18 October 2004.

ACCOMMODATION WITHOUT TRANSFORMATION

The Naxalite emissaries Varavara Rao, Gaddar and Kalyan Rao handed over an agenda for the 15 October 2004 meeting. Prominent amongst the issues for deliberation was the issue of land reforms and socio-economic justice.[84] The details of the issues are in Appendix I. The Naxalite group's delegation to the 15 October deliberations was headed by PW Andhra State Secretary Ramkrishna and Janashakti State Committee leaders Riyaz and Amar.[85] The Government of AP's delegation included the state Home Minister K. Jana Reddy and seven other members of the government and senior Congress leaders.[86]

The modalities for dialogue and the creations of a conducive atmosphere for peace figured prominently with both sides clarifying their positions. The home minister mentioned that the objective of the deliberations was to articulate and accommodate the demands 'within the constitutional framework'.[87] In other words, the deliberations were to be an exercise to learn about the issues that the Naxalites were agitating for and how they could be addressed through the policies of a government. This would be an exercise for the fulfilment of the 'people's mandate' that the government secured in the election.

This of course was contested by the Naxalites who saw it as putting conditionality and limits to the scope of the deliberations. For the Naxalites the understanding reached during the deliberations should have priority over constitutional and legal propriety. The AP home minister argued that there was a constitutional limitation upon the power of the state government and that it could not amend the constitution. Both parties therefore agreed to keep the disagreement over constitutionally contentious issues like Clause (7) pending and move forward to the issues of land and the democratic rights of the people.

In the debate about democratic rights, the Naxalite parties sought assurance that the government would revise and withdraw many of the anti-naxal measures introduced by successive governments in AP. They argued that many of these measures, such as, 'rewards on the heads' of Naxalites, cases against people alleged to be Naxalite sympathizers for providing food and shelter to them, cases booked under AP Public Security Act and POTA were inimical to democracy and therefore should be withdrawn. Besides this, criminal cases against those who participated in the land occupation campaign and famine raids should be reviewed as they were not made for personal gain but were for the benefit of the 'people' and therefore 'political' in nature.[88]

On the issue of land the CPI(Maoist) representative suggested reducing the ceiling limits on land holding, appointing a committee to go into land distribution, the allotment of lands identified as surplus to Dalits and women, and strict implementation of the Land Transfer Regulation Act of 1970 in *adivasi* dominant areas. The Maoists focused on issues such as regularization of land occupied by poor with the help of Naxalite parties. A detailed list of agricultural land alienated for industrial and business purposes was also submitted by the CPI(Maoist) and was emphasized by both the Naxalite leaders and the 'mediators' during deliberations. It was argued that because the minimum safeguards provided by law to the land rights of the poor had not been implemented, it was necessary to protect some of the land that the people had occupied by assigning regular ownership rights to them without any 'compensation' to the landlords.[89] Additional surplus lands should also be identified. The Naxalite parties estimated that around 12 million acres of land were available for distribution among 4 million landless agricultural labourers in the state.

The government representatives broadly agreed with the case made by the Naxalite leaders and the mediators on the issue of land. The revenue minister suggested that the government was committed to identifying surplus land for allotment to the poor. He, however, stressed that 'in a democratic set up taking of decision was somewhat complex and the governments can even fall on the issue of land'.[90]

At the end of the deliberation the government proposed to study many of the demands raised by the Naxalites. On the issue of land the AP home minister announced the creation of 'a high power body' to identify the land available for distribution amongst the poor.[91] In light of protests from the Naxalites and mediators about rising vigilante violence the AP home minister made a carefully worded statement that 'the Government expresses its firm resolve to control anti social, armed mafia groups and "other armed outfits"'.

All through the negotiations the state government's initiative received 'critical support' from the central government led by the Congress party. The Union Home Minister Shivraj Patil stressed that the AP government should maintain 'caution' while engaging the Naxalites in dialogue aimed at resolving 'difficulties faced by the people'.[92] Later, the report of ministry of home affairs on internal security in India maintained that to tackle Naxalism the states should engage Naxal groups in 'peace dialogue', if the latter were willing to 'shun violence'. The report attributed the decline of Naxalite-related violent activity in AP to the 'peace talks' between the AP government and the Naxalites.[93] The lifting of the ban on the PW in AP caused some anxiety amongst the adjoining states of Orissa, Madhya Pradesh, Chhattisgarh and other states experiencing Naxalite activity.[94] The AP peace talks, they believed, allowed the PW to regain their strength in other states as many of the cadres from AP went to organize political activity in other areas.[95] In AP, however, all the parties to the peace talks—the government, Naxalite leaders and the mediators—felt that the dialogue and code of conduct followed by both the Naxalites and the government had restored peace in rural areas.

BEYOND ADVERSARIALITY: ANTAGONISM RECONFIGURED

The political strategy of the Naxalites in AP came under closer scrutiny after the relaxation of police operations following the state Assembly elections in 2004. The Naxalites were charged with intensifying their cadre recruitment drive all across AP as the police were asked to suspend 'combing' operation in the villages and forests.[96] At many places, the Naxalite leaders and cadres were charged with occupying private as well as forestland and distributing it among the people.[97] Amidst growing reports of occupation and distribution of land, the AP DGP S.R. Sukumara said that the law would take its own course if the Naxalites resorted to 'unlawful' activities; the police department could not wait till the talks were over.[98] Soon after the peace talks, the Minister of Municipal Administration Koneru Ranga and one of the government representatives in the talks alleged that the Naxalites' attitude towards the land issue was 'unhelpful' and that they were making impossible demands for distribution of forest land. Such demands were beyond the authority of the state government.[99]

Earlier the CM of AP, Rajasekhar Reddy, expressed dismay that

Naxalite parties had not agreed to lay down arms in the course of the negotiations between 15 and 18 October 2004. The CM suggested that there was no scope for 'private arms in a democracy'.[100] The statement of the CM came in the backdrop of the peace talks and occupation of the land of a TDP legislator, P. Kasha, by the CPI (Maoist) in Anantpur district. Earlier in response to the demand by the Naxalites for verification of land deals around the twin cities of Hyderabad and Secundrabad, supported by Boja Tarakam, one of the mediators, the CM cautioned the Naxalites against making 'meaningless' demands. The CM asserted that since the government had allotted these lands to entrepreneurs for setting up industries there was no need for enquiry.[101]

Irked by the Naxalites' land-occupation campaigns and their moving around with arms in the villages, the AP government decided to 'informally' reverse the code of conduct understanding. The AP police meanwhile was getting restive. Police officers believed the idea of peace talks provided the 'stressed' Naxalite groups a breathing space which allowed them to enlist fresh recruits. The police claimed that having committed the folly of going into dialogue with the PW, the AP CM was looking for 'the first exit'.[102] At a meeting of police officers of the Naxalite-affected districts in Hyderabad, instructions were given that the police should not allow armed Naxals to enter the villages and organize political meetings.[103]

As the environment of peace was getting vitiated, the Naxalites demanded immediate distribution of the ceiling surplus, forest and temple lands to the poor.[104] In December 2004 the Government of AP set up a land committee headed by Koneru Ranga Rao to assess the over-all land distribution programme of the government and suggest more effective ways for implementation of land reforms. The committee suggested that the implementation and working of the land-reform programmes of successive governments had a number of defects.[105] Later, the land agitation issue was taken up by the CPI and CPI(M) in April 2007 through a *Bhoomiporatam* (land struggle) campaign.[106] Leaders of the agitation, including the CPI state secretary, were arrested on charges of 'sedition' in relation to the *Bhoomiporatam* agitation. The flare-up between the government and the agitators peaked with firing upon the agitators by the police on 28 July 2007 at Khammam district; seven agitators were killed. The government claimed the firing was the result of incitement by a former Naxalite, Bandi Ramesh, who was among the agitators.[107]

Earlier, however, the CPI(Maoists) and the CPI(ML) Janashakthi decided to pull out of the peace talks in January 2005, alleging that the Greyhound forces of the government had intensified combing operations.[108] The prospect for peace in AP received a major jolt with the killing of Riaz, one of the CPI(ML) Janashakthi leaders who participated in the negotiations with the state. He was killed in an alleged encounter at Karimnagar district on 1 July 2005. Finally, on 16 August 2005 the government of AP re-imposed the ban on the CPI(Maoist) under AP Public Security Act 1992 in response to the killing of a senior Congress legislator Narsa Reddy by the Maoists on 15 August 2005 in Mehboobnagar district.[109] With the imposition of the ban on the CPI(Maoist) and its front organization, the AP CM suggested his cabinet take a 'tough' stand against the Naxalites. This eventually ruled the possibility of a negotiated peace.

The Andhra Pradesh experience of negotiations, despite falling short of transforming the nature of the conflict or checking the spiral of violence and counter-violence, is of remarkable significance. Much of the debate around dialogue, deliberation and communication as necessary components of democracy accord priority to engagement between groups that broadly adhere to liberal ideological doctrines.[110] 'Extremists' therefore are usually excluded from such processes because they are regarded as having convictions at odds with such liberal ideas or are perceived to make 'unreasonable', untenable moral claims.[111] The Andhra Pradesh experience demonstrated the resilience of Indian democracy on one hand and the impact of a politically mobilized public opinion and relentless civil society activism on the other. It is equally significant that notwithstanding the politico-ideological asymmetry, the CPI(Maoist) developed much of the debate around land relations and socio-economic issues in language that emphasized the constitutional obligations of the state. Consequently, the government of Andhra Pradesh announced a stock-take of land relations in the state soon after the conclusion of first round of deliberations.[112] Deliberative engagement—negotiations—put the question of land relations at the centre of political debate in Andhra Pradesh. The political mobilization and militant struggle around land that followed the talks was deeply influenced by the deliberative engagement that had gone on.[113]

Issues around land relations and ideological polarization were important factors that strained the deliberative process. For Maoists, allotment of huge tracts of urban land to big companies and firms was a serious issue to be studied and reviewed. The CM of Andhra Pradesh on the other hand considered such demands 'meaningless' and contrary to the developmental imperative of the state.[114] The political-ideological polarization around issues of land relations prompted the government to question the legitimate political existence of the CPI(Maoist). The CPI(Maoist) had proved resolute enough to engage in debate with the dominant discourse of the ruling parties. When the negotiations broke down, the Maoists' political existence was seen as inimical to public order. Consequently, the deliberative space was eroded once again and overtaken by militant confrontation. Eventually the CPI(Maoist) was banished from the 'legitimate' public domain and banned under the Andhra Pradesh Public Safety Act.

APPENDIX: DEMANDS OF THE PEOPLE'S WAR UNDER 10 CATEGORIES

I. A democratic atmosphere should be created in the state. The government should respect people's right to fight for their democratic demands.

- The government should not prevent agitations, peaceful demonstrations and meetings.
- Lift the ban on the Communist Party of India (Marxist-Leninist) PW and other organizations.
- Scrap the system of rewards on workers of PW, People's Guerrilla Army and other mass organizations.
- Scrap Grey Hounds, Special Security Forces, and the Special Intelligence Branch (SIB) and withdraw the central paramilitary forces.
- Release all political prisoners.

Scrap the system of giving acceleratory promotions and unofficial incentives to police officers who kill Naxalites in fake encounters.

- Scrap the informant network in villages. The government should end the practice of winning over PW workers and using them as covert agents.
- Control 'lumpen' gangs such as Green Tigers, Kranti Sena, Palnadu Tigers, Tirumala Tigers and Nayeem Gang.
- Order a judicial probe into all fake encounters and punish the police officers responsible.

- Lift all cases registered against workers of mass organizations and other revolutionary parties.

II. Implement reforms in the agricultural sector.

- Implement land reforms. Hand over to the occupants the endowment, government, and forestland, and lands belonging to landlords, already occupied by people.
- Implement the Land Ceiling Act.
- Complete all pending irrigation projects. Farmers should be given irrigation facilities and supplied adequate power.
- Waive all private loans taken by the farming community to stop suicides by farmers.
- Prepare a permanent and integrated plan for tackling the drought situation.
- Scrap corporate agriculture.

III. Implement policies of industrialization and other schemes based on local resources in place of the liberalization, privatization and globalization policies being followed now.

- Withdraw all World Bank projects and schemes supported by imperialists.
- Stop the retrenchment of workers and the privatization of the public sector enterprises.
- Protect small- and medium-scale industries from competition by multinational companies.
- Withdraw user charges on drinking water, education and health services.
- Scrap all agreements with the World Bank, MNCs and other countries.

IV. Recognize the tribal people's rights on forest.

- Announce autonomy for the tribal people.
- Implement the '1/70 Act', which provides protection against the alienation of land held by tribal people in scheduled areas to non-tribal people. Stop settling of non-tribal people in areas inhabited by tribal people.
- Initiate steps to develop and support tribal languages

V. Form a separate Telangana state.

VI. Formulate an integrated plan for the development of backward regions of north coastal and Rayalaseema areas.

VII. Punish those who belittle the self-respect of Dalits. Take action against police officers and upper-caste members responsible for attacks on Dalits in Karamchedu, Tsundur, Neerukonda and Vempenta.

- Provide job reservation for Dalits in the private sector.

VIII. Equal property rights for women.

- Reservation for women in the private sector.
- Stringent punishment for those who commit atrocities on women.

IX. Implement total prohibition.

X. Order a probe into the illegal amassing of wealth by officials, politicians and capitalists; corruption scandals by officials and politicians.

- Recover money from the affluent who evade taxes.

Source: *Frontline*, 13 August 2004, pp. 30-2.

NOTES

1. *Development Challenges in Extremist Affected Areas: Report of Expert Group to Planning Commission* (New Delhi: Government of India, 2008).
2. While CPI (Maoist) is a historically specific entity, CPI (Marxist-Leninist) is a prefix that many Naxalite groups except perhaps the MCC used Naxalite is a blanket terminology which all the groups owing allegiance to the Naxalbari peasant revolt of 1967 use. I use these terms quite interchangeably in this paper. I have been cautious in using CPI(Maoist) to the specific party that it is.
3. P. Sundarayya, *Telengana People's Struggle and its Lessons* (Calcutta: Communist Party of India [Marxist], 1972) and Mohan Ram, op. cit., pp. 1025-32.
4. Mohan Ram, 'The Telengana Peasant Armed Struggle: 1946-51', *Economic and Political Weekly*, 9 June 1978, p. 1028.
5. Ajoy Bose, 'Naxalites: A Change of Focus', *Indian Express*, 12 June 1988.
6. *Shakamuri Apparao and Others vs Government of AP and Others*', W.P. 6473 of 1996 in The High Court of AP, Hyderabad, 1996 (3) ALD 493.
7. Justice N.M. Vekatchaliah, 'Letter to the CM Regarding the Procedure to be Followed in the Case of Deaths in Encounter', National Human Rights Commission, New Delhi, 1997.

8. *In Search of Democratic Space*, Hyderabad: Committee of Concerned Citizens, August 1998, p. 5.
9. Ibid., p. 7.
10. Ibid.
11. Ibid.
12. 'First Report of the CCC', in ibid., pp. 9-18.
13. Ibid., p. 17.
14. Ibid.
15. Ibid., p. 34.
16. Ibid., p. 36
17. Ibid., p. 33.
18. 'Letter of the CM, N. Chandrababu Naidu to S.R. Sankaran (Convener) CCC', in *In Search of Democratic Space* (1998), op. cit., p. 19.
19. 'Second Report of the CCC', in *In Search of Democratic Space* (1998), pp. 37-8.
20. Ibid., p. 38.
21. Ibid., p. 39.
22. Ibid.
23. Ibid., pp. 9-45.
24. K. Balagopal, 'People's War and the State: Did the Police Have Last Laugh', *Economic and Political Weekly*, 8 February 2003, pp. 513-17.
25. Ibid., p. 513.
26. 'Meeting of the CCC with Political Parties at Hyderabad', in *CCC: Third Report, 1997-2002*, vol. II, Hyderabad, 2002, pp. 66-9.
27. 'Summary of Discussion with the CM of AP on 10th April 1998', in *In Search of Democratic Space* (1998), pp. 71-81.
28. *Janmabhoomi* (literally meaning birthplace) was a social welfare programme introduced by the Chandrababu Naidu government in AP in 1997. It covered areas like primary health care, education and family welfare, etc., and stressed 'people's participation'. Chandrababu Naidu considered *Janmabhoomi* to be his flagship programme. Critics considered it to be an ideological-political programme for realizing a neo-liberal agenda with World Bank assistance. G. Krishna Reddy, 'New Populism and Liberalisation: Regime Shift Under Chandrababu Naidu in AP', *Economic and Political Weekly*, 2 March 2002, pp. 871-83.
29. 'Revolutionary Resistance: Liberal Democrats' Response—Our Task', 'CC Circular No. 2/1998: 15.3.1998', in *In Search of Democratic Space* (1998), pp. 82-96.
30. 'Correspondence with the NHRC', in *CCC: Third Report* (2002), pp. 77-101.
31. 'Open Letter to the CPI(ML) PW', in *New Indian Express*, 3 June 1999.
32. 'An Appeal by Ten Senior Editors', 23 April 2000, in *Third Report of the CCC* (2002), vol. I, pp. 10-11.

33. Ibid.
34. *Hindu*, 7 April 2000.
35. 'Record of the Discussion of the CCC with the CM', 3 June 2000, in *Third Report of the CCC* (2002), vol. I, pp. 20-7.
36. Ibid.
37. *Hindu*, 11 March 2000.
38. The APCC President said, 'While the Government attitude to naxalites and their transformation movement, though spilling over as law and order problem in certain areas, continues to be repressive, with fake encounters, custodial deaths, covert support to private vigilante groups, etc., the failure of naxalites to perceive the changing socio-economic realities, and democratic aspirations of the people, by their increased violent acts, death threats to the public representatives, attacks on public property, police stations, resulting in loss of life is equally agonising'. *Hindu*, 28 December 2001.
39. *Hindu*, 28 December 2001.
40. K. Balagopal, 'People's War and the Government: Did the Police Have the Last Laugh?', *Economic and Political Weekly,* 8 February 2003, p. 516. The Telugu daily, *Vaarta* in 2002 invited letters from its readers expressing their opinion on the 'talks' between the government and the People's War. An overwhelming number expressed anxiousness and hope that the talks would take place. CCC, *Third Report*, Hyderabad, 2002, pp. x-xi.
41. *Frontline*, 6-19 July 2002.
42. The PW in a letter to the CCC said: 'We are not setting any pre-condition for talks. We only request the government to stop encounters, arrests, raids and combing operations at least for two to three months'. *Hindu*, 19 January 2002.
43. *Hindu*, 22 January 2002 and 25 January 2002, http://www.hinduonnet.com/thehindu/(accessed on 18 March 2006).
44. The AP governments' offer to hold talks with the PW was backed unanimously by all opposition parties. *Indian Express*, 13 February 2002.
45. *Indian Express*, 13 February 2002.
46. The CCC made an appeal to both the government of AP and the PW to initiate certain 'confidence building' measures by abjuring violence from second week of February 'for a period of at least three months' to create 'mutual trust' and facilitate dialogue. CCC Third Report, pp. 94-5. The PW offered to observe a ceasefire from the second week of February if the Andhra government came forward for talks. *Indian Express*, 25 January 2002. http://www.indianexpress.com/archive_frame.html (accessed on 18 March 2006).
47. *Hindu*, 12 March 2002.

48. *Hindu*, 12 March 2002. Even after the 12 February 2002 announcement of talks between the PW and the government of AP, there had been instances of 'encounters' involving cadres of the CPI-ML-Janashakti (another Naxalite party in AP) (e.g., on 16 February 2006). *CCC, Third Report*, vol. I (2002), p. 112 and *Hindu*, 24 February 2002. However, the Tupakulagudem encounter assured that the 'ceasefire' declared by the PW on 25 January 2002, which came into effect in the second week of February, was withdrawn on 14 March 2002. *CCC, Third Report* (2002), vol. I, pp. 122-4.
49. In announcing the withdrawal of the 'ceasefire', the PW highlighted the continuation of 'encounters' by the police and deliberate negligence by the government which did not convene the proposed all-party meeting that it proposed on 12 February 2002. *CCC, Third Report* (2002) vol. I, pp. 122-4. *Indian Express*, and *Hindu*, 12 February 2002.
50. After the withdrawal of the 'ceasefire' by the PW, violence both on the part of the police and the PW went up rapidly. While the police continued 'encounter killings', the PW carried out land mine blasts, destroying government installations and killing constables. *Hindu* 23 March 2002.
51. *Hindu*, 23 March 2002.
52. The initial dialogue was between representatives of the government of AP and PW to finalise the modalities for direct talks between the leadership of the PW and the government of AP. *Hindu*, 1 and 6 June 2002.
53. The first rounds of talks were held on 5 June 2002 followed by 9 and 20 June.
54. The representatives of the PW during the negotiation urged relaxation of the ban on the PW, withdrawal of rewards on the heads of Naxalite leaders and an end to encounters and combing operations to facilitate the direct participation of the PW leaders in the process of dialogue. *Hindu*, 6 June 2002.
55. The government agreed to withdraw the 'cash awards' on the heads of the PW leaders and to provide 'safe passage' to them to come into the open for talks with the government. *Hindu*, 21 June 2002.
56. There were several 'encounters' in AP after the talks began on 5 June 2002. These encounters mainly involved cadres of CPI-ML-Janashakti group (hereafter Janashakti). See *Hindu* and *Indian Express* for 6 and 10 June 2002.Following the third round of negotiations between the PW and the government of AP there were 'encounters' involving PW cadres in which important senior leaders of the PW were killed. The first of these encounters was on 24 June 2002 in which two women cadres of the PW were killed. *Hindu*, 25 June 2002.
57. *Hindu*, 7 July 2002.

58. K. Balagopal (2003), op. cit.
59. *Indian Express*, 1 September 2002.
60. *Hindu*, 2 October 2003.
61. Ibid., 14 November 2003.
62. 'Chief Minister's Letter to AP Governor', 14 November 2003, in *Negotiating Peace: Peace Talks between Government of AP and Naxalite Parties*, Hyderabad, December 2006, p. 5.
63. Ibid.
64. 'Election Manifesto of the Congress Party' (*Extract*), 5 April 2004, in ibid., p. 13.
65. Ibid., pp. 11-12 and *Hindu*, 20 March 2004.
66. *Hindu*, 6 April 2004.
67. Ibid., 2 March 2004.
68. The Ibid., 17 March 2004.
69. Ibid.
70. The TDP along with its allies could only win 49 out of 294 seats in the Assembly election, a loss of 160 seats compared to its 1999 performance. Similarly in the Lok Sabha election, the TDP with its allies could only secure 5 out of 42 seats. http://WWW.indian-elections.com (accessed on 23 March 2006).
71. *Hindu*, 15 May 2004 and http://sify.com/news/fullstory php?id=13472740 (accessed on 29 March 2006).
72. *Hindu*, 29 May 2004.
73. *New Indian Express*, 5 June 2004.
74. *Indian Express*, 22 July 2004.
75. *National Common Minimum Programme of the Government of India*, May 2004, p. 10.
76. *Indian Express*, 22 June 2004, p. 3.
77. *Negotiating Peace* (2006), pp. 53-158.
78. Ibid.
79. 'General Administration (SC.A) Department, G.Q. Rt. No. 5607', 30 September 2004, in *Negotiating Peace* (2006), pp. 149-51.
80. Ibid., p. 64.
81. *Hindu*, 30 July 2004.
82. *Hindu*, 18 October 2004 at http://www.hindu.com/2004/10/18/21hdline.htm (accessed on 30 March 2006).
83. *Hindu*, 30 October 2004.
84. *Indian Express*, 6 October 2004, p. 3.
85. It is noteworthy that while the government of AP and the PW emissaries were discussing the modalities of the dialogue that was proposed by newly elected Congress government of AP in May 2004, the PW had merged with the Maoist Communist Centre on 14 October 2004. The merged group was named the CPI(Maoist) and the PW participated in the deliberation with its merged identity. *Hindu*, 15 October 2004.

86. These representatives were D. Prasada Rao, D.S. Redya Naik, K. Ranga Rao, all Ministers, Paladugu Venkat Rao, T. Purushottama Rao, K. Keshav Rao and K. Karunakar Reddy, all senior Congress leaders. *Hindu*, 14 October 2004.
87. 'Welcome Speech of the Home Minister Jana Reddy', 15 October 2004, in *Negotiating Peace* (2006), p. 170.
88. Ibid., pp. 184-5.
89. Ibid., pp. 189-98.
90. Ibid., pp. 192-3.
91. Ibid., p. 202.
92. *Times of India*, 9 August 2004.
93. *Annual Report of The Ministry of Home Affairs* (New Delhi: Department of Internal Security), 2004-5.
94. *Times of India*, 29 October 2004.
95. Ibid.
96. *Hindu*, 9 July 2004.
97. *New Indian Express*, 30 October 2004.
98. Ibid., 29 October 2004.
99. *Hindu*, 30 October 2004.
100. *New Indian Express*, 21 October 2004.
101. *Hindu*, 19 October 2004.
102. *Indian Express*, 1 November 2004.
103. *Times of India*, 9 November 2004.
104. *Hindu*, 7 November 2004.
105. *Land Committee Report: Government of Andhra Pradesh*, 2006.
106. *Frontline*, 11-24 August 2007, pp. 25-8.
107. Ibid., p. 27.
108. *Hindu*, 18 January 2005.
109. *Frontline*, 27 August-9 September 2005, pp. 44-5.
110. John S. Dryzek, *Deliberative Democracy and Beyond* (New York: Oxford University Press, 2000), pp. 8-30.
111. Ibid., p. 22 and Maleha Malik, 'Engaging with Extremist', *International Relation*, vol. 22, no.1, March 2008, pp. 85-104.
112. The committee to take stock of the land relations was appointed under the chairmanship of Koneru Ranga Rao, a minister in the government of Andhra Pradesh. The committee submitted its report in 2006. The report highlights extensive landlessness in rural Andhra Pradesh. Much of the land allotted to socially and economically powerless beneficiaries in earlier phases of land reforms has been alienated from them. This trend of land alienation was noticeable amongst both the Scheduled Caste and Scheduled Tribes. The situation was far more rampant in tribal tracts where legal protections and judicial intervention were supposed to entrench tribal land rights. The report suggested that a

high proportion of superior quality double cropped and irrigated land was no longer in possession of the tribals, even though the constitution, protective legislation and judicial pronouncements at the highest levels forbade transfer of land from tribals in the scheduled areas. *Land Committee* (2006).

113. K. Balagopal, 'Land Unrest in Andhra Pradesh: Ceiling Surplus and Public Land', *Economic and Political Weekly*, 22 September 2007, pp. 3829-30.

114. In the course of the deliberations, the CPI(Maoist) submitted a list of the names of some industrialists whom they claimed to be major land grabbers around Hyderabad city. This list included the name of the chairperson of Satyam computers, who was eventually found to be involved in a huge cover-up which included financial bungling and spurious land deals.

PERCEPTIONS

How does one become familiar with—comprehend, understand—something as diverse as 'the Maoist question'? The title of this book, 'More Than Maoism', emphasizes that diversity. But to learn about leaders and their ideas, and followers and their motivations, is difficult and dangerous. Isolated and inhospitable places are often the scene of violence and exploitation. It requires patience, hardiness and courage for most people to go to such places.

In this section, we present the work of six journalists who have followed and lived with the people whose lives are at the heart of these stories. Each of their accounts contributes towards an understanding of the circumstances of security forces, the causes of revolt and the motivations of combatants.

CHAPTER 15

Red Star Over Bastar?: 34 Days with Guerrillas

SUVOJIT BAGCHI

ENTRY

The king of Jagdalpore, Kamal Chandra Bhanj Deo, is an honourable man. He is appalled by the condition of his subjects, the tribals, and repeatedly refers to his great grandfather Pravir Chandra Bhanj Deo who died fighting the Indian state for the tribal cause. But on being asked specific questions related to Maoist or tribal issues, this refined gentleman, who studied in twenty-first-century Britain, says: 'I can't tell you much, I have been told not to talk to the press'. Bhanj Deo allows me to take a photograph of him, with his grandfather, in black-and-white, in the background. But he refuses a video interview or even an audio byte. Bhanj Deo never specified who asked him to maintain such a royal silence and why.

The story of south Chhattisgarh in 2011, a hundred years after probably the biggest tribal uprising in modern India is *this* story of silence. In south Chhattisgarh, nobody talks about the left wing rebels plan to overthrow the state or the state's plan to 'cleanse' the vast swathe of forest land, to a journalist who clearly looks an outsider. Even if they do, the opinions are finely balanced, forbiddingly guarded.

But the silence prevails, I later realized, only as long as you travel on the highway—dotted with police and paramilitary camps—which cuts through Dantewada district in the extreme south of Chhattisgarh. In Dantewada town, things are perceptibly 'pro state'. Everyone—from ice-cream vendors to primary school teachers—will make sure, they tell you about the 'good work' of the district's administration. They will tell you, in quality Hindi, about the road, school and toilet construction projects undertaken by the civil administration. Knowing you are from the press, they will take you to a local school run under the Indian national government's education-for-all scheme, Sarva Shiksha Abhiyan, and will introduce you to the children whose parents were killed by the Maoists.

So, by the time your assignment is complete, and when you start back for Raipur, the busiest city and capital of Chhattisgarh, you are more or less convinced that the Maoists are the contemporary *avatars* of the dacoits from central India.

But if you can manage to elude the men in *khaki* swarming all around, stay put in Dantewada without informing your driver, start walking early the next morning down National Highway 16 towards Andhra Pradesh and without much plan, slip into the forest to your right, you will hear another version of the same story.[1]

The more you move away from National Highway 16 into the forest towards the main river Indrawati, the more changes you begin seeing. You will see fewer and fewer police camps till they finally disappear; you start feeling uncomfortable about your clothes and haversack as more and more people ask overtly indignant question: '*Aap yahan kyon aaye ho*?'—Why are you here?

'I study rivers.' I said that thrice as I reached the Indrawati.

These are the fringe areas—located between Maoist-controlled forests and paramilitary controlled highways—and are the most hostile areas. I was later told that a large number of villagers in these areas act as police or party informers. The informers themselves take huge risks—they are often caught, threatened, tortured and eventually made to disappear by both sides—by operating in these areas. No wonder, an outsider with a branded haversack will always be suspect.

By the time I reached the Indrawati and paid Rs. 20 to a young boatman with a green bandana and an abstract tattoo on his left shoulder to row me across the river in a *donga* (a narrow wooden boat that often capsizes) I realized that I could no longer understand the language spoken around me. It was *definitely* not Hindi.

The boatman said without being provoked: 'Hindi is our national language. Everybody should know it. I know Hindi very well.'

On the opposite bank of the river, the language is totally alien—it's Gondi. And occasionally Halbi. The boatman with the tattoo too switched to his natural tongue as we sailed to the northern shore of Indrawati.

I made the first entry in my notebook:

River Indrawati is the LOC [line of control] of south Chhattisgarh; the closer to the highway you are, the more Hindi you are . . . deeper into the forest, you are more Gondi. While I saw some Gond tribals travelling in a bus on Highway 16, most passengers were from mainland India—Biharis, Bengalis, Rajasthanis, Chhattisgarhis and Marwaris; road workers, barbers, contractors, sub-inspectors, mobile phone vendors and drivers. But, in here, I see only the Gond tribals. They are thin and muscular and speak a language I have no idea about.

Soon, a group of about 40 Maoist cadres, in olive green battle fatigues, welcomed me. Most of them were in their twenties, all had rifles slung over their shoulders. They sang a welcome song, which I realized through my stay, is a Maoist ritual:

Lal lal salaam, lal lal salaam
Aanewale sathio ko lal lal salaam
Patrakar sathio ko lal lal salaam.

(Red salute to the friends who have come and to the journalists.)[2]

A tall, thin and strongly built man in his forties, armed with an AK-47, introduced himself to me as Gudsa Usendi *alias* Sukhdev. Usendi is the spokesperson of the Maoist party in Dandakaranya (DK).[3] I was surprised. I had a different mental picture of Usendi. From the texture of his voice, I thought of him as a tall, plump man. He used to call the BBC studio in Delhi nearly every fortnight to give his side of a story. His voice was an inspiration to reporters on a dry day when there was a dearth of stories. His calls filled airtime, and hence he was as important and popular in a newsroom as the Home Ministry's spokesperson. Around the world, news is not always driven by content or style, but by deadlines. Usendi sometimes helped us to meet those deadlines. 'But he is so thin', I thought. 'He looks like a martial arts instructor and not an irate spokesperson of a revolutionary party. He is younger too.'

Usendi is also one of the 20 members of the Chhattisgarh state committee of the Maoists, called the Dandakaranya Special Zonal Committee (DKSZC). He gave me the first instructions of guerrilla life: 'Akash will be your guard, stick with him. In case of an attack, if I say Bastar you will move towards the enemy and if I say Narayanpur you will move away from the enemy. Akash will cover you.'[4]

Akash, my bodyguard, an 18-year-old Gondi boy, originally from central Chhattisgarh, had an unusually pleasant smile and treated me almost like a baby while he was with me. 'As we move forward or backward, while under attack, make sure that you are always behind me so that I can take the fire on me', he repeatedly told me.

I had never imagined I would discover someone in the remotest part of central India who would tell me that he would 'take the fire' for me. On being asked why would he do that, he told me it was his 'job'. I wondered if he would have been equally efficient if he had been asked to shoot me.

Akash carried my luggage and even got me lunch and dinner, as I was almost incapable of swinging my legs after walking for hours. He followed me to the loo behind tightly knitted shrubs, infested with strange insects, and stood close while I recorded goings on with my camera. Akash showed the blue and yellow plastic tents we would sleep in and introduced me to the basics of guerrilla warfare: 'The tents are placed in a semi-circle to keep the line of fire open. They are in clusters in and around the hill to ensure safety of the Section B.'

If there are three tents in a cluster, then Section B will be in the middle and called headquarter. I stayed for a week, in one such Section B, with Akash and nine others. Slowly it sank in, that I was supposed to move towards the origin of fire when someone shouts, 'Section B, Bastar', and reverse the movement if it was, 'Section B, Narayanpur'. The codes changed from camp to camp.

THE PARTY AND THE GOVERNMENT IN METTAGAON

I mostly stayed with two divisions of the Maoists in south Chhattisgarh, the Madh/North Bastar Division, headed by the lean and burly Rajmon, and the East Bastar Division headed by Niti, a woman in her thirties, seemingly malnourished, but who works for 18 hours at a stretch. I stayed in various other blue and yellow tents under several divisions but was always with the North Regional Committee. The divisions, a bit like elbows, connect upper arm (regional committees) to the lower arm (area committees). There are similar connecting ligaments and tendons between area committees to the gram party committees (GPC) at the village end.

The Maoists have three regional committees in DK called North, South and West. The regional committees have 8 divisional committees supervising 25 to 30 area committees. The size, name, number and jurisdiction of the divisions change as per strategic and political requirements.

A flowchart of the party's structure in DK is shown below.[5]

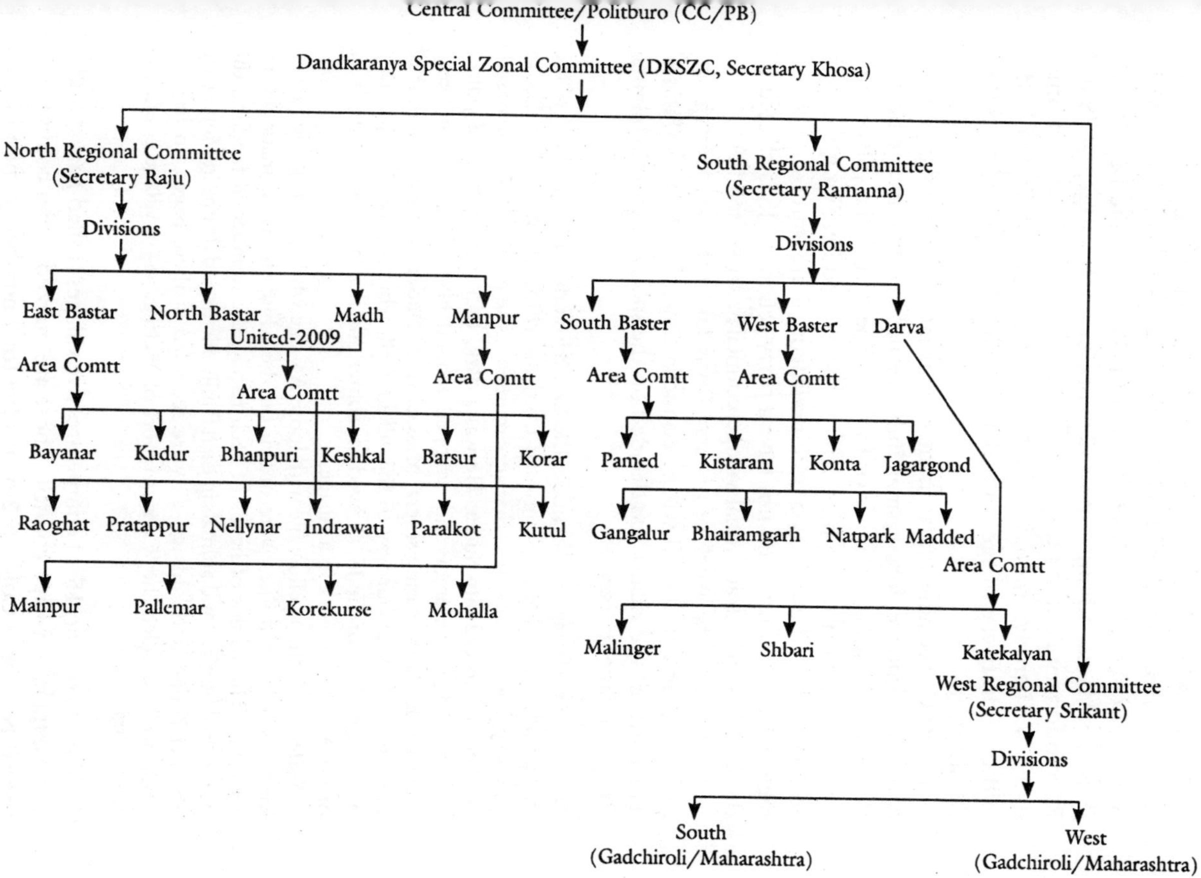
Central Committee/Politburo (CC/PB)
Dandkaranya Special Zonal Committee (DKSZC, Secretary Khosa)
North Regional Committee
(Secretary Raju)
Divisions
East Bastar
North Bastar
Madh
United-2009
Manpur
Area Comtt
Area Comtt
Area Comtt
Bayanar
Kudur
Bhanpuri
Keshkal
Barsur
Korar
Raoghat
Pratappur
Nellynar
Indrawati
Paralkot
Kutul
Mainpur
Pallemar
Korekurse
Mohalla
South Regional Committee
(Secretary Ramanna)
Divisions
South Baster
West Baster
Darva
Area Comtt
Area Comtt
Pamed
Kistaram
Konta
Jagargond
Gangalur
Bhairamgarh
Natpark
Madded
Area Comtt
Malinger
Shbari
Katekalyan
West Regional Committee
(Secretary Srikant)
Divisions
South
(Gadchiroli/Maharashtra)
West
(Gadchiroli/Maharashtra)

The party's state committee in DK is called DKSZC. It has two arms, the Janatana Sarkar (JS) and the People's Liberation Guerrilla Army (PLGA). The party controls both the JS and the PLGA. The JS is the Maoist administrative network in a DK village. 'A JS is a Revolutionary People's Committee (RPC). We call it RPC in other states but here we thought of a Gondi name and so we call it JS', said Usendi. Every village council has its own RPC. RPC has its own constitution.

An RPC has nine units: finance, judiciary, defence, agriculture, education/culture, forest, small industry, public relations and health. Each of these units has three or four members from the village. The unit chiefs report to the president of the JS who heads a governing council. The council has a vice-president, a treasurer and a few members. The units need not have a party cell in it. 'JS is elected by the Gram Sabha (traditional village council)', said Usendi.[6]

During the first week of my stay I was taken to visit Mettagaon, one of the few thousand village councils controlled by the Maoists. The name of the village was decided on the spot, like its inhabitants, to camouflage its *identity*.

Diary Entry: Mettagaon was under the East Bastar division. The head of the JS in Mettagaon was a young man from the community. He decided to change his previous name at that very moment as all his aliases were exposed. We decided to call him Suder. He was a dark, thin man with a red-yellow scarf folded in a triangle and wrapped around his forehead, a bit like a bandana. He was wearing several brass earrings. Suder took me on a tour of Mettagaon and on our way to the village well, which he claimed was dug by the members of the JS, showed me something that may well be the basis of the Maoist network in a village.

Suder took out a yellow file with loose A4-size white paper neatly tucked inside. Vertical red lines were drawn on the white sheets to mark several columns. The names of heads of each family, the number of families, the number of humans and animals in each family, births and deaths in Mettagaon and per-family landholding—all were recorded in these pages. In brief, it could well be called the 'Census report of Mettagaon—a village council in East Bastar'.

The chart (Fig. 15.1) enumerates five villages (called *paras*) under the Mettagaon village council. Those are marked under column 1 as 'Serial Number'. Column 2 marks the total number of men in each village and column 3 marks the number of women. Columns 4 to 8 mark the number of animals: column 4 for cows, 5 for buffaloes and the rest for goats, pigs and chickens.

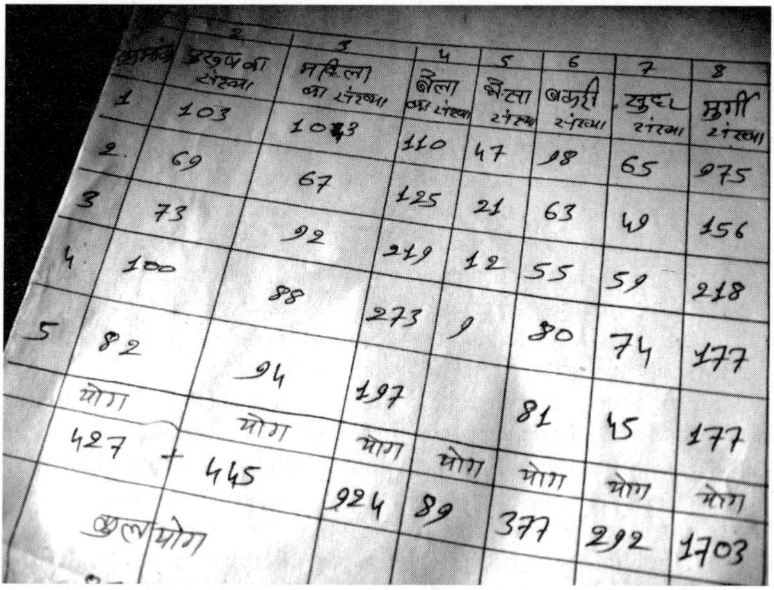

क्रमांक	2 पुरुष की संख्या	3 महिला की संख्या	4 बैल की संख्या	5 भैंसा संख्या	6 बकरी संख्या	7 सुअर संख्या	8 मुर्गी संख्या
1	103	10[illegible]3	110	47	98	65	975
2	69	67	125	21	63	49	156
3	73	92	219	12	55	59	218
4	100	88	273	9	80	74	177
5	82	94	197		81	45	177
योग	427	योग 445	योग 924	योग 89	योग 377	योग 292	योग 1703
कुल योग							

Fig. 15.1: Suder's chart

Three things, I felt, are significant in this chart. First, the household animals are registered so that after every paramilitary/police offensive a comprehensive analysis of 'missing' animals can be made and the cumulative damage calculated. Thus each village unit has a ready database that keeps an account of the collateral damage of the conflict.

Second, the census is also conducted to document if any villager has abandoned the village. Such unwarranted disappearances are potentially dangerous if such villagers are picked up by the police or worse if they join the administration as 'special police officers'.

Third, the total number of men to women was 427/445 in Mettagaon village council.

This was the 'macro' census of Mettagaon. There is a micro census as well. The micro list documented the number of members each family had in each of the five villages. It recorded the number of births and deaths in each family over the last year, and the number of animals a family had acquired or lost. The *micro* list thus tells us about each family.

I spent a day in the Mettagaon village council and spoke to the president of the council, Suder, and other members of the Mettagaon

JS, like Suklu (member, defense unit), Mahesh (member, forest unit) and Chander (member, agriculture unit). I also spoke to a few villagers in the presence of the JS members.

Suder and the team told me that they have 153 families in the Mettagaon village council. The total occupied land is 543 acres. Each family has land for farming and constructing a house. There was a difference of opinion among the JS-Mettagaon members about the exact size of unoccupied land. It could be between 150 and 200 acres. Five families in Mettagaon region were given five acres of land each by the party. However, I could not locate any of the beneficiaries in Mettagaon who were given land; rain and other logistical reasons, like time and security, prevented such meetings.

Instead, I met a farmer called Sahitram, in the village Kilem in the Maoist council Kharenar, somewhere north of Indrawati. Sahitram showed me his farmland and mud-and-thatch house and told me that he used to be a landless farm worker six years ago. But the party gave him eight acres of land, five for farming and three for erecting a house. He said that he had joined the party because he got land from it. He informed me that five families in his village council got land from the party.[7]

The CPI (Maoist) proclaims that in the guerrilla zones with the 'development of the people's political power' their objectives of 'land to the tiller (and) all power to the Revolutionary People's Committee' will be met.[8] Maoists claimed that so far they had distributed 300,000 acres of forest land in Chhattisgarh.[9]

And that's what made them a potentially dangerous party for the companies wanting to acquire land for setting up mining industries in south Chhattisgarh. This fear was highlighted in a report published by the Federation of Indian Chambers of Commerce and Industry (FICCI):

> [Maoist insurgency] would add risk significantly to companies mulling investments in affected areas, and worsen the overall investment climate . . . India has lots of unmined iron ore and coal—the essential ingredients of steel and electric power. Anxious to revive their moribund economies, the poor but resource-rich states of eastern India have given mining and land rights to Indian and multinational companies. Yet these deposits lie mostly in territory where the Naxals operate. Chhattisgarh, a hotbed of Naxalite activity, has 23 per cent of India's iron ore deposits and abundant coal. It has signed memoranda of understanding and other agreements worth billions with Tata Steel and Arcelor Mittal (MT), De Beers Consolidated Mines,

BHP Billiton (BHP), and Rio Tinto (RTP). Other states also have similar deals. And US companies such as Caterpillar (CAT) want to sell equipment to the mining companies now digging in eastern India.[10]

I walked for about 10 km on average everyday and did not see any mining activity in Bastar or Narayanpur. Lawyer-activist from Bilaspur in north Chhattisgarh, Sudeep Srivastav, claimed that while substantial mining had taken place in north Chhattisgarh, especially Bilaspur, south Chhattisgarh was relatively free of big projects. 'Of course . . . the lack of mining is because of resistance by the Maoists and the tribals', he said.[11]

THE MAOIST MILITIA

The defense unit member of the Mettagaon council, Suklu, gave me some idea about his unit. He told me that it has three members, including him. The unit has one platoon of militia under its command. The militia platoon, which is smaller than a conventional platoon, has its own commander.[12]

In Mettagaon, the militia, also called the 'base force', has 24 members in the platoon, of which 13 are women. The platoon has five single-shot gunpowder rifles, 10 bows and sufficient arrows, and 10 knives. The militias are also trained to make homemade pressure bombs using ammonium nitrate. The knives and arrows are all accounted for. Tribals traditionally used bows, arrows or knives. Maoists have taught them to maintain an inventory of the arsenal.

Suklu told me that the militia is a local force and is different from the Maoist army, the PLGA. The militia, according to him, provides primary cover to PLGA, collects and disseminates information as and when required. When asked about the militia's advantage over state forces, Suklu told me, 'We move faster than the forces as we know the terrain better'. On the basis of my interviews with Suklu and other militia members in other divisions I noted:

Maoists' information gathering seems to work like this:

1. A company of paramilitary/police comes out of a camp and moves north or south.
2. A boy, who was watching the camp, makes his primary logistics survey.
3. He starts running towards the forest. He runs at a speed of 8-10 km/hour, at least double the speed of the security forces.
4. He informs his counterpart in the next village or reaches the PLGA squad and passes on the information.

5. After receiving the information regarding troop movement, Maoists make an on-the-spot survey of their: (a) own strength—manpower and firepower; (b) opposition strength; and (c) time and distance of the troop from the camp.
6. They may stay put, mobilize the militia and take the police force head on, which is unlikely, or plan to encircle them. They may escape right away—if they have a squad.
7. They can have any kind of formation. They can move in pairs, in multiple squads or platoons. They can break the formation to make a new formation during an ambush.

Hence, getting information on time is of primary importance. This is an area where the PLGA is entirely dependent on local boys and girls between 15 and 20 years. The support of these militias is the main area of strength of the Maoist military. Thousands of young boys and girls of the community operate as militias. However, they always said that they were above 16 years of age. These militias periodically attend training workshops and keep a close watch on every house of the village to ensure that the guest in the village is not a police informer. While most of the militias are Gond tribals, unlike the members of the community, they don't indulge in nightlong song-and-dance soirees or heavy drinking sessions. Rather, they are well disciplined and aspire to join the PLGA.

What is fascinating is the sense of responsibility of these tribal boys and girls. They are fully aware that if they fail to carry a small item of information to the party, they may endanger the lives of many tribals, whom they consider as family members. A huge sense of bonding and camaraderie is driving these militias. I was told that if the militias make mistakes that lead to deaths of tribal comrades, members go into a state of depression and insist that they be punished. These small characters—Suklu, Gassi, Vishal, Suni—have made the party what it is today in DK.

The militias actively assist the PLGA in combat. Being a hunter-gatherer society, the Gond militias are adept at setting traps to snare animals. Traps, which are holes 2 ft deep and 4 ft wide, are set up along the likely routes of the security forces (Fig. 15.2).

The cavities are covered with shrubs and inside are finely chiselled wooden spears and iron rods inserted vertically. The objective is to make at least one soldier fall into the trap during a paramilitary operation. The entire opposition platoon slows down if one of them steps into the cavity.

Fig 15.2: Cavity in the ground

Militias, I felt, were barely informed about Mao's dialectics, but undertook risky assignments for the party. One such assignment, to ferry me safely through the police-controlled areas and hand me over to the Maoists, was undertaken by a man named Gassi. Curious as to what could drive someone to take such risks, I enquired about Gassi's motivation.

'My family has been systematically tortured by the forest and revenue officials of the Indian government', Gassi said in broken Hindi. Allegedly, government officials have for decades been harassing tribals for 'chopping trees' or 'killing wild animals', which the locals think is an 'infringement of their rights'. Forest officers settled allegedly trumped up cases 'illegally' by accepting bribes or by demanding other benefits such as the company of tribal women. A large number of the locals, who now work as the militias, joined the party to express their solidarity with the Maoist movement to drive away the officials.

I interviewed close to 100 men, women and children in south Chhattisgarh. Literally everyone told me on the record that one of the main reasons for them to support the party was torture by *patwaris* (land revenue officers), *nakedars* (forest guards and police). These three categories of government officials used to work *in tandem* with the *mangujars* (zamindars) in the villages. Maoists managed to break this nexus. A member of the local farmer's unit of the Hindutva organization, the RSS, Ramdayal Mishra, of Kondagaon, told me that one of the main reasons for the Maoist success is that they have been able to 'break the nexus between the rural rich and the urban government officers'.[13]

The PLGA, the militia, the members of various units of JS and the villagers are fairly integrated. It is difficult to differentiate a party person from a tribal and a tribal from a party member. While it is not very difficult to identify a PLGA member wearing an olive green shirt or a holster, it is impossible to identify someone who is not wearing a uniform. The militias don't wear a uniform and make life difficult for the administration. PLGA members on the other hand never go to police-controlled areas wearing battle fatigues. An officer of Chhattisgarh police told me they feared this 'hidden army' the most.

CULTURE AND HEALTH

The party came into Bastar in the early 1980s and virtually had a free run for the first 20 years. One Maoist leader claimed that 'we were noticed centrally in the media only when the Tatas wanted to set-up steel plant in Lohandiguda in 2004'. This is a bit exaggerated, but not entirely wrong.

During this period, the party not only consolidated itself in the region but convinced the average villager that India, led by an upper-caste and upper class-government, aims to seize 'the water, the forest and the land' of the tribal people. The reference to the 1910 or the 1965-6 uprising by the Gond tribals against the state is made often in meetings and cultural programmes.

Songs, an intrinsic part of a Gondi life, have been used by Maoists to disseminate political messages. The party's cultural wing, Chaitanya Natya Manch (CNM), uses traditional tunes for revolutionary lyrics. The songs valorize great Gond warriors; the lyrics often compare, albeit aggressively and positively, the Bhumkal [revolt] of 1910 with the present uprising. There are songs on every aspect of revolutionary tribal life—from women's role in the movement to glory of guns, from death of martyrs to the role of police and the PLGA. I recorded more than 50 songs—both live performances and recordings. The one on the PLGA, sung by 16-year-old Anusha, has a nice lilting rhythm:

Naru Naru Naru Naru bayan police kin, bayan police kin
Kappi pite leke minji kar dehi mutro

Lakho karor police batke bhumi birshala, naru birshala
Usurudi kal tereski ladai maye kaal

....

PLGA sena the leya leihar kin, leya leihar kin
Bharti kisi PLGA badli kiya kaal

(Watch the police when they arrive from hideouts and attack with arrows
They will come in millions but we won't leave our land and village
[To fight them] we need to bring in more people to the PLGA
They [police] will finally go back as they are here for money.)

The three-minute song is immensely popular with the villagers and the cadres. The other popular songs start with the refrain *re rela re re rela re re rela*. There is a lovely non-revolutionary song about the monsoon in Bastar that is sung often in the party and Gondi civil society. 'The way it rains in Bastar', the song says, 'makes it seem as if the skin of the sky has been shredded'. In the monsoon in DK, it rains without a break for 72 hours or more. It is impossible to see someone standing a couple of feet away. I was in DK at the peak of the monsoon, and while it is fascinating to watch the rain, it is painful to be constantly wet. All activities stop during the monsoon—military offences and Maoist ambushes. This is the safest time for 'adventure tourism' in Bastar, but an arduous time for a journalist who is paid to walk and work.

In the DK, the cadres kept up an unending supply of revolutionary songs. The songs, old and new, are copied time and again into thick diaries and letter pads.[14] Chandu, the CNM's state committee member, spent time with me. A singer, lyricist and composer, he has a vast repertoire of *gana-sangeets* (people's songs) from across the country. I often compared him with the Indian music maestro, Salil Chowdhury, who also was a product of the communist movement in the 1940s and was thrown out of the undivided party. 'Soon after the revolution, you will go to Bombay and become a notoriously famous music director like Salil-da—and the party will revoke your membership', was my standard joke.

Chandu used to play lot of Salil Chowdhury numbers from his mp4 player sitting under plastic canopies in heavy rain, deep into the night. CNM members play a crucial role in reaching people through Chandu's and his friends' songs. Chandu, unlike Chowdhury, is also a filmmaker and capable of making short documentaries using his ragtag equipments.

The other popular wing of the JS was the health unit. This unit is one reason for the Maoists' popularity in the forest. Almost every village in the Maoist-controlled area lacks basic health care. The nearest health centre is 5 to 10 km away from any village and is closed most of the time. The district hospital is normally 20-5 km from any village that I visited in East Bastar. The patient and the family needs to cross hills and rivers to reach a health centre. The health workers are also often not available. ('Often' is an understatement: they were available only a 'few times a month'.) A Chhattisgarh government health survey conducted in 2004 says: 'State level data as reflected in the commonly used indicators suggests that on many counts Chhattisgarh does not compare very well with the national averages'.[15] Thus the Maoist 'doctors', a few hundred young boys and girls in their early twenties, are a huge hit in the villages of DK.

The 'rebel' doctors carrying boxes full of medicines for malaria, snake bites, itching, dysentery, skin allergy or high fever are greatly respected amongst the villagers. I spoke to five such doctors who told me that 'some men from the city came to impart basic training a few years ago'. The doctors from the city prepared a list of diseases and corresponding medicines, the 'trainee' doctors more or less follow the list delivered to them by the 'docs with degrees'. They have developed an idea about symptoms as well. I was treated with a strong drug called Reziz, meant for acute falcipuram malaria, purely on the basis of symptoms. I was diagnosed with malaria much later.

One of the barefoot doctors, Prakash, a 23-year-old young man, with a serious, oval face, told me while having a casual conversation one evening:

> I generally used to hang around with the boys. I was not doing anything. Nobody took me seriously and no one had any hope for me. Then the division secretary asked me if I would like to be a doctor. I thought he was joking but took a chance. He sent me to a training camp and after two weeks of training I came back as a doctor. Now the entire village, mine and others, runs after me. It gives me a strange sense of purpose and hope—I feel I am doing something for *my* people, *my* land.

Imparting this 'strange sense' of purpose into a group of illiterate, ill-fed, sickle-cell-ridden, frightened and half-lost tribal people and organizing them against the world's third largest military power is what the Maoists' success is about.

The present movement is seen more as a continuation of a hundred-year-old struggle against the Indian state. The tribal boys and girls, who are part of the party, were told that if their land was lost, their culture, language and songs and 'way of living' would disappear as well. While the Maoists define the relationship between the Indian state and the Gondi tribals as that between 'colonizer' and 'colonized', they do not project the insurgency as a Gondi or tribal-identity movement. The Maoists have always supported nationality movements in India from the north-east identity and liberation movements to Kashmir. The political resolution adopted after the unification of the party in 2004 outlines the policy. But the resolution is silent on the nature of Gond uprisings. The tribal uprisings are seen almost always as resistance movements to retain land, water and forest.

CADRES, RULE BOOKS AND COMMUNICATION

The Maoists in Chhattisgarh can be broadly divided into two groups: leadership and the cadres. The leadership is 5 to 15 per cent and is made up predominantly of Telugu-speaking men and women from Andhra Pradesh. However, there are members from Bengal, Orissa, Karnataka and Maharashtra. Most of the central, state (DKSZC) and regional committee members are from these states. The rest of the cadres, 85-90 per cent, are Gondi tribals.[16]

While I was always keen to meet the Maoist bosses in the central committee, my primary objective was to interact with ordinary cadres to find out what exactly they did. I interviewed several cadres and wrote the following note:

- Getting up early in the morning.
- Brush, freshen up and have tea with a good portion of milk and sugar.
- Roll Call—assignments are given. It is decided who is going to work in the kitchen and who is going to look after the camp security. The PLGA cadres are assigned to go to village and help in community welfare activities.
- Comrades are also assigned to get firewood, water and vegetables from the forest for lunch or dinner.
- Lunch & studies.
- Rest and recreation.

I combined the interviews and instructions to structure the daily routine (Fig. 15.3):

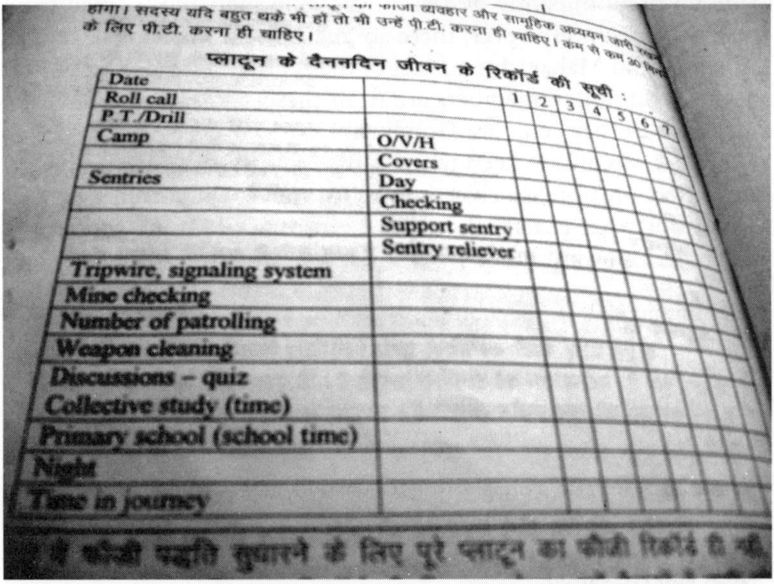

Fig. 15.3: The PLGA handbook, also called the Platoon Handbook, gives a detailed description of a fighter's daily routine

8 to 11 a.m.	Physical drill and arms training
	Breakfast while listening to radio news
	Cleaning of guns, a must
	Group studies of party literature and other newspapers, magazines
	A section goes to work in the village
12 noon	Assemble for lunch and rest after food
2 to 5 p.m.	Start planning the dinner (those who are on kitchen duty)
Studies	
5 p.m.	Evening drill
6 p.m.	Personal work, community studies, writing to family
8.30 p.m.	Dinner, listening to radio news
9 to 10 p.m.	Retire for film screening, radio news, rest[17]

An average cadre is supposed to guard the camp for 90 minutes every night and two hours in the afternoon. This is called 'doing a

Fig. 15.4: Maoists watching the movie, *Do Bigha Zameen*, after a day's work

sentry'—a must for any camp member. Leaders may not participate in this routine as they have other responsibilities.

Maoists have another handbook that they use more commonly. It is called the *Area Committee (AC) Handbook.*

Nothing surprised me more than the *Area Committee Handbook*—the Maoist rule book. Detailing every aspect of their cadre's life, this book lists a number of instructions and details that offer an insight into the organization of a communist guerrilla force.

For example, chapter 17 charts all the things that a Maoist cadre needs for survival.

Accounts/Quota	*Women*	*Men*
Soap for washing clothes	1½ per month [pm]	1 pm
Bathing soap	½ pm	½ pm
Also listed are some of the essential items for the guerrillas:		
• coconut oil (for both)	100 gm/month	
• rubber bands	1 packet/month	
• hair clips (for women)	1 pair/not mentioned	
• brassieres (for women)	2/year	
• *ghamcha* [towel]/*lungi* [sarong]	1/year	1/year
• vests		3/year
• innerwear	3/year	4/year
• slippers	3/year	3/year
• socks	3/year	3/year
• petroleum jelly [referred to as 'Vaseline']: quantity not mentioned		
• needle, thread, plastic sheets: quantity not mentioned		
• sweater, muffler, blanket: 1/every three years		
• milk powder: 400 grams/month		
• tooth brush: 2/year		
• toothpaste [referred to as 'Colgate']: 50 gram tube in three months		
• torches: 3 for every squad		
• watches: 3 for every squad		
• gun cleaning oil: 100 ml every two months		
• radio: 2 for each squad		
• *bidis:* 20 packs/month with a warning that smoking is discouraged		
• groundnuts: 2 kilograms		
• *gurh* (molasses): ½ kilogram for women		
• Rs. 300 every year, each member for mutton, sweets, etc.		

This is only a part of a long list.

Maoist squads maintain a record of whatever they consume and send the accounts weekly or fortnightly to their area commander.

The *Handbook* also lists the responsibility of a guerrilla in the chapter 'Permanent Instructions'. Besides it has chapters on responsibility of the Area Committee (AC) secretary, structure and role of the local organizing squad (LOS) and local guerrilla squad (LGS), structure and role of Area Command, Militia and Militia Command.

LETTER-WRITING

A guerrilla writes several letters every week to family and friends. In addition, official letters are religiously exchanged to finalize appointments, discuss work plans and resolve operational problems. Most letters are written in Gondi using the Devanagari script; a few are written in English and Hindi.

These letters are not delivered by post. Normally written on A4-sized paper, the letters are folded and pressed several times to become small rectangular pieces of paper. They are then sealed. Young boys travel between squads and villages to deliver these letters. They are called *couriers.*

Besides professional and strategic information, the couriers carry personal mail, perhaps written by a young wife to her guerrilla husband, or mother to daughter, brother to sister or father to son. Such correspondence imposes a strong sense of 'family' in communist villages. Couriers also carry sensitive information like, 'Comrade, please meet Mr X. the journalist with a Kinley water bottle from Y. Paper waiting at place Z'. It is through these couriers such information goes out and comes into DK.

My guard, 18-year-old Akash, read some of his personal letters to me. Every letter began with the line, 'May this letter find you in good spirit and health'. Akash told me that this line is understood to mean, 'I hope you are alive'. He is very fond of his elder brother who is also in the party. Akash told me they exchange several mails a month and he feels sad and worried when he does not receive mail.

One of the most dramatic letters was written to 9-year-old Manju by her mother. She let me video her while she was reading it. As I play the video, this is what I see and hear:

Dear Manju

Hope this letter finds you in good spirit. I am sure the Dada-Didis [elder brothers/sisters] are taking good care of you. You please take care of yourself and listen to [what] the senior comrades tell you. We know they love you and will take good care of you. We are fine here. You would be happy to know that last month we have killed some of the miscreants who tortured and killed your aunt Kumbhli. We got two of these police officers and killed them. Please do not lose hope. You do your work, we will win some day. Please send a letter through this courier and let me know everything about yourself.

With revolutionary greetings,
Ma.[18]

I received two letters during my stay with the guerrillas. The first one was from a Central Committee member, Comrade Sonu, in charge of the DK region. The comrade rebuked me for not being able to see him at an agreed place and time, but did so in a very official tone: 'We waited for you in heavy rain for three days but you never turned up. That was bit unexpected.'

The second letter was from Gudsa Usendi. I had spent my first two weeks in DK with him and received his letter when I was leaving the area after five weeks. He wrote the letter to my friend, Rukmini. Usendi wrote that he had left the north Telengana region to join the Maoist party in the mid-1990s. Since then he had worked mostly in DK. The letter had nothing about the revolution, policies or ideologies. Rather, Usendi wrote about his mother, with whom he lost touch a long time ago. Usendi wrote 'I think we learn the basics of living or survival from our mothers. And I also feel while we all are different—our language, culture or politics are all distinct and divergent—we tend to think on the same line on one issue, ***mother***.'

There was another mode of communication. The computer-proficient comrades, who had an understanding of English and Hindi, used this mode. They key in a letter on a laptop, then cut-paste it onto a pen-drive. The memory chip of the drive, a few millimeters in size, is extracted and delivered to the recipient. But this is expensive and its use limited.

I noticed several young guerrillas making copious notes from books and literature supplied by the party. Some of them told me they did this as part of their community-studies workshop. Once I even saw Manil, a 9-year-old boy, copying the portrait of the slain leader, Azad[19] (or Madhu, as he was known in the Bastar), from a photograph in a party magazine. Manil told me, he did not know the identity of Madhu until he was killed but always loved him because Madhu had been friendly to him.

PARTY MAGAZINES

The CPI (Maoist) publishes several magazines. Twelve are published in the DK region alone. All the comrades—young and old—are expected to read and study from these magazines that are also intended for public distribution. *Prabhat* (Dawn) is a Hindi quarterly, *Sangharsrat Mahila* (Fighting Women) is an irregularly published magazine focusing on women's issues, *Jhankar* (The Beat) is a bi-annual literary magazine, *Janatana Raj* (People's Government) is a bi-annual periodical in Gondi, *Padiyora Pollo* (Fighting Voice), also in Gondi, is an irregular publication about the PLGA, and *Viyukka* (Morning Star) is an annual periodical on political theory. A military magazine published for internal circulation discusses strategic mistakes committed during operations and related military information. In addition to these, the various divisions of the party in DK publish their own magazines: the East Bastar Division publishes *Bhumkal Sandesh* (Uprising Report), the North Bastar Division publishes *Bera* (Dawn), South Bastar Division publishes *Pituri* (Uprising), Gadchiroli Division publishes *Pordu* (Morning), and Darva Division publishes *Moyul Gudrum* (Spring Thunder).

These magazines are typeset to be printed on A4-size paper. There are also a few silk screen printing plates used to print these magazines.

Maoist cadres are exposed to literature or films prescribed by the party. The rules are changed *only* when a long commentary of Arundhati Roy appears. Her writing is immediately translated into Hindi by comrades. Each word of every article is dissected and debated, scanned and analysed, by cadres and leaders. Roy is a star in Bastar, loved and adored. Often comrades used to tell me stories about her—'she used to wear my trousers' . . . 'she gave me this song [Faiz Ahmad Faiz's *Hum Dekhenge,* sung by the legendary Pakistani singer Iqbal Bano]'. Roy is a serious aberration in a party that abhors cult status for individuals. 'I think she can dislodge your party secretary if there is a fair election', I started saying after cadres time and again deluged me with *Royisms.*

STUDY GROUPS

Evenings are normally dedicated to reading magazines and party literature. I often joined the members in their study groups. A range of topics was discussed over cups of sugary tea. We had debates on all kinds of subjects—from the crisis in Kashmir and Afghanistan to the communists' role in China and West Bengal, from the rise of corporate India to the benefits of the welfare state or even the relevance of Mao's politics in today's India. We had differences of opinion about a number of issues, but the Maoists were articulate and coherent in putting forth their point of view. They always listened to me carefully, even taking notes at times, and framed an argument before responding. I told myself, 'It is not possible to argue so systematically unless one takes part in Marxist study circles'. While the Maoists would not deny or confirm that they have formal study circles, I felt they must have interactive sessions with politically informed leaders.

Later, I met Badri, a member of the Maoist education department, who confirmed that they had political classes. I listened to recorded speeches of the late Anuradha Ghandy, the lone woman in the Maoist politburo. Ghandy stayed in DK for three years and was tremendously popular among the cadres. She was called Janki *Didi*. In the recorded speeches, she spoke effectively about the history of women's movements across the world and their relationship with the class struggle. While she spoke passionately about slain cadre, especially women, and about life and work, she also spoke in detail about the struggle of women activists in India. She explained complex thoughts clearly and precisely.

'I did not know many of the things she is saying about women's liberation in India and Europe', I conceded to Usendi, while listening to her one evening. Ghandy died in 2008 after returning from the forest, from malaria.

My interactions with the cadres were not rigid, and the leaders never stopped the cadres when they asked me about the life in big cities or even personal questions regarding my marital status, earnings or property. The exchanges were free-flowing and friendly. I realized that it was not important to start a discussion with a preconceived notion ('Let's be on guard . . . these are underground guerrillas') or restrictions. Junior cadres, men and women, were ready to talk as long as one was not pushing one's point in an aggressive way. In fact, I soon realized even my jackass jokes, reminiscent of Bollywood actor Salman Khan, were becoming a hit in the forest: 'Now I will kidnap you guys and ask for ransom. The Party will give it since I am positively irritating.' Or: 'Two things I like about you guys—*gaan* (song, in

Plate 1: A village near Dantewada, Chhattisgarh, where Maoists set up camp (April 2010).
Photo: Shailendra Pandey, *Tehelka*.

Plate 2: The final day of a week-long Maoist camp in Abuuj Maad in south Chhattisgarh. Before leaving, the group sang the *Internationale* and observed a two-minute silence facing the red flag. Photo: Suvojit Bagchi.

Plate 3: Maoists shifting base, a daily practice to evade security forces. Photo: Suvojit Bagchi.

Plate 4: A portable DVD player run on battery provides entertainment and propaganda in Chhattisgarh. Photo: Shailendra Pandey, *Tehelka*.

Plate 5: An Adivasi woman, her child and an armed Maoist cadre in a hamlet in south Chhattisgarh. Photo: Suvojit Bagchi.

Plate 6: 1500 people assembled in east Bastar in August 2010 to attend a meeting to mark the Maoists' 'Martyrs' Day'. Photo: Suvojit Bagchi.

Plate 7: A bus set on fire by Maoists in Morangi village, 6 km from Hazaribagh city, on National Highway 33 (14 May 2011). Photo: *Prabhat Khabar* team.

Plate 8: Three police jeeps burnt by Maoists in the Saranda forest in Chaibasa district of Jharkhand (7 April 2004). Photo: *Prabhat Khabar* team.

Plate 9: A bombed police jeep in the Saranda forest in Chaibasa district of Jharkhand (7 April 2004). Photo: *Prabhat Khabar* team.

Plate 10: Indian Home Minister P. Chidambaram at the funeral of paramilitary police killed by Maoists in Dantewada in April 2010. Photo: Shailendra Pandey, *Tehelka*.

Plate 11: Adivasi children near Dantewada help Maoists to identify ‘enemies of the village’
Photo: Shailendra Pandey, *Tehelka*.

Plate 12: A hut, a child and three firearms in a village in Bastar. Photo: Suvojit Bagchi.

Bengali) and gun', were the favourites of the guerrillas, who, as the most potent security threat in India, are not usually credited with a sense of humour. Gudsa Usendi presided over many of those wacky meetings.

The study group discussions always ended abruptly with the announcement on the radio: 'This is the BBC and you are listening to the daily news from London'. The BBC Hindi radio service is the window to the world for thousands of Maoists and tribals in Bastar who have no other access to news from outside. 'We listen to BBC Hindi, All India Radio, Radio Teheran or even German Radio's language broadcasts. But BBC is a priority', said Usendi. Normally, while listening to the evening news, the guerrillas planned their next day in more detail, assigned duties and wrote letters. When the BBC decided to reduce Hindi radio's air time in 2011, I was hardly surprised when a Maoist sympathizer called to say, 'As an Indian citizen I am requesting you to revive the radio—and we can raise funds, if you want'.

SLEEPING ARRANGEMENTS

Both men and women cadres of all ages sleep in a common lodging. There was no separate tent for kids or young women. During my stay, I never noticed any hesitation on the women guerrillas' part when sleeping alongside their male comrades. Women are accorded no special privilege in terms of work and are supposed to do all the duties that men do. For example, both men and women cadres are assigned duties to guard the camp for 90 minutes every night. The bed is a plastic sheet spread out on the ground under a plastic canopy held up with a rope tied to the tree trunks. There is no concept of a pillow, but the guerrillas do use shawls to shield themselves against the forest cold and insects, which include mosquitoes carrying the dangerous falciparum malaria virus.

Because it was the monsoon, most nights turned surreal when the plastic roof of the tents collapsed under torrential rain. I woke in a drenched stupor. The duct tape covering holes in the roof was not strong enough to counter the rain, and I often needed to haul out my belongings and get out of the tent into the wet, pitch-dark open ground. Once, while standing in the rain at night, we were informed that a nearby river, the Koram, was flooded and that it would be wise to move to a higher ground. While shifting camp at night through a dense forest, wet to the bone, I couldn't help asking myself, 'Would the Maoist guerrillas have chosen this painful life if they had a chance to aspire to better living conditions?'

On less dramatic nights, we would manage a good sleep under the canopy. On many nights I would wake up to the sound of Akash trying to get Anusha, a female comrade, to get up to relieve him of his guard or sentry duty. Akash would gently nudge her feet and keep repeating in a monotonous sleepy tone: 'Anusha, please wake up, you have to do sentry now. . .'. It normally took him a quarter of an hour to wake Anusha, but I never heard Akash raise his voice.

* * *

The camp functioned remarkably smoothly. Nobody who was a party member quarrelled or fought in my presence. It looked like everybody knew what they were supposed to do. However, it is difficult to say whether this was because of discipline inculcated by the party or inherent camaraderie traditionally encouraged in Gondi society. It might well be both. In any case, the Maoists have gained immensely from tribal society's organization.

'Quarrels in the dormitory are strongly condemned', wrote British anthropologist Verrier Elwin in 1947. His book *The Muria and Their Ghotul* helped me to form an opinion that the integrated social fabric of the community helped the Maoists form a strong network of communist tribals.

Elwin writes:

> To the Muria [a sub-group of Gonds], as to most aboriginals, tribal solidarity is the supreme good and anything that breaks this precious unity and fellowship must be condemned. Individualism is the great sin. For this reason quarrelling and homicide is rare, theft is almost uncommon. There are few who refuse to share the common work and interests of the community. Adultery is bad, not only because it infringes the rights of another Muria, but breaks up the carefully regulated system of the people and threatens to disrupt it by jealousy and hatred.[20]

Maoists nicely coalesced with the Elwinian world when they arrived in south Chhattisgarh in the 1980s.

LOVE, MARRIAGE AND CELEBRATIONS

This is what Maoists preach in their communes—to share, work together, co-exist peacefully and never have illegitimate affairs. All males are called *bhaiya* (brother) by the women guerrillas. Most women categorically denied having any romantic inclinations towards their male peers. Sex outside marriage is taboo among the guerrillas. Free mixing, dating or any kind of sexual advance, even a friendly one, is not accepted inside the party. So how do the Maoists manage to keep thousands of boys and girls, aged between 15 and 25 years, together, without any of them, or at least a majority of them, getting physically intimate? I could not probe this question in detail because of the formal nature of my relationship with the party and its cadres. However, one woman, Rehmati, from the cultural wing of the party told me that when comrades were 'attracted' to anyone in the party, they would propose marriage:

> If we both agree, we seek the party's consent. If the party allows it, we get married and are allowed to stay in a separate tent for a short period of time. The party tries to give the couple common assignments so that they stay close. But that is difficult to arrange, so eventually within a few months or so, many couples separate. However, when the newly married couples are together, the party and their comrades try their best to give the couples some additional space and time. The same thing happened with me. The women are quite comfortable with this arrangement. Simply because we did not earlier have the right to choose our partners in the village.

The Maoist party, it seemed, treated women differently from local social norms. Several women associated with the women's wing of the party, Krantikari Adivasi Mahila Samiti (Revolutionary Tribal Women's Organisation or KAMS), told me they felt 'free' within the party. Sukaldai, mother of three who was informed on to the police by her disgruntled husband for being with the Maoist party and consequently jailed for a while, told me that women are severely exploited in tribal communities. She said: 'Women are forced by their father and husband to do all the work and are denied all rights to property. That is a part of the exploitation. They are also exploited sexually as men tend to "keep" women outside marriage. That woman are exploited less in tribal cultures is all bunkum!'

Her views regarding the exploitation of women in tribal society were corroborated by several women in KAMS and also by party members who were predominantly Gonds.

One male member of the party, on condition of anonymity, told me that the party encourages men of all ages to undergo sterilization. He also said that he had 'willingly' undergone a vasectomy. Other members acknowledged that the party encouraged vasectomies among men and birth control pills among women. However, it is not mandatory. Bringing up a child is a serious problem in a guerrilla life, and it would be even more of a problem to protect a pregnant woman.

The *Area Committee Handbook* also details a marriage oath, which says that the couple will 'remain faithful to each other and the party' and fight the 'system that is feudal and patriarchal' following the 'norms set up by Marxism-Leninism-Maoism' for the liberation of the masses. The bride and the groom hold automatic weapons in their left hand and raise their right fists in a 'Red Salute' as they repeat the oath read by a senior comrade. I witnessed one such marriage.

Having said that the Gond notion of community and Maoist ideas of a commune have overlapping areas, I also witnessed differences between the party and the community. Tribals frequently indulge in late night soirees. Animals are slaughtered for dinner, a good amount of local liquor called *mahua* is arranged (*mahua* is made from the fermented flowers of the *mahua* or *Madhuka longifolia* tree) and a few drums are taken out to play the beat for the dancing and revelry. Tribals used to drink *mahua* during the day on most days.

But alcohol consumption is banned in the Maoist party. My friend and I were keen to have a swig of *mahua*, 'You can't do that—you

Fig. 15.5: PLGA cadres Sukmati and Somudu getting married

are with us', we were told. Even otherwise amiable Chandu sounded a little stiff.

That a party member cannot drink is a clear message. While quite a few erstwhile members of the party feel uncomfortable with this practice, the party is of the opinion that 'a stone cannot fight'. The party believes that it would be impossible to control tribals if alcohol were 'legalized' within the party since most tribals are addicted to local liquor. Hence, drunkards will eventually find themselves distanced from the party howsoever skilled as workers or fighters they may be.

But I noticed that the party did not resist or question late night festivities or other celebrations of the people in the villages. Party rules were not imposed on the locals. I stayed in several villages where many members of families were drunk. They welcomed the Maoists and were happy to see them, invited the Maoists for dinner and accepted invitations. But neither was alcohol offered, nor was it demanded. When Maoists stayed in a peasant's house, they cooked the rice and lentils they were carrying and preferred to sleep outdoors, even in heavy rain. It never appeared to me that the farmers were scared of the guerrillas or that the Maoists were wary of villagers. Villagers never inform the police, I was told.

But what if they do?

Diary entry: It was an unusually sultry evening. I think my fever is slowly disappearing. Maybe the parasites are 'under cover' in the spleen. As I was about to doze off, I met Mungeri. He gave me his real name and requested me several times not to use it. The comrades got him here in the camp to have a word with me. He seemed rattled. It took him a little time to organize his thoughts and narrate his story in the presence of a couple of party cadres.

Mungeri worked for 10 years for the party's mass organization for tribals, farmers and workers, Dandakaranya Adivasi Kisan Mazdoor Samiti (DAKMS). After being systematically 'influenced by a woman relative who also works in a government-aided organisation', Mungeri made 'the mistake' of his life.

'I went to the police and started giving them information about the party', said Mungeri. The police extracted all the information and dumped him. Maoists arrested and interrogated him. 'I was under the evil influence.' He is still under Maoist surveillance and is under tremendous psychological pressure from both sides.

It was not clear to me why Mungeri became a police informer. The reason—'evil influence'—did not sound convincing. The Maoists feel he was paid for divulging secrets. It could be money, women or coercion—what could it be? A man in his late forties cannot go back to his family, his hand shakes, he fumbles while walking and even talking. Is he neurotic? Before he slowly disappeared in the rain Mungeri told me, 'I think my life is over'.

The police push the locals to share information—they lure, threaten and torture—but refuse to rehabilitate the spies after extracting the information. Moreover, rehabilitation is not easy as it means uprooting spies from areas controlled by the rebels and settling them in some other part where they may not have an agency to support them socially. They will lose land and possibly livelihood, like Mungeri. But if Mungeri does not divulge the location of Maoists in the village he may well be branded a sympathizer. His family will be threatened, houses burnt, wife molested and in all probability during one spell of Green or Red Hunt, his entire family will be made to disappear.

To the Maoists Mungeri is a *mukhveer* or a spy. He has botched his brothers' trust and joined the enemy ranks. He has sold himself for money or succumbed under pressure. He lacks the moral fabric that holds a community together during a war. In addition, he risks the lives of his friends, he has exposed his comrades. A defector, a spy. In any war such men lose sleep, become neurotic and finally disappear. Mungeri has become a neurotic. 'Hope you guys will only watch him', I said to the guerrillas.

A MAOIST SCHOOL

The children of the guerrillas are part of the Maoist camps. They stay with party members and travel with a platoon or company. Their parents normally live in other camps and they write to each other often. Children of slain guerrillas too stay with the other camp members and in most cases women in the camp take care of them. Older children with a basic understanding of language go to the Maoist school called the Basic Communist Training School.

A close look at the syllabus reveals a mix of life-skills training, basic education and theory that may help raise volunteers for the party (Fig. 15.6). These schools began operating only a couple of years back and the education wing of the party runs at least one session every six months. Some of these children had also attended the local *ashram* (residential schools) set up by the Indian government. I have visited two residential schools funded by the state government—in Tirkanar in Narayanpur district in East Bastar and in a place called Rohtaar in the Abuj Marh area. In both places, villagers complained that the teachers rarely visited the schools. Hence, while the schools

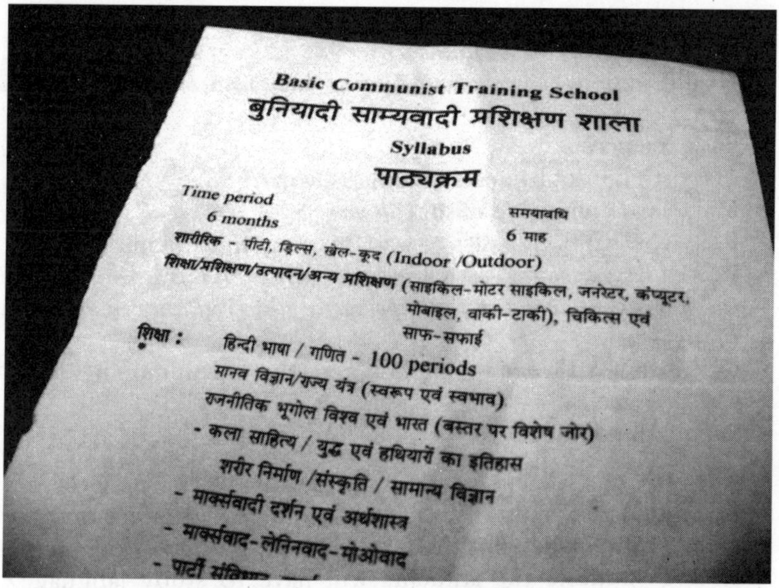

Basic Communist Training School

बुनियादी साम्यवादी प्रशिक्षण शाला

Syllabus

पाठ्यक्रम

Time period 6 months — समयावधि 6 माह

शारीरिक - पीटी, ड्रिल्स, खेल-कूद (Indoor /Outdoor)

शिक्षा/प्रशिक्षण/उत्पादन/अन्य प्रशिक्षण (साइकिल-मोटर साइकिल, जनरेटर, कंप्यूटर, मोबाइल, वाकी-टाकी), चिकित्स एवं साफ-सफाई

शिक्षा : हिन्दी भाषा / गणित - 100 periods

मानव विज्ञान/राज्य यंत्र (स्वरूप एवं स्वभाव)

राजनीतिक भूगोल विश्व एवं भारत (बस्तर पर विशेष जोर)

- कला साहित्य / युद्ध एवं हथियारों का इतिहास

शरीर निर्माण /संस्कृति / सामान्य विज्ञान

- मार्क्सवादी दर्शन एवं अर्थशास्त्र

- मार्क्सवाद-लेनिनवाद-माओवाद

- पार्टी

Fig. 15.6: The school's syllabus

were funded by the state government, they were run by the villagers. Maoists visited the schools at times and played with the children. The state government paid for a teacher, an assistant, a cook and the meal. The teacher went to district headquarters to collect the money. The Maoists maintained the schools—a remarkable example of great Indian coexistence. (For safety reasons, I have not identified the schools.)

The following are life-skills training, as described in the printed syllabus (emphasis in italics is mine):

- Physical training, drills, sports (indoor/outdoor)
- Education/Production/Other Training (*I feel these are what the state defines as 'vocational training'*): Cycle and motorcycle riding, use of generator, computer, mobile phone and walkie-talkie, basic medical course, cleaning and hygiene
- Education: Hindi and Maths—100 periods
- Human science/State science (*Anthropology and political science*), Political geography, world and India with special courses on Bastar (*this again is about formation of states and evolution of the world and India*)

- Art, literature and culture
- War and history of weapons
- Health and hygiene (*about human body and basics of environment*)
- Basic sciences
- Marxist philosophy and economics (*basics*)
- Marxism-Leninism-Maoism (*all basics*)
- Party constitution, basics of warfare, party functioning.
- Recce (*Reconnoitre*) as intelligence (*I think this is training to make the students understand the importance of surveillance in guerrilla life*)
- Organizational work among non-agricultural communities
- Couriering
- Supply of goods

The two-page syllabus mentions that sessions will start in February and continue till August. This has two months of extensive outdoor activities that include working in the fields to produce food grains.

It also suggests the students will have to study language/ mathematics for the full-time (i.e. 100 periods) and the next four months will be dedicated to other subjects.

Names of the teachers and their responsibility *vis-à-vis* subjects are allotted. Total working days with leave are 130.

Usendi told me that the schools' sessions are subject to the existence of a 'peaceful atmosphere'. According to him, many courses remain incomplete due to 'floods and police offensives'. The Maoist Education Committee (EDC) runs three categories of schools. These seem to be the most organized cell of the party. 'We have teachers, syllabus and sessions—everything in order, more or less', said Badri, an important member of the education cell.[21]

RECREATION

The guerrillas also organized film shows in villages. Films are played on a laptop powered by a solar charger.

The films being played repeatedly were the Hindi classic *Do Bigha Zameen* (Two Acres of Land) on the plight of landless labourers in Nehruvian India; the 2008 remake of Mao's *Long Walk*; Giulio Pontecorvo's 1960s' classic on the Algerian freedom struggle, *The Battle of Algiers*; and strangely, the fantastically entertaining *Enter the Dragon*. The films have English subtitles and are stored on a pen-drive. One member of the cultural wing, Chandu, sits next to the screen and translates all the English subtitles into Gondi. Watching Chandu, whose mother-tongue is Telugu, translating English subtitles into colloquial Gondi was a humbling experience. When I complimented Chandu on his Gondi skills, he simply told me that he had watched each film hundreds of times. Several villagers told me that they did not know until the Maoists introduced them to films that any such thing as a 'film' existed. The Maoists can be credited with introducing several commodities born in the market—films, playing back of songs, mp4 cameras—to the tribals of Bastar.

MILITARY ORGANIZATION

Keeping vigil, protecting leaders and other comrades, involving local youth in the militia and maintaining a guerrilla army are principles laid down in Mao Tse Tung's theory of *Yu Chi Chan* (Guerrilla Warfare). Mao has laid down guidelines for guerrilla warfare that were simple to adopt and implement. Such guidelines largely evolved from a combination of common sense and Mao's reading of ancient Chinese warfare. For example, Mao says that for a guerrilla, equipment requirements cannot be based on what the guerrillas want or even what they need, 'but must be based on what is available for their use'.[22]

The Maoists of India follow this assiduously. They don't (and can't) ask for a weapon of their choice. After being seized, weapons are accounted for by the Central Military Commission (CMC) and then distributed to the Regional Command. The Command gives them to Division or Area Command on the basis of strategic requirements. While I was not exposed to the Maoist arsenal, I have come across steel containers with Maoist literature—collected over decades—stashed 10 or 15 ft below the ground. The books and pamphlets are wrapped in plastic sheets, taped and placed in the ground. I assume weapons are stashed in a similar way in many places in DK.

I identified nine kinds of guns: the Insas Standard Rifle 5.56 mm, the Carbine 9 mm, the AK-47, .303 rifles (antiquated), 12-bore guns, the SLR 7.62 mm rifle, the LMG 7.62 and 5.56 mm, pistols 9 mm and 8 mm and old country-made rifles that are used to kill wild game. Most Maoist fighters carried the .303 and 12-bore rifles, which, however, deadly, are single-shot and far less effective than automatics.

There are locally-made, obsolete muzzleloaders, mostly carried by militia in the villages and used before the Maoists arrived. The senior leaders carry more sophisticated weapons, and personal and camp guards are also given semi-automatics or automatics.

By no standard can the Maoists' weaponry be called modern. There are a few semi-automatics and even fewer AK-47s. I did see a couple of two-inch mortars and one land-mine detector. I was told repeatedly by everyone that 90 per cent of these arms were snatched from the state forces during ambushes and raids.

I was always sceptical about the Maoists' theory of arms 'collection'. The arms, they maintained, were almost entirely snatched from the security forces. 'We also procure and make a few but mostly it belongs to police', said Jagesh, the member of the State Military Commission (SMC), DKSZC and North Regional Command.

A gun's life, if oiled regularly, is more than that of its user. Hence a gun has many owners, it travels many miles and serves many governments and regimes, non-state actors and rebels. So it was not unusual that the guns that Maoists had 'accumulated' included some from the Srikakulam or the Naxalbari uprisings of 40 years ago!

It is my job to be sceptical, and I asked the same question about military supplies—arms and ammunitions—to many people.

'Where do you get your guns from or do you think the supply comes from some other country?'

Every time, the answer was the same: 'We do not know; you ask the Central Committee (CC)'. Or: 'Yes, we snatched it from the police'.

But my questions seriously irked Comrade Jagesh.

Diary entry: Jagesh called me in the evening while I was resting after a dose of Reziz. He took me close to his camp. Comrade Kolu, another SMC member, was present. Jagesh used cryptic but unambiguous sentences: 'I would like to know why you are here? You have been asking the same question to every senior member regarding military supplies. I told you, it comes from police. We snatch these guns. But you are cross-examining. That is why I am asking you.' His cheek muscles were stiff.

'I am a journalist and trying to find out the source of the procurement. It is not necessarily for writing but maybe because of my training I am pushing a little hard. Sorry.'

'You will get the same answer from every one.' Muscles loosened.

Then he went on to brief me about the past and present of the Maoist movement in India—ideas and ideologies that I knew. But Jagesh spoke with a disciplined but irrepressible emotion. 'Do you think we are doing all these by guns? Do you think we really use guns to control these people? Do you think it is possible to run a system like this . . . to have so many people with us . . . using fear?'

'Nope, I don't.'

'Then please don't ask so many questions about guns. Guns are there to protect these people, not to destroy them. If we were not protecting their land, their language, their culture . . . if we were torturing them, as media is reporting, do you think they would have protected us like their kids?'

'No, I don't think so.'

'Then please don't ask about firepower. Please try to understand we are trying to do what your government has not done in 60 years. Please try to understand we are not *rakshas* [demons] in the forests trying to rotate civilization backwards. Please stop projecting us as mercenaries who are aided by other countries. Please write that and please tell the civil society in the cities—who have stocks in the mining companies, who build opinion to send the army to raise that stock—that butchering the majority for the interest of a small minority has never been tolerated in history.'

His six-and-half-foot frame was leaning forward with a setting red sun in the backdrop. He looked like Clive Lloyd, I thought. At Lords, 25 June 1983. . . .

'Will you be able to win this war?'

'We don't care. I don't care. When I joined the communist movement I was not contemplating whether I will win or lose in my lifetime. But the question for me was—whom I should I spend my life with—the rich or the poor. I have chosen the poor not because I wanted to win but that is how I wanted to spend my life. And . . . you call us enemy of the people. . . .'

We kept silent till it started raining and then went back to our blue tents.[23]

FUNDING: A 'FUNNY COUNTRY'

Maoist funding is an area that is still quite unknown to me. I do not have conclusive evidence to prove mining companies or multinationals operating out of Chhattisgarh pay a 'levy' to the Maoists. Neither Maoists nor multinationals accept the allegation of giving or receiving money. Undoubtedly, the Maoists have a revenue model. Without it, providing meals for a few thousand comrades would have been impossible.

I was not exposed to the fund-raising process, but, I formed an idea about funding by probing the business of *tendu*-leaf cultivation. *Tendu* leaves are one of the main forest products in central and eastern India. The leaves are used to make *bidi*s (local cigarettes). The relationship between *bidi* and revolution is complicated and fascinating.

I spoke to several people—ranging from financiers of this million-dollar industry to *munshis* (the managers employed by *tendu* contractors) to cultivators to try to understand the business.

It works like this. The Government of Chhattisgarh gives a piece of land (called *beat*) for one season to a contractor on the basis of an open tender. The contractor takes a loan from a financier and pays the tender amount to the government. The contractor then appoints one or more *munshis* to collect leaves from the cultivators—the tribals. The leaves are dried and sealed in jute bags called *boras* and delivered to the contractors. The government pays the cultivators from the tender money deposited by the contractor. There is one standard bag (*manak bora*) which has 1,000 *gaddis*. A *gaddi* is a roll or a bunch of leaves. One *gaddi* normally has 50 leaves. Depending upon the area, one *gaddi* may have 70 or even 100 leaves.

Piyush Guha was arrested for allegedly aiding and abetting the Maoists and kept in custody for four years. In May 2011, Guha was granted bail by the Supreme Court. The court ordered a suspension of his punishment. Meanwhile, he had lost the business that he started from scratch. He described how it worked:

> In 2007, when I was working in Chhattisgarh, as a financier, the government was paying cultivators at Rs 45 (US $1) for 100 *gaddis* (5,000 leaves). The Maoists told the contractors that they will have to pay Rs 25 in addition to Rs 45 to the cultivator. This made the poor villagers very happy. They were already supporting the Maoists, now they started adoring them. In addition, for each standard bag or Manak Bora the contractor had to pay Rs 125-150 to the Maoists as a levy. I used to finance the contractor so that he can get the tender from the government and sell the leaves to me. Of course they used to sell to me at a rate cheaper than the market since I was financing them. Then I used to transport the entire consignment of *tendu* leaves, sold to me in kilogram and not in *gaddis*, to Murshidabad in West Bengal to my factory where hundreds of workers make *bidis* from those leaves. We used to market it in eastern India under our brand name. But that was 2007, I am sure the earning has increased.

Murshidabad, the last capital of Bengal before British era, is now the *bidi* hub of eastern India. The Muslim-majority district is one of the poorest in the country where the main industry is to roll flat *tendu* leaves into brown cigarettes. There are hundreds of thousands of people associated with an industry that has a turnover in millions of dollars. The industry is completely dependent on supply of quality *tendu* leaves from central, western and eastern India—the area which is largely dominated by the Maoists. Hence, a good portion of the capital generated by the *bidi* industry goes to finance the revolution.

The base line is even more spectacular: The major *bidi* magnets, who scream against the armed Maoist uprising, buy *tendu* leaves from contractors who in turn pay the rebels. However, if that source of Maoist funding were cut-off, it might affect the revenue of the government, livelihood of at least a million families and seriously depress the economy in pockets like Murshidabad. A friend and a security expert said: 'It's a funny country!'

I was told Maoists collect similar levies from other forest produce and even tax the mining industry. The industry pays indirectly—and willingly—through their contractors. Top officials of the Chhattisgarh police told me that the mining companies (they named one specifically) unofficially asked the government if they could pay the government to 'raise battalions' to secure their projects in Dantewada. The state government declined the offer. The mining industry has never shown an interest in to diverting funds to improve the living condition of the people of the area. The chief minister of Chhattisgarh, Raman Singh gave a proposal to the prime minister of India in July 2010 to 'use 10 per cent of the profit of the public and private sector mining companies for local area development'. According to Raman Singh, the prime minister took the proposal 'very seriously'. Little appeared to happen in the succeeding 12 months.[24]

VIOLENCE: THE STATE'S RESPONSE

Si La Justicia No Limpia El Pueblo
Nosotros Lo Haremos

(If the Justice does not clean out the town
We will do it ourselves)

MICHAEL TAUSSIG,
Law in a Lawless Land: Diary of a Limpieza in Colombia

I had the privilege of travelling on National Highway 16 through southern Chhattisgarh with several people who had decided to take the law into their own hands, albeit with state assistance. Dileep Sethia—a shaggy-bearded, stocky man in neatly-pressed white shirt and trousers—used to be with a Maoist squad till the mid-1990s and was definitely one of the main strikers of the Dantewada police.

Sethia took his orders, he told me, directly from the 'boss', the

Senior Superintendent of Police of Dantewada (SSP), S.R.P. Kolluri. He carries in his back pocket a 9 mm pistol that fires 12 rounds. He walks around with a group of local boys as bodyguards and often says that the war against the Maoists can never be won 'without the support' from these local boys. Dileep Sethia and his 'boys' are called Special Police Officers (SPOs). Technically, however, Sethia was not an SPO when I met him, rather he headed a wing of SPOs with 65 fighters. He was called an *Arakshak* (a constable). His team of SPOs were armed and maintained by the state and the central government.

Dileep Sethia was supremely happy with his present existence—an existence that had put the local police chief just a phone call away, and given him bodyguards with semi-automatics, connections with the national and international press and certificates from senior officials.

Sethia took his 'expert' status seriously enough to refuse work that he did not feel like doing. At first he refused to accompany me on a tour of Dantewada district. It was only after being 'convinced' by his seniors—the order came from Mr Kolluri—that he agreed to come along. Sethia reminded me of a couple of police inspectors I met in Mumbai years back. They told me several times that they could call up any police officer, government secretary or film actress at any time of the night. Sethia could not call actresses because Dantewada does not have a film industry, but he could call the SSP—as he told me a couple of times.

'How much is he paid?' I asked myself but could not ask him. May be I was awestruck by Sethia's machismo, his eagerness to resolve the crisis single-handed using semi-automatics.

'If they [the police] get 50 or 60 like me things will change', he told me.

Well protected in my hired air-conditioned car, Sethia and I set-off on our tour of Dantewada. It was worth crossing continents for a drive with Sethia. I pressed the red button of the audio recorder:

Sethia: . . . I was promoted. Because I took part in lot of Naxal operations . . . killed them (Maoists) also in various places. . . . I led the group to operations . . . we did that in various places . . . so we were promoted . . . like two-three boys . . . we were made constable from SPO. . . .
Q: People you killed were Naxalites?
Sethia: Yes, Naxalites. . . .
Q: How many have you killed so far?

Sethia: I have lost count (of how many I have killed). Killed in several places. Entered Andhra and killed them . . . with Greyhound force . . . killed them in Maharashtra. . . .[25]

Is he lying? Is he overstating facts about himself for more phone calls from bosses? Is he showing off? I don't know. Neither can I cross-check. But what matters is Sethia's confessions: ***I have lost count of how many I have killed.***

Dileep Sethia is invincible. He knows that the law that criticizes him has also given him complete immunity. He pointed at the state police officials and said: 'Look at their paunch. They cannot fight the guerrillas. Only we [the local boys] can fight the guerrillas . . . we are tough. We know the terrain.'

The white Maruti van escorting us screeched to a halt close to a place called Kasauli. We—six men in early to mid-twenties and I—got down from the van and took positions at a little distance from it. The six young men circled the area with my car in the centre. I lit a cigarette and tried to get friendly with Yogesh, Sethia's bodyguard. He was a strong, muscular man with serious innocence in his eyes, thick lower lip and an Insas (Indian Small Arms System weapon). He answered me in monosyllables.

I get 3,000 rupees as salary. It's a very little amount but I had to manage. One can make little more [money] by going in for more operations. I am not scared [about operations] but situation is *scary.* I have parents and a sister. I meet them occasionally. I always wanted to join the police and so I joined. I hope to become a constable some day. I agree with you that tribals and Maoists are also like brothers and I don't necessarily feel like killing them but I have a compulsion. If I don't, they will kill us. So I had to fire. However, I have not been in any major or very violent encounter.

Some of the SPOs are ex-Maoists, others are local unemployed youths and yet others are leftovers from the Salwa Judum campaign.

While the Supreme Court of India, has objected to arming local tribal boys to fight another set of tribals,[26] the appointments are done in accordance with established provision of Indian law. The Police Act introduced by the British in 1861 states that 'special police officers' can be appointed in case of 'unlawful assembly or riot or disturbance of the peace'. So, legally speaking, there is nothing wrong in appointing Yogesh.

But with or without the Supreme Court's objection, SPOs will remain in Konta, Sulinga, Kutru and in all of south Chhattisgarh.

On the one hand, the law has ensured for the last 150 years that local boys can be used to fight a 'local war'. And the removal of SPOs would make men like Mohammad Karimullah vulnerable.

I met Md Karimullah, a 52-year-old CRPF officer of Narayanpur, at Kanker's Counter-Terrorism and Jungle Warfare College. On 29 June 2010, he was crossing a *nullah* with 63 colleagues at Kongera, Narayanpur, when the CRPF platoon came under fire from three sides. Twenty-seven of Karimullah's comrades were killed. He could not recollect how he managed to survive. 'I started running through the trees', he said. But Karimullah made one thing absolutely clear, they did not have any information about the Maoists.

> We didn't have the information that the Maoists may well be hiding in the village. If we have had any idea, we would not have gone to that village. However they had the information that we will be crossing the village. We had an SPO with us, whose family stays in that village. Obviously, the family would have informed him, if they had known . . . I don't think they knew either. There is serious shortage of information.[27]

Listening to Karimullah telling me how they were ambushed by the Maoists, I experienced a haunting moment: exactly two months earlier, the Maoist commander, Jagesh, had described the same Kongera ambush to me. Now Karimullah gave his version. Both men claimed, 'with guns in their hands, and God on their side', they would win this local war.

But to win you need to have the local boys on your side—boys who can move fast, carry intelligence, form a second layer of resistance. These are the 'boys' the state defines as SPOs—or would-be-SPOs who interned in the sister organization of Salwa Judum.

Karimullah and the administration needed more boys to win. Hence, there will be more smart boys in Bastar who can flick the magazine of a rifle and say like Dileep, 'Only we can fight the guerrillas'. Losing the boys means losing the war.

VIOLENCE: A VIEW FROM THE OTHER SIDE

During my stay in the forest close to the village of Kudurgaon, a Maoist militia commander called Budhu came to see me. He said he was attached to East Bastar Division. He was wearing a *khaki* shirt and a tightly fitted holster. Over three hours Budhu told me why it is absolutely necessary 'to kill'. Unlike Dileep he had not 'lost count' of how many he has killed. Rather, he was very specific and said he had killed three people over the last seven years.

Since I became affiliated to the party, in our panchayat area we have killed three men. The last execution took place three years back. People commit small or minor mistakes and they are warned and then we let them go. But there are people who are traditionally class enemies. We give them death sentence. However, we warn them several times before executing a death warrant. We request them and their families to leave the village permanently. But if they stay put we tell them not to divulge information about the party and the members to the police. But some start acting as informers and then we had to kill them. Like those who were killed in my area were warned for five years and then neutralized. One of them was shot and the others were lynched.[28]

Budhu told me that a number of these killings in recent years were videotaped. Like any other region struck by prolonged conflict, south Chhattisgarh was developing an obsession with the glorification of violence.

Both the Maoists and the members of security forces illustrate the process of 'neutralization'. They refer to each other as 'enemies', and as happens in any conflict area, the fighters are immensely proud of their job. Both sides record killings and distribute videos. Young boys rush to ambush points to click photos of dead soldiers which they circulate among friends and journalists. One aspect of this is to use violence—on both sides—to grab attention in the form of more air time or print space to provoke public outrage locally or nationally. But another objective is to highlight personal achievements: to get a pat on the back from the local police chief or Maoist commander.

The violence slowly becomes an industry. Documentary filmmakers from Europe, Latin America, the US and India flock to the hamlets of Tadmetla, Gidam, Orcha or Kongera to buy grainy footage of headless bodies. A market for photos of lower torsos, gouged eyes, chopped fingers and gang-raped women has evolved. It makes career for outsiders and money for local boys. A distributor of water pumps in a remote village asked me, 'What is the best documentary camera these days—Sony Z?' Neither the government nor private education enterprises has thought of starting a cinematography course here; but the conflict has taught locals the difference between a pan and a tilt. I met these photo-journalists-cum-story-suppliers-cum-police-informers around Highway 16, and months later they were still calling me around midnight to offer me footage of decomposed bodies and burned houses.

Inside the forest, Maoists have their own set of documentation professionals. They document any act of police violence and produce videos which circulate in Bastar. One such video, which has acquired an iconic status, is on the rape and murder of a woman named Kumbhli. The secretary of the Madh division, Rajmon, showed me this 84-second video. The opening shot shows the head of a woman detached from the torso. As the camera gets close to the face, the detached head shakes a bit and rolls off establishing that the head is not attached to the neck. Loud sounds of voices crying at very high pitch can be heard. One sees villagers and a few Maoist cadres with their trademark green sari surrounding the lifeless body. I was told this was Kumbhli who was raped and murdered by security forces on 16 February 2010 in a village called Pyware in Dumnar, Narayanpur.

Recall the letter to 9-year-old Manju quoted earlier in this essay: 'You would be happy to know', Manju's mother had written, 'that last month we have killed some of the miscreants who tortured and killed your aunt Kumbhli.' Perhaps someone has also recorded the revenge killing.

The Kumbhli video is carried by a large number of young cadres who have access to a mp3 or mp4 recorders and players. They watch it and will make you watch it if you start admiring the culture of violence. They downloaded it onto my pen-drive.

The Maoists carry quite a few still cameras of 4 or 6 megapixels. There are also a few handy-cams. The cultural wing processes these pictures, adds music if required and cuts some sort of a rough documentary. I saw two such films—on Salwa Judum in Dandakaranya and on an attack on a place called Chinnari in April 2010. Both videos highlighted the paramilitary and SPO-led violence committed against Gond tribals.

But besides these videos, Maoists systematically documented the impact of Salwa Judum and Operation Green Hunt on the villages. A few cadres were detailed to document the atrocities committed by the state forces. A little like the census officials of the government, these cadres moved from village to village to record disappearances and looting of livestock and food grains. They photographed the houses burnt and recorded the testimonials of the targeted families.

I met one man, Vijay, who had documented the impact of atrocities committed by the Salwa Judum and state forces around the Indrawati River. He was one of very few tribals who had been to Mumbai to attend the Mumbai Resistance of 2004. Hence, he had a clear understanding that the world did not begin and end in south Chhattisgarh. Perhaps his encounters with rights activists around the world convinced him that one day there will be a commission—something like a Truth and Reconciliation Commission—to listen to him. He would address such a commission and the world would listen. Such thoughts were perhaps what pushed him to list every quintal of rice looted, every finger chopped off and every dead person's identity along the Indrawati River. 'It makes me nervous when I cannot establish the identity of a dead man', he told me.

Vijay's list told me that between National Highway 16 and the Indrawati River, 1,570 houses had been burnt down and 64 people killed between 2006 and 2009 (Fig. 15.7). He listed how many quintals of paddy, rice, *mahua*, *tora*, turmeric and mustard had been burnt or looted. He documented the amount of gold and silver looted and the number of animals killed. He said that he had visited most of these houses but 'not all'. I was not sure why someone would pursue the record of a dead man or woman in a Gond village where the tradition is to bury the belongings of the deceased. Families in the past wanted to forget a dead Gondi, but Vijay resisted. Why?[29]

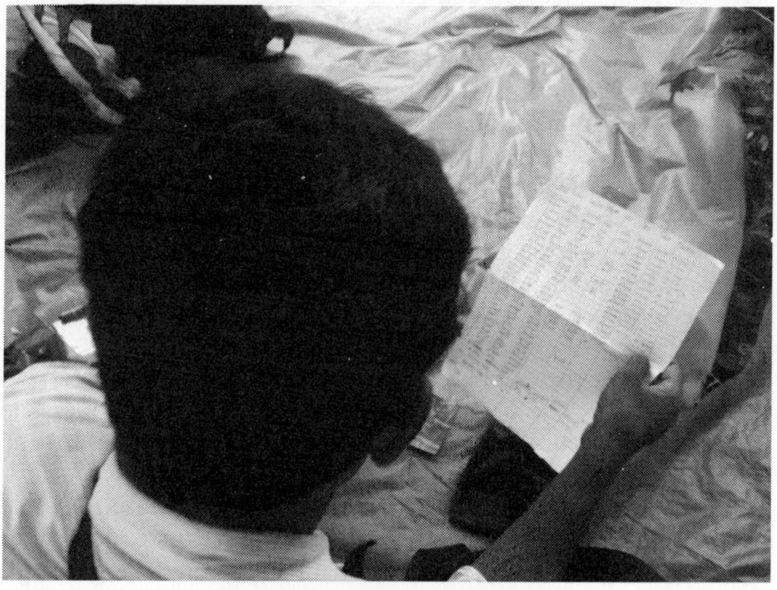

Fig. 15.7: Vijay and his list

'Yaad rakhne ke liye',—to remember, Vijay told me.

One village that Vijay wanted me to visit was Takilore on the southern side of the Indrawati inside Dantewada. Takilore is like any other village of DK, but perhaps a little bigger and more affluent. I reached there around nine at night after walking for about eight hours. Fever, marathon walks, monotonous food, incessant rain, malnourished kids and weeping women had sapped my energy—physical and emotional. I wanted to rest for a night in Takilore before I moved out of this vast, claustrophobic forest.

TAKILORE

Instead of a sleepy village, about a dozen women, toddlers and elderly couples greeted me as I reached Takilore. Moments later, others emerged from mud and straw houses. They set about telling me what happened to the men of Takilore on 3 February 2010.

Several 'men in *khaki*' arrived in the village in the early morning when most males were working on their land. The farmers were rounded up and taken to Bhairamgarh police station, a few kilometres south-west of Takilore. A few hours later, all that the women found were the bound, gagged and lifeless bodies of their husbands lying on the police station grounds. 'I could see ants swarming on my husband's face. I lost my mental balance and started swearing at the police', said Jaymoti, a Takilore widow, whose husband Anitram Kalmami was among those killed. The police claimed that the men supported the rebel Maoists, said Jaymoti.

'I did not know if my husband was a Maoist', said Jaymoti. 'Even if he was, is it reasonable for a government to kill its villagers for supporting a political party?' The words were getting blurred in my head. My mind, addled by quinine, was switching off like a fading television screen. I was trying to reconstruct the morning of 3 February, but the questions were getting blunt.

'Did you get the dead bodies?'

'Yes, we did. The bodies were given to us. The legs, hips and spines were broken. We put them on a stretcher (made of cane) and some how got them home.'

My mind was fading out intermittently. When I focused, I could see characters replacing Jaymoti on the coir-bed in front of me. Bhima replaced Mangri who replaced Rukhmati. They were telling a single story that started in the early hours of 3 February 2010: 'My husband'... 'Bhairamgarh'... 'the jaw'... 'the ribs' ... 'the pelvis' ... 'the stretcher,' were words I could register.

'Are you alright?' asked Rajmon, the secretary of the Maoist Madh division.

'I am.'

The security forces released the men's bodies only in the evening. A year later, no enquiry into the Takilore incident had taken place. The village is now referred to in colloquial Gondi as 'the village of widows'.[30]

EXIT

Takilore was my last stop before I headed for National Highway 16—this time to move out of Dandakaranya. A small squad of three girls and four men came to see me off as I stepped into a narrow, wooden boat for the final time. There was no song and no clapping. Each one shook hands with me and whispered: 'Red Salute'. The doctor, Prakash, came to see me. We shook hands and he hugged me suddenly, whispering, 'Please tell your friends in the city, we are not *rakshas*'. He smiled, so did I.

The boat was pushed into the river and it slowly moved away from the shoreline. It started raining again and the Maoists in their olive fatigues blurred from my vision. I reached the other side and walked for about 1 km to reach a specific house in the village. I was told to contact the owner of the house by the Maoists. The owner came out to meet me. He had a red tumour under his left eye. He did not shake hands and his smile was sad. The great Gond hug was missing. He took me to the verandah, recently plastered with cow-dung. Children were playing with cows and an Enfield motorbike leaned against the wall. He was not a poor man, but he seemed to be a Maoist sympathizer.

I dropped onto a plastic chair, drank coconut water and realized that my muscles were giving up. My legs were heavy and my reflexes were slowing. I couldn't walk any further. I started hallucinating that I was pillion riding on the Royal Enfield on National Highway 16.

The man with red tumour shook me. 'Are you alright?' he asked in clear Hindi. 'I think you have a fever.'

'Then you must make a move, it's getting late. And you must leave all that you are carrying in your backpack.'

'Like?'

'The Platoon Handbook—I can see its edge. May be you should drop everything that may put you in trouble, in case you are picked up by the police.'

I had a lot of things that could put me in trouble. I had close to 80 hours of audio and video material. I had photos; I had diaries with notes, cameras and a dozen cassettes. Should I go back to the forest, I thought.

Then came the most appropriate advice. 'You start walking now. If you walk south, in another three hours you will hit Highway 16. Get a bus and head for Orissa or Gadchiroli—wherever you wish. I can't take you to the Highway 16. I am sorry. The Maoists are *friends* but they don't realize one simple thing. We live with families on the border. We call this area, India. The other side of the river: Pakistan. There are villages close to the highway, controlled by the police and *not* by the friends from the forest. The police have informers there. If any of them see me with you, an outsider, I will be summoned . . . we live with families, *bhaiya* (brother).'

'You speak good Hindi, though you're a Gond', I said.

'We are Indians. We are not Gonds. Hindi is our national language.'

Our eyes met and I felt for the first time that mine were moist. Maybe his as well.

By the time I reached National Highway 16, I was interrogated several times by the villagers about my credentials. Who am I? Why am I emerging out of a forest that houses bandits? When did I go inside? They asked me in pure Hindi. I realized I was getting closer to my country. I also felt good that I didn't push the man with an Enfield and three daughters to see me off. I hit the main road by late noon at a place called . . . but I was told not to disclose the names.

I got on a bus. CG17F 0752. What I witnessed made me record its number. There were more than a dozen of SPOs, mostly carrying semi-automatics, along with six children, eleven women and thirteen men who, I think, were all civilians. Was this using civilians as human shields? I thought of putting the question to the police chief, if I got to see him.[31]

CG17F0752 picked up speed. My phone, switched off for last two months from fear of being stalked by middle-aged men with moustaches, delivered its first messages. They told me that I can now be a neighbour of cricket star Gautam Gambhir by investing in a property that costs $300,000.

The bus honked and took a sharp turn. It picked up speed, and the forest on either side began to blur. I requested the SPO sitting next to me to push the backpack, with photographs of the Maoists, under the seat.

'Please push it gently. . . it has some fragile items in it.' I smiled at him and went to sleep on National Highway 16.

NOTES

1. If one enters the forest from the left while walking on National Highway 16, from east to west, one may have similar experience. But I slipped into the forest on the right and unknowingly, at that point, slipped into the territory of the North Regional Committee of the Maoists. If I had slipped into Dandakaranya (DK) from the left, I would have been in the territory of the South Regional Committee.
2. I was accompanied by friend and journalist Rukmini Sen, who filmed almost the entire trip.
3. For more on Dandakaranya, see http://en.wikipedia.org/wiki/Dandakaranya. DK has managed to irritate India since the time of the Sanskrit epic, the *Ramayana*. The majority of the *rakshas* (demons) of the *Ramayana* were said to be from DK. I have called Dandakaranya south Chhattisgarh or DK.
4. The names I use are the pseudonyms that people told me.
5. The chart is prepared on the basis of my conversations with Maoist cadre and state committee leaders. According to one police officer, whom I consider the most informed in Chhattisgarh, the chart is 'more or less correct'. However, I could not locate all the places on the map—places like Natpark, Mohalla or Nellynar. They could be wrongly spelt as I sometimes could not follow the villagers' pronunciation. Two more issues are worth mentioning. First, the names of leaders in any underground organization may change periodically. Hence they may not be using the names I have mentioned. Second, the North Regional Committee broadly covers the administrative divisions of Kanker, Bastar and Narayanpur, and the South Regional Committee covers Dantewada and Bijapur.
6. Refer to Chapter 26 for the interview with Gudsa Usendi.
7. For Suder's and Sahitram's interviews in Hindi, see http://www.bbc.co.uk/hindi/india/2011/03/110309_maoists_suvojit_psa.shtml.
8. Central Committee (Politburo), CPI (Maoist), *Strategy and Tactics of the Indian Revolution*, Chapter 7, p. 49. Retrieved from http://www.satp.org/satporgtp/countries/india/maoist/documents/papers/strategy.htm#7.
9. In a press release, 23 November 2010, Maoists claimed that 'over three lakh acres of land has been confiscated from the government forest department and landlord classes. Thus there is no landless peasant in the

areas of struggle, here in Dandakaranya.' The release was jointly signed by State Military Commission (SMC) chief, Sudhakar and Gudsa Usendi.

10. Federation of Indian Chambers of Commerce and Industry, *Task Force Report on National Security and Terrorism*, vol. 1, pp. 36-8. Retrieved from http://www.ficci.com/SPdocument/20032/terrorism-report.pdf.
11. A lawyer-activist from Bilaspur, Sudeep Srivastav has brilliantly documented corruption associated with mining in Chhattisgarh. A critic of the state and central government's mining policy, Srivastav says that 'mining is a bigger scam in India than [radio frequency] spectrum and it benefits [everyone from] ministers to Maoists'.
12. Refer to Chapter 25 for interview with Comrade Jagesh, military instructor, DK, and member, State Military Commission (SMC) of CPI (Maoist).
13. Part of this interview can be heard in Hindi at http://www.bbc.co.uk/hindi/india/2011/03/110309_maoists_suvojit_psa.shtml.
14. The other song which is a roaring hit in the tribal, Maoist and mining belt of central and eastern India is *Gaon Chodob Nahin, Jangal Chodob Nahin* (Won't leave my village, won't leave my forest). The song can be heard at http://www.youtube.com/watch?v=8M5aeMpzOLU.
15. Government of Chhattisgarh, Human Development Report Chhattisgarh. Retrieved from http://cg.gov.in/book/hdr.pdf. Also check the Hindi interviews with patients and Maoist doctors at http://www.bbc.co.uk/hindi/india/2011/03/110309_maoists_suvojit_psa.shtml.
16. The percentage of Telugu-speaking Maoists to Gondi Maoists is calculated on the basis of my observations. There is no data available. The secretary of the CPI (Maoist), Ganapathy said that they were 'striving to have more leadership from the oppressed classes'. In an interview released by the CPI (Maoist) on 16 May 2011, he said that 'the vast majority of them (cadres), i.e. more than 80 per cent, belonged to the oppressed classes and castes. Comrades from rich peasants and upper middle class are less in number'.
17. For more details on Maoist life in the forest, see http://www.bbc.co.uk/news/world-south-asia-12637562
18. This is the synopsis of a long letter. The translation from Gondi to Hindi was done by journalist Lingaran Kodopi in Delhi, March 2011.
19. Refer to Chapter 24 for Azad's interview with Siddharth Varadarajan.
20. Verrier Elwin, *The Muria and Their Ghotul* (New Delhi: Oxford University Press, 1991, rpt.), p. 133.
21. Refer to Chapter 27 for an interview with Badri on Maoist education.
22. Samuel B. Griffith II, *Mao Tse Tung on Guerrilla Warfare (Great War Stories)* (Champaign: University of Illinois Press, 2000, rpt.).
23. That was the only time when I had some kind of a confrontation with

the party. I realized I should have been cautious. Whatever I had been asking the cadres or the middle leadership was getting reported to the local chiefs. Jagesh, otherwise, was an exceptionally warm person. He used to laugh very loudly and very often. He took good care of me while I was down with fever, arranged for medicines and gave long structured interviews on strategic planning. For the structured interview of Jagesh, refer to Chapter 25.

24. The Government of India is planning to introduce legislation that will charge mining companies an additional tax for development in tribal and Maoist areas. Mining companies are opposing the bill.
25. Refer to Chapter 32 for Dileep Sethia's interview.
26. Record of Proceedings, Supreme Court of India, http://supremecourtofindia.nic.in/outtoday/we25007.pdf (accessed on 10 July 2011).
27. For the Karimullah interview, see http://www.bbc.co.uk/hindi/india/2011/03/110309_maoists_suvojit_psa.shtml.
28. For the Budhu interview, see http://www.bbc.co.uk/hindi/india/2011/03/110309_maoists_suvojit_psa.shtml.
29. The villages in Vijay's list feature Priyakote, Pushal, Pallowaya, Niram, Orchapara, Ekheli, Kiringa, Bangoli, Markapal, Belnar, Gungemar, Kolnar, Palli, and five others. All are located above the Indrawati River on the district planning map of Dantewada.
30. Refer to Chapter 31 for the Chief of Police of Dantewada, Vishwa Ranjan's statement on killings in Takilore. For testimonials of Takilore widows, see http://www.bbc.co.uk/hindi/india/2011/03/110309_maoists_suvojit_psa.shtml.
31. Long after that ride did I ask the Chief of Police of Dantewada, Vishwa Ranjan, about 'human shielding'—ferrying armed men in a passenger vehicle through a civilian area. 'No—it is not human shielding. It happens across the world', he said.

CHAPTER 16

The Naxal Movement: Internal Contradictions and Possibilities

HARIVANSH*

This is not an analysis by some sociologist, political pundit or economist. These lines are the experiences of a journalist, as a witness, judge of human affairs and neutral observer, of the Naxal-affected areas of Orissa, Bihar, Andhra Pradesh, Jharkhand, Maharashtra (the Chandrapur region) and Chhattisgarh for the past 33 years. The experiences have been gleaned from visiting some areas a number of times and of meeting some top-level Naxal leaders and supporters of their cause. I had the chance to listen to and discuss things with the legendary Vinod Mishra who, as soon as he was released from jail, came to speak at the public meeting organized by the *Prabhat Khabar* Readers' Forum. When Nagbhushan Patnaik—who had been condemned to death by hanging—was released and was on his deathbed in his village in Orissa, I had the opportunity to meet him in his remote home (Gunpur, which is on the Andhra-Orissa border).

*Harivansh has edited *Prabhat Khabar*, a Hindi daily based in Ranchi, the capital of Jharkhand, for more than 20 years. He made the paper, in Sevanti Ninan's words, 'a champion localiser' [*Headlines from the Heartland* (New Delhi: Sage, 2007), p. 104], and he draws on his long local experience for the reflective and highly personal essay below. He emphasizes the growing role of capitalism and consumerism, both in strengthening and, paradoxically, undermining Maoist causes and appeals. Written in Hindi especially for this volume in 2011, the essay presents local stories that Harivansh came to know first hand. The essay has been translated by veteran translator, Vimal Mehra, of Varanasi.

We cannot call Dr. Vinayan a direct Naxal. He was basically a Gandhian and was under Jayaprakash Narayan's influence. However, he also remained underground and was considered a Naxalite because he raised land-related questions in the Jehanabad district of Bihar. I have memories of long meetings with him during his underground days in Bihar and of relations with him going back years.

Thereafter came the brief experience of working in a bank in Warangal in Andhra Pradesh. I have memories of meetings and discussions with the intellectual guides of the Naxal movement in 1981-2 during my stay in Hyderabad, and memories of being in their company. I also had the experience of being a member of the Independent Citizens' Initiative team that went to study the Salwa Judum in 2006 and coming face to face with the ground realities. This team that went to Chhattisgarh in 2006 had six members: Ramachandra Guha (historian and columnist), Farah Naqvi (writer and social worker), E.A.S. Sarma (former secretary, Government of India), Nandini Sundar (professor of sociology), B.G. Verghese (ex-editor, *Hindustan Times* and *Indian Express*). I was the sixth member. This team gave its report titled 'Civil War in India's Womb: An Enquiry into the Ground Realities in the Dantewara District of Chhattisgarh', which was much debated in several forums including the Government of India.

This article contains the experiences of that which I saw and learned and found during all this, as also the experiences gleaned from many years of going to the locale and seeing firsthand and meeting the people involved in the bloody conflicts that took place in Bihar.

This article also embodies the experience of reading the literature of and becoming familiar with the movement that attracted me and provoked my curiosity in my student life. After reading Mary Tyler's *My Years in an Indian Prison*, I learned in 1978 how this movement lent a new spark to the dreams of the youth; how the most brilliant minds from the renowned academic institutions of the country came to be associated with this movement, and sacrificed themselves; how they gave up a life of comfort, renounced their elite family background, and chose the path to the villages, the jungles and the hills. It also contains the experiences of visiting, observing and living in the remote Naxal areas of Bihar-Jharkhand for the last 23 years, as also the anecdotal experience reaped by personally being in the midst of the prevailing conditions, because of having resided in these states.

Where does the Naxal movement that began in the Naxalbari

village of West Bengal in 1967 and shook our generation out of its complacency stand today? What did the commentators and strategists of Naxalism want? How did a generation of talented youth jump into this movement in its initial phase? The talented students of the best colleges of metropolises such as Mumbai, Kolkata, Delhi, etc., became a part of this movement. What were the dreams that gave pace and impetus to this movement? How and why has this movement that emerged from the Naxalbari village spread to about 200 districts? In spite of the spread what are the changes and the divisions that have come into this movement? What decline has come about in its guiding principles and ideology? What are its internal paradoxes? These and numerous such questions are being raised in the entire country today about Naxalism.

A group believes that by 2025 Naxalism will rule a large part of India, directly or indirectly. The Kesroli Group, a think tank, which had India's top under-50-years-old professionals from business, finance, policy, public affairs, media and NGOs, was busy searching for the possibility whether or not India was becoming a superpower. This group gave its report, and it has been called India's demographic tsunami. This report says that by 2025, Maoists will come to control the mineral-rich states of India on the strength of their 10,000-strong armed cadres. According to intelligence sources,[1] the Maoist guerrillas are making a new red corridor. This corridor is in the forest areas of West Bengal and Orissa. The book titled *Maoist Handbook on Strategies and Tactics of the Indian Revolution*, prepared in 2004, notes that, 'we will be able to build these areas into a contiguous area of armed struggle, with each area influencing the other'. According to this news, the extremists have nineteen military companies, and each has three light machine guns, fifteen automatic rifles, mortar rockets, and a huge number of hand grenades.

Analysts believe that in the era of coalition politics, India is continuously becoming anarchic. Institutions are collapsing. An example of how the Indian state has become helpless was the incident in which the Naxals blew up a train—the Gyaneshwari—near Kharagpur in West Bengal on 28 May 2010 and killed many hundreds of innocent people. This happened to the most important train on the Kolkata-Mumbai rail route. From May 2010, no trains travelled this route at night. Due to immense public pressure, the railways said that it would start running trains on this route from the middle of January 2011. The day after this announcement the Naxals attacked a small station near the Rourkela railway station in Orissa, kidnapped five railway employees and smashed the railway control cabin. The government took back its announcement that it would run trains at night. This is how helpless the Indian state is.

In this belt, it has been quite common for the Naxals to hijack trains and to bomb them. That's why, when the Naxals call for a *bandh*, the train services of many states become disturbed. Trains on many routes are cancelled. This is the undeclared power of the Naxals. They commit an act in one state and escape into another state. There is no coordination between states. The states blame the centre for this problem. Many non-Congress chief ministers of Naxal-affected states have blamed the centre for this. It is a matter of vote politics. Every party is eager to get the help of Naxals in order to come to power. In 2004, the United Progressive Alliance (UPA) created a climate against the National Democratic Alliance (NDA) using the Terrorist and Disruptive Activities Act (TADA), and it gained and used the support of Naxals. In the last state elections in Chhattisgarh, the state-level Congress leaders openly took a stand in favour of Naxal groups. The Congress party felt that the anti-Naxal campaign started by the Home Minister P. Chidambaram is adversely affecting its vote bank, so a prominent leader of the Congress—Digvijay Singh—opened a campaign against his own home minister. In West Bengal, it was believed in 2011 that Mamta Banerjee was openly supporting the Naxals due to election politics. In this way, at the level of Indian politics or governance, there is no consensus about the Naxal problem. This is the Naxal's biggest strength.

In the history of Naxalism, the year 2010 is believed to be the most violent. In this year, 998 people died in Maoist violence, in nine states affected by Naxalism. These numbers include the 285 policemen. The 2010 number is five times more than the number of people killed in extremist violence in Jammu & Kashmir and the north-eastern states. In 2009, the Maoists killed 908 people. But what is the state of health of this movement? From what areas is it facing challenges? Is it becoming stronger or weaker? Is state power the only threat for the Naxals? Maybe not.

Some new trends are visible, which are soaking up this movement's energy. For example, the socio-economic values that are arising from economic liberalization; the era of 'depoliticalization' [*sic*]; the incalculable wealth reaching the Naxal groups in the form of levies and commissions. According to a news item in the ***Dainik Bhaskar*** on 15 December 2010, the Naxals extorted Rs. 2,400 crore (US $600 million) in a single year from eight states and 223 districts under their sway. The growing hunger for money among their cadres due to the unimaginable sums of money is a challenge for the Maoists. Numerous important Maoists are slipping away from the party unnoticed, taking money with them. Rs. 400,000 in cash (US $9,000) was confiscated by raiding a village near Bokaro. Where on the one hand the Naxals are getting stronger due to the money, on the other, their old-time commitment is also getting challenged. Earlier, the Maoists of Gandhian bent of mind were mostly above temptation and the profit motive, but no more.

According to newspaper reports and Maoist statements issued from time to time, the Maoists have also joined hands with rebels in Bangladesh, Pakistan, Bhutan and Sri Lanka. For years we have also been getting reports of Naxal contact with the militants in Kashmir and the north-east. The cover story in *Outlook's* 7 February 2011 issue was 'China's Secret War with India'. This issue contained confessions by top militant leaders of the north-east as to how they are receiving weapons and aid from China. The same issue also told us how Chinese weapons are being used in Naxal areas. People have raised the point that China, which has emerged as a superpower, is using Naxals to create chaos in India, and is helping them. Old documents coming to light recently show how, after India's Independence, five communist leaders went to Russia without passports to meet Stalin. Their aim was to prepare the ground for a bloody revolution in India. The Naxals have also been making frequent trips to China. Vinod Mishra had also been to China via Nepal. But today's world is not one of ideological polarization. Therefore if the fact that the Naxals are becoming powerful with China's help were to reach the ears of the common public, it will go against them. In order to succeed in India, the 'Indianization' of Naxals is necessary, which hasn't happened so far.

On the other hand, the Naxals have suffered their biggest setback due to the rise of new social forces—Mayawati in Uttar Pradesh, Nitish Kumar in Bihar, Lalu Prasad in Bihar, the coming to power of tribal leaders through organizations like the Jharkhand Mukti Morcha, etc. The classes that support these movements are becoming sharers of democratic power. Earlier, too, there were very few reports of indecent behaviour with women in Naxal organizations. The Naxals say that news items of rape or indecent behaviour are police propaganda. But right from Lalgarh in West Bengal to Jharkhand, numerous such matters have become public which are hurting the Naxals' cause. In Jharkhand, 22 incidents of atrocities against women extremists have been recorded between 2001 and 2008. The recorded statements given by these once-Naxal women to the police are proving fatal for Naxal groups. Now when the Naxal groups are looking for new female cadres, they don't find any.[2]

From time to time we get news of social polarization among Naxals. For example, in 2009 an officer of the special branch in Jharkhand, Inspector Francis Induwar, was brutally murdered. Then in 2010, right before the Bihar elections, four policemen were kidnapped by Naxal groups from the Naxal area of Lakhisarai. They killed one of them who was a tribal policemen named Lucas Tete. These policemen were residents of Simdega in Jharkhand. These actions sent a message among tribals that Naxal groups are actually oppressing them. One group raised the question that both the tribals that were killed were Christians. In this way, Naxal groups who look at society from the angle of class distinctions are forced to confront issues related to caste, religion, region and backward-forward caste issues that echo in our politics. It's not easy to find answers to these internal paradoxes.

Anti-Naxal voices are also being raised in classes that were not against them earlier. Take, for example, the anti-Naxal campaign started by the first chief minister of Jharkhand, Babulal Marandi. Babulal is a politician who has tribal roots. In 2005, he wrote a booklet titled, *Hai re! Ugravad* (Alas, This Extremism).[3] His point was that 'the reason for extremism is not social or economic, . . . it is a purely political problem.' 'This book,' he wrote, 'is dedicated to all those innocent children, women, men, and brave policemen and officers of Jharkhand who lost their precious lives due to the cowardly, senseless and born-of-despair acts of extremists and to those brave villagers who, even today, stand firm like a rock in front of the extremists.'

These kinds of exhortations and resistance are not an easy challenge for the Naxal movement because the voices behind this resistance give the message: how can Naxals who attack the proletariat be their friends? In this way, Naxals are being challenged from new quarters all the time, and their internal paradoxes are emerging.

I cannot say whether my personal experiences are right or wrong, but those experiences have taken me to the conclusion that the economic liberalization of 1991 attacked the very foundation of the politics of ideology. Political groups have fragmented and cracks have appeared in their formation. At the level of thought, reflection and organization, political groups are today unable to find party workers who are ideologically committed to their cause. This situation ranges from the extreme left-wing groups to the extreme right-wing groups. The MLA and MP fund[4] has converted political workers into contractors.

On the other hand, the information revolution and advertisements being aired on TV channels have changed the ways society thinks and understands things these days and also lifestyles and the traditional mindset. Naxalism has not remained untouched by such changes. A few examples can explain this point. From where and how is Naxalism being issued new challenges?

The first example is near Jamshedpur. This region is contiguous to West Bengal, Orissa and Chhattisgarh. All these states are under Naxal sway. Nearby is the famous Lalgarh of West Bengal. The incident took place at the end of 2006 in the village Khatimari under the jurisdiction of Gudabandha police station.[5] It is an extremely thickly forested area. In this area, the Naxals had killed the MP of Jamshedpur, Sunil Mahato, on the day of Holi. In Khatimari village, Ghatshila subdivision, the Maoists had warned the villagers against building roads, but ignoring the threats, the people of Majhotolia, the most thickly forested area of Gudabandha police station area, and many other villages, made a road by cutting through a mountain as per their pre-announced programme. Women participated more in making this road which was built by voluntary donation of physical labour. Because of there being no road, the lives of the villagers had become difficult. If someone fell ill suddenly, it was impossible to get medical treatment for him or her. The patients used to die while being taken to the hospital. Villagers of Majhotolia, Dumatola, Barisaitola, Tiriabeda, Lephokocha, and Jaraghotu remained associated with this voluntary donation of physical labour for an entire week. Due to the lack of road access, this area had remained a safe haven for Maoists. When the villagers started building the road, Maoists put up posters warning them not to build this road. The villagers took this threat as a challenge and got down to building the road, bringing their food from home.

The Maoists can convince themselves that this was a police-inspired campaign, but if throngs of people emerged from villages, then one must understand the hidden message behind this, and that too in an area where police or the administration are conspicuous by their absence, an area which is pure forest, surrounded by mountains. An area where the gun rules. Those who were earlier Naxal supporters came out against them. After all, why were people demanding a road in such an area? When the government was not making the roads, they came forward themselves and blasted mountains to make a road. The meaning is clear: the hunger for a better life was building up inside them.

The Naxals have had a hand in creating this political consciousness. The economy of liberalization and advertisements aired on TV channels have intensified the hunger for better life among the people, and now emphasis is being laid on children's education. There is a search for a better standard of living. The common man of the village wants to be a part of the world of consumerism. Whether this is right or wrong is a wholly different question, as is whether the model of American development is suitable or unsuitable for India. Will the people of these backward villages attain prosperous and happier lives via this model of development? This question is unanswered, but this much is certain: the dreams of economic prosperity have inspired people to take to a different path than hitherto, and this is the biggest challenge faced by the Naxals.

If the Indian constitution, governments and the democratic system are able to deliver the bright light of development to every village, then the Naxals are going to be faced with a big challenge. But corrupt ruling systems, the collapse of governance, the fact that politics has become unethical, the fact that political parties have become private limited companies, give the impression that it is impossible that the light of development will reach every single village. If this does not happen, then this population and these very dreams of the common people will prove to be the biggest energy source for the Naxals in the future.

In Jharkhand, Panchayat elections took place after 32 years at the end of 2010. A large number of young people of Naxal background have won in these elections. The Naxals gave the call for boycotting these elections, and at some places they killed people, intimidated them, but the people refused to be afraid. If these young people who have won in the Panchayat elections want to, then they can change the grammar of grassroots politics by cleaning it up and by ridding it of corruption. However, there is very little possibility of this happening because people bid crores of rupees to become the chairman of district councils. People who won in these elections have been given expensive cars because they were going to elect the district council chairman. The process of buying and selling of Members of Parliament that began during the term of Narasimha Rao has finally reached the level of Panchayats and districts via members of state legislatures.

It is undeniable that political power has reached the villages due to the recent decentralization of politics. How much good this institution of village chiefs and so on will be able to do for the people can only be found out by assessing the ground reality. However, what is certain is that the idea that politics is the easiest way to earn money has reached the level of the village. Satisfying the hunger of becoming prosperous overnight and living a five-star lifestyle is possible only via this route. The Sonbhadra area of Uttar Pradesh (UP), which is contiguous to Jharkhand (and has been affected by Naxalism for many decades), also saw Panchayat election in the year 2010. There, the slogan was 'The post of the village head means that you can make one crore rupees in a year,' that is to say, one can earn Rs. 40 lakh honestly by getting Rs. 1 crore worth of public works done. If this is the way, how useful will be the decentralization of political power that has trickled down from Delhi (parliament/central government) to the state capitals (state legislative assembly/state governments)? This will only be found out later, but the process has already delivered the decentralization of corruption from Delhi to the villages.

Simultaneously, television and media have created the hunger for a consumerist lifestyle. Corruption is no longer a social issue. All the old moral taboos have collapsed. The Naxals are also affected by this process. In the Panchayat elections in UP (where there are Naxal affected areas), the supporters of Naxals or their cadres—who used to reject the parliamentary process, calling it a bourgeois process, and heap abuses on the parliament and resolve to change society by violence alone—also got associated with these elections. People breaking away from their roots is a new challenge for Naxalism.

In this era of liberalization, the politics of ideological commitment has collapsed. This correspondent toured village after village in the Naxalite affected areas of Bihar in the years 1985 to 1995 and saw the conditions there. Today, the appearance of villages in Jehanabad,

Gaya, Arwal and Arrah (Bihar) has changed. Road connectivity, the arrival of electricity, the presence of schools and a change in the old style of landownership, have changed these areas.

One more important reason has made a difference. In the places where the most backward and neglected people of society have obtained a share of political power, conditions are changing. Mayawati and Nitish Kumar in UP and Bihar represent those social forces which used to be considered the very backbone of the Naxal movement. When Lalu Prasad was in power, he used to proclaim, 'I am the biggest Naxal, now we Naxals are in power'. His links with Naxal leaders were public knowledge. The Naxal movement has faced new challenges from the participation of the socially backward in the democratic structure. The fact that Nitish Kumar, the chief minister of Bihar, has given political participation to the extremely backward will also affect the Naxal movement.

Naxalism does not face these challenges only from the Naxal-influenced areas of north India. The situation is similar even in the south. There are similarities with Gudabandha in Jamshedpur. How are the dreams of a better life changing the mindset of the people of Naxal-influenced areas? On 18 January 2004, the first bus ever arrived in the village Gangpur in Adilabad district of Andhra Pradesh.[6] This first bus journey opened a whole new world for the people of this and surrounding villages. Was it John F. Kennedy who said about America that roads were like wings that enabled Americans to fly and thereby see a new world? The government in India did not provide these wings, but the people are demanding wings—roads. In this village of Adilabad, too, people came face-to-face with a new world via the road. This report comes to the same conclusions that were drawn in the Gudabandha road issue in Jamshedpur. The two places are geographically distant from each other, but the direction of people's thought, dreams and sentiments are identical.

Extensive work has been done in the developed countries of the world to document how roads write the history of development and how they transform entire regions. The story is similar in India too. It used to be a full day's journey by bullock cart to reach the small town of Penbi from the village of Gangpur, a distance of mere 40 km. In the rainy season one had to cross the river adjoining the village, followed by many small brooks, often filled with waist-high water. All that was needed was to connect Gangpur to the main road by making an approach road a mere 12 km long. The Naxals warned against building this road, but the villagers stood their ground. Some 1,800 people of the village built an unpaved road under police supervision and made many small bridges the entire task completed in about 25 days. Gangpur is surrounded by fertile land and has sufficient underground water. Farming used to take place in the old-world fashion. There were no facilities for education and health care. It was a young man from the village who told the *Hindu* that many pregnant women died due to lack of medical treatment, and snake-bite victims did not receive treatment on time and often died.

Thereafter began the road issue. Gangpur and its nine surrounding small settlements, inhabited mostly by Gond, Kolma and Lambada tribesmen, were once a stronghold of Maoists. But after the road-building episode their stranglehold broke down. The villagers became opposed to the Maoists and in a bloody skirmish around 2003, the Naxals had to back down. The villagers wrested a handgun from a commander of the Naxal platoon. The next day they walked 60 km to the police station and handed the pistol over and said that they now wanted a better life. The villagers began collecting donations and laid the foundation for making the road. For two months 100 villagers carved hillocks under the watchful eyes of 30 policemen, to make 37 small bridges that culminated in the building of the road itself. Thus began the bus service between the towns of Kadam and Uttanoor on 18 January 2004. Exactly five days before, on 13 January, the Naxals attacked the village. The villagers were united as one. The Naxals had to retreat.

As soon as the road was built a whole new world of economic activities opened up for the villagers. Prior to this middlemen controlled the paddy, cotton, corn, turmeric, etc., grown in the village. As soon as the road opened the villagers began bringing seed from traders in the city, as also fertilizers and advance loans. Thereafter they began selling their produce directly to the very same big traders, who earlier accessed them via middlemen. The middlemen used to pay low rates and also levied 3 per cent interest on loans.

The *Hindu* was informed about this by Madhu, an ex-Maoist. He was a drop-out from the tenth grade and had been a member of the regional council of the Maoists. Rajeshwar Reddy, a farmer from the village, said that now they (the farmers) go to the city of Kadam to find out the market rate. Due to the road they now earn an extra Rs. 300-50 per quintal. One road changed the villagers' way of thinking and working.

According to this report, the dream of armed revolution began to feel like a burden to the villagers. More than 100 television sets came to be owned in surrounding villages. The villagers mostly watched Telugu soap operas on these TVs. By then 70 VCDs had found their way to the village. This spread of popular culture did not appeal to the Maoists. They killed a villager, Damodar Rao, who had played a leading role in this endeavour. Then the villagers began an agitation demanding that the government provide them with a paved rather than unpaved road, so that they would be able to buy their own autorickshaws, begin their own businesses and join the mainstream.

Andhra is not the only place with this new mindset in regions earlier considered the strongholds of the Naxals. In the first term of Nitish Kumar's government in Bihar (from 2005 to 2010), major road-building projects were undertaken. We have before us the example of a village a mere 20 km from the city of Gaya. Earlier when the people of this village reached Gaya at night, they used to stay the night at the Gaya train station. This 20-km journey was unsafe after 5 p.m. The road was also in a bad shape. The police and administration lay prostate in government offices. Naxal terror ruled the roost, their domination was unchallenged in the entire region. But as soon as the road was built, people got the chance to farm this fertile land. On the political front, backward and neglected people began getting the chance to partner in political power. Due to three decades of Naxal agitations, a change had already come about in the form of landownership. When they got the chance to earn, the same Naxals of yore got down to farming, growing vegetables and many other productive occupations. Due to the road having been built, it became possible to visit Gaya four times a day. Vegetables began to be carted to and fro on motorbikes. Their vegetables began to reach Gaya city in a big way. Where earlier there was no scope for income, farming of crash crops now began. Once the capital came into individual hands, new dreams and new needs arose.

The Gudabandha village of Jharkhand near Jamshedpur, the Gangpur village of district Adilabad in Andhra Pradesh and villages near Gaya in Bihar, all of them once under the influence of Naxals, are different places today. Some are in the plains; some in hilly areas. How come the dreams and aspirations of the people of these three areas are similar—dreams of progress, of becoming associated with new economic activities and becoming a part of the consumerist economy?

People associated with the Naxal movement admit that the successful market economy of contemporary China is a blow to the original class-struggle concept of Maoism/Naxalism. They categorize all Chinese leaders after Mao (and including Deng Xiaoping) as 'revisionist', and Mao alone is held to be leader of the Maoists of India. However, the section of Maoists that is entering politics due to being influenced by power politics, or that wishes to improve the quality of life by demanding roads, education and hospitals, takes refuge in the principles of Deng. These people quote an important statement by Deng Xiaoping: 'What difference does it make whether the cat is black or white? Whether or not it possesses the strength to catch the mouse is what is important.' Deng said this around 1977-8 when he was putting China on the path of the market economy, having freed it of Maoism. By 'cat' he meant 'ism' or ideology. Using the language of hints and symbols, he asked: what is the difference between communism and capitalism? The real issue is that prosperity should arrive, wealth should come and there should be economic progress. The logic is that if capital is not created in the first place, then how is its distribution possible? Wealth distribution is only possible after wealth creation.

Today the dreams of becoming rich via Western-style free-market economy are reaching village after village of India. They are posing more of a challenge to Naxalism, at least in the context of India. Weak, corrupt political power is not able to pose that much of a threat to the Naxals. The structural cohesiveness of political parties has gone awry. Earlier every village had political workers: Congress, Communist, Socialist, Jan Sanghi, etc. There was no political vacuum. It's not the same any more. This kind of political structure has collapsed. Now party workers have become political contractors. At this level there is a political vacuum in the villages, which has been filled by the Naxals.

But how did Naxalism become strong? In the year 2003 *Prabhat Khabar* had done a case study on the mountain named Jhumra. The Jhumra mountain is situated in Jharkhand in a forested area. It had long been considered an impenetrable stronghold of the Maoists. In the last 30-40 years the police have been able to reach there barely two or three times. When the police raided the place, they found evidence of Naxal camps. Fierce skirmishes took place. It is believed that Naxals from Nepal as well as all over India had been receiving training there. This place is some distance away from Lalgarh in West Bengal. How did this entire belt come to be afflicted by Naxals? If we find this out, we will learn that the cause behind the flourishing and spread of Naxalism and its taking root lies in the failure of the present-day political establishment.

The Jhumra mountain is connected with the mountain Lugu and the Uperghat hill. This place is near Steel Authority of India Limited's Bokaro plant. According to police documents, the Maoist Communist Centre (MCC) used to operate from the Jhumra mountain. This is the same place where around 1927 the British used to cultivate tea. The local residents were tea plantation workers. Thus, the local residents were economically connected to the tea industry. Even though it's a mountain, yet even today farming takes place on it.

In 2004, a resident of Jhumra—Biseshvar Mahato—told ***Prabhat Khabar*** that his forefathers had come to a tea plantation near Ramgarh around 1927 to work there. Quite a few people from Rohtas or the districts around the-then Bihar arrived there. After Independence, a paper factory was set up in Dalmianagar, near Rohtas in Bihar. Raw material for it came from the Jhumra mountain. That is to say, bamboo, the raw material, was cultivated on the Jhumra mountain. Local residents received employment on a large scale. The life and economic activities of the local populace was affiliated with producing and farming. Biseshvar Mahato said that he returned to his village in Jhumra mountain after having passed his exams in the Honsir Middle School in 1967. His education got him the job of a permit accountant in a Dalmia factory. But a few years later the factory closed down. The bamboo business also diminished. Since bamboo was not being harvested, people associated with the bamboo industry on the mountain were on the verge of starvation and unemployment. The three company officials living atop the mountain were also plunged into a financial abyss and passed away once the company shut shop.

Seeing the worsening condition of the region, the Bihar Rajya Van Vikas Nigam (Bihar State Forest Development Corporation) began public works on the mountain. The forest department began harvesting ***sakhua*** wood, teak wood, mango, ***karanj*** trees and bamboo. Daily 10-15 truckloads of wood began to be harvested and sent to depots in Hazaribagh and surrounding areas. Due to this economic activity the faces of the people settled on the mountain began to glow again with health and hope. The farmers and agricultural labourers settled there and got busy making their lives better.

Moneylenders and small and big businessmen also arrived there seeing farm-worthy land and potential for trade. The moneylenders set up shop by giving the villagers money. Thereafter they trapped them in the web of interest. Usury increased to such an extent that big businessmen began confiscating the local people's hard-earned money as interest. Alongside the usurers, lathi-wielding henchmen living at the bottom of the mountain began arriving to assist them. They would take away goats, cows, oxen, chicken, and food grains stored at home as interest payment. Farmers and farm workers began yearning to be free of the terror of usurers.

Politics did not come to their aid. Nor did the administration, the courts, or institutions like banks, which were intended to lend money to the farmers. The democratic and constitutional framework could not resolve the crisis faced by the people and could not save them from exploitation. Thus ground was laid for the situation to flare up. In 1972 the influence of the MCC reached this region. It began to be considered the headquarters of the MCC. The MCC needed a safe haven and an exploited populace exactly like this.

The MCC began its fight against the usurers. Numerous big businessmen and usurers were killed. When the villagers were freed from the terror of the usurers' *lathaits* (lathi-wielding henchmen), they naturally took refuge with the MCC. When the police occasionally raided the place to capture the militants, they would beat up the innocent villagers. The militants instilled their own share of fear in the hearts of the villagers. Thus, the public came to be trapped between the police and the militants. Slowly, farming came to a standstill.

Earlier the government used to get a lot of revenue from the Jhumra mountain. The plots on the mountain on which farmers once grew paddy, corn, chickpeas are barren today. Now militancy is being cultivated on the same land. The people 'growing' militancy here are not the local farmers, agricultural workers or villagers. The credit for the birth of militancy goes to failure of the government and the role of big businesses and usurers. No government to this day has provided education, health care, medical facilities, roads, electricity, irrigation or drinking water on the Jhumra mountain.

When people with Naxal ideaologies came to the mountains from outside and sowed the seed of a revolutionary farmer-labourer movement, the people associated themselves with them more and more. After reading the posters and handbills put up by the MCC, the mind of youth suffering from starvation and unemployment began leaning towards militant ideas. If the government wanted, it could have connected this entire area to the Kedla colliery, the washery in Vasantpur, and the big market of Jharkhand and the Laiyo colliery, via economic productivity. Turmeric, mustard and green vegetables can be cultivated on Jhumra mountain on a large scale.

Because of Jhumra being reduced to such dire straits, people settled at the bottom of the mountain do not forge marriage links with the mountain-dwelling folks, citing the extremists' presence for their decision. Difficulties come in the way of marriages as outsiders hesitate to marry their daughters into Jhumra. Thus Jhumra is a case study in how government failure has resulted in Naxalism gaining strength and flourishing.

What are the sources of the Naxals' power? How have they been getting stronger? Will the Home Minister Chidambaram or the Indian government be able to weaken or eliminate them in the next five years as part of their policy on Naxalism?

Actually the strength of the Naxals lie in the villages, in the poor, the have-nots, the exploited. Systemic failure and corruption fuel them. Their torchbearers are clear in their minds about their functioning style, vision and ideology. They know that the source of their strength is the deepening, spreading socio-economic disparity.

Is it possible to find a solution to the challenges posed by the Naxals within the framework of democracy?

It is certainly difficult, but not impossible. First, the judicial system will have to be brought into shape. Given a system where 30 or 40 million lawsuits are pending in the courts, people wander desperately seeking justice for 20 or 30 years. The Naxals set up courts, on the strength of their terror, and hand out speedy verdicts. People of villages and forests and those living in regions within their influence seek them for justice.

The second task will have to be fulfilled on the governance front. Governance ought to be snappy and efficient: computerization of land records and reports; time-bound disposal of land disputes; large-scale reform in the police department; harsh laws to control corruption.

Alongside these administrative steps the political parties also need to change. They should not become one or the other family's private firm. There ought to be a democratic structure within each political party, the way Congress was until 1972. That is to say, there should be possibility within a party for someone to disagree with the leadership. Party workers should spread out to villages with their respective agendas; there ought to be the possibility of mass politics. Parties should fight for the poor, as the CPM, the CPI, the socialists or Jana Sangh (the earlier incarnation of the Bharatiya Janata Party) used to fight for public issues. Thus, there should not be a political vacuum at the grassroots. If all this happens, then there will be a hindrance to the spread of Naxalism.

There can be three possible sources for alternatives to the challenges posed by the Naxals: first, political parties; second, the government, ministers, bureaucrats (i.e. the ruling elite); and third, the legislature. If we base our statements on the experience in Jharkhand, which is deeply affected by Naxalism, then what new feature can we expect from these three? Political parties have become 'malls' along American lines. Huge malls are coming up in Indian marketplaces, wherein there are diverse kinds of shops. Similarly, every political party's political 'mall' contains thousands of 'shops', i.e. a single party has a thousand segments. Every person has his or her own 'shop'. Individualism and ego have become primary in political parties. There is no space any more for ideology. These parties have more to fear from inner conflict than from their political foes. A *Mahabharata* (the legendary fratricidal war) is on in full swing inside each party itself. When this is the condition of institutionalized parties, then it is no wonder that the world witnessed the miracle performed by independent MLAs in Jharkhand.[7] Neither does any political party have an ideology, nor a different character. On the other side, Naxal groups have firebrands who have a clear notion of their goal, who go among the people carrying with them questions about the establishment and who write handbills.

In today's system corruption is no longer an issue, but if you ask people who work at the grassroots about their experiences, they will say in one voice that corruption is the biggest issue blocking the path of development. The corruption in Naxal-influenced areas is stunning. The Naxals raise this delicate issue. They offer the logic that if they extort levies, they fund the struggle for change with this money. They pay every party worker a monthly salary, but politicians or bureaucrats earn money only to fill the coffers of their families. These arguments penetrate deeply into the minds and hearts of the people. The unemployed youth are attracted. They get weapons and a monthly salary. In regions that are anarchic and where political power is conspicuous by its absence, it is not only guns that come into one's hands; political power also comes along with the gun. As soon as the gun comes into one's hand so does the terror that is born of it. Mao is credited with the famous quote that political power comes out of the barrel of a gun. In villages and jungles, it is the guns of the Naxals that give rise to political power.

No senior political leader or party has taken the initiative to study this problem. In this sense, Jayaprakash Narayan (JP) was the first senior leader who went among the Naxals in the Mushari area of Bihar when the Naxals were spreading their influence there. JP was ill. He was recuperating in Dehradun. At that time, a worker of the Sarvodaya movement wrote a letter informing him about threats from the Naxals. Upon receiving the letter, JP immediately returned to Bihar. He went to Mushari and remained in those villages for four months with his wife, Prabhavati Devi. He only had an ordinary jeep to travel around that area. He used to stay in the primary schools of the villages that he visited or a similar public place. He had to go to the open fields to relieve himself in the morning. A great leader like JP, whom the country and the world had come to recognize and respect way back in 1942, who was considered 'the heir to Nehru', went and lived among the Naxals, stayed in the villages and studied the problems there. He met the Naxals and then wrote the booklet *Amne Samne* (Face to Face). JP conceded that it was because of bad governance and corruption that this problem was growing. People were not getting justice. JP said that the seed for the birth and encouragement of the Naxals lay in the failing political establishment. It lay in the corruption rampant in the delivery mechanism. In spite of JP saying these things, no efforts were made to solve these issues.

After coming to power in 2004, Manmohan Singh has often said that Naxalism is the biggest challenge faced by the country post-Independence. People ask 'Is this a *prime minister's* statement? Is he the leader of the opposition that he is telling the country about this condition?' The prime minister should say: 'Yes, it is a serious challenge, but as a prime minister I am taking such and such solid steps to solve it.' The truth is that from the central to the state governments, no one has any solid strategy for solving this problem.

The central government, believing it to be a law and order problem, shifts responsibility to the states. The state governments say that it is a problem which has spread over 10 states, which is not within the powers of these states to tackle on their own, and that the centre is not taking any firm steps.

The ruling elite of the country was stunned by the murder of the MP Sunil Mahato, on the day of Holi in 2007. Mahato was the MP from Jamshedpur in Jharkhand. Jamshedpur, which is well known as the city created by the Tata business family, is the very same industrial city where, after the rise of Naxalism in 1969, Naxals formed groups in the surrounding areas. They raised questions related to water, forest wealth and land. Mary Tyler, a foreigner associated with a Naxal, was incarcerated in the Jamshedpur jail and wrote the famous book *My Years in an Indian Prison* based on her experience.[8] It is from the same area that Sunil Mahato got elected to the parliament on the ticket of the Jharkhand Mukti Morcha (JMM). People were astonished at his murder because the JMM was never a declared enemy of Naxal groups. In the 2009 state elections Naxal groups silently supported the JMM. Two Naxals, while incarcerated in jail, contested the state elections on the ticket of JMM. One of them was elected an MLA, but he is still in jail in 2011.

Sunil Mahato was guarded by trained police commandos, but the operation mounted by the Naxals was so professional that within the blink of an eye, everything was finished. The commandos were killed and some of them ran for their lives. The Naxals took away with them the ultra-modern weapons wielded by the commandos. The Naxals did not suffer even a scratch. The security arrangements for people holding political power vanished within the blink of an eye. This was the most serious aspect of the entire incident.

The fact is that leaders of urban India are immersed in 'the rise of new India'. They are busy discussing 'India becoming a superpower', but India's villages, mountains and jungles are agitated. The late Vinod Mishra, the famous Naxal leader of the 1980s and later general secretary of the Communist Party of India (Marxist-Leninist), wrote a book entitled *Dhadhakate Khet Khalihano Se* (From the Blazing Farms and Farmyards). At that time, he was underground. In those days, a bloody struggle was going on in the plains of Bihar. Although the situation has changed in these areas now, the Naxals have spread into new areas. Governments from time to time claim that the Naxal problem is under control, but on the lines of ***marz ya rog badhata*** *gaya, jyon-jyon dava ki* (the disease or ailment kept getting worse as one kept taking more medicines), the problem is continuously expanding.

For the time being Naxal-influenced areas are confined to areas around forests. Will they be able to occupy India on the strength of this strategy? In this context, the statement made by a senior leader, the late Comrade Kanhai Chatterji, is clear in itself:

> From 1968 to 1975 we used to undertake limited, sporadic actions only in the areas surrounding the Koderma jungle, which caused us to be discussed a lot, but we did not succeed in bringing about any serious change. Then we assessed ourselves and we got the impression that success was right in front of us for the taking. But after wasting seven years, we felt that we are not an outfit of holy men that has renounced normal life and adopted forest dwelling. Revolution is nothing if not organizing common people into our movement and getting people to stand up in our support, then what are we doing? Eventually we rectified our modus operandi and came out of and down from hills and forests and began to become one with the villages.[9]

But the top leadership of this movement believed that soon there would be a red revolution in India. The following statement by Charu Majumdar is interesting:

> The Naxalites and their farmers are the surrounding mountains in whose midst there is the jungle. In this atmosphere, approximately 20 young men are sitting on a boulder in front of a house. They have no claim to fame, no India-wide prestige. They are young, they are dreaming of securing liberation from exploitation, liberation from darkness, liberation from poverty and starvation for the millions and millions of Indian farmers. They believe in revolution. It is their firm belief that only armed farmers can make the revolution successful. They are residents of Srikakulam of Andhra Pradesh. They have come from the Warangal, Nalgonda and Adilabad districts of Telangana. They have come from districts of Rayalseema. Unlike lazy folk they don't only dream. The story of Srikakulam has confirmed the belief that in the very near future Yenan will be formed.[10]

These two statements make it clear how it seemed to Charu Majumdar that revolution was virtually knocking on the door, but after the military action undertaken between 1968 and 1975, Kanhai Chatterji admitted that the strategy needed to be changed.

In the heyday of Charu Majumdar an unwritten idea had formed among the Naxals—that by 1975 revolution will take place. However, lack of unity within the party made Charu Majumdar sense the ground reality and he said: 'Going by the way in which the struggle is going forward under our party's leadership, the country will not be able to get liberated even in 2001, let alone 1975.'[11]

After Charu Majumdar and Johar, Vinod Mishra, a brilliant student of the Durgapur Engineering College, took over the reins of the party. Under his leadership a big change occurred in the party. He and Nagbhushan Patnaik joined together and got busy putting up open people's groups. Eventually, the Indian People's Front (IPF) was formed. It remained widely discussed for 10-15 years and emerged as a major force. Its sphere of influence ranged from Bihar to Jharkhand, West Bengal, Andhra Pradesh, Orissa, Uttarakhand and the north-east. Here, Naxals busy trying to occupy political power through violence or military action once again began to strengthen their strongholds around forest areas. Areas which contain the country's mineral wealth. Local tribesmen could not benefit from this mineral wealth. Major industries and factories were set up. But yes, the Naxal groups also began to receive a large income from these mines and industrial centres. They strengthened their base in these areas. The forests and plateaus of Jharkhand, Orissa, Chhattisgarh and Andhra Pradesh became their strongholds. Now the central government—following the strategy of Home Minister P. Chidambaram—is busy trying to weaken them, by simultaneously working in these areas on many fronts.

Post-1980, the Naxal movement took a significant turn. On 22 April 1980 the People's War was set up in Andhra Pradesh. The underground CPI-ML (Liberation) took its first step towards parliamentary politics and decided to create a nation-wide front. In 1982 it jumped into the election fray under the banner of the IPF. In 1989, the first ever Naxal leader—Rameshwar Prasad—was elected to the parliament from the Arrah parliamentary seat. The IPF made the right to vote an election issue in Bhojpur. In 1992, the CPI-ML (Liberation) openly emerged as a parliamentary political party. At that time its general secretary was Vinod Mishra. This was the era when one by one many private militias arose in reaction to the struggle of the rural poor under the leadership of the Naxals: the Kunvar Sena, Lorik Sena, Brahmarshi Sena, Bhumi Sena, Sunlight Sena and later the Ranveer Sena. Apart from the Ranveer Sena, all the rest became defunct one after another due to their own internal paradoxes.

Many violent skirmishes took place between Liberation, the MCC and Party Unity, in which they attacked each other's supporters. The MCC murdered many high-caste people in villages such as Dalelchak

Baghaura, Bara and Senari. In reaction, the Ranveer Sena and other private militias attacked the residential areas of the weaker castes or the Dalits. Among these, the Laxmanpur Bathe genocide in the Arwal district and the Bathani Tola genocide in Bhojpur were the cruellest, where even newborn babies and pregnant women were murdered.

In 1998, the Party Unity and People's War merged and the new party was named CPI-Marxist-Leninist (People's War). Thereafter, People's War and MCC merged in September 2004, which now functions as the CPI (Maoist). Of course, theoretically, there are several other Naxal groups also active in Bihar, namely the Shantipal outfit (which has influence in some districts of eastern Bihar), the CPI (Marxist-Leninist) New Democracy (mainly active in Kaimur and Muzaffarpur), CPI-ML (Kanu Sanyal), etc.

In Bihar, the police admitted in a muted voice that in 2005 Naxals were active in 31 of the 38 districts of the state. From among these, they wielded substantial influence in 13 districts. After Jharkhand separated from Bihar, it was believed that it would be difficult for the Naxals to conduct guerrilla warfare in the plains of Bihar. But this belief has been proved wrong. The CPI (Maoist) formed after the merging together of the MCC and the People's War made itself militarily strong enough to be able to attack a prison and release its supporters or to occupy an entire settlement for 3-4 hours. On 13 November 2005, armed units of the CPI (Maoist), which must have been around one hundred in number, executed the Jehanabad jailbreak. It was the first incident of its kind in the entire country. Before this, they had simultaneously attacked a bank, a post office, a police station and the house of an MLA belonging to the Rashtriya Janata Dal (RJD) party, in Madhuban of Champaran district. They occupied the entire area unchallenged for several hours. The Naxals' strategy of robbing the bank and police station in Jandaha of Vaishali district on 29 April 2006, however, did not succeed.

It is mainly the responsibility of the Peoples' Liberation Guerrilla Army (PLGA) of the CPI (Maoist) to attack the symbols of political power—the railways, banks, police stations, government offices, etc. They have developed many 'guerrilla zones' in Bihar.

In the beginning, the Naxals entered the rural areas by making minimum wage, honour, equitable land distribution and opposition to the feudal system its issues. Many a time their fight for these causes got bogged down in the vicious circle of Bihar's complex caste structure. In Bihar, Naxalism did not remain an issue confined to merely law and order problem. Land was concentrated in a few hands. After the Green Revolution in Punjab, Bihar became a victim of regional disparity. A continuous fall in the development of agriculture was recorded in the state. By the latter half of the 1990s this process virtually demolished the agrarian system of Bihar.

The state produces approximately tens of thousands of graduates each year. The names of 1,500,000 people are registered in the employment bureau. Government schemes are up for grabs by corrupt wheeler-dealers. A handful of officials, contractors and politicians, have become billionaires by looting government funds. Given this background, young men are attracted to the armed rebellion of the Naxals. A politics run by weapons excites them. To pay for the expenses incurred on their cadres and weapons, the Naxals extort a fat levy from officials and contractors associated with government-run development schemes. Political parties have become less and less dependent on struggles undertaken for the common man. Given this situation, it has become a custom to take up arms even for minor issues.

It is worth noting that in Bihar and Jharkhand the traditional left-wing is shrinking in size and influence. The leftists were wiped out in the 2010 elections in Bihar, but Naxalism is spreading in north Bihar. For the moment, two separate streams, both born of the Naxal movement, are flowing in Bihar. One route is symbolized by the CPI (Liberation), which attempts to coordinate parliamentary and non-parliamentary struggle. The CPI (Maoist), which has chosen the path of armed struggle to establish the political power of the common public, represents the other stream.

However, in 2011 there was new writing on the wall. On one hand, the Naxal movement was expanding, and on the other it was being challenged from within itself. Just as political parties suffered ideological and organizational decline, so the Naxals were victims of this phenomenon.

I have seen some of the highly-publicized heroes of this movement from a close range and know that there was once a Gandhian phase to this movement as well. The use of the words 'Gandhianism' and 'Naxalism' in the same context sound weird, but the early leaders of this movement had definite marks of Gandhian lifestyle and philosophy. Their mutual disagreement was intellectual, but in their personal lives they were living symbols of simplicity, commitment and intellectual clarity. The simple, ethical lifestyle and commitment of these political leaders attracted people to them in a big way. Regardless of the fact that these leaders belonged to the upper castes in the caste structure, but—in the jargon of sociology—they had 'declassed' themselves. They had become the centre of inspiration for social groups around them.

I remember that in 1981 I was living in Hyderabad, having moved there from Bombay. That same year I went to meet Nagbhushan Patnaik (died 1998) in his village of Gunupur in Orissa. It is contiguous with the Srikakulam district of Andhra Pradesh. I travelled there from Vishakhapatnam in an extremely old and ramshackle bus. Then I crossed five rivers, big and small, getting wet in the process. I walked for miles. No one understood Hindi or English. I was scared, too, travelling in a totally unknown, wild and uninhabited region. But it was motivated by an overpowering desire to meet Nagbhushan Patnaik. I was young. In the village I met an extremely old man. He did not know Hindi. With a Hindi-knowing person acting as my interlocutor, I asked him which politicians of the country he knew. His answer was: Mahatma Gandhi. I asked him: 'How and why?' That elderly tribal from Nagbhushan Patnaik's village with his hair and beard all completely white gave a reply that still rings in my mind even after 20 years. He said: 'Gandhiji had come to my village. He was dressed like us. He talked in our interest, not about his family, not about his party.'

Nagbhushan Patnaik's character had a similar aspect, which inspired me to travel 800 km to his village to meet him. He was an extremely well-read, livewire of a man. His father wanted him to be an Indian Administrative Service (IAS) officer. His political consciousness made him become a Naxal. He had a long underground life. Incarcerated in a prison for 12 years. Three years of solitary confinement. Escape from jail. Sentenced to death by hanging. The hanging stayed due to his illness. Victim of dozens of fatal illnesses. A slim, tall and dark-skinned body. I remember to this day that when I met Nagbhushan Patnaik, there was a gleam in his eyes. His failing body was unable to keep up with him but the face had the glow of resolve on it. There was an air of purity and determination about him. He was the very epitome of courage. I had a long talk with him. At that time he was suffering from a 102-degree fever. He said to me: '***Rogon ne nishchay hee filhaal mujhe naakaam banaa diyaa hai, par ichchhaa shakti aur bhee drdh aur mazboot hui hai***' (Diseases have certainly incapacitated me for the time being, but the willpower has become even firmer and stronger).[12]

I wrote the report of our meeting in *Dharmyug*, the highest-selling Hindi magazine, published by the *Times of India*, Mumbai, under the penname 'Ajay'. At that time I used to work in a bank. I was forbidden to write, according to my service rules. For many years the tape of the long conversation remained with me. Nagbhushan Patnaik had also written a letter to me from the Cuttack Government Hospital. Usually I don't keep anything with great care, but that letter remained with me for years. I had to wander to many parts of the country like a vagabond as part of my job and somewhere along the years it went missing.

The village of Gunupur is in the Koraput district of Orissa. Surrounded by rivers, crouched in the lap of mountains, poverty, unemployment and an incompetent system did not let the living standard of the people rise above the level of primitive living. Here, in a zamindar family, was born Nagbhushan Patnaik. I asked him about his background. He said:

> My father was a big zamindar. His personality was totally feudal. Right from childhood a feeling of alienation began to take hold of me due to the way the servants were treated in our household. I could feel the pain of the victims of suffering. When I became a firm communist, I discovered that my father and his cronies were tormenting many helpless poor in a variety of ways. I sided with the downtrodden. A close relative of my father had filed a lawsuit against him. I helped the poor against him. Here I would like to make it clear that a communist is [also] most certainly the son of a father, as well as the father of his own children. As a result, he has love towards his father, and cordiality inside him, but there is no place for feudal sentiments in this relationship. I gave my father every respect that a father deserves, but on political issues I wholeheartedly opposed him and his tenants.

Brilliant by birth, Patnaik always stood first in his class. His memory was outstanding. He became interested in studying philosophy, science, culture and revolutionary literature only in his college days. He would read all night. He said: 'That was the time when I did an intensive and detailed study of the Gita, the Koran, the Bible, the Ramayana and Aurobindo.'

After graduating from college, at his father's wish, he went to Banaras to study:

> In those days I was studying at the Banaras Hindu University. My father's inner wish was that I become an IAS [officer]. But by that time my ideas had matured. Upon finding out about my ideas he stopped funding my education. From there I came to Cuttack. I finished my law studies by teaching private tuition to pay for it. That was the time when I became an

active participant in the activities of the All India Students' Federation. At that time I received inspiration and soul-strength from my brother-in-law. He is my friend, philosopher and teacher.

After this his life became one long hide-and-seek game with conflict. Alongside his legal practice his political activism also grew. Nagbhushan Patnaik did his level best to stop the smuggling of rice across the Andhra-Orissa border that was going on with the connivance of a few powerful and prosperous officials. He would lie down in the path of the bullock-carts carrying the rice and would refuse to move. Until 1964 he remained associated with the CPM.

In 1965-6 he was incarcerated in Tihar jail. He said:

As soon as I stepped out of jail I again jumped into a workers' movement. As a result, I was ordered to leave that place or be arrested. I disobeyed the order and went underground. Then, of course, being underground became an unavoidable part of my life. I was arrested in 1969. Just a few months later, on the night of 8 October, we got together and freed ourselves. The prison walls could not bind us.

Telling me about his arrest and the events following it, he said:

In July 1970, I was again arrested, in Calcutta. With me was another important comrade—Appala Suri. The police alleged that we were on our way to meet Charu Majumdar. In the police station, our hands and feet were tied up and we were thrown on the ground. We were beaten mercilessly. We were strung up upside down. We used to get only a nominal amount of food. My feet had become totally wounded, they had lost all sensation, but they couldn't make me cough up anything. This period of excruciating torture continued nonstop for five days. The torture did come to a stop, but then began the period of harassing us mentally.

He said that scholars well-versed in Marxism and Maoism were brought from far and wide to question him. 'I was quite steadfast in my views, hence they could not make me spill anything on the question of organizational structure. They had to go back disappointed, but they found debating with me quite interesting and fruitful.'

He confessed his love for books:

I love books the most. Right from my student days, the seeds of Marxism and Maoism had begun sprouting in me. I was a student of serious literature. As it is, I have read the entire body of ancient English literature—Dostoevsky, Tolstoy etc., but the revolutionary, blazing poems by Qazi Nazarul Islam lit the revolutionary fire inside me.

Refreshing memories of his underground life, he said:

During the time underground, struggling for our cause, death was face-to-face every single moment. It is mere coincidence that today I am before you. Numerous times bullets have brushed past me, piercing and tearing through friends standing nearby, separating them from us permanently. We used to weep at the passing away of our friends. At the same time, we would also vow to take revenge against a system where there is exploitation and inequality.

During our underground living we had to subsist for months on meat, wild roots and berries, but this is an everyday experience for any revolutionary.

I was a lawyer by profession and politically active, therefore my face was well known to the police and the majority of people. After going underground I had to remain alert and cautious every single moment. At that time innumerable young men struggling against exploitation were killed in Andhra, Kerala and Bengal under the pretext of 'armed encounter [with the police]'.

Whether Nagbhushan Patnaik was underground or in jail, his family members had to face a variety of problems. One of his brothers was in a government job. He would often get transferred for no rhyme or reason. Another of his brothers was tortured by the police. The family faced problems at every step in getting his brothers, sister and daughter married. On the occasion of his sister's marriage—just one day before the wedding—the groom's family refused to go through with it. A senior police officer of that area came to know of this. He himself went to the groom's family and persuaded them to change their mind.

But these incidents did not disturb Nagbhushan. He told me:

I remember I was about to be hanged. My daughter was about to get married. Just a few days before the wedding she came to visit me. She suggested that I apply for parole to be able to attend the wedding. I asked her if I should bow before the government. She understood my feeling and holding her head in her hands she cried out in quite a loud voice. She seized my hand, kept crying for hours, but she clearly told me not to compromise with my beliefs. I looked on silently, stunned.

My father died. I was disturbed. Since I was the senior member of the family, mother requested the government to release me on parole. That order came 15-20 days later. I was asked to leave under the supervision of a few police officers, but I refused. When I was informed that the court had sentenced me to death by hanging, I was not at all surprised, nor did it disturb me. Rather I smiled. The family members appealed to the president for mercy. I opposed this. I never hired any lawyer for my defense, but yes, I did give shape to my internal feelings in the form of poetry. I wrote quite a few poems.

Even today tears flowed from his old mother's eyes from remembering those scenes. I had met her too. She told me:

When I went to meet Nagbhushan after his death sentence, I burst into tears as soon as I saw him, but he was unperturbed. He reasoned with everyone: 'If you want to cry, then don't come to visit me.' He said to me: 'What would you have done if I had died in an accident? There is nothing confusing about death by hanging, no suffering involved. Everything comes to an end in an instant.'

A similar Naxal comes to mind. Vinod Mishra was a brilliant student of the Durgapur Engineering College. From there he joined the Naxal movement and declassed himself. He lived among the people of the villages for whom he was waging his struggle. In 1991 Lalu Prasad Yadav (chief minister of Bihar) commented a few times: 'I come from the poor class [he meant 'caste'], hence I understand the pain of being a Naxal. Those who are not Naxal leaders of this class [he was referring to upper-caste Naxal leaders] are without a mass base.'

But in the elections that took place during his term in office, the public gave massive support to CPI (M-L) in Naxal-influenced areas. They did so because there was not a big gap between Vinod Mishra's life and philosophy. There was ideological difference of opinion among the Naxals of that generation, but they were always guided by the Gandhian philosophy of unity between ends and means. In his underground days, 'Vinod Mishra' was a myth. For years the debate raged about whether it was a Naxal pseudonym or a real name. When he gave up his underground existence and entered public life, his party made up its mind to take part in electoral politics and started walking the path of changing society by means of elections.

Thus the earlier Gandhian character of Naxalism was a source of inspiration for society. It is now on its way out. It could be the effect of liberalization. It could be the growing effect of consumerism and materialism or the effect of the breakup of Russia and the changes in China. The Naxal movement is also now not attracting talent on the large scale that it used to earlier. This is true not only for the Naxal movement, however. Today from left-wing to right-wing, no political party is able to find workers. The RSS is not getting new entrants. In a way this is the era of depoliticalization. So what is it about the Naxals that attracts the poor?

Where there is large-scale unemployment, food shortages, absence of social justice and starvation, the ideas propagated by the Naxals attract people. People have lost faith in political parties. They see the statements made by them in their election manifestos about the steps that they promise to take against poverty and starvation—and then they see their conduct as soon as they come to power. Given this scenario, Naxals—who live in the jungle, choose a hard life and live every moment on the edge of life and death—even now inspire them.

NOTES

1. *Hindustan Times*, 28 January 2011.
2. *Times of India*, 29 January 2011.
3. Babulal Marandi, *Hai re! Ugravad* (New Delhi: Prabhat Prakashan, 2005). Marandi's son was killed, apparently by Maoists, in 2007. *Times of India*, 11 November 2007.
4. The Member of Parliament Local Area Development Scheme (MPLADS) provides Members of Parliament with a fund which can be spent on projects in their constituency. It has been copied in some states. http://mplads.nic.in/welcome.html (accessed on 1 May 2011).
5. See *Prabhat Khabar*, 5 November 2006.
6. See K. Srinivas Reddy, 'A Road that Changed Their Lives', the *Hindu*, 10 June 2006, on which the following account is based.
7. The allegiance of independent MLAs was keenly contested when Jharkhand government was formed in 2005. *Times of India*, 9 March 2005, http://articles.timesofindia.indiatimes.com/2005-03-09/india/27859456_1_jharkhand-mlas-trust-vote-senior-bjp-leaders (accessed on 1 May 2011).
8. Mary Tyler, *My Years in an Indian Prison* (London: Gollancz, 1977).
9. Author's own notes.
10. *Deshvrati*, 13 March 1969.
11. Author's own notes.
12. *Dharmyug*, 8 November 1989, p. 13.

CHAPTER 17

The Maoist Rebellion: A Journey to Out-land

SUDEEP CHAKRAVARTI

It is increasingly difficult for me to accept the notion that rebellion will disappear in India even if the current cycle of extreme left-wing rebellion ends. There is reason to believe there will be other cycles—as has been proven several times over since the outbreak of peasant rebellion in Naxalbari in 1967—until governance, justice and development are delivered instead of corruption and inefficiency.

Since 2009, several key Maoist leaders have been apprehended in India, and many killed in operations and extra-legal covert action undertaken by intelligence operatives and special forces of police and paramilitary. The list includes members of the Politburo of the Communist Party of India (Maoist), the leading left-wing rebel conglomerate, as well as members of its Central Committee, and several zonal and state committees that span the country. In late April 2011, three leaders of the party's Central Committee were arrested in Bihar. It was the result of a joint operation carried out with the security apparatus of two other rebellion-affected states: centrally-located Chhattisgarh and southern Andhra Pradesh. Increasing interaction, sharing of information and coordination among central and state government, police, intelligence and special force networks have marked anti-Maoist operations since 2009. And my discussions and interviews with rebel insiders, security officials and security analysts confirm that the current cycle of extreme left-wing rebellion had not previously been pushed to the wall in the way that it has been in 2011.

The reason for my disquiet is rooted in India's recent history. I would term the present cycle of rebellion Mark IV. This follows Mark I, the 'original' 1967 spark lit over sharecropping disputes in the northern part of West Bengal state that was co-opted by the radical

Communist Party of India (Marxist-Leninist) and rapidly exported to other parts of the country, riding on farmland anger and urban intellectual angst that provided much of the leadership. That was brutally suppressed across much of India by the early 1970s. But Marks II and III surfaced in the 1980s and 1990s in several radical incarnations, to be also put down, splintered, and dissipated—but not fully ended. Enough anger and resentment remained over skewed agriculture policy, societal mistreatment of low-caste citizens and indigenous tribal populations, and staggering levels of corruption, to rebuild and grow into a force that in various degrees affects a third of India's districts, and led Prime Minister Manmohan Singh to famously declare in 2006 that 'Maoism' was India's 'greatest internal security threat'.

The prime minister deliberately missed the point: India's socio-economic ills and deficiencies pose the greatest threat to internal security. Even as Mark IV is under pressure, we need to consider why people—Indians with no wish to secede from India, unlike rebels in Jammu & Kashmir and India's troubled 'Far-East'—choose to go up against the undeniable might of India's state apparatus. After all, Maoist rebels in India are decidedly Indian. What drives them to repeatedly pick up bows and arrows, spears, axes, and largely looted weapons ranging from ancient .303 rifles to more modern INSAS carbines and Kalashnikov automatic weapons to defend their position and everyday aspiration? It is now beyond doubt that serious flaws exist in a system that has repeatedly annihilated left-wing movements since the time of India's Independence only to have these rearing their heads more emphatically with each cycle of resurgence, alongside India's explosive economic growth, enhanced social mobility, and greater presence on the global stage.

Much resentment is rooted in inefficient administration, corruption and even the severely fractious caste system that frequently triggers outrageous acts that range from brutalizing or killing people of a lower caste for taking water from a community well, or crossing the fields of a person from an upper caste. The roots of rebellion, however, remain deeply embedded in the system and attitudes of governance that two decades of economic reform and media revolution have not been able to significantly diminish. This drives official strategy and tactics in a range of areas, from economic policy to decisions about how the Maoist issue should be dealt with.

In February 2007 I heard Raman Singh, chief minister of

Chhattisgarh, compare a vigilante force aimed at eroding Maoist rebel influence in largely tribal-inhabited areas of Chhattisgarh to Mohandas Karamchand Gandhi's way of non-violence. Singh was addressing a security conference in the state capital of Raipur, a half-day's drive from areas under Maoist sway.

Called Salwa Judum (updated as 'Koya Commandos'), this state-sponsored vigilante group comprising tribal inhabitants participates with state police and central government paramilitary to carry out operations in villages and hamlets to flush out Maoist sympathizers and frighten the rest into flight, incarceration or submission. As a matter of record documented by Indian civil and human rights groups and acknowledged by the Supreme Court in several cases, this entailed destroying homes and food stock, rape, torture, maiming and killing. Tribal people were set against each other by exploiting legitimate anger against the heavy-handedness of Maoist rebels in these areas and turning it into a cynical exercise of reclamation. This ranges from innocents caught in the crossfire—what security experts and practitioners term 'collateral damage'—to innocents attacked in revenge for, say, rebels killing security forces. Such violence can also be pre-emptive, to frighten people from offering support to rebels.

'Salwa Judum cannot be defeated', the chief minister asserted at one point in his speech. He carried on without missing a beat, even as several police and paramilitary officers in the room had the grace to look elsewhere: 'It will be written a hundred years from now. Salwa Judum is showing Gandhi is alive, showing non-violence is alive. . . . Salwa Judum is like the fragrance of the forest in summer.'

As India raucously claims the decade of 2010s as its own, Salwa Judum—and the Chhattisgarh government—have been censured by judges of the Supreme Court, alongside continuous criticism by civil and human rights activists and prominent commentators in India's media. Several senior serving police officials that I interviewed in the course of researching my 2008 book *Red Sun: Travels in Naxalite Country*—Maoists are often interchangeably referred to as 'Naxalites'—have gone on record to say that the battle against Maoist rebels cannot be won using such approaches. These officers, from Chhattisgarh as well as states like West Bengal and Maharashtra, both affected by extreme left-wing movements, said that, at best, police and paramilitary were mere firefighters in a situation brought about by long years of non-governance, mis-governance, corruption, and lack of socio-economic development. Similar sentiments were expressed by other police officers directly engaged in combating Maoists when I travelled in these states and Orissa state in 2009 and 2010 to update *Red Sun* and report for my columns on human rights and business in the New Delhi-based *Mint* financial daily (www.livemint.com).

Such sentiments are underscored by a document of the Planning Commission of India. 'It becomes more vital in the eyes of the administration to prevent the strengthening or growth of Naxalite influence than to answer that just aspiration', recorded *Development Challenges in Extremist Affected Areas: Report of an Expert Group to Planning Commission* (2008). 'Often,' it continued, 'any individual who speaks out against the powerful is dubbed a Naxalite and jailed or otherwise silenced. . . . What is to be pointed out here is that the method chosen by the Government to deal with the Naxalite phenomenon has increased the people's distrust . . . and consequent unrest.'

The heavy-handedness of the anti-Maoist battle includes scant regard for collateral damage and extends to economic activity. All too often, resettlement and rehabilitation for projects are undertaken without understanding the dynamics that operate in areas where a project, whether extractive or manufacturing, inevitably displaces people. This happens physically, economically and emotionally and in ways that remote CEOs, business planners, accountants and engineers either do not, or may not care to, understand.

In India, as in several other places in the world, businesses also feel strengthened, even invulnerable, if they are in partnership with a government entity. Several high-profile cases fall into this category in the mining and metals industries and automobile and power sectors in West Bengal, Orissa, Chhattisgarh, Jharkhand and Karnataka. All these states are deeply affected by the Maoist rebellion and prospecting agenda. They also feel powerful compulsions to exploit natural and industrial resources that are often in zones inhabited by tribal and other disadvantaged people.

In these situations, the doctrine of Eminent Domain—which permits government to expropriate land for the 'greater good'—is often abused in spirit and execution. Resettlement takes precedence over rehabilitation. It is an open secret that state governments typically look to a Memorandum of Understanding as a policy achievement and set out to make arrangements for tax breaks and to acquire and clear intended land on behalf of business. These five resource-rich states have proved particularly susceptible to the MOU *mantra*.

In these places, deliberate, lamentable misunderstandings lead to negative energy—the sort that local activists and their more aggressive cousins, Maoist rebels—are increasingly adept at leveraging. I travelled in the Kalinganagar area in Orissa in mid-2010, the centre of a massive work-in-progress industrial area of largely iron and steel manufacture owing to its proximity to iron ore-bearing regions. Villagers who feared displacement spoke to me of the option of aligning with Maoist rebels to hold their ground. It is a volatile area. In January 2006 a dozen tribal villagers were shot dead by state police forces as they protested acquisition of land by the Orissa state government on behalf of Tata Steel. In the south of the state, activists and villagers spoke of similar options to protest against the acquisition of their land—three villages' worth, along with forests—for a mega project by South Korea's Pohang Iron and Steel Company (POSCO). In the state's north-west regions, in the Niyamgiri hills, tribal inhabitants refuse to allow representatives of Vedanta Plc. to mine bauxite from a mountain they worship as holy. It is unsurprising for people to seek redress, or turn to violence, if they do not receive administrative or judicial endorsement—let alone understanding—of their constitutional right to land and livelihood.

Such realities of exclusion lie at the core of my belief that India is very likely heading for more churn, not less. This is the reality of what I call 'Out-Land'—out of sight of the urban, middle-class India (In-Land) and so, less worthy of policy and media attention.

If India proves incapable of dealing with such intense dynamics, greater schism is inevitable. India is already a country of vast city-states. The National Capital Region that radiates from Delhi, Mumbai-Pune, Mumbai-Ahmedabad, Chennai-Bengaluru, Kolkata and other emerging metropolitan hubs will grow steadily. Special Economic Zones proximate to these areas are also a reality. It isn't far-fetched to foresee these 'In-Land' hubs becoming autonomous areas with controlled access, and with vast less developed spaces becoming lawless, impoverished zones beyond the pale of governance by the Republic of India—an 'Out-Land', ruled by armies of rebels and ambitious warlords.

But that lies in a future that may yet seem too distant for India's policy makers and its somewhat giddy middle classes, content that they belong to the 500 million or so that are now counted as members of India's development party. The Maoist blueprint may offer a more immediate agenda.

While no movement can remain unaffected by the hits the Maoist rebellion has recently suffered, it is reasonable to expect the rebellion to reach out to more recruits in both rural and urban areas, consolidate their areas of operation, spread propaganda and recruitment in new areas, and train and develop leaders. It is also reasonable to expect Maoists to become more elusive as they attempt to counter penetration of their ranks and leadership by security and intelligence agencies.

This is in keeping with the Maoist strategy. Several strategy-and-tactics documents of the erstwhile Communist Party of India (Marxist-Leninist) People's War, and the entity it merged into in 2004, the Communist Party of India (Maoist), point to the necessity of recruiting cadres in cities both to support and provide recruits for the People's Liberation Guerrilla Army—the cadre-based, largely rural force that India's Ministry of Home Affairs estimates at 20,000. These documents also speak of the need to build alliances with civil society groups, and infiltrate police, paramilitary and administrative machineries. Such documents dwell on the need to spread and consolidate the rebellion in rural areas and, whenever practicable, break into urban India.

A media release from the Communist Party of India (Maoist) in mid-April 2011 reiterated this philosophy, seizing upon a renewed spate of corruption scandals:

> Our Party believes that only through the united, well-organized and militant mass struggles, corruption can be put to an end. Our Party calls upon the people of our country not to get satisfied by the namesake laws and forming new committees to frame such laws by the government and not to end these struggles, but to continue with firm conviction. We call upon workers, peasants, students, intellectuals, employees, pro-people Gandhians and all other patriotic forces to come forward and to form a broad alliance to fight against corruption which has affected our country. Our Party appeals to raise voice against all these thieves and dacoits who are involved in endless corruption, scams and plunder and who have stashed trillions of rupees of black money in Swiss banks, [and] have no right to be in power even for a moment.

The Maoist rebellion is less about Mao and more about a mirror it holds to India's failings as a nation. This country has much to celebrate each day as it moves ahead. But Maoists, and others like them, will continue to remind us of India's unfinished agenda of all-round development and progress. I fear that the battle will get more intense and bloodier as Maoists fight back and gather tinder from the exploitation of common folk in the jungles and rural areas.

There, innocents find themselves caught, on the one hand, in the middle of a war between Maoists and the state, and, on the other hand, as the victims of compacts between governments and businesses to acquire land, aggressively and indiscriminately, for mining and manufacturing. It is tragic, and, more than Maoism, such practices will likely bring untold socio-political grief.

CHAPTER 18

Weapons of Mass Desperation*

SHOMA CHAUDHURY

On 22 September 2009, India woke up to the news that the Delhi Police had captured a top Naxal ideologue, 58-year-old Kobad Ghandy. Ghandy was a South Bombay Parsi who had grown up in a giant sea-facing house in Worli, attended the Doon School and then studied accountancy in London before returning to India to work with the most destitute of Indian citizens in Maharashtra. He went underground in the 1970s. Home Minister P. Chidambaram called Ghandy the state's 'most important Naxal catch'.

Over the year 2009, the Home Ministry had been planning a major armed offensive against the Naxals, particularly in Chhattisgarh. According to reports, the plan involved stationing around 75,000 troops in the heartland of India, including special Central Reserve Police Force (CRPF) commandos, the Indo-Tibetan Border Police Force (ITBP) and the Border Security Force (BSF). Scattered newspaper accounts spoke of forces being withdrawn from Jammu & Kashmir and the north-east; there is also talk of bringing in the feared Rashtriya Rifles—a battalion created specially for counter-insurgency work—and the purchase of bomb trucks, bomb blankets, bomb baskets, and sophisticated new weaponry. Home Minister P. Chidambaram has also said that if necessity dictates, he will bring in the special forces of the army.

The decision to launch such a massive armed operation on home ground should have triggered animated political, civil society and media debate. But Operation Green Hunt—as the offensive is being termed—has been gathering force in almost-complete silence. Prime Minister Manmohan Singh and Home Minister P. Chidambaram have variously called Naxals or 'Maoists' 'the gravest threat to India's

*First published in *Tehelka*, 3 October 2009. Edited and reproduced with permission.

internal security'. Perhaps a military offensive against them is the answer, but is it the only answer? Is it the best answer? Will it provide a solution? Who will be impacted by this offensive? What will be its repercussions? Who are we really declaring war on? What are we declaring war on? Are we going into this with eyes wide open? Is there anything we should have learned from the seemingly irreparable psychological mess in Kashmir and the north-east? These are the questions a democratic society should be asking. With such a significant operation looming on the horizon, what can excuse the complete absence of debate from national political parties?

But silence, perhaps, is only the lesser worry. In September 2009 the government announced an ad blitzkrieg as part of its psychological offensive. 'Naxals are nothing but coldblooded murderers', the ad screamed across all major news dailies. The visual showed a series of men, women and children brutally killed by Naxals.

On the night of 22 September, a 24-hour news channel, Times Now, hosted a prime-time debate on the significance of Ghandy's arrest. Watching the show was like straying into a child's playroom, watching the grave judgements of infants playing at Good and Evil. As an individual point of view it would have counted for nothing, but as the voice of Times Now, currently deemed the most popular English channel, the television show's unthinking edit line seems symptomatic of a wider, urban, English-speaking constituency. Coupled with the government ads, it presents the disturbing prospect of a public discourse that is marked by reductive official propaganda on the one side and infantile ignorance and simple-mindedness on the other. We can afford neither.

At the heart of the Naxal riddle, there are three primary questions: Who is a Naxal? What is one's position on violence as a tool of struggle? And why is Naxalism on the rise across the country? To understand the first, try a useful metaphor. Imagine fish in water. Naxal leaders are the fish, finite, identifiable (even punishable) and the water is the vast, infinite constituency they speak for and swim in.

As Kobad Ghandy proves, a Naxal ideologue, commander or politburo leader can come from any milieu: the disempowered Dalits of Andhra Pradesh, the destitute tribals of Chhattisgarh, the middle-class intellectuals of West Bengal or the privileged rich of Mumbai. These 'informed revolutionaries' function at two levels. At a political level, they do not believe in parliamentary democracy, where they see power still concentrated in the hands of the feudal upper class and their long-term objective is to seize state power for the people through armed struggle. In this, they threaten the sovereignty of the Indian state. Many humanist thinkers including men like K. Balagopal of the Human Rights Forum, who was involved in brokering peace talks between the government and Naxals in Andhra Pradesh in 2004, believe the state is within its rights to confront them. He says, 'The Maoists themselves would not tolerate such a challenge if they came to power.' Balagopal is also critical of Naxal leaders creating 'liberated zones' where the Indian state cannot function. 'If they claim to be the voice of the people, can they pursue a political agenda that injures people—either by their actions or the repercussions they invite? Does the current tribal generation of Chhattisgarh want to sacrifice itself for a utopian future that may never come?'

It is true that in this prolonged ideological war, many Naxal attacks like the horrific one on the Ranibodli police station in 2007 and the more recent one in Rajnandgaon embrace brutal tactics and almost fetishize violence. Even if these attacks are against an oppressive and corrupt police, it is a no-brainer to condemn them and say one is opposed to this violence. Or that the perpetrators should be punished.

But like dozens of other intellectuals, Balagopal points out that it is suicidal to focus only on this ideological war or resort to extrajudicial means alone to quell it. Can Naxalism really be wiped out by brute counter-force? If that were so, Siddhartha Shankar Ray's crackdown in West Bengal in the 1970s should have nailed it for all time. But the fact is, while stories of their own coercions are true, Naxal leaders enjoy wide support because they also espouse socio-economic causes and empower people that the Indian state has ignored—criminally—for 60 years. Most Naxal cadres, therefore, are not 'informed revolutionaries' fighting a conceptual war: they are beleaguered tribals and Dalits fighting local battles for basic survival and rights. Bela Bhatia, an activist, says she met a *mazdoor* (labourer) in Bihar who was part of the cadre. 'You can call me a Naxal or whatever you want,' he said, 'I have picked up the gun to get my three kilos of *annaj* (grain).'

The point is, should the Indian state be declaring armed war on its most despairing people? Is there no other way to empower them and wean them away from the gun and the seduction of the 'informed revolutionary'?

Lalgarh, in fact, is a textbook case for the Naxal riddle. Since early 2009, mainstream Indian media had been agog about the 'Naxal menace' in Lalgarh. But almost no one thought to ask, was the flare up in Lalgarh in May 2009 *sui generis*? Does an entire society become Maoist overnight? Very few bothered to report that the trouble in Lalgarh began after the Maoists attempted an assassination of Chief Minister Buddhadeb Bhattacharya earlier in 2009. In retaliation, the West Bengal police rounded up and brutalized scores of innocent tribal boys in neighbouring Lalgarh, who had nothing to do with the attack. After several months of general, untargeted police oppression, angry and desperate, the tribal community spontaneously organized themselves as a resistance force, fighting the might of the Indian state with nothing more than traditional tools—pick-axes, bows and arrows. A few weeks later, Kishenji, a Maoist leader from Andhra Pradesh, arrived to raise the ante, teaching tactics of struggle, meshing solidarity with guns and advice. The state responded with increased force and brought in paramilitary forces—a dry run for Operation Green Hunt. After several days of heavy fire the state, ironically using Maoist jargon, declared that Lalgarh had been 'liberated'. But the truth is it has been on burn ever since.

As Himanshu Kumar, a Gandhian and the only human rights activist on ground zero in faraway Dantewada where Operation Green Hunt was launched, said,

> We can all be agreed on the premise that Naxalism is a problem, but why are these poor people attracted to a politics that will end in death? Have we created such a heinous system that death is more attractive than the deprivations and humiliations this system doles out? If that is so, why should I defend this system? All that these people want is food, health care, school, clothes and their legitimate right over their land. Yet, instead of weaning them away by strengthening the democratic process, if we are going to run our democracy only on the strength of weapons, I fear we are entering a dangerous and irreparable state. We are headed for civil war.

Men like Himanshu should know. For 17 years, he has functioned like an Intensive Care Unit on the edges of a wounded society, providing education and health care, painstakingly drawing tribal people into the electoral and constitutional process. The government, loath to undertake the trouble, has been happy to outsource its functions to him. Yet now, it is deaf to his wisdom. Worse, it hasn't even consulted him.

Which brings us to the element of water in the Naxal metaphor. People who say human rights activists and the questions they raise are anti-national would be surprised to know what men like Prime Minister Manmohan Singh and Finance Minister Pranab Mukherjee themselves have had to say earlier about the Naxal riddle. Not to mention a galaxy of judges and constitutionalists.

In 2006, the Planning Commission asked an expert committee for a report on development challenges in 'extremist affected areas'. The committee comprised senior officers like former Uttar Pradesh police chief Prakash Singh; former intelligence head, Ajit Doval; senior bureaucrats like B. Bandopadhyay, E.A.S. Sarma, S.R. Sankaran and B.D. Sharma; and activists like Bela Bhatia and K. Balagopal. The report submitted in October 2008 had some visionary analysis and recommendations.

'The main support for the Naxalite movement', it said, 'comes from Dalits and adivasi tribals'—the element of water, the infinite constituency in which Naxal leaders swim. Dalits and *adivasis* comprise a staggering one-fourth of India's population, yet are disproportionately destitute and low on the Human Development Index scale. Worse, they suffer the most humiliation and indignity: the proverbial insult to injury. The report is an exhaustive anthology of the causes for rural discontent and violence—recording meticulous data and case studies—but at the heart of its argument, it places the 'structural violence implicit in our social and economic system' as the key explanation for Naxalite violence. Slamming the neo-liberal directional shift in government policies, it urges a 'development centric' rather than 'security centric' approach to the Naxal problem.

Curiously, in 2005, human rights lawyer Kannabiran had written a letter to Dr Manmohan Singh reminding him of his own report as a Planning Commission Member in 1982 and one written by Pranab Mukherjee in 2002 that had come to the same conclusion. As Bela Bhatia says, 'With all this insight and understanding already with them, it is completely mystifying why they should go against their own intuition and recommendation and take a security-centric route. Actually,' she adds, 'it is not mystifying. It only makes the character of the Indian State more clear.'

This 'character' gets even more depressing when you know that on 15 September 2009, Arjun Sengupta, former economic adviser to Prime Minister Indira Gandhi, also wrote that 'Naxalism is a cry that must be heard'. Responding to Manmohan Singh's admission that despite the state's best efforts to contain the 'Naxal menace', violence was still on the rise, Sengupta wrote powerfully,

> It is important to understand why this is so and in what sense Naxalite violence is different from other violent outbursts. Although it has always expressed itself as a breach of law and order with violence, murder, extortion and acts of heinous crimes, it may not be prudent to think of every protest movement of the disaffected people as a simple issue of law and order violation, and calling for its brutal suppression. This form of extremism, indeed, goes beyond law and order, fanning some deep-seated grievance. We must try to resolve those problems first, as otherwise the violence will remain insurmountable.

Way back in 1996, Justice M.N. Rao of the Andhra Pradesh High Court had also remarked in a judgement, 'While left-wing extremism is viewed as a problem by the administration, it is increasingly being perceived as a solution to their problems by the alienated masses.' Why is this so? That's a question every self-styled jingoistic nationalist must ask themselves.

As Sengupta reminds the prime minister, he is right to fear that Naxal violence will raise its head again and again, because at its heart is the deeper structural violence that our democratic republic refuses to address: a violence that forces 77 per cent of Indians to live on less than Rs. 20 a day while 5 per cent enjoy lives that border on obscene excess.

Structural violence: that's an imaginative vacuum. For most urban Indians, the lives of tribals and Dalits have no meaning, no face, no flesh. Our books no longer write of it, our films no longer evoke it, our journalists no longer cover it. It's not just the poverty; it's bumping into a face of the Indian state you have never seen before: brutal, illegal, pimped out to serve the interests of a few. Unless one travels into the silent smoky hole in the heart of this country, the remote jungles of Chhattisgarh, Orissa, Jharkhand, Andhra Pradesh, the desolate corners of Uttar Pradesh, Bihar and Rajasthan, one cannot feel the dread of this question: how will Operation Green Hunt solve this? You might stealth-march a mythic army of COBRA commandoes into this imaginative vacuum, but how will that dissolve the 'two categories of human beings' our nation has created? Operation Green Hunt may kill several hundred 'informed revolutionaries' and several thousand of the despairing poor who have taken up arms, but how will it address the birth of new anger—anger born out of an old wound?

As anthropologist and historian Ramachandra Guha says, 'It's like a house with three rooms. One room was already on fire. Instead of dousing that, you willfully set fire to another room, then bulldoze the whole structure down.'

One of the key architects of Operation Green Hunt, Home Secretary G.K. Pillai sits in a giant office in powerful North Block. At first meeting, he doesn't seem the average cynic you expect Indian bureaucrats to be. An amiable, thoughtful man, he says he's seen long years of service in the north-east and knows what a security-centric approach can do to a people, how it can trigger a world of smoke and mirrors where nothing is what it seems and everyone is chasing someone's shadow. He seems open and ready to listen. More, he is full of surprisingly honest admissions: Manipur is a society in collective depression, he says. Yes, raising the Salwa Judum in Chhattisgarh (which human rights activists have been crying hoarse about) was wrong; yes, the Naxals have often taken up causes and done work that the government should have. But, he adds, their violent disruptions are a real deterrence for governance. You have no argument with that.

According to him, then, Operation Green Hunt was planned as a kind of 'area domination'. 'We want to take back control of the land; but we will only fire if we are fired against. Lalgarh is the model; we want no collateral damage. Our real success will be in restoring civil administration in this area. Public Distribution System, mobile medical vans, stronger police *chowkis*, schools—that's our goal.' You feel eager to believe him.

Part of the problem of administering the tribal villages in the jungles of Chhattisgarh is that they are lonely and farflung; also few in the district or political administration know the tribal languages. In 2009, Operation Green Hunt had been long in the planning. Battalions of CRPF men and paramilitary forces across the country were given crash courses for the impending operation. The centre sanctioned 20 new schools in jungle warfare; invited crores worth of bids for military equipment. Is there a similar hot-foot programme for training, sensitizing and incentivizing the civil administration, you ask. Has he invited civil society activists in the region for their inputs? Mr Pillai has a sudden shocked moment of self-recognition.

No, he admits, and scribbles 'training' and 'dialogue' on a yellow notepad.

There is a month to go before Operation Green Hunt is launched. A familiar despair sprouts: the gap between stated intention and action. And miles of paper and good advice gathering dust in the Planning Commission.

Today, the biggest riddle for anybody concerned about a just and equal world is the dilemma of violence as a tool of political struggle. When the government shows such poor intention, when it is completely deaf to peaceful people's movements like the Bhopal gas victims', or the tribal resistance to bauxite mining in Niyamgiri, or the Narmada Andolan, is one justified in asking the poor to defang themselves, unless one is willing to step out of one's comfort zone and share their lives of helpless *status quo*?

Should one distinguish between Naxal violence and spontaneous rural violence? Yet, in a democratic society, how can violence of any kind be condoned? Where does that leave democratic practice?

Despite these internal tussles, almost the entire human rights community is agreed that not only is Naxal violence to be condemned, but subdued. Increased and international access to weaponry has led to escalating violence. As Prakash Singh, a widely respected retired police chief, says, 'The Naxals used to move in *dalams* [cells] of 20. That's gone up to a 100. They have sophisticated weapons and their attacks have become more brutal. We have to show that such armed insurrection will not be tolerated.'

The disagreements arise over strategy and efficacy. A top security expert who wishes not to be named but is generally considered a hawk, has serious doubts over Operation Green Hunt. Ironically, he voices the anxiety of a wide range of human rights activists.

> To attempt this kind of an action by police forces against your own land and people is a dangerous trap. We usually reserve such operations for hostile territory. The police are supposed to go after particular individuals—say, Ram Lal, a criminal. But in an operation of this kind, you don't even know who Ram Lal is, it is very difficult to know who he is or get accurate intelligence on his movements. You might end up killing Ram Lal's relatives or his whole village. And if you don't hold inquests, you'll never know who you killed.

Kashmir and the north-east are bleeding, painful reminders: once paramilitary forces or the army moves in, you can never really withdraw. No bureaucrat or military strategist or powerful minister can control the vicious logic of paranoia, fake killings, genuine mistakes and revenge that sets in. When friend and family can be an informer, everyone is an enemy.

Already, this helpless cycle had started to turn in Chhattisgarh. In September 2009, in the first of its assaults, a company of 100 COBRA commandos set off to destroy an alleged Naxal arms factory in Chintagufa area. They were caught in Naxal fire. Seven COBRAs were killed. In turn, they claimed to have killed nine Naxals (whose bodies they say they have) and many more they claim the Naxals dragged away. The government has tried to pass this off as a big triumph. But the deadly smoke and mirrors game has already begun. Villagers claim the COBRAs made no kills and had dragged innocents out of villages to tot some up, among them an old man and woman. Chhattisgarh Director General of Police (DGP) Vishwaranjan does not help matters by refusing to answer questions: 'I don't have any details', he says. An odd answer for a DGP. Plus, there's the wound of six COBRAs dead in the first sortee.

As Operation Green Hunt kicks into top gear, all these problems will magnify. The hallucinations of the impregnable forest. Extremists who disappear, leaving villagers to bear the brunt of the commandos' ire. Paranoia within and without, revenge and, as in the Salwa Judum, innocent tribals caught between the fury of the Naxals and the fury of the state.

Pressure will create equal and opposite counter-pressure. Prime Minister Manmohan Singh can't seem to grasp this simple physical equation. The impact of the Salwa Judum was to drive more tribals into the arms of Naxals. Operation Green Hunt promises to set the place on fire. When Binayak Sen spoke against the Salwa Judum, he was jailed. Now, when Himanshu Kumar is warning about impending civil war, no one is listening.

Himanshu Kumar implores that government sends in 'Not commandos. Send in health workers and schoolteachers protected by the CRPF. Show the tribal people hope and they will choose life over death.' But the weight of his voice does not sway even a mote of dust in the corridors of the Home Ministry.

There is one final silent piece in the escalating Naxal violence that has gripped the country: neo-liberal land grabbing and tribal rights. It is no coincidence that a majority of the Naxal leadership today is from Andhra Pradesh. According to journalist N. Venugopal, the roots of this go back to the Telengana movement of 1946-51, which was abruptly withdrawn by the Communist Party. In the Andhra Second Five-Year Plan (1956), 60 lakh acres of surplus land was identified. Yet by the time the Land Ceiling Act was passed in 1973, and enough concessions had been made to rich landowners, the state said only 17 lakh acres of surplus land was available, and it distributed only four. Land, livelihood and liberation were the clarion calls then. Still driven by that unfulfilled aspiration, most leaders today are from the families of the 1946-51 movement.

E.A.S. Sarma, former commissioner of tribal welfare and former secretary, expenditure and economic affairs, unlocks the real heart of the matter. 'I am totally against violence of any kind and a firm believer in democratic process,' says he.

> But Left extremism is a secondary issue. How many tribals even know there is a government? Their only experience of the state is the police, contractors, and real estate goons. Besides, the Fifth Schedule of the Constitution grants tribals complete rights over their traditional land and forests and prohibits private companies from mining on their land. This constitutional schedule was upheld by the Samatha judgement of the Supreme Court (1997). If successive governments lived by the spirit of the Constitution and this judgement, tribal discontent would automatically recede.

Sarma is probably right. Human rights activists have long argued that the real intention of the Salwa Judum in Chhattisgarh was to capture tribal land—brimming-rich with minerals—and hand it over to private companies. The fact that 600 tribal villages have been evacuated in the last few years gives credence to this theory. If tribal people no longer live on that land, the inconvenient Fifth Schedule of the Constitution will not apply.

Given that the Supreme Court directed that the Salwa Judum was to be dismantled, perhaps, Operation Green Hunt is the second lap. In any case, whether for ill-intention, poor execution, or unplanned collateral damage, there is much to fear in the impending operation.

In the meantime, we would all do well to read the Fifth Schedule of the constitution.

CHAPTER 19

Soundings from Maoist Territory

KUNAL MAJUMDER

On 6 April 2010, Maoists ambushed a heavily armed Central Reserve Police Force (CRPF) battalion in the jungles of Dantewada in Chhattisgarh, and blew up an armoured vehicle. Within hours, 76 soldiers were dead.

Four days later we received an anonymous call. It was an invite from the Naxals. My photographer and I flew down to Raipur, the capital of Chhattisgarh, and took a bus as instructed by the caller. At no point along the 400-km stretch that links Raipur with Dantewada did we sight a single major blockade or armed guards.

Though Bastar is a backward area, the road was pleasantly broad and level—no doubt to service the large number of mining multinationals that operate in this iron ore-rich region of Chhattisgarh. In the bus I was really surprised to find no talk of the recent carnage—other than a stray comment from the driver towards the journey's end when we were about to reach Dantewada of how not the Maoists but the CRPF men were in hiding due to fear that it could be their turn next time. After an eight-hour journey, we got another call telling us where to get down and which guest-house to put up in. We were picked up by an escort the next morning, who took us to the edge of a forest.

Our guide Geeta, in her late twenties, clad in a faded sari and armed with a single-barrel gun spoke hardly a word despite all my tries. She was also an expert in the art of delaying. Each time one of us asked her how much further we are going, she would dodge us with half-liners like, 'Let's cross this hillock first', or 'Just across the field'.

Women form a major chunk of the Maoist cadres and many of them are among the top commanders. Even during my visit, I found an equal proportion of men and women in the party cadre. Apart from women participation, quick tribunal justice has been a key attraction for the tribals. A poor tribal is petrified to go to a police station when his hen is stolen or his cycle goes missing. The corrupt policeman asks him for bribe and harasses him. The Maoist gives him instant justice.

As we went up and down the hillocks, groups of 8 to 15 year-old tribal kids would stop to greet us with their customary *lal salaams.* They could have been mistaken for your neighbourhood children; only their bows and arrows gave them away. It was much later, during our interface with the Maoist leaders, that we learnt they were actually members of the party's Balak Sangathan, a large roving network of young members who are involved in health care, education, and cultural activities—and, most importantly, in 'identifying enemies'.

After eight hours of walking, which included a lunch-cum-tea break, we reached a village—wooden huts with thatched roofs, a few coconut and mango trees, and idle cattle ambling all around: the usual Chhattisgarh pastoral scene. Geeta pointed to the hut in which we would be spending the night and said we are going to start again tomorrow morning. Saying that, she disappeared into the hut. Minutes later, she emerges dressed up in battle fatigues.

It was stifling hot when we had started, but by around 7 p.m., it started getting cooler. As we chatted and sipped the tea made by the tribal women—our hosts of the moment—the Maoists 'guarding' us sprang up and ran towards one of the huts. It was already quite dark and had started drizzling.

In a few more minutes two men, both in their mid-forties, dressed in civvies, AK-47 rifles swinging from their shoulders appeared. After the customary *lal salaams*, one of them introduced himself as Ramanna *alias* Ravula Srinivas, the 44-year-old chief planner of the Dantewada attack. Accompanying him was 48-year-old Ganesh Ueike, the party's political strategist.

Both Ramanna and Ganesh were from Andhra Pradesh. They came to Chhattisgarh some 30 years back. Since then they have never gone back. Not even once did they revisit their village or keep contact with their parents or relatives. During the 15-hour interaction that followed we were told in great detail of how the attack was planned and executed. Ramanna, secretary of the south Bastar regional committee of the CPI (Maoist), at times became ecstatic as he told us about the 'highest casualties our cadre has ever inflicted on the Indian anti-Naxalite security forces in a single day'. Ramanna's father was a farmhand; he had been only to school and spoke in Telugu-accented Hindi. But Ueike, a B.Sc. from Osmania University, was quite fluent in English. In the last few years, there has been an increase of Gondi-speaking leaders in the party hierarchy in Chhattisgarh. All the second-rank leaders are locals.

Even though the Maoist movement in post-independent India began in West Bengal, most of the key leaders in the movement today are Telugu. After the crackdown by Siddhartha Shankar Ray, Chief Minister of West Bengal in the late 1960s and 1970s, many leading Naxal leaders including Kanu Sanyal moved to Andhra Pradesh. Top leaders like Ganapati, Krishenji and Azad (now dead) are Telugu. I must also mention that the number of incidences in Chhattisgarh increased only after the 2004 crackdown on Naxals in Andhra. We will get to the Andhra incident later.

After the usual pleasantries, even before we could start questioning them on the attack, they had their own set of questions. They wanted to know where did we work before, where is our home? How many members in family? Which university we went to? How much we are paid?

And then finally, we began. Our first natural question: Why did you kill the 76 CRPF jawans?

Ramanna took the lead and started complaining that media always thinks the Maoists are a military organization but the fact is they are a political party. So for the next two hours, both of them explained the CPI (Maoist) party structure and hierarchy. (See the chart of CPI (Maoist) Party structure on page 227.)

Finally Ramanna returned to our first question: What exactly happened on 6 April 2010? I will not go into the details of what the Maoist version of the attack is. Information on it has already appeared in the *Hindu* and even I have written about it in my piece 'Amongst the Believers'.[1] However, I would like to share with you in detail the reasons given by the Maoists for the attack and my observations:

- Operation Green Hunt: Killing of 115 innocent *adivasis*, who are not Naxals.
- Maoist leaders had been arrested in vicious countrywide crackdowns and killed in 'fake encounters'. Azad was still alive then.
- The Raman Singh government had signed 96 MoUs with various multinational mining firms in just the Beladila hill region.

Ganesh asked me: 'Tell me, are these companies going to give proper jobs to the poor *adivasis*?' I really didn't have an answer. When I looked around at ordinary villagers, the only luxury they had was a radio. There wasn't even a cycle in the scores of villages that I walked in my 30-km journey to meet Ramanna and Ganesh. The reason for violence is the standard one: 'We have taken up arms to safeguard the rights of the hapless tribals.'

I could actually see the pride in Ramanna's eyes for having planned and implemented such a big attack. He even went on to call one of his comrades and made him display how they plant pressure bombs by using a syringe and camera flash.

At this point I must point out a few things. First of all, it's important to differentiate between Maoists and tribals. Following the typical Marxist-Leninist-Maoist (MLM) strategy, the movement adopted the causes of the downtrodden. The Maoist movement in Chhattisgarh grew only after a systematic and consistent work done by Maoist leaders like Ramanna and Ganesh for the last 30 years. We very conveniently say Maoism is growing in tribal areas because the Indian state has failed to bring in development. But the story is somewhat different. If you look at the lifestyle of the tribals in India, you will realize the definition of development is very different for tribals compared to the Western model we in urban India have adopted. A tribal's needs are very simple. Usually he depends on his *tarri* (an alcoholic drink) and simple produce from the forest. Now the government banned manufacturing of alcohol and stopped tribals from using forest goods. Tribals were even asked to move out of their ancestral homes inside the forest. The tribal is not going to destroy the forest. He has been living there for generations. What has now happened is tribals who earlier sustained themselves have moved to moneylenders and fallen into a vicious circle of poverty.

In the last few years, there has been a struggle to acquire the mineral-rich land here for mining. Ramanna is not wrong when he mentions the number of MOUs signed between the Raman Singh government and the private companies. In an interview, Singh proudly announced Chhattisgarh had a GDP increase of 10 per cent. But the question is 10 per cent of growth among whom? The tribals still continue to be the most impoverished and neglected. And now they are caught in a battle between the state and the Maoists. They can escape neither.

Mining as a cause of unrest has been acknowledged by none other than ex-Union Mines Secretary Santha Sheela Nair. She retired in August 2010. But in May, she told me how the central government realizes that mines have become an issue of contention and is a possible reason for the Maoist conflicts. A new Mines and Minerals Bill, vigorously opposed by the mining lobby, will, if enacted, make it mandatory for 26 per cent of the profits to be shared with the locals. Under it, licenses can only be given to companies that make a full disclosure of their Corporate Social Responsibility (CSR) activities even before they start mining. The bill is still pending, I don't know if it is ever going to see the light of day.

Now, two days before Azad's killings on 29 June 2010, Ramanna calls me up early morning and starts complaining how the CRPF has been raping and torturing young girls. Ramanna goes on to issue a threat against the security forces and tells me that they will conduct a similar ambush like the one they did on 6 April. Within hours of the call, Maoist cadres ambush 63 security personnel, killing 26, just 3 km from the CRPF camp in Narayanpur district.

Once again, there is some truth in Ramanna's complaint. Just a few weeks back, my senior colleague Tusha Mittal had visited the village of Mukram, just a few kilometres from where the April massacre of 76 CRPF jawans took place, and found the whole village deserted. Facing a blacklash from the troops, most of the 115 families had fled to neighbouring Andhra Pradesh and Orissa. Villagers told her three girls were raped and five people including the *Sarpanch* picked up. That day in the evening, I called up Vijay Raman, the Special Director General of CRPF. He was furious. Since January 2010, more than 450 lives—including around 150 security personnel—had been lost in anti-Naxal operations. He completely rubbished the rape allegations against the security forces.

Of course, two days later on 1 July, prominent Maoist leader Cherukuri Rajkumar *alias* Azad was killed by the Andhra Police. Azad was the person negotiating on behalf of Maoists with Swami Agnivesh, a social activist, on a peace process. Agnivesh just couldn't get over his guilt. He says that it is possible Azad let his guard down because of his last letter and that Azad was a key person and most favourably disposed to the peace process. However, the Home Ministry has completely rubbished this claim. Chidambaram repeatedly said Maoists had not shown any inclination for talks.

Meanwhile, the focus shifted to West Bengal. As the Communists struggled to retain power after 35 years in government, there was an all-out battle between various political forces. Mamata Banerjee, then in opposition but who was to become Chief Minister after her election victory in 2011, displayed her strength by organizing a rally in the heart of Maoist territory—Lalgarh. The ruling Communist Party of India (Marxist) (CPM) accused her of siding with the Maoists. The issue of Azad's death played out at Banerjee's rally. She spoke about justice, equal rights and reconciliation. The upshot was that the CPI(M), which had held 41 assembly seats in the Jangalmahal area, lost heavily in the state elections of May 2011.

Mamata Banerjee began her tenure in government by promising reconciliation. She appointed interlocutors headed by activist Sujato Bhadra to talk with the Maoists. The honeymoon soon ended with the killing of ruling Trinamool Congress worker Lalmohan Mahato in West Midnapore district in September 2011. Banerjee said 'politics of killing' would not be tolerated. Her party organized a 6 km long protest rally against the Maoist violence.

Coming to what happened in Lakhisarai in Bihar in September 2010: out of the four policemen kidnapped by Maoists, only the tribal policeman was killed; the Yadav policemen were released. The Maoists are conscious of the issue of caste, especially in Bihar. It goes back to the MCC days when the Maoists were fighting against the Ranvir Sena, an upper-caste militia. Maoists from Delhi to Chhattisgarh condemned the killing of constable Lucas Tete. The killing of activist Niyamat Ansari in Latehar in Jharkhand further showed the contradictions in Maoist organization.

Maoist supporter G.N. Saibaba wrote a piece in *Tehelka* raising key issues:

- Why did the Maoists demand the swap when they knew that ordinary policemen have no importance for the government?
- Why did they kill Lucas Tete, a Jharkhandi *adivasi*, and not the Yadav, Sinha or Khan among the four abducted men?

To conclude, the Maoist movement has found fertile ground wherever there has been some form of injustice. In Bengal, the Naxal movement started over land; in Bihar, the Maoists found their bases among lower caste people; in Andhra, again it was landless peasants; in Jharkhand, it's forest and mining; and now in Chhattisgarh, it is mining and forest. The causes have been right, though the method wrong. Probably because of the rightful nature of the cause, the Maoist movement has managed to survive. It has also managed to thrive and expand. Many urban middle-class Indians have even supported the movement because of its just causes. If the movement is to be crushed, it is only possible by taking away the causes, not by eradicating the followers.

NOTE

1. Kunal Majumder and Shailendra Pandey, 'Amongst the Believers', *Tehelka*, 1 May 2010.

SECURITY

From the beginning of the twenty-first century, governments have sent increasing numbers of police and paramilitary police to combat Maoist-led insurgencies. The effectiveness of the training and deployment of these forces became a crucial issue for analysis. The essay in this section provides a constructive critique from a widely experienced security specialist. Numbers are not enough. Training, discipline, energetic leadership and local knowledge are essential.

CHAPTER 20

India's Maoist Movement: Trends and Security Implications

P.V. RAMANA

INTRODUCTION

Since 1967, India has been facing an armed revolution being waged by extreme left-wing elements. On 2 March 1967, the Naxalites, who were then members of the Communist Party of India (Marxist) and led by Charu Mazumdar, Kanu Sanyal[1] and Jangal Santhal, led a tribal peasant uprising in Naxalbari village, Siliguri sub-division,[2] Darjeeling district, West Bengal. Since then, all those who subscribed to the idea of an armed overthrow of the state have been generically referred to as Naxalites, the term having its origins in Naxalbari village. The objective of the rebels is the armed capture/seizure of state/political power through the method of guerrilla warfare by waging protracted people's war (PPW).

MERGER AND CONSOLIDATION

The Naxalite movement continues to witness a number of mergers while there have been a few insignificant splits. These mergers are listed below:

- Maoist Unity Centre (MUC), formed in 1997, is itself an amalgam of Naxalites of the Kerala Communist Party and Maharashtra Communist Party.
- 1998: Party Unity merges with PWG after years of negotiations, and PWG is renamed as Communist Party of India-Marxist-Leninist (People's War), heralding the first major and significant merger among competing and rival Naxalite groups.
- 1999: CPI-ML (Naxalbari) and MUC merge. Later, a faction of Red Flag merged with CPI-ML (Naxalbari).

- January 2003: Revolutionary Communist Centre of India (Marxist-Leninist-Maoist) merges with MCC and the resultant group is named as Maoist Communist Centre of India (MCCI).
- May 2003: CPI (ML) 2nd CC merges with MCCI.
- CPI-ML (Naxalbari) and CPI-ML Red Flag and Maoist Unity Centre (MUC) merge.
- 21 September 2004: PW and MCCI merge, resulting in the formation of the largest and most lethal Naxalite outfit in India—the CPI (Maoist) with a then estimated strength of 9,500 underground, armed men and women.
- 2008: CPI-ML (Naxalbari) merged with CPI (Maoist).
- January 2008: CPI-ML (Janasakthi) Kerala unit merged with CPI (Maoist).
- Strong possibility exists of the other state units of the Janasakthi merging with CPI (Maoist) in the months ahead.

With these mergers, there has been a consolidation of forces. It is argued here that at least some of the mergers had occurred in the wake of operations against rebels, internecine clashes among the groups, and the so-called repressive measures adopted by the government such as imposing a ban on the Naxalites. In this wake, the Naxalites could have possibly come to the conclusion that 'strength lies in unity'. At the same time, it could also be argued that, with these mergers, one group gained a presence in an area far from its habitual zone of operation. The consequences of the merger were explained by Narayan Sanyal after his Party Unity merged with the then PW: 'This is the most significant incident in the CPI-ML history after the martyrdom of Charu Mazumdar. . . . It was the desire of the rank and file that there should be a unified leadership so that the revolution can be quickened.'[3]

In a separate interview, the general secretary of the then Communist Party of India-Marxist-Leninist (People's War) and of the present CPI (Maoist), Muppala Lakshmana Rao *alias* Ganpathi, said, 'In our agenda for a new democratic revolution, there are two aspects—the agrarian revolution and fight for nationality. For the development of a new democratic revolution, the unification of the two (PW and Party Unity) is needed. Our merger is a cue for such unification.'[4]

INCREASING MILITARIZATION

The increasing militarization of the Maoists becomes evident from the high number of fatalities in the violence perpetrated by them during the past few years and the modern arms and equipment they are now fielding. When they launched their violent campaign in 1967, in Naxalbari village of West Bengal, the Maoists fought with ordinary weapons such as spears, sickles and farm implements. Now they boast of .303 rifles, SLRs, LMGs, AKs, INSAS rifles, mortar—all looted from the security forces—and rockets and rocket launchers, and anti-personnel pressure mines and explosive devices including landmines, claymore mines and directional mines. Another report said that the security forces recovered a hand-held thermal imager from a Maoist hideout in Jharkhand.[5] Along with increasing militarization, fatalities in Maoist violence have been fairly high and consistent over the past few years, as Tables 20.1 and 20.2 indicate. If anything, the numbers are going to rise for a few succeeding years as the security forces mount operations against the guerrillas and the latter indulge in bizarre and mindless killings to blunt security operations.

URBAN MOVEMENT AND TACTICAL UNITED FRONT (TUF)

An important trend currently being witnessed in the Maoist movement is urban penetration. This should be seen together with the Maoist plan of forming TUF activities, because the presence in towns and cities would boost TUF activities.

The Maoists always had a presence in towns and cities to cater to logistics needs and stay in safe houses during medical treatment or

TABLE 20.1: FATALITIES IN MAOIST VIOLENCE, 2005-9

	2005	2006	2007	2008	2009
Andhra Pradesh	208	47	33	82	18
Bihar	96	45	53	88	72
Chhattisgarh	168	388	311	320	290
Jharkhand	119	124	123	256	208
Madhya Pradesh	3	1	2	1	–
Maharashtra	53	42	22	31	93
Orissa	14	9	16	109	67
Uttar Pradesh	1	5	3	1	2
West Bengal	7	17	3	26	158
Kerala	0	0	0	0	–
Karnataka	8	0	5	7	–

Source: Ministry of Home Affairs, ***Annual Report***, various years, New Delhi.

TABLE 20.2: MAOIST VIOLENCE PROFILE, 2010

State	2010 (January 1 to July 15)				
	No. of Incidents	Civilians Killed	Security Forces Killed	Naxalites Killed	Naxalites Arrested
Andhra Pradesh	46	7	0	7	165
Bihar	174	40	5	4	218
Chhattisgarh	357	88	144	50	402
Jharkhand	279	70	12	9	206
Madhya Pradesh	6	0	0	0	0
Maharashtra	43	10	2	2	33
Orissa	119	29	16	1	85
Uttar Pradesh	4	1	0	0	75
West Bengal	203	117	32	28	257
Others	1	0	0	1	42
Total	1,235	362	211	102	1,483

Source: Statement Referred to in Reply to Parts (a) & (b) of Lok Sabha Starred Question No. 23, 'Naxal Attacks', 27 July 2010, New Delhi: Lok Sabha Secretariat.

in transit. Because of the anonymity it accords, it becomes easy for the Maoists to stay and operate in urban centres.

On 10 January 2007, the police in Bhopal, Madhya Pradesh, busted an R&D-cum-arms making unit of the rebels. The interrogation of the arrested persons brought to light that the rebels earlier ran similar units in other towns in Madhya Pradesh such as Jabalpur and Indore. Barely a few days later, the police in Rourkela, Orissa, unearthed another similar unit.

On many occasions important leaders belonging to the Central Committee were arrested from towns and cities. These include, for instance:

- Malla Raji Reddy *alias* Sattenna, arrested on 17 December 2007, in Angamaly town, Ernakulam district, Kerala.
- Sridhar Krishan Srinivasan *alias* Vishnu, arrested on 19 August 2007 in Mumbai. Vernin Gonsalves *alias* Vikram, member of the Maharashtra State Committee, arrested on the same day, separately, in Mumbai.

The detection of Maoist activities in towns such as Surat, in Gujarat, earlier in 2006, clearly indicates that the Maoists are attempting to penetrate the urban-based working class movement in the country. In their earlier *avatar* as the People's War Group (PWG), the Maoists had gained good experience in penetrating and spearheading the working class movement. The Singareni Karmika Samakhya (SIKASA), a Maoist front and trade union of miners in the Singareni Collieries in Andhra Pradesh, had a near total control over mine labourers and had successfully fought for better wages to miners. At that time, its influence was such that all mining activity came to a grinding halt when the SIKASA issued a strike call for better wages and implemented it for 58 days at a stretch.

Maoist presence and/or activities have been detected in a number of towns and cities across the country, including in Delhi,[6] the national capital. These towns and cities included Bhopal, Jabalpur, Indore, Rourkela, Bhubaneswar, Kolkata, Ranchi, Patna, Gorakhpur, Allahabad, Lucknow, Varanasi, Raipur, Bhilai, Nagpur, Shirdi, Bangalore, Chennai, to name a few.

As an analyst observed: '[These] efforts are part of a grand strategy to mobilise a section of the discontented population, especially industry workers . . . by aiming at heightened "mobilisations" around industrial establishments and simultaneously indulging in disruption strategies.'

Thus, the Maoists seem to be acting on a long-term perspective plan. In their scheme of things, they hope to gain control over the working class movement and use it appropriately at a later stage when their so-called New Democratic Revolution advances and furthers. In the immediate to short-term the objective is to gain control over key (strategic) industries with a view to inflicting 'damage' on the state's capacity to fight the Maoists, either through organizing sabotage activities or bringing production to a halt. According to an internal document of the CPI (Maoist) they envisage penetrating the working class movement in industries such as communication, oil and natural gas, coal, transport, power, defence production, etc.

According to the Maoists, United Front is one of the three magic weapons that the outfit necessarily requires to take the revolutionary agenda to its logical conclusion (the other two are strong party and strong army). Through forming coalitions with persons and groups that are opposed to the state and its policies, on one issue or the other, the Maoists seek to fight the state through 'peaceful' means, as well as broaden their support base.

The TUF is a secret committee. It functions directly under the guidance of the Sub-Committee on Mass Organisations (SUCOMO), which itself is a sub-set of the all-powerful and apex Central Committee of the CPI (Maoist). In fact, the then Communist Party of India-Marxist-Leninist (People's War) [CPI-ML (PW)] considered forming the United Front in 1995. However, these efforts did not take concrete shape for a variety of reasons.

At their 9th Congress/Unity Congress held in 2007 in Bihar, the Maoists passed resolutions on a number of issues, which indicates the TUFs they would have already formed or shall form in future. The resolutions passed covered issues such as Dalits, formation of Special Economic Zones (SEZ), agrarian crisis and farmer suicides, secessionist movements which they claim are nationality struggles, and minority rights, etc. Thus, the calls given by the Maoist organizations or affiliates since then against the massacre of Dalits in Khairlanji, their vocal and reported/alleged physical support to displacement struggles of Singur, Nandigram and POSCO, and the impasse and violence in Lalgarh, etc., should be seen in this light.

A TUF serves the following functions:

- Consolidate various 'anti-imperialist' struggles and bring them on to one platform on the basis of a common working understanding;
- Expand the reach of the Maoists to various sections of the society by building contacts with them;
- To expand over-ground cadre strength, thoroughly indoctrinate them, and then completely incorporate them into organizational work, especially in urban areas;
- Poach partners for potential leaders and ideologues;
- Serve as a good cover from the long arm of the state;
- Essentially being a political activity, it reinforces the military activities, i.e. armed struggle.

Besides, the Revolutionary Democratic Front (RDF), a front organization of the CPI (Maoist), which is proscribed by the union government under the Unlawful Activities Prevention Act, is a key component of the TUF. Among its various activities, besides issuing calls and statements on various issues, including one on 16 December 2007 calling the people to 'Lend support to the ongoing revolutionary movement in Dandakaranya, India!', an RDF representative presented a paper entitled 'Nandigram: The Road to Sovereignty of India', at the Conference against SEZs and other industrial projects displacing people, held on 2-3 June 2007 in Kolkata. In December 2007, RDF all-India leader G.N. Saibaba gave an interview to a Norwegian journalist, Lars Akerhaug, which was subsequently published and also posted on the RDF blog. In 2007, it also launched its own blog, http://rdfindia.blogspot.com.

Moreover, RDF was principally involved in the founding of a broad front known as the People's Democratic Front of India (PDFI), which was founded in July 2006. Its members include Medha Patkar, Nandita Haksar, S.A.R. Geelani, B.D. Sharma (President, Bharat Jan Andolan), Maoist ideologue P. Varavara Rao, and RDF leader Darshan Pal. Some of its constituent organizations include Samyukta Sangram Committee (West Bengal), Indian Federation of Trade Unions, All India Federation of Trade Unions, Chhattisgarh Mukti Morcha, Daman Virodhi Manch (Orissa), Jharkhand Progressive Students Union [an affiliate of the All India Radical Students Federation (AIRSF)], etc. While the various constituent organizations of the PDFI organized their activities in their respective areas of operation, the PDFI hosted a meeting on 12 May 2007, in Delhi, to commemorate the 1857 First War of Independence, and a conference to debate on the 'need to initiate the third wave of independence struggle'.

The Maoists have made attempts to form a TUF with the Muslims. This effort has been on since the past few years. In the wake of the proscription imposed on the Students Islamic Movement of India (SIMI), which has been involved in a series of bomb blasts in different cities and towns of India. According to media reports of 23 August 2008, Azad, spokesperson of the Central Committee of the CPI (Maoist), said 'it was a reiteration of the (government's) policy to continue its brutal war on Muslims'.

INFRASTRUCTURE ATTACKS

Since quite some years the rebels have been targeting and blasting infrastructure—damaging railway lines and setting on fire railway wagons and stations, blasting telecom towers, setting on fire state-owned passenger buses, etc. The objective of these attacks is to challenge the authority of the state, dictate terms of living to the populace in their strongholds and to cause hardship to the people, as well as hamper development. This has also caused a huge drain on state finances as re-building the infrastructure is a welfare function of the state, but an expensive and avoidable proposition. The details of these attacks in the past few years are listed in Table 20.3.

TABLE 20.3: ATTACKS ON INFRASTRUCTURE BY MAOISTS: JANUARY 2006-JUNE 2009

		1 January to 31 December 2006	1 January to 31 December 2007	1 January to 31 December 2008	1 January to 30 June 2009
Economic Targets					
Bihar	Uranium mines	1	0	0	0
	Essar Steel	1	1	1	0
Chhattisgarh	NMDC	11	4	0	1
	Essar pipelines	2	1	3	2
	BRO	4	1	0	0
	Gramin Sadak Nirman Yojana	0	0	1	1
Orissa	Essar pipelines	1	0	0	4
Maharashtra	BRO	2	0	0	0
Jharkhand	Steel plant	1	0	0	0
Bihar	Cement plant	0	1	0	0
	Solar plate	0	0	0	2
Total		23	8	5	10
Railways					
Andhra Pradesh		1	1	2	0
Bihar		12	9	11	3
Chhattisgarh		5	18	6	3
Jharkhand		13	15	7	3
Maharashtra		1	0	0	0
Orissa		1	2	0	5
West Bengal		0	2	1	1
Total		33	47	27	15

Telephone Exchange/Towers				
Andhra Pradesh	2	0	1	0
Bihar	0	0	14	12
Maharashtra	1	1	2	1
Chhattisgarh	1	3	15	5
Jharkhand	0	0	10	3
Orissa	1	2	4	5
Total	5	6	46	26
Power Plant				
Andhra Pradesh	2	3	0	0
Chhattisgarh	2	0	0	0
Maharashtra	0	0	1	2
Total	4	3	1	2
Mining				
Orissa	1	0	0	0
Jharkhand	0	4	4	0
Chhattisgarh	0	1	2	0
Andhra Pradesh	0	1	0	0
Total	1	6	6	0
Pole/Transmission				
Chhattisgarh	5	10	23	3
Orissa	0	0	1	0
Total	5	10	24	3
Grand Total	71	80	109	56

Source: Annexure 3 referred to in reply to para (a) to (c) of Lok Sabha starred question no. 41 for 7 July 2009 regarding 'measures to check naxalism'.

TABLE 20.4: ATTACKS ON INFRASTRUCTURE BY MAOISTS: 2010

		2010 (January 1 to July 15)	
			Total
Economic targets			
Andhra Pradesh	Uranium mines	0	
	Essar steel	0	
Chhattisgarh	NMDC	3	
	Essar pipelines	0	
	BRO	0	
	Gramin Sadak Nirman Yojana	2	
Orissa	Essar pipelines	1	
	Gramin Sadak	2	
Maharashtra	BRO	0	
Madhya Pradesh	PM Sadak Yojana	1	
Jharkhand	Steel plant	0	
Bihar	Cement plant	0	
	Solar plate	0	
	Gramin Sadak Nirmal Yojana	0	9
Railways			
Andhra Pradesh		0	
Bihar		11	
Chhattisgarh		2	
Jharkhand		12	
Maharashtra		0	
Orissa		6	
West Bengal		4	35
Telephone Exchange/Tower			
Andhra Pradesh		2	
Bihar		7	
Maharashtra		0	
Chhattisgarh		[illegible]	
Jharkhand		6	
Orissa		12	
West Bengal		1	29
Power plant			
Andhra Pradesh		0	
Chhattisgarh		0	
Maharashtra		1	1
Mining			
Orissa		0	
Jharkhand		0	

Chhattisgarh	0	
Andhra Pradesh	0	
Maharashtra	1	1
Pole/Transmission		
Chhattisgarh	0	
Orissa	0	0
Panchayat Bhawan		
Chhattisgarh	1	
Jharkhand	1	
Andhra Pradesh	0	
Maharashtra	1	
Bihar	2	
Orissa	6	
West Bengal	3	14
School Building		
Chhattisgarh	4	
Andhra Pradesh	1	
Jharkhand	4	
Bihar	8	
Maharashtra	0	
Orissa	3	20
Forest road, culverts, etc.	62	62
Total	171	171

Source: Statement referred in reply to part (a) and (b) of Lok Sabha starred question no. 23, answered on 27 July 2010.

CONCLUSION

The union government has initiated a number of security and development measures to squarely address the Maoist challenge. In a December 2007 address, the Indian prime minister outlined the strategy of the government to defeat the Maoists: 'security and development'. These measures are just about consolidating and gaining momentum. At the same time, the various affected states, too, are slowly getting their act together. However, there has been no uniform policy, strategy, perception and consensus among all the affected states. This has hampered security operations as well as come to the advantage of the rebels. There are indications that the situation is changing for the better and it is assuring that the affected states are gradually getting their act together.

On the other hand, the various high officers of the Union Ministry of Home Affairs have made grand and rather unrealistic claims on how early the Maoist challenge could be defeated. The claim that this could materialize in about two to three years is grossly unrealistic. Possibly, the Maoist challenge could be defeated in approximately seven to ten years. The various state governments and the union government are evincing greater political will than ever in the past to address the Maoist challenge headlong. It would take some more time to arrive at a consensus among all the affected states. Further, it requires a few years' time to build the combat and intelligence capabilities of the security forces in the various Maoist-affected states, and for development initiatives to make a perceptible impact. However, it is incontrovertible that the Maoists would have to shut shop in the years ahead. The government and the people should evince patience, not panic when the Maoists stage a spectacular attack or a chilling massacre, and work silently. In short, the watchwords are 'patience' and 'silent action'.

NOTES

1. The legendary Naxalite leader committed suicide at the age of 81 on 31 March 2010. He disagreed with Charu Mazumdar's 'class line' (annihilation of class enemies) and supported 'mass line' (building a people's/mass movement). Owing to his ideological differences he parted ways with Charu Mazumdar.
2. Siliguri is now a district in West Bengal.
3. See http://www.rediff.com/news/1998/oct/05nxl.htm
4. See, 'Unification is the only way to advance the cause of the Indian revolution', http://www.rediff.com/news/1998/oct/07gana.htm.
5. *Indian Express*, New Delhi, 15 September 2010.
6. See P.V. Ramana, 'Maoists in Delhi: Is the Police Prepared?', IDSA web commentary, http://www.idsa.in/idsacomments/MaoistsinDelhiIsthePolicePrepared_pvramana_030510.

MEDIA

When Mao's Chinese Communist Party came to power in 1949, television was in its infancy. When the Indian state struggled with the Khalistan movement between 1981 and 1993, television in India was a government-run, middle-class luxury. In the twenty-first century, however, India experiences its first 'television insurgency'. Governments and rebels strive to disseminate sympathetic versions of events to an ill-defined entity called 'the public'.

The two essays in this section describe how a television newsroom copes with 'Maoist stories' and emphasizes the pressures of time, access and competition in the presentation of television news. The second piece attempts to place the peculiar problems of Indian coverage of Maoist-related events in the context of media coverage of conflict in recent times.

CHAPTER 21

Media and Maoism

ROBIN JEFFREY

The 'Maoist insurgency' comes at a time when India lives in a totally new media environment. Every group in this drama struggles with these conditions and seeks to use them to achieve its aims.

Such attempts to 'make the media work for you' were illustrated in Arundhati Roy's vivid account in *Outlook* of days spent with Maoist-led tribals in the forests of Chhattisgarh.[1] Maoist leaders calculated that giving someone of Roy's global reputation first-hand experience of their activities would help their cause. Few other writers appear to have had similar access (see Suvojit Bagchi in Chapter 15 of this book and Gautam Navlakha in the *EPW*).[2] Roy would have had to weigh up the extent to which she was being used. Was there a hope on the Maoist side of her becoming a twenty-first century Edgar Snow and writing a *Red Star Over India*? (Snow's *Red Star Over China*, published in 1937, brought Mao Tse-tung to world attention).[3] Indeed, Roy's long sympathetic piece generated a surprising number of supportive responses from *Outlook* readers, as well as predictable calls for her prosecution as a traitor working for India's enemies.

How *new* is the media environment in which the Maoist insurgency unfolds? Comparisons with earlier crises of the Indian state make clear how much things have changed. At the time of the Telangana insurgency of 1948-52, India produced 2.5 million newspapers for a population of 360 million (111 people to a daily newspaper). There was no television; the two dozen radio stations were government-run and tightly controlled. Telephones and radios were rare.

In 1968-74, when 'Naxalites' challenged governments in West Bengal, Andhra Pradesh and elsewhere, television was almost non existent and, like radio, controlled by timid bureaucrats and politicians. Newspapers sold nine million copies a day for a population of 550 million (60 people to a daily newspaper), and India had one million telephones.

In 1984, when the Indian army battled Khalistan insurgents at the Golden Temple in Amritsar, the only television was the government's Doordarshan which broadcast pictures of the temple only days later. The contrast with the live and out-of-control television coverage of the Mumbai terrorist attack of 26 November 2008 could not be more striking.

Even at the time of the Kargil war of 1999—India's 'first television war'—commercial television was just beginning to escape from various government controls and there were perhaps 30 million homes with televisions. Newspapers sold 58 million copies a day for a population of 1,000 million (17 people to a daily newspaper), and telephones had pushed beyond 20 million. These changing conditions meant that military authorities had to look for different ways of dealing with media than they had deployed during earlier war experiences in 1962, 1965 and 1971.

By 2010, another new medium had spread throughout India: 580 million cell phones. Every owner of a cell phone was a potential photographer, filmmaker, radio listener and keeper of audio recordings. India also had close to 130 million television households: more than half the country slept each night in a place with a television set. India had more than 50 television news channels, many of them plugging particular lines which were not necessarily those of governments. India published 100 million newspapers a day for 1,150 million people (11 people to a daily newspaper). Up to 15 per cent of the population had access to the Web.

This media environment enabled ordinary people to tell their stories—and hear the stories of others—as never before. Fierce competition among scores of owners of media outlets drove these changes. The businesses and organizations included the biggest newspaper and telecom companies of Mumbai and New Delhi. At the other end of these invisible threads of communication were hundreds of millions of cell phone users, television viewers and newspaper readers.

Both Maoist ideologues and governments struggled to devise ways of telling their stories through these varied media. One of the 'marketing' issues in this environment was the very name of the insurgent movement itself. The term 'Maoist' suited both sides. The mergers of revolutionary communist groups in 2004 agreed on Communist Party of India (Maoist) as the name for the new consolidated organization. Why did they do so when a good Indian label, 'Naxalite', was available? The answer may lie in the perception that 'Maoist' provides a vision for the oppressed people whom ideologues seek to recruit: a brave hero, Chairman Mao led struggling peasants for years before encircling the cities, capturing power and creating the modern Chinese giant (and inspiring a successful revolution in neighbouring Nepal). It is a communicator's dream: a rousing (and selective) story told in 25 words or less.

From the standpoint of India's 'patriotic' media, aiming to paint the insurgents as traitors, 'Maoist' also works. The word suggests something un-Indian and foreign—Chinese. Sinister and scary, it echoes with the humiliation of the 1962 war.

The opposing sides experiment with ways of influencing India's publics. One example was the access the Maoists were prepared to give Arundhati Roy. Another is the written question-and-answer exercise that the Maoist spokesperson, Azad, undertook with the *Hindu* (Chapter 25 in this book).[4]

On the government side, state media outlets seemed to present more varied opinion than would once have been the case. Governments appeared to realize that slow, dreary, unconvincing reporting and tried-and-true spokespersons do little to engage or convince audiences. Panels on Doordarshan in 2010, on the other hand, featured various analysts and opinions in ways that would once have been too controversial for government media-minders to tolerate. Governments appeared to be experimenting with more effective ways of 'manufacturing consent'.

Governments also seek ways to control trigger-happy commercial media, particularly since the terror attack on Mumbai in November 2008. Commercial television at that time groped for standards: how does a medium dedicated to the fast news-break deal responsibly with a terrorist attack on a global landmark like the Taj Hotel? As it was, live feeds helped the terrorists. And in 2010, such evidence of 'media irresponsibility' strengthened the hands of those who wanted to put tighter bonds on all Indian media in the name of national security.

YouTube videos promote causes and provide material for security forces and insurgents to study. Both sides video-record ambushes and devastation—to analyse and learn and to use as propaganda. A policeman showed Arundhati Roy a PowerPoint presentation of Maoist carnage—mutilated policemen and blown-up schools. Gory photographs are mailed on compact disks to Members of Parliament. Intercepts of radio messages get recorded and are used either for their intelligence or propaganda value. Roy tells of Maoists recording a police message instructing officers to shoot journalists who want to cover Maoist activity. The recording, when disseminated, made further media fodder for the Maoists—and no doubt gave journalists in remote towns even greater reason for caution. The dangers of being a small-town journalist in Bihar, Chhattisgarh and Jharkhand are well known. 'I earn around Rs. 5,000 every month by not writing', a reporter with a Hindi daily in Chhattisgarh told Shubhranshu Choudhary to explain the perils of the profession. 'Journalism here is the art of *not* writing.'

The bloodshed in remote India plays out in front of urban, middle-class India. Mediated guerrilla war is something Mao and Ho Chi Minh did not contend with, though one can see parallels with the awakening of United States public opinion through television to the horror of the Vietnam War. Governments and insurgents will calculate how much exposure to destruction and violence helps their cause. What sorts of media provide the most effective outlet for telling their versions? And how does one determine the effects of particular kinds of media on 'the public', security forces, insurgent cadres and the outside world?

Analysts will watch how governments and insurgents develop media policies. Governments will struggle to control media yet keep media credible and timely, because without prompt credibility, media lose the power to persuade. Indian media, under scrutiny for irresponsible television coverage of breaking events and for 'pay for coverage' scandals in newspapers, need to find ways to police themselves—or face clumsy but constricting attempts by government to control them. And where does the New Equalizer, the mobile phone, fit into this equation? Is it a crucial device for mitigating—or promoting—insurgency? Media will not decide how this insurgency ends; but they will profoundly influence the unfolding.

NOTES

1. Arundhati Roy, 'Walking with the Comrades', *Outlook* (29 March 2010), pp. 24-59.
2. Gautam Navlakha, 'Days and Nights in the Maoist Heartland', *Economic and Political Weekly*, 17 April 2010, pp. 38-47.
3. Edgar Snow, *Red Star Over China* (London: Victor Gollancz, 1937).
4. *Hindu*, 'Edited text of 12,262-word response by Azad, Spokesperson, Central Committee, CPI (Maoist)', 14 April 2010, http://beta.thehindu.com/news/resources/article396694.ece.

CHAPTER 22

Maoism: Seen from the Newsroom

DIVYA IYER

5 October 2009. The Newsroom. I was rushing against time to finish a special report I had laboured on for three days. I had less than an hour to put it on air. Between our frantic exchanges, my editor and I heard nothing unusual in the highly charged clamour that defines a regular television newsroom. Till we heard someone scream, '*His body has been found. They killed him.*'

It happens every time, without fail. With uncanny precision, the trouble-makers of the world decide to strike on the day I flog myself over a tough report. End result: my story gets dropped as breaking news takes over the airwaves. I felt a sense of *déjà vu*. Only this time the trouble-makers were too close home. And the visuals that came in made me forget my story.

The Naxals had beheaded Francis Induwar, a special branch inspector of the Jharkhand Police, whom they had abducted five days before. Induwar's mutilated body had just been found lying on a highway.

Television news works like well-oiled machinery, so even as most people in the office took a while to gather their thoughts on what this episode meant, the channel was abuzz with all the elements of breaking news. Shock and awe are feelings that journalists don't recognize for more than 30 seconds. They can't afford it. There was no time to sit and ponder. Producers got busy getting map graphics made of the exact location of the incident; the research team was digging out the chronology of what happened in the last five days since Induwar was picked up. And even as reporters in New Delhi frantically worked the phones to get responses from the Home Ministry, the Maoist cadre and the police, on air, the anchor kept the story going with a phone interview of an official giving preliminary details of the murder.

Reactions started pouring in. The government condemned the Naxal brutality; the Naxal sympathizers were critical of the violence but blamed it on the continued state cruelty. I saw the usual suspects (read: the Home Minister P. Chidambaram, Home Secretary G.K. Pillai, Naxal sympathizers Varavara Rao, Arundhati Roy, Medha Patkar) mouthing the same rhetoric on various news channels. Nothing had changed since 6 April when the country witnessed the worst Maoist attack ever. At least 75 men of the Central Reserve Police Force (CRPF) and a state policeman were killed in an ambush in the thick Mukrana forests of Chhattisgarh's Dantewada district. Nothing had improved on the ground in the last six months.

Except the media coverage of the Naxal issue. Television news by definition is about immediacy and visual impact. Something that the Indian media first discovered during the Kargil War when violence entered middle-class India's drawing rooms for the first time. War was soon followed by communal violence during the Godhra riots. The media, especially broadcast news, that were practically absent (except for the state-owned Doordarshan) during the 1984 anti-Sikh riots that broke out after Indira Gandhi's assassination, were out in full force during the Gujarat riots. These were the first and the biggest televized communal clashes in the country's history and an immense training for television media. But years later, the 26/11 Mumbai terror attacks proved how much the commercial media in the country have yet to learn. The nascent industry groped to find a balance between fast news breaks and reporting responsibly on a live terrorist attack that continued for three days. The television channels came under severe attack for 'media irresponsibility' as live feeds from ground zero helped terrorists figure the coordinates of the security forces. 'But the Indian media have learned their lessons. At least the television channels', says Radhakrishnan Nair, the executive editor of CNN-IBN. 'Look at the restraint all channels, including the Hindi media showed during the Ayodhya verdict. It was a benchmark which was followed for the Godhra verdict as well.'

The Maoist issue has been no different. As the man largely responsible for all the news coverage at CNN-IBN, Nair is well aware of the challenges that the Maoist coverage poses. He hit the nail on the head when he identified the problem for me. 'This is very different from covering terrorism. A terrorist is seen by all as a terrorist. There is no debate. No motives are attributed to us. But who is a Maoist?

It is a complex question that makes it all the more difficult for us to report.'

It is indeed, as my colleague Rupashree Nanda found out while reporting in Salboni in Lalgarh, West Bengal. She had travelled all the way from Delhi to try to capture the 'greys' of the debate that the mainstream media had so far failed to reflect effectively. In between the black-and-white, water-tight compartments of brute Maoist violence and state apathy, nobody reported on the predicament of the local tribal population that was caught in between the two—a huge population that was living in the country's most mineral-rich regions but with absolutely no access to basic education, livelihood and health care. Rupashree went to report on the ground realities. She was picked up by the police and detained for two days. Today, villagers are seen to be the legs of the Maoist movement and suddenly to be seen with a 'Maoist' is to be a Maoist. And journalists were not the only target. The government meted out the same treatment to entire villages. Rupashree later reported:

> Linga seen meeting Naxalites does not make him a Naxalite. Linga seen roaming in market places with the police does not make him a police informer. But in Dantewada, it is the Rashomon effect at work. When the partial truth masquerades as the whole truth and the only truth, it is a lie. Open to exploitation by all sides.

Linga was a young Muriya tribal from Sameli, a village in Dantewada. On the morning of 31 August 2010, he was picked up from his home by plainclothes but armed policemen.

Sitting here in the newsroom, listening to the calls made by the office to concerned officials to rescue my colleague in Lalgarh, I could only wonder what was making the state so insecure about journalists reporting on the Maoist issue. On one hand, the media are accused, and sometimes rightly so, of being limited in their understanding of this complex issue. But if the journalists are denied the access and freedom to report the truth from the ground, can you blame them for the arm-chair understanding of the issue, churned out from news desks in New Delhi? This is not, however, an excuse for the kind of reports that come out in the media today.

'It is free, fair and flaky' says Rohit Khanna, executive producer at CNN-IBN. Producing long-format documentaries for the channel, Khanna's biggest grouse against the media is their limited and shortsighted coverage of the Maoist issues. 'It is mostly seen as insurgency or violence. The channels and papers are only doing lip service by saying the issue is connected with the tribal people. The fact is they don't understand how.' It's the same kind of shallow reporting that comes out of conflict zones in Kashmir and the north-east, he feels.

H.R. Venkatesh, a senior anchor and copy-editor at CNN-IBN, agrees. As part of the desk that decides on headlines and stories, Venkatesh knows it's the numbers that matter, not the issue. 'It's not meaningful reporting. If the death toll is less, drop it. That's how we operate at the desk. But if the educated Indian middle class is involved, we go berserk. Then numbers don't matter.'

Such a criticism was also levelled at the centre for the way it negotiated the release of R. Veenil Krishna, the district collector of Malkangiri district in Orissa. The CPI-Maoist cadres abducted the Collector and his junior engineer on 16 February 2011, two days before Union Home Minister P. Chidambaram's scheduled video-conference with the collectors of 60 Maoist-hit districts. What followed were lengthy and elaborate negotiations with the Maoists ending in the Orissa Chief Minister Naveen Patnaik agreeing to all their demands. The nine-day hostage crisis ended with the state giving into the biggest-ever prisoner swap involving hardcore CPI-Maoist cadres to secure the release of the district collector. The Maoists released Krishna just 3 km from where they had abducted him. This was a complete contrast to the way Francis Induwar's mutilated body was found on the highway five days after he was abducted.

Critics denounced the way the centre (and therefore the media) handled the two situations differently. Their charge: caste bias in the centre's approach and media's coverage. One victim was a low-ranking police officer and the other an educated middle-class IAS officer. It was seen as a sad comment on the government—it did everything for the district collector, but couldn't save Francis Induwar. Though one can't comment for the state, the media were certainly not discriminatory in their coverage. Here, I speak strictly of the national television news channels. If anything, the criticism we faced, both from within our own channel and outside, was of going overboard with the coverage. Some even termed it as milking the issue by 'emotionally exploiting' the families, asking them to appeal for their loved ones' release. This was especially true in the case of Francis Induwar's family. It was something that had disturbed a lot of us, including me, for days. Francis Induwar's nine-year-old son, promising to take revenge through his tears, was splashed across all television channels. It was as frightening as it was heart-wrenching. A young kid wanting to kill the Maoists for his father's death was not something the nation needed or could afford, because that would mean hundreds of kids in the interiors of the country growing up with anger and hatred. There have been nearly 1,800 deaths in the last three years in Maoist violence, the majority of them being policemen. That is a lot of angry children. This is not the future one wanted to give them. And this was definitely not the solution to the 'Maoist problem'.

But what made the child's outburst so disturbing for me were the rumours that filtered in the next day. There were reports that a local stringer (freelance reporter) had prodded the boy to make the statement. A lot of us were appalled, though not surprised. It's an uncomfortable truth of reporting these days: feed the answers, the bytes and the lines to the case studies and record it. It's not about reality. It's what makes good TV. The practise is more rampant in small towns and interiors of the country than in urban centres where the mushrooming of media houses (and therefore the mikes at the location) provides automatic checks and balances. There was no way to verify the rumours. But it gave rise to a heated debate in the newsroom on what should be done. A whole day had gone by with the nation watching the young son of Francis Induwar wanting revenge. A whole day when the centre had used this video to drive home the point that Maoists are no longer social revolutionaries wanting a caste-less, class-less society, but violent, anti-national elements who simply wanted to kill honest Indians. The answer to this dilemma came in a dramatic way—in Rahul Gandhi's visit to Induwar's house. Gandhi told the slain cop's sons that he understood their pain, as he too had lost a father in similar fashion. The media got their day's headline and the earlier dilemma was forgotten. But the journalistic question still remains. How much is too much in such sensitive hostage situations? Vishakh Rathi, the former executive producer of CNN-IBN, says it's a decision that has to be taken on a day-to-day basis.

> As a practitioner and a viewer, I feel we should not show women and children crying and appealing for help. I agree that this puts pressure on the system to act, but my concern is the *nature* of the act. If the police or the government acts out of media pressure and arrests the wrong person, who will be responsible? By constantly showing distraught families on TV, one is not necessarily helping the system do the right thing.

Though a legitimate concern, Rathi is aware that it is not always possible to pay heed to it in the news business. Competition drives the electronic media industry and one will do anything to get the eye-balls. Then there is the other danger: of becoming numb to excess. It's what many believed happened to the coverage of Kashmir and the north-east. Critics argue that the media get bored with similar stories till big-ticket death-tolls jolt them into escalating the news. They predict a similar future for the Maoist coverage. But Rohit Khanna disagrees. He says, 'We are numb to the phenomenon, not to incidents. So every Maoist attack and Naxal violence would get carried, but there will still be no real understanding of the issue. It's like the media reports on the 2G scam, but is numb to corruption.' Channel heads get defensive on the issue. As Radhakrishnan Nair clarifies, 'News is a priority business. Interest levels of the viewer are very important in this profession. And of course, availability of resources plays a huge role in how much coverage we do of a certain issue.'

This is the simple truth. Regardless of how well or poorly the electronic media in India cover the Maoist issue, the fact is it is extremely challenging to report. Most of the Naxal attacks owing to the nature of their operations are in remote parts of India. For news channels which are based out of urban centres, getting credible information from these locations becomes the toughest task. The visuals are networked from the local channels, but getting the news right (and fast) on this extremely sensitive and complex issue becomes the biggest determining factor for the electronic media.

Television as a medium falls short of giving in-depth coverage of any issue. It has immediacy but lacks depth and perspective. The average Indian therefore has to depend on multiple modes of information like electronic media, newspapers, magazines and the internet to get his/her news. But the majority of the intelligentsia in the country feel that none of the media in India is able to give the whole picture. While the newspapers tend to give more details than the news channels (owing to the medium), it is widely believed that neither gives a balanced and comprehensive report. An online article that quoted findings of a Hoot-Panos study, funded by Hivos says,

> When covering the Maoist insurgency in West Bengal, the rule seems to be, use whatever information is made available. Be it the Maoists or the police, the stories had one-sided versions and conclusions based on whatever

speculation, suppositions and assertions could reach the media at the time of filing the stories. *Anand Bazar Patrika* had a story on September 19th claiming *'Maowadira chheledhora noi, dabi vibriti te* (Maoists not child lifters, claims statement), without a word on the origin and the authenticity of the statement. Another said, *'Shilda's Ananta murdered by Maoists'*, again raising doubts about who were the real perpetrators of the crime in an area also infested by political rivalry. The *Telegraph* too in a similar fashion carried incidental or one-sided versions of the stories that was made available to the media. It has been found that the police or suspected Maoists' statements singly make up the source for reporters, so there was always doubt about their authenticity.

In comparison, the national news channels covered the Maoist-state conflicts responsibly and without sensationalism. Well, for the most part. A leading national news channel though surprised everybody by suddenly choosing not to report the Binayak Sen trial. It looked like the channel had already taken a stand that Binayak Sen was a 'Maoist' and therefore anti-national. It defied all journalistic ethics which demand that news, no matter what, must be reported. And Binayak Sen—a doctor working with the poorest of the poor in Chhattisgarh's tribal regions, branded a Naxalite and given life sentence by an Indian court—was NEWS. Not reporting the trial and the consequent public outrage was not self-censorship. It was plain dangerous.

But the larger concern is not so much about how a Maoist incident is being reported in the Indian media. Silence of the press when there is no incident is perhaps, a bigger worry. The weakness of television news today is that it covers events and not the issue. So there are no follow-up stories on the policy implications of an attack or what happens in the Maoist camps through the year, no fact-finding or analysis on what the state machinery is doing (or not doing) for developing these regions or curbing the violence. What one sees on the telly today is what some call 'band-aid' reporting: it gives the viewer the facts but no context. In a powerful visual medium like the electronic media where stories can have great impact, this is a bad miss.

But not everything is wrong with the medium. On the brighter side, most of the Maoist coverage is bereft of any reporter bias or slant. With in-built checks and balances in the system the journalists are able to filter out the propaganda that both the warring factions—

the Maoist camp and the government—start to feed the media soon after an attack. There has been some learning as well. Some channels like CNN-IBN have taken a policy decision to not interview a Maoist leader live on air. Instead, they prefer recorded interviews which minimizes the chances of putting Maoist propaganda on the channel. The safeguard against becoming a Maoist mouthpiece has become more crucial in recent times with the emergence of a new leadership in the CPI (Maoist) that is 'less conservative and reclusive than has historically been the case. Far from being media shy, the new West Bengal-based group has chosen to undertake bold and brutal actions calculated to garner media attention'. From Francis Induwar's beheading to the capture of Lalgarh in West Bengal to a dramatic train hijack during India's election campaign, there seems to be 'a remarkable reorientation in the Naxalite tactics.'[1] This new face of Maoism has been best personified in Kishenji, the Andhra-born, West Bengal-based rebel. Kishenji is a new kind of Naxalite leader, actively courting media attention by holding press conferences. This tactical change has also led to the Maoist leader giving interviews and access to some prominent faces. Arundhati Roy's article in the *Outlook* magazine recounting days spent with Maoist-led tribals in the forests of Chhattisgarh is part of the Maoists' new plan of publicizing their work and gaining public support and sympathy.

Predictably, Roy's article found a lot of empathy but an equal measure of criticism. India's forgotten war had suddenly become the central focus. And everyone had an opinion on it. In May 2009, India's Home Ministry threatened to prosecute intellectuals and civil society groups who help 'spread' the Naxalites' ideology. It wasn't clear what 'spreading' Maoist ideology would involve. As Spacek observes, 'The term is so nebulous and meaningless that it could apply to anyone who is not just sympathetic to the Maoists but who is critical of the government's actions.' This could easily include news channels. But Roy, sharp, opinionated and widely read, was the preferred target. While a lot of people, including Human Rights Watch, criticized these threats, Arundhati Roy went on giving print and television interviews about how she felt about the Naxal issue. She was fearless, passionate and brutal in her observations. But even she fell short of the much needed but elusive 'balance'. Vishakh Rathi was the producer on location for Roy's interview to CNN-IBN. He says, 'People like Arundhati Roy have confused and muddled the debate so much that there is no middle ground anymore.' Rathi echoes the general opinion that intellectuals like Roy have polarized the Maoist debate. And now, somehow, the middle ground has to be struck by the media.

The media have brought the war raging in India's hinterland to urban, middle-class India. But the question that determines the regularity and depth of the coverage is this: how much does urban India care about this story. Or is the story too deep in the jungles, too far removed from their lives, for them to agree with Prime Minister Manmohan Singh when he called Maoism 'the gravest internal security threat that our country faces'? The media will not decide how this insurgency will end. They cannot bring about a solution that has evaded the government for decades. But the media can, and will profoundly influence how a nation responds to the unfolding crisis.

NOTE

1. Michael Spacek, 'India's Forgotten War-blogging Naxalism', http: naxalwar. wordpress.com (accessed on 20 October 2011).

INTERVIEWS

How do those involved in conflict, or close to the people and places caught up in conflict, explain their involvement or understand what they see around them? In these five interviews, two deceased Maoists analyse their party's positions and their own roles, and a fine scholar, an experienced security specialist and a young journalist discuss their involvement and views.

CHAPTER 23

When I Met Kanu Sanyal

AVIJIT GHOSH

I met Kanu Sanyal only once. In May 2007 I was assigned to do a full-page story on the 40 years of the Naxalbari movement. I knew that talking to one of the tallest leaders of the armed struggle would be invaluable for my story. A journalist-friend from Kolkata had given me Mr. Sanyal's landline number. On reaching Siliguri in north Bengal, I called him up from my hotel room. Sanyal himself picked up the phone. 'Come in the evening. We will talk,' he said. The bus dropped me off at a point that I don't remember by name. When I mentioned Kanu Sanyal and Hatigisha to villagers, they immediately showed me a narrow road that snaked past bamboo groves, a rivulet and small hamlets. It was a 2-km walk in tranquil surroundings.

Sanyal, then 75-plus, was sitting outside a sparse mud house, which also served as a one-room party office in Hatigisha. The sun was dying and fearing it would get dark soon, I immediately took some photographs of him.

Sanyal said he had been ailing for some time. He looked frail. In the 1960s, the bylanes of Calcutta and the paddy fields of Naxalbari echoed the slogan, *'Jail ka tala tootega/Kanu, Jangal chhootega* (The locks of prison will break, Kanu and Jangal Santhal will be freed). One wondered how he would have looked then. What followed was a 60-minute interview. It could have been longer but I was worried that I wouldn't get a return bus. 'Don't worry,' he said, 'I will send someone to escort you back.' Two things were clear during that interview—the radical left leader's mind was as sharp as ever and that he remained committed to the revolution through mass struggle.

AG: *What are your memories of 25 May 1967, the day the Naxalbari movement began?*

KS: For us, 24 May is the Naxalbari day. That day, the police were informed that some leaders of the Naxalbari movement were hiding in Boro Jhorojote village. There were no leaders there but a huge gathering of peasantry and tea garden workers. One police officer was killed there. Since the peasants understood and accepted our politics and took up arms on their own, we celebrate that day as a victory of our political ideas. Other groups observe 25 May as Martyrs' Day, when 11 activists were killed.

AG: *In retrospect, do you think that Charu Mazumdar's 'annihilation of class enemy' line was a historical error?*

KS: It was not only a historical error but also a fundamental deviation from Marxism-Leninism and the thoughts of Mao. But, remember, we did not follow the annihilation line (forming small squads and killing landlords, policemen and other class enemies) in the Naxalbari struggle. Only one landlord was killed during the struggle. In practice, the annihilation line was first followed in Srikakulam area of Andhra Pradesh in late 1969.

AG: *Why did the Naxalbari movement fail?*

KS: We had a strong base among the peasants and the tea garden workers. But we carried on the movement without a proper party structure. That was the main reason.

AG: *What are the long-term gains?*

KS: There was no protection to sharecroppers earlier. We captured land in Naxalbari and the peasants are still in control over the land. After 1977, the West Bengal government was forced to bring the Bargadari Act through which some hereditary rights were given to the sharecroppers. Another question that came up was that if we wanted to lead an agrarian revolution, we needed a strong party. Consequently, the Communist Party of India (Marxist-Leninist) [CPI (ML)] was formed in 1969. But that too wasn't successful in the long run because Charu Mazumdar's annihilation-of-class-enemies line prevailed. In a very subtle way, he said that peasant committees and associations were not necessary. Neither were mass organizations necessary. Only form small squads and start annihilation of class enemies. So I don't agree that after forming CPI(ML) (the) agrarian struggle started in new areas. Mobilizing and organizing peasants and taking them ahead in the struggle was not done.

AG: *Did you meet Mao secretly in 1967?*

KS: Yes. It was a 45-minute meeting. We went by road to Kathmandu. From there Chinese comrades took us by jeep to Peking. We stayed in Tibet too. We reached China on 30 September. The next day we saw them celebrate 1 October as National Day. I could see people weeping after seeing Mao. We met Mao, Zhou Enlai and the commander-in-chief. Mao's advice was: whatever you learn in China, try to forget it. Go to your own country, try to understand the specific situation and carry the revolution forward.

AG: *If you were the chief minister of West Bengal today, how would you have dealt with Nandigram?*

KS: I can only answer the question from a peasant organizer point of view. I feel the issue cannot be resolved. If you think deeply, Nandigram isn't just about the 14 March police firing. It is a question of policy. They say that agrarian reform is done. So we are opting for industrialization. But the truth is that they have not completed the task of agrarian reform in West Bengal. Besides, thousands of industries have been closed. The entire 150-year-old tea industry is facing a deep crisis but the Communist Party of India (Marxist) [CPI(M)]-led state government has been unable to resolve the problem. We should be asking whom does the industrialization benefit. During the French Revolution, under the leadership of the bourgeoisie, land was given to the tillers. They should follow the French model.

AG: *What is the larger point emerging from Nandigram?*

KS: India still needs an agrarian revolution. Without solving the agrarian problem, you cannot develop the country by industrialization.

AG: *The Maoists are present to a greater or lesser degree in over 150 districts. What is their future?*

KS: The Maoists are sure to meet with failure. In an Andhra Pradesh village, where they are very powerful, I found out that some peasants were not tilling their land. I asked them, why? They said, 'If we do so, the landlords will come and ask for the produce. And if we do what the Maoists tell us, the forces will come.' The Maoists, in spite of having guns, have failed to assure the peasants that they should serve a radical land reform in the countryside. Back in 1969, when CPI(ML) was formed, we used to say after one action in a district that agrarian revolution is going ahead. And that guerrilla warfare has started. The Maoists have started the same thing in a wider form. Only now guns are more easily available. But I can say that they are detached from the people. The Maoists cannot see. Earlier this month people revolted in Ranchi against Reliance Retail. The Maoists are active in the areas in and around Ranchi but they cannot see what is happening. They just want state power first. They feel that by killing some policemen and blasting some police jeeps, the agrarian revolution is going ahead. In Iraq, people have no option but fight the American forces. That's what the Iraqi people are doing. They feel if we kill more and more foreigners, they will go back to their own country. Such an option is justified in Iraq. But not in India.

CHAPTER 24

Maoist: Azad talks to Siddharth Varadarajan

Until he was killed in July 2010, Azad was the spokesperson for the Central Committee, CPI (Maoist). An interview with him was published in the *Hindu* on 12 February 2010. Siddharth Varadarajan of the *Hindu* describes how the interview came about:

When I arrived in my office at the *Hindu* one morning, there was a man waiting for me whom I could not place. He said he was a student of the Maoist insurgency. He mentioned an interview I had conducted in 2006 with the Nepali Maoist leader, Prachanda, when he had been 'underground' and asked whether I would be willing to interview Azad, who was then the spokesman of the Communist Party of India (Maoist). I said yes, but what I would like even more was an interview with the Maoist leader Ganapathi. The man smiled and said that would not be possible. I said in that case, the Azad interview should at least be face-to-face, the way Prachanda's had been and that I would be willing to travel to anywhere they said. He replied that even a written interview with Azad would be extremely difficult to organize logistically and that if I did not give him the questions right away, there was no guarantee a message could be sent to him. Since our newspaper discourages written interviews I sought the concurrence of my editor, N. Ram, and then quickly typed out some questions. My mysterious visitor took the printout and vanished.

A few weeks later, news came that Azad had been killed in an encounter. But the news turned out to be incorrect. About seven weeks after I handed over my questions, a CD finally arrived on my desk with the words 'Azad interview to Hindu' written on it with a blue marker.

Varadarajan: ***In recent weeks one has seen statements by the Government of India and leaders of the Communist Party of India (Maoist) saying they are in favour of dialogue and talks but each side seems to lack seriousness. There has also been an element of drama or more precisely, theatre, with Kishenji and P. Chidambaram exchanging statements*** *through the media. Our first question is whether Kishenji's statements can be treated as authoritative pronouncements of the CPI (Maoist) central leadership in pursuance of a national strategy? Or are these tactical announcements by him keeping only the specifics of the Bengal situation in mind.*

Azad: It is true our party leadership has been issuing statements from time to time in response to the government's dubious offer of talks. But to generalize that there is lack of seriousness on both sides does not correspond to reality. To an observer, exchanging statements through the media does sound a bit theatrical. And it is precisely such theatrical and sensational things the media relishes while more serious things are swept aside. Now the stark fact is lack of seriousness has been the hallmark of the government, particularly of the Union Home Minister P. Chidambaram. It is Chidambaram who has been enacting a drama in the past four months, particularly ever since his amusing 72-hour-abjure-violence diktat to the CPI (Maoist) in the course of his interview with *Tehelka* magazine some time last November. As regards Kishenji's statements, they should be seen with a positive attitude, not with cynicism. Though our Central Committee has not discussed our specific strategy with regard to talks with the government at the current juncture, as a Polit Bureau member, Comrade Kishenji had taken initiative and made a concrete proposal for a ceasefire. Whether Comrade Kishenji's statements are the official pronouncements of our Central Committee is not the point of debate here. What is important is the attitude of the government to such an offer in the first place. Our Central Committee has no objection to his proposal for a ceasefire. But as far as the issue of talks is concerned, our Party will pursue the guidelines given by our Unity Congress held in early 2007.

Varadarajan: *Both the government and the Maoists are also laying down preconditions. Chidambaram says the Maoists should 'abjure violence and say they are prepared for talks. . . . I would like no ifs, no buts and no conditions'. Now 'to abjure' can mean to renounce or forswear violence, or even to avoid violence, i.e. a ceasefire. What is your understanding of Chidambaram's formulation? What do you think is the implication of what he wants the Maoists to accept?*

Azad: It is a very pertinent question as no one knows exactly what Chidambaram wants to convey by his oft-repeated, yet incomprehensible, 'abjure violence' statement. Hence I can understand your confusion in interpreting Chidambaram's 'abjure violence' statement. It is not just you alone but the entire media is left in a state of confusion. His own party leaders are a confused lot. Some interpret Chidambaram's statement to mean that Maoists should lay down arms. Some say it means unilateral renunciation of violence by Maoists. Yet others say what this could mean is a cessation of hostilities by both sides without any conditions attached.

It is indeed very difficult to understand what Chidambaram wants to convey. This seems to be a characteristic trait of Chidambaram whether it be his pronouncements on Telangana, which are mildly described by the media as 'flip-flop' behaviour and interpreted by both pro and anti-Telanganites according to their own convenience; or on Operation Green Hunt which he describes as a 'myth invented by the media' even as the entire political and police establishment, and the entire media, give out graphic descriptions of the huge mobilization of the security forces, and the successes achieved by Operation Green Hunt; or on MOUs signed by various MNCs and Indian corporate houses with the governments of Chhattisgarh, Jharkhand, Orissa, West Bengal and others.

The home minister himself had displayed his split personality, not knowing what exactly he wants when he says Maoists should 'abjure violence'. To a layman what this proposal obviously implies is that the state too would automatically put a stop to its inhuman atrocities on the *adivasis*, Maoist revolutionaries and their sympathizers. But not so to our home minister!

When you ask us what our understanding of Chidambaram's formulation is, our answer is: we are very clear that the real intent behind his rhetoric is not a ceasefire between the government and the Maoists, like that with the NSCN, but an absurd demand for a unilateral renunciation of violence by the Maoists. Anyone with a bit of common sense would understand the unreasonableness of the home minister's demand.

It is not that our so-called political analysts and others who appear on TV channels or write articles in the print media lack this common sense. It is their vested interests that come in the way of questioning the home minister in a straightforward manner. Can they not put a simple question why the government cannot stop its brutalities on the people, adhere strictly to the Indian constitution by putting an end to the police culture of fake encounters, abductions, rapes, tortures, destruction of property, foisting of false cases and such indescribable atrocities on the people and the Maoists? Chidambaram is cosy in studios and press conferences before English-speaking TV anchors and correspondents but can never answer the questions put by illiterate *adivasis*. That is the secret behind his skipping the *Jan Sunwaayi* in Dantewada in December 2009. Drama and real life are entirely different.

The implication of what Chidambaram wants the Maoists to accept is crystal clear. He wants the Maoists to surrender. Or else [the state's] paramilitary juggernaut would crush the people and the Maoists under its wheels. It is total surrender, pure and simple. While repeating that he never wanted the Maoists to lay down arms—as if he had generously given a big concession—he comes up with an even more atrocious proposal: Maoists should abjure violence while his lawless forces continue their rampage creating more Gachampallis, Gompads, Singanamadugus, Palachelimas, Dogpadus, Palods, Tetemadugus, Takilodus, Ongaras, and so on. Not a word does he utter even as scores of inhuman atrocities by his forces are brought to light by magazines like *Tehelka*, *Outlook*, a host of websites, and, to an extent, some papers like yours. What is it if not sheer hypocrisy on the part of the home minister to ask Maoists to abjure violence while his paramilitary forces indulge in crimes everyday, every hour, in gross violation of the very Constitution by which he swears?

Varadarajan: *The Maoists also have their preconditions for talks. In his recent interview to Jan Myrdal and Gautam Navlakha, Ganapathi made the following formulation on the issue of talks: 'To put concisely the main demands that the party has placed in front of the government [of India] for any kind of talks are: (i) all-out war has to be withdrawn; (ii) for any kind of democratic work, the ban on the party and mass organizations have to be lifted; (iii) illegal detention and torture of comrades had to be stopped and they be immediately released. If these demands are met, then the same leaders who are released from jails would lead and represent the party in the talks.'*

My question is whether these are realistic preconditions. For example, the 'all-out war' can be suspended first before it is 'withdrawn', i.e. a ceasefire, so why insist on its withdrawal at the outset? Are you asking for a ceasefire or something more than that?

Secondly, you want the ban on the party and its mass organizations lifted and prisoners released. Usually in negotiations of this kind around the world between governments and insurgent groups, the lifting of a ban is one of the objects of talks rather than a precondition and the release of political prisoners an intermediate step. Is the Maoist party not putting the cart before the horse, making demands that the government may be unlikely to accept as a starting point, rather than positing the same as one of the end points of the proposed dialogue?

Azad: I concur with the logic of your arguments. It is logically a valid argument that such demands could be resolved in the course of actual talks and not as a precondition for talks. But you must also understand the spirit of what comrade Ganapathi has said in his interview given to Jan Myrdal and Gautam Navlakha. Some clarification is required here. I will try to clarify what comrade Ganapathi has said.

Firstly what he meant when he said the government should withdraw its all-out war is nothing but a suspension of its war, or in other words, mutual ceasefire. Let there be no confusion in this regard. What Chidambaram wants is unilateral ceasefire by Maoists while the state continues its brutal campaign of terror. On the contrary, what the CPI (Maoist) wants is a cessation of hostilities by both sides simultaneously. This is the meaning of the first point. A ceasefire by both sides cannot be called a precondition. It is but an expression of the willingness on the part of both sides engaged in war to create a conducive atmosphere for going to the next step of talks.

Secondly, if peaceful legal work has to be done by Maoists as desired by several organizations and members of civil society, then lifting of ban becomes a prerequisite. Without lifting the ban on the party and mass organizations how can we organize legal struggles, meetings, etc., in our name? If we do so, will these not be dubbed as illegal as they are led by a banned party? According to us, the ban itself is an authoritarian, undemocratic, and fascist act. Hence the demand for the lifting of the ban is a legitimate demand, and, if fulfilled, will go a long way in promoting open democratic forms of struggles and creating a conducive atmosphere for a dialogue.

Thirdly, what Comrade Ganapathi had asked for is that the government should adhere to the Indian constitution and put an end to the illegal murders in the name of encounters, tortures and arrests. We must include the term 'murders' which is missing in the third point. There is nothing wrong or unreasonable in asking the government to stick to its own constitution. As regards the release of political prisoners this could be an intermediate step as far as the nature of the demand is concerned. However, to hold talks it is necessary for the government to release some leaders. Or else, there would be none to talk to since the entire party is illegal. We cannot bring any of our leaders overground for the purpose of talks.

Varadarajan: *Would the Maoists be prepared to establish their bona fides on the question of talks by announcing a unilateral ceasefire or, perhaps the non-initiation of combat operations (NICO) after a particular date so as to facilitate the process of dialogue?*

Azad: It is quite strange to see intellectuals like you asking the Maoists to declare a unilateral ceasefire when the heavily armed Indian state is carrying out its brutal armed offensive and counter-revolutionary war. How would unilateral announcement of ceasefire or NICO after a particular date establish the bona fides of our party on the question of talks? What purpose would such an act serve? It is incomprehensible to me why we are asked to 'display this generosity' towards an enemy who has the least concern for the welfare of the people and derives vicarious pleasure in coldblooded murders, rapes, abductions, tortures and every kind of atrocity one could ever imagine. And how would this 'generous Gandhian act' on our part facilitate the process of dialogue with the megalomaniacs in the Home Ministry who do not spare even non-violent Gandhian social activists working in Dantewada and other places?

Varadarajan: *What do the Maoists hope to achieve with talks? Are you only looking to buy time and regroup yourselves—which is what the government said the CPI (Maoist) did during the aborted dialogue in Andhra Pradesh? Or is it part of a more general re-evaluation of the political strategy of the party, one which may see it emerge as an overground political formation, engaged in open, legal activities and struggles, and perhaps even entering the electoral fray directly or indirectly at various levels in the kind of 'multiparty competition' that Prachanda says is necessary for the communist movement? When you say you want the government to lift its ban on the party, are you also undertaking not to indulge in methods of struggle (e.g., armed struggle) which led to the imposition of the ban in the first place? There are other Maoist and revolutionary communist parties across India that are mobilizing workers and peasants through mass politics. They have not been banned. Why does the CPI (Maoist) not believe those are legitimate forms of struggle? In Kashmir, the Hurriyat Conference stands for the self-determination of J&K and seeks to mobilize people for this but the Indian state, which may use violence and repression and excessive force against people who peacefully protest, has not banned the Hurriyat. Does this not indicate that there is some space in the system for the Maoists to press their demands through peaceful political means?*

Azad: Your question, or rather, a whole set of questions, requires a detailed answer. I am afraid it will take much space but I will try to be as brief as possible. Before I proceed, let me clarify at the very outset that the proposal of talks is neither a ploy to buy time nor regroup ourselves, nor is it a part of the general re-evaluation of the political strategy of the party that could lead to its coming overground, entering the electoral fray, and multiparty competition as in Nepal. Our CC had already dealt in detail with the question of multiparty competition in our Open Letter to the UCPN (M) and various articles and interviews by our party leaders. So I will not go into it again here.

Now let me take up each of the points that you had raised.

First, you asked me what we want to achieve with talks. My one-sentence answer is: we want to achieve whatever is possible for the betterment of people's lives without compromising on our political programme of new democratic revolution and strategy of protracted people's war. People have a right to enjoy whatever is guaranteed under the Indian Constitution, however, nominal and limited these provisions are. And the government is duty-bound to implement the provisions of the Constitution. We hope the talks would raise the overall consciousness of the oppressed people about their fundamental rights and rally them to fight for their rights. Talks will also expose government's hypocrisy, duplicity, and its authoritarian and extra-constitutional rule that violates whatever is guaranteed by the Constitution. So talks would help in exposing the government's callous attitude to the people and may help in bringing about reforms, however, limited they may be.

Another important reason is: talks will give some respite to the people who are oppressed and suppressed under the fascist jackboots of the Indian state and state-sponsored terrorist organizations like the Salwa Judum, Maa Danteswari Swabhiman Manch, Sendra, Nagarik Suraksha Samiti, Shanti Sena, Harmad Bahini, and so on. Those who sit in studios and insulated rooms, and make their expert analyses about how Maoists want to buy time or utilize the respite to regroup themselves, can never understand the ABC of revolution or the ground situation. This is actually not an argument at all. If the Maoists try to utilize the situation, so would the police and the government. Wouldn't they? They created an extensive network of police informers during the six-month period of ceasefire in Andhra Pradesh in 2004. The intelligence hawks attended every open meeting and activity of the Maoists, took videos of people, and could easily target them after the clampdown. Maoists had definitely increased their recruitment but so did the enemy. It doesn't need much of a common sense to understand that both sides will utilize a situation of ceasefire to strengthen their respective sides. Then could this be called an argument at all? These cynics, or, I would rather call them, war-hungry hawks, itch for a brutal suppression of the Maoists and the people they directly lead, even if it means genocide. They do not care if in the process thousands of police and paramilitary personnel too perish for they are nothing but cannon fodder in the eyes of these gentlemen.

So let me make it crystal clear: the proposal of talks is meant neither to buy time nor to regroup ourselves but to give some respite for the people at large who are living under constant state terror and immense suffering. How many of our countrymen know that three lakh *adivasis* were driven away from their homes, that half the *adivasi* population in our country is already living under conditions of chronic famine and even the rest of the population is now pushed into famine condition? And why? Because of the insatiable greed of the corporate sharks that is fuelling Chidambram-Raman Singh's war in Chhattisgarh, Chidambaram-Naveen Patnaik's war in Orissa, Chidambaram-Buddhadeb's war in West Bengal,

Chidambaram-Shibu Soren's war in Jharkhand, and so on. Whoever has the minimum concern for the well-being of the masses, no matter what his/her ideology is, would naturally think of how to save them from being decimated. But those who have nothing but sheer contempt for the poor and helpless people and only think of how to maximize the profits of a tiny parasitic class, put forth weird and cynical arguments deliberately to confuse the people. They depict the Maoists as terrorists, create a fear psychosis in the middle and upper classes that the Maoists would soon come to your cities and disturb your supposedly secure lives; that they would seize power by the middle of this century, and what not. By such hysteria whipped up by the rulers through the various means at their disposal, they justify the brutal war on the people and make the massive displacement, mayhem, massacres, rapes and atrocities appear like collateral damage in the larger noble objective of achieving peace, progress and prosperity for all.

Varadarajan: *On the question of re-evaluation of political strategy of CPI (Maoist), demand for lifting of ban, and the issue of legitimacy of open, legal forms of struggle?*

Azad: There are a lot of questions related to the above and I feel this needs some detailed explanation keeping in mind several misconceptions doing the rounds. Firstly you are wrong in assuming that it is the forms of struggle (armed struggle) pursued by the CPI (Maoist) that had 'led to the imposition of the ban in the first place'. On the contrary, it is the other way round. It is the imposition of the ban that had led the party and mass organizations to take up arms in the first place. People are easily misled to believe that it is the violence of the Maoists that had compelled the government to impose the ban. This is a classic example of how a white lie can be dressed up and presented as the truth by endless repetition. If you have even a cursory glance at the history of the revolutionary movement in our country you will find that the forms of struggle adopted by the Maoist revolutionaries from time to time basically corresponded to the forms of suppression pursued by the rulers.

A stark example of the transformation of a peaceful mass movement into a violent armed struggle is right in front of our eyes. Lalgarh's peaceful mass movement with simple demands for an apology from the police officials and an end to brutal police repression had transformed into a revolutionary armed struggle due to the brutal suppression campaign unleashed by the state and state-sponsored terrorists like the Harmad Bahini. So was the case of the movement in Kashmir and various states of north-east. Even in Naxalbari in 1967, the first shots were fired on unarmed women and children by the police. The people retaliated in their own manner and the party took birth and evolved a correct political line for the Indian revolution. In Srikakulam, Koranna and Manganna were the first martyrs and these murders transformed the movement into an armed struggle. Even during the first great armed mass uprising of Telangana during the late 1940s, the spark was first lit when the cruel feudal lords murdered Doddi Komaraiah.

If you take the case of the transformation of the movement led by the erstwhile CPI(ML)[PW] or MCCI or the present CPI(Maoist), you will find the same pattern. The revolutionaries go to the oppressed, make them conscious of their inherent strength and the reasons for their misery, make them aware of their fundamental rights, organize and unite them, mobilize them into peaceful forms of protest and struggle. Then the state enters with its baton in defence of the class of big landlords, contractors, industrialists, land mafia and other powerful forces that control the state and economy. Everywhere, the peaceful struggles are crushed brutally, entire areas are declared disturbed, fake encounters, abductions, disappearances, rapes, burning down villages, and untold atrocities become the order of the day.

The Indian Constitution is consigned to the dustbin by the rulers and is not even worth the paper it is written on. At that point of time any revolutionary party has to quickly switch to non-peaceful and armed forms of struggle if it is really serious about transforming the lives of the people and the oppressive conditions in the country. The alternative is to surrender the revolutionary aims, make adjustments with the system and sail with other parliamentary parties albeit with some revolutionary rhetoric for a while. This, however, will not work for as long as people cannot distinguish between the bourgeois feudal parties and the ML party that had turned into a new parliamentary party. When people are fighting a do-or-die battle you cannot turn your tail but will have to provide them with new appropriate forms of struggle and forms of organization. And this is what our party had done right from the days of Jagtyal Jaitra Yatra.

What shook the rulers at that time and compelled them to declare Jagtyal and Sircilla taluks in Karimnagar district of north Telangana as disturbed areas in 1978 was not the armed struggle of the Maoists (which had suffered a complete setback after the setback in Naxalbari, Srikakulam and elsewhere by 1972 itself) but the powerful anti-feudal militant mass struggle that upset the hitherto established feudal order in the countryside. And one of the main forms of struggle at that time was social boycott of the feudal lords and their henchmen, which witnessed the unity of over 95 per cent of the people in most villages. Social boycott had disturbed the peace and tranquillity of the feudal barons who functioned like a state within a state. From then on, undeclared ban has been in vogue in parts of north Telangana until 1985 when it encompassed the entire state. CRPF was deployed for the first time to suppress the peaceful mass struggles that broke out against liquor. I remember how the mainstream media like the *Indian Express* published stories of policemen selling arrack at the police stations and forcing people to consume liquor in order to foil the anti-liquor agitation of the revolutionaries.

We find the same story in the urban areas too. The Singareni colliery workers organized themselves into a trade union called Singareni Workers' Federation (SIKASA) in 1981 but it was unofficially banned within three years. An undeclared ban was imposed on students' and youth organizations, women's organizations, workers' organizations, cultural organizations and every form of peaceful, democratic protest was brutally suppressed. One must see the development of armed struggle in the background of the strangulation of even the limited democratic space available in the present semi-colonial, semi-feudal set-up, and the brutal suppression of the movement by unleashing the lethal instruments of the state.

To cut a long story short, it is not the forms of struggle and forms of organization adopted by a party that had led to the imposition of ban but the very ban (whether declared or undeclared) on every type of open, legal activity including peaceful public meetings that had compelled the revolutionaries to adopt non-peaceful and armed forms of struggle and underground forms of organization. Our party appeals to all independent observers and unbiased media personnel to look at this phenomenon historically and analyse this with an open mind. You will realize that what I have said is 100 per cent correct. We are prepared to enter into a debate with anyone on the course of development of the revolutionary movement led by our party in our country and how, why, and when armed form of struggle had to be adopted by the party.

Revolutionaries never mince words. There is no need to. We believe that ultimately people have to take up armed struggle to seize power. But this does not mean we take up armed struggle at the cost of all other forms of struggle and thereby invite the state to unleash its brute force on the people. On the contrary, it is only when all other forms of struggle fail to achieve the objective, when these are crushed under the iron heels of the state that we resort to non-peaceful and armed forms of struggle. It is very important to understand this as it has become a common practice for some so-called political analysts and representatives of the ruling classes to charge the Maoists as responsible for all the violence since their very ideology talks of armed struggle. Hence, they conclude, there is no use of talks with the Maoists. These simpletons resort to the method of simple reductionism: Maoists believe in violence and armed struggle to overthrow the state; hence they indulge in endless violence; there is no use of talking to people whose very ideology is rooted in violence; and hence there is no other way than to crush the Maoists with all the means at the disposal of the state. Such goes their argument. I will deal with this later on.

I didn't quite understand what you meant when you said referring to other open Maoist and revolutionary communist parties across India that are mobilizing workers and peasants through mass politics: 'Why does the CPI (Maoist) not believe those are legitimate forms of struggle?', you ask. Who has said we do not believe these are legitimate forms of struggle? We consider all forms of struggle as legitimate, right from social boycott as we had practised in Jagtyal, hungerstrikes as our comrades in various prisons are frequently taking up besides other places, and various militant demonstrations. Armed struggle is also a form of struggle and assumes importance depending on the tactical moves by the enemy. While all forms of struggle are legitimate in our eyes, some so-called revolutionaries, veterans of yester-years, surprisingly exclude armed struggle from the forms of struggle and lay one-sided emphasis on peaceful forms of struggle. They can well join the Gandhian organizations and fight for some reforms instead of calling themselves as part of the ML stream or as Maoists aiming for the revolutionary transformation of society. For some of them, ML ideology or label is only a fashion. They do not wish to bring about the revolutionary transformation of the society and state but only a few cosmetic reforms.

The question of imposing or not imposing a ban on a certain party or organization depends on several factors. It would be too simplistic to conclude that just because a party believes in armed struggle and indulges in acts of violence it is being banned while those who pursue open, legal forms of struggle are allowed to function freely. During the Emergency, as we all know, both the revolutionary Left as well as the reactionary Right parties were banned. Even at the height of sectarian violence indulged in by the Hindu fascist gangs, they are allowed a field day. They carry arms, display them openly, threaten the religious minorities with genocide, indulge in violence against the Muslims and Christians, and yet are deemed as legitimate organizations since they are part of the ruling classes and their integral culture of violence.

The acts of destruction in the violence that was organized in a planned manner [in Andhra Pradesh] by a faction of the Congress in one day far surpassed the so-called violent acts carried out by Maoists in an entire year! Yet our Union Home Ministry issues advertisements against Maoist violence while keeping mum about the mayhem and arson by his own Congress party hooligans. Thus the question of how you look at violence is coloured with a class bias. The violence by the ruling class parties is considered legitimate while those by the oppressed masses and their organizations are dangerous and a threat to the security of the rulers. This has been true right from the time of Charvakas.

Varadarajan: *If the government believes the Maoists 'misused' the Andhra talks, your party believes the dialogue there was abused by the authorities to identify and then target your leaders. How, then, do you hope to deal with the risks of once again entering into a dialogue with the Indian state?*

Azad: The talks we held with the Congress regime in AP provided us with important lessons. And these lessons would guide us in any future talks with the governments of the exploiting classes. It would be too simplistic to conclude that the police could identify and target the leaders by utilizing the talks interregnum. They used it to some extent just as we used it to take our politics widely among the people in the state and outside. The setback we had suffered in most parts of AP is not a fall-out of talks but due to several inherent weaknesses of our party in AP and our failure to adopt appropriate tactics to confront enemy's tactics. This is an entirely different subject and can be dealt at some other time.

What is of relevance here is that the talks in AP have given us a rich experience and important lessons. If at all a situation for talks arises once again—which we do not foresee in the near future given the inexorable compulsions on the government from the corporate sharks for total control of the mineral-rich region—we can instruct our leadership in various prisons to take the responsibility. Our general secretary had explained this in the course of his interview with Jan Myrdal and Gautam Navlakha. The mistakes committed in AP during talks with the government will not be repeated.

Varadarajan: *There is a contradiction between the recent offer for talks made by Kishenji and the spate of violence and killing by the Maoists, which has followed that. The Home Ministry has compiled a list of such incidents and circulated it to the media. No doubt there has been no letup in the government offensive during this period and you could produce your own counter-list but many of these attacks by the Maoists do not appear to be 'defensive' but 'offensive'. Can the offer of talks go hand in hand with the intensification of offensive Maoist military activities?*

Azad: This is not as complicated as it is made out to be. The crux of the matter is: no ceasefire has been declared either by the Maoists or by the government. The Maoists had made an offer of talks which was immediately dismissed by the government as a joke and spurned by Chidambaram himself who wants nothing short of total surrender, whatever be the language he uses. When the government is not serious about a ceasefire and dialogue, and is placing a condition that Maoists should abjure violence without spelling out whether it will reciprocate with a simultaneous declaration of ceasefire, then what is the use of grumbling about acts of violence by Maoists? The acts of violence by both sides will cease from the day a ceasefire is declared.

Now I am not going into the innumerable atrocities by the police forces and the paramilitary gangs sent by [the state]. There has been a wide coverage in magazines like *Tehelka*, *Outlook* and our own Maoist information bulletins. The statements and fact-finding committee reports by various organizations and Gandhians like Himanshu Kumar clearly show how savage the state has become.

Equally atrocious is the list compiled by the Union Home Ministry regarding the violent acts by Maoists to justify its rejection of the Maoist offer. The annexure appended to your questionnaire speaks volumes about the duplicity and lies spread by the warmongering hawks in the Home Ministry as part of their psy-war. This is meant to lend an element of legitimacy to their rejection of the ceasefire offer by Maoists and also to their war waged for nipping in the bud the alternative organs of people's power, the alternative development models, and for grabbing the resources in the mineral-rich region for the benefit of the class of tiny parasitic corporate elite they represent. I will not go into all the incidents listed therein.

The very first 'heinous act of violence' cited by the Union Home Ministry in its annexure circulated to the media to manufacture consent for its dirty war, goes like this: 'In West Bengal (22 February 2010)—attack on a State Police CRPF Joint patrol party in PS Lalgarh, district West Midnapore. In the ensuing gun battle Lalmoham Tudu, President of the Police e-Sangharsh Birodhi Janaganer Committee (PSBJC) was killed.'

The above incident was said to have taken place within three hours of the offer of a 72-day ceasefire made by comrade Kishenji. Chidambaram himself had gone on record repeating several times this fabricated 'heinous act' in a desperate bid to justify his rejection of the Maoist offer. Earlier too, Chidambaram had deliberately hurled an accusation against the CPI(Maoist) of massacring villagers in Khagaria district. Coming to the so-called attack by Maoists on the joint patrol party, it is a 100 per cent lie. There was no such attack at all. Ask anyone in Narcha village or Kanatapahari. Every villager, and not just the family members of Sri Tudu, will tell you how a 100 odd CRPF men lay in waiting at his house on the night of 22 February, how they caught the three, and carried out the cold-blooded murder. That there had been no firing by the Maoists was corroborated even by the CRPF men guarding the camp.

Initially, the SP of Paschim Mednipur asserted that Tudu died when the CRPF men 'bravely' retaliated to an attack by the Maoist guerrillas on the fortress-like CRPF camp in Kantapahari. Later, realizing the hollowness of his own story and fearing that it would evaporate like dew drops with the first rays of the sun, they changed the version by [saying] that Tudu and other two were killed when a Maoist guerrilla squad attacked the CRPF's raiding party. This lie is being propagated consciously, with a clearly worked out strategy of justifying the gruesome offensive by our own brand of George Bushes and Donald Rumsfelds.

Tehelka magazine, Star Ananda and other media sources have graphically exposed this lie.

As for your question regarding offensive and defensive actions, I wish to clarify to every well-meaning person who desires a reduction of violence on the part of the Maoists that there is nothing like defensive and offensive actions once the war has commenced. However, our revolutionary counter-violence is overall defensive in nature for a considerable period of time. This does not mean we will retaliate only when we are fired at and keep silent the rest of the time when the police, paramilitary and the vigilante gangs unleash terror and engage in all-round preparations for carrying out genocide. To make this clear, let us suppose the men sent by Chidambaram are combing an area. When we come to know of it, we will carry out an offensive, annihilate as many forces as possible in the given circumstances, and seize arms and ammunition. We will also take prisoners of war where that is possible. This will be part of our overall defensive strategy although it is a tactical counter-offensive.

In the war zone, if you do not take the initiative, the enemy will seize the initiative. Likewise, we may have to attack ordnance depots, trucks carrying explosives, guards at installations such as NMDC, RPF personnel, and even outposts and stations far beyond our areas to seize arms, as in Nayagarh, for instance. To fight a well-equipped superior enemy force that has no dearth of arms supplies and logistical support, what other option do we have but to equip ourselves with the arms seized from the enemy?

Some of these men are killed when they offer resistance. We feel sorry for their lives but there is no other way. Chidambaram may yell that innocent CISF jawans were targeted even though they were in no way related to the state's offensive against Maoists. But that is how things would be in a war zone. The war would get dirtier and dirtier, engulf new areas and affect hitherto unaffected regions and sections of society. But this is precisely what [the ruling] coterie want. We will also destroy the informer network built by the enemy, his supplies, bunkers, communication network and infrastructure. We have to confiscate money from the banks and other sources for funding the revolution. There is no use of yelling about the indiscriminate destruction by Maoists. We have to paralyse the administration, immobilize the enemy troops, cut-off his supplies and perhaps even target the policemen engaged in removing the dead bodies of the enemy. There was a hue and cry when our guerrillas placed mines under the dead bodies.

But why such a hue and cry? Where are the rules in this war? Who has defined the rules? If there were rules, then why are the peace-chanting pigeons in the Home Ministry completely silent about the beasts in police uniform who had chopped off the breasts of 70-year-old Dude Muye before killing her, murdered in cold blood over 120 *adivasis* since August 2009 in Dantewada, Bijapur, Kanker and Narayanpur, and yet roam freely and continue their atrocities without hindrance? Chidambaram, Pillai, Raman Singh and their like should first define the rules of engagement and then, and only then, they have a right to speak of violations of the rules. I am sure they would never dare to discipline their own forces while preaching meaningless sermons about Maoist 'atrocities'.

We appeal to all peace-loving, democratic-minded organizations and individuals to ponder over this question, pressurize the government to adhere to the Geneva Convention, punish those who are creating Gompads, Gachampallis, Singanamadugus, Palachelimas, Tetemadugus, Takilodus, Dogpadus, Palods, and several other massacres. If it is to be a war, then let it be, but the state should clearly state whether it would abide by its own constitution and the international conventions on the conduct of war.

Varadarajan: *The Maoists are engaging in armed struggle but have not hesitated in using violence against non-combatants. The beheading of a policeman, Francis Induwar, while in Maoist captivity, shocked the country and was a blatant violation of civilized norms and of international humanitarian law, which the Maoists, like the government, are obliged to adhere to. If civil society condemns the security forces for killing civilians in places like Gompad village in Chhattisgarh and elsewhere and demands that justice be done and the guilty punished, it has an equal right to condemn the Maoists whenever they commit such crimes. There have been some reports that the Maoist leadership has apologized for the killing of Induwar but what steps have you taken to punish those who were involved? What steps have you taken to ensure such crimes are not committed by your cadres? If your answer is that the state has also not punished those among its ranks who have committed crimes, are you then admitting that the political culture and moral universe the Maoists represent is the same as that of the state which you decry as illegitimate?*

Azad: I have already covered part of your question in my answer to your earlier question. Our attempt will always be to target the enemy who is engaged in war against us. Non-combatants are generally avoided. But what about the intelligence officials and police informers who collect information about the movements of Maoists and cause immense damage to the movement? It is true most of them do not carry arms openly or are unarmed. What to do with them? If we just leave them they would continue to cause damage to the party and movement. If we punish them there is a furore from the media and civil society. Caught between the devil and the deep sea! Our general practice is to conduct a trial in a people's court wherever that is possible and proceed in accordance with the decision of the people. Where it is not possible to hold the people's court due to the intensity of repression, we conduct investigation, take the opinion of the people and give appropriate punishment.

I agree there is no place for cruelty while giving out punishments. I had clarified this in one of my earlier interviews while referring to the case of Francis Induwar. But it is made into a big issue by the media when a thousand beheadings had taken place in the past five years by the police, paramilitary and Salwa Judum goons. You are saying the beheading of Francis Induwar was a blatant violation of civilized norms and of international humanitarian law which both sides in the war are obliged to adhere to. Do you really think the government is adhering to the law? And has the media ventured to ask Chidambaram why [the state] hasn't been following the international law or at least the Indian constitution when dealing with the people in the war zone or citizens elsewhere? Just ten days ago, two of our party leaders—comrades Shakhamuri Appa Rao and Kondal Reddy—were abducted from Chennai and Pune respectively by the APSIB and the Central Intelligence officials and were murdered in cold blood. What cruel tortures these comrades were subjected to by the lawless goons of the Indian state no one will ever know. I can give a thousand such examples of killings of our comrades in cold blood while in police captivity in the past five years. Why is the media silent about these murders but becomes hysteric when one police inspector is beheaded? What is the civil society doing when such cold-blooded murders are taking place in police custody? Why single out a rare case of the beheading of one Induwar and play it up whenever you need an excuse to bash the Maoists?

When our comrades hear of these cold-blooded murders committed by the APSIB or other officials of the state, it is natural that their blood would boil and they will not bat an eyelid to hack any of the perpetrators of these inhuman crimes, say a man from APSIB or Grey Hounds, to pieces if he fell into their hands. In the war zone, the passions run with such intensity which one cannot even imagine in other areas or under normal circumstances. Could someone who has seen women being raped and murdered, children and old men being murdered after hacking them to pieces in the killing fields of Dantewada and Bijapur, ever give a thought to your so-called non-existent (I say non-existent as none of the combatants know what these are nor would follow these conventions as the history of fake encounters by the Indian state shows) international laws when the perpetrator of such crimes happens to fall into their hands? The pent up anger of the masses is so intense that even the party general secretary will perhaps fail to control the fury of the *adivasi* masses when they lay their hands on their tormentors.

Maoists are not for crude and raw justice as some are trying to make it appear. Maoist guerrillas are not thugs and mercenaries like the men who carry out their brutal heinous acts in the name of democracy and the 'rule of law'. Maoists have great respect for human life. Democratic values and norms are an integral part of socialist and communist ideology. Yet at the same time we think it is necessary to destroy the few poisonous weeds to save the entire crop.

I once again request you and all others to think by imagining yourselves what would you have done when your mothers, sisters and daughters are raped in front of your eyes, your father, brother and sons are murdered after being hacked to pieces. And worst of all, when there is no guardian of the 'rule of law' to receive your complaints and the complainant himself/herself is abducted. When we do not understand the feelings of the affected people, it is better to imagine ourselves in their place. This may help us in getting nearer to the truth.

Varadarajan: *The Supreme Court has asked the petitioners who filed a PIL against Salwa Judum atrocities to draw up a rehabilitation plan for those displaced by the violence perpetrated in Chhattisgarh by Salwa Judum, the regular security forces and the Maoists. Is the CPI (Maoist) prepared to give an undertaking that it will allow the rebuilding of schools and the establishment of basic government services (primary health care,* anganwadi, *PDS, etc.) as part of a court-backed plan for the welfare of the tribals affected by the conflict? Will you agree not to attack government employees and officials who enter to provide services to the tribal masses?*

Azad: Asking us to give an undertaking that we will allow the rebuilding of schools and establishment of basic government services in the areas we control and that we will not attack government employees and officials is quite bizarre, to say the least. The welfare of the masses is the first priority for the Maoist revolutionaries. You should request Chidambaram to allow you to visit the areas in Dandakaranya, Jharkhand, Orissa, or the villages of Jangalmahal by controlling his paramilitary forces, the SPOs, the Salwa Judum, Shanti Sena, Nagarik Suraksha Samiti and Harmad from obstructing you. Then you will see with your own eyes a hitherto hidden story of how the *adivasis* are prevented from pursuing their normal activity by the state and state-sponsored terrorists.

You will find how the forces had occupied school buildings for six months to a year, thereby preventing the children from pursuing their studies. You will find how the *adivasis* are prevented from buying their daily necessities from the weekly bazaars most of which were forcibly closed through threats and intimidation by the so-called security forces. Who is blocking the development of the *adivasis*, who is preventing them from carrying on their normal activity like cultivating the fields, tending the animals, collecting minor forest produce, picking *tendu* leaves, obtaining their daily necessities, and so on will become as clear as daylight once you visit these remote villages. Hence the government, its 'security' forces, and vigilante gangs are hell bent on preventing independent observers and fact finding teams from visiting these areas.

It is worthwhile to keep in mind that it is not the lack of development that has become the problem in the rural areas, particularly *adivasi*-inhabited areas. On the contrary, it is its imperialist-dictated anti-people development model that is driving them to displacement and deprivation, death and destitution, and extreme desperation. There need be hardly any doubt that the poor *adivasis* have been a happier lot before the civilized [corporate] goons set their foot on their soil. The development model pursued by [the rulers] displaced them and made them aliens in their own land.

The so-called development that you are referring to is the development that India had seen under the British colonialists. The talk of roads in remote areas is not for the benefit of the people, who are without food and drinking water, but only for the speedier movement of raw materials from the hinterland to the cities, to help the mining sharks to transport the mineral wealth and forest produce. And, of course, for rushing in the state's troops to quell any militant people's struggle against the rapacious plunder by the tiny parasitic class of bloodsucking leeches. The entire world knows that a George Bush invaded Iraq for oil even as the media in the US barked about Saddam's non-existent Weapons of Mass Destruction. Entire India knows that [the rulers] and the vultures they represent are itching to lay their hands on the abundant reserves of iron ore, coal, tin, bauxite, dolomite, limestone and other minerals of Chhattisgarh, Jharkhand, Orissa and other states where their Operation Green Hunt is launched.

Lastly, banding together Maoists with the state and vigilante gangs, and equating their revolutionary counter-violence in defence of the rights of the people with the counter-revolutionary violence of the state and vigilante gangs like the Salwa Judum, is a despicable trick played by the rulers and those so-called democratic forces to obfuscate the stark reality of the brutal violence of the state and state-sponsored terrorists. I can say with full confidence that there was no displacement, whatsoever, of innocent people due to the revolutionary counter-violence by the Maoists. It is only a handful of anti-people exploiters, tribal heads and landed gentry who had fled the villages in the course of the class struggle.

Many, however, had surrendered to the people, mended their behaviour, and continue to live in the villages like others.

The Supreme Court should know that the displacement of the *adivasis* was done in accordance with a premediated plan to evacuate the villages and settle them in Vietnam-type strategic hamlets. And this policy is being continued by the BJP government in Chhattisgarh with full assistance from the Congress-led government at the centre. The Supreme Court, if at all it is serious about the displacement of the *adivasis*, should direct the central and state governments to immediately halt its brutal armed offensive on *adivasi* villages in the first place, which is resulting in the massive exodus of the people estimated at around three lakhs since the current brutal war began in the name of Operation Green Hunt.

Varadarajan: *Human rights groups have condemned the security forces and the Maoists for not respecting the sanctity of schools. If the security forces take them over and convert them into barracks, the Maoists have also been guilty of destroying school buildings and infrastructure. Even in the absence of a ceasefire or dialogue, don't you think both sides need to come to an understanding that schools and school children should not become targets of this war?*

Azad: It has now become a fashionable thing for some human rights groups and the media personnel to play the role of referees in a sports event. By criticizing both sides equally they imagine they are being impartial or neutral in the war. If someone says that both Indians and the British were responsible for the violence in India during the two centuries of British rule would you accept it? Or that both Iraqis and the American occupiers are responsible for the violence in Iraq? Any freedom-loving person would unequivocally say it was the British colonialists that caused the bloodshed in India and it is the American aggressors that are the cause for the unending violence in Iraq.

By criticizing both, the so-called security forces and the Maoists, for not respecting the sanctity of schools, these human rights groups imagine they are playing a neutral and impartial role. But they do not even see the cause-and-effect chain of events. They do not ask themselves the simple question: if the police and paramilitary do not occupy schools, then where is the need for the Maoists to destroy them? Do you know the fact that in many villages it was not the Maoist squads but the people themselves who had demolished school buildings since they did not wish to see the security forces create insecurity in their villages? How can you ask the Maoists and the people to assure you that they will respect the sanctity of schools occupied or likely to be occupied by their tormentors?

My request to media people like you is: please do not be misled by an act, by how it happened, but go deeper into why it happened. Only then you will reach the truth.

However, we also agree with your proposition that even in the absence of a ceasefire or dialogue, both sides should come to an understanding that schools and school children should not become targets of the war. We take this occasion to convey to the GOI that it should immediately withdraw all its forces from school buildings and stop recruiting school children as SPOs and as police informers. If they withdraw their forces and assure they would not reoccupy school buildings, then our party will desist from targeting schools. And if the government stops recruitment of school children as SPOs and police informers, then the very basis for punishing these people disappears.

But the more important thing and the larger issue is: can schools function even if the buildings are intact when the parents of the school children are murdered, raped, abducted, tortured, and are forced to flee? What do you have to say of the children of the three lakh people who had fled the villages due to Operation Green Hunt I and II? What use are the school buildings and the talk of sanctity of schools when the villages themselves are deserted? A more rational proposal would be to ensure that the inhabitants of the villages are resettled with the assurance that the police and paramilitary would not continue their atrocities and let them live in peace. This is the most important thing and should assume first and foremost priority in the war theatres all over India, particularly Dandakaranya.

Varadarajan: *Is the Maoist party and leadership under pressure because of recent top-level arrests like that of Kobad Ghandy? Is there also a wider crisis of leadership with fewer activists from the intelligentsia getting attracted to Maoists?*

Azad: I did not understand what pressure you are referring to. Is it the pressure for a ceasefire and talks? If so, then I would say you are completely off the mark. One cannot overcome pressure through such tactics. Actually the party and leadership will grow rapidly in times of war. Several new leaders are emerging out of the struggle. War is giving birth to new generals and commanders, which we never anticipated in normal times. While it took several years to produce a leader of calibre in relatively peaceful times, it is taking a fraction of that time in the midst of the war situation.

Today we find even children acquiring high level of consciousness at an early age. War is transforming the world outlook of the illiterate people, their understanding about the class nature of the state and its various wings, and how they have to get rid of the anti-people state and establish their own organs of power. People have begun to understand from their own lives what Comrade Lenin had taught in his *State and Revolution*. This transformation has contributed to the development of leadership at all levels. At the central level, I agree there is some problem, though not very acute, after the losses in the past two years.

Overall, it is not true to say that there is a wider crisis of leadership due to drop in recruitment from the intelligentsia. You will be surprised to know that contrary to the assessment of various analysts and media personnel, the appeal of the Maoist movement has actually grown stronger in the intelligentsia. And it is precisely this fact which is rattling [the rulers] and [their] trumpeters in the media. The threats and attacks on intellectuals have been increasing in tenor and there are growing attempts at isolating the intellectuals who seem to sympathize with the Maoists. The more the growth in popularity of the Maoists and their politics, the more is the cacophony about the erosion of the mass base of Maoists, especially among the intellectuals.

You must also look at it from another angle, instead of concluding that [a] lack of intelligentsia has created a crisis of leadership. The mass base of the Maoists has actually grown stronger, notwithstanding the attempts of the rulers to destroy it by brute force. The more you try to crush it the more it bounces back. Our leadership is drawn basically from the oppressed class of *adivasis*, Dalits, agricultural labourers and poor peasants. It is precisely because of this circumstance that our movement has become invincible. Intellectuals are a good asset for the party but it is the basic classes that are the lifeblood of the party. And we have plenty from these sections.

Varadarajan: *In Ganapathi's interview to Jan Myrdal and Navlakha, he said: 'I reiterate that at present no one party or organization is capable enough to be a rallying centre for all revolutionary, democratic, progressive and patriotic forces and people. Hence, at present juncture our party can play a significant role in rallying all revolutionary, democratic, progressive and patriotic forces and people.' This suggests you see the Maoists as one part of a wider force of progressive, patriotic people. Who else do you consider part of these forces? Which organizations or parties do you regard as progressive and patriotic part of these forces? Does this not include the CPI and CPI(M)? Why then have Maoists in Bengal been involved in assassinating cadres of other communist parties like CPI(M)?*

Azad: It is not only now, but all along we have been considering ourselves an indivisible part of the broader force of other revolutionary, democratic and patriotic sections of people. Firstly, we are one of the several revolutionary detachments in the international detachment of the world proletariat and we see ourselves as a part of the broad worldwide anti-imperialist front. Our mass organizations are a part of the International League of People's Struggles (ILPS) and are in the forefront of the struggle against American imperialism.

Within India, our party took birth in the midst of the revolutionary upsurge of the late 1960s, particularly with the glorious Naxalbari uprising, and hence we are an indivisible part of all that is revolutionary in the Indian political stream. We are also an heir to the great Telangana Armed Agrarian Uprising (1946-51), the Tebhaga uprising of 1946, and all the revolutionary struggles led by the Communist Party since its birth in 1921, notwithstanding the betrayals by its central leadership at every critical turning point in the revolutionary political history of our country.

Second, and the one more pertinent to your query, is the fact that the communist revolutionaries are politically (i.e. in terms of its programme), a part of the wider democratic stream of all anti-feudal and anti-imperialist forces in the country. This is the essence of our programme of new democratic revolution (NDR), which seeks to unite all those opposed to imperialism, feudalism, comprador bureaucratic capitalism into one broad front to overthrow these enemies and establish a government comprised of the four-class alliance of the working class, peasantry, urban petty bourgeoisie, and the national bourgeoisie. Once you grasp this political basis of our NDR it will not be difficult to understand why we are trying to form numerous tactical united fronts as part of forming a strategic united front in various states and at the all-India level.

To identify the organizations or parties that can be called progressive (usage of the term 'democratic' would be more appropriate) and patriotic, one has to see not only whether they have any anti-imperialist, anti-feudal and anti-state or anti-authoritarian aspect included in their political programmes, but also their actual practice. We consider most of the ML revolutionary forces as part of this front.

We consider national liberation organizations like the NSCN, ULFA, PLA of Manipur, and the JKLF in Kashmir as part of the wider democratic forces fighting the Indian state. We consider the various non-parliamentary trade union organizations, various progressive organizations belonging to the religious minorities which are persecuted by state-backed Hindu fascist organizations; various organizations of Dalits and other oppressed castes, *adivasis* and women; the non-parliamentary organizations that are fighting for demands like separate Telangana, Gorkhaland, Vidarbha, Bundelkhand, and so on; the organizations that are waging struggles against SEZs, mining and other so-called development projects leading to massive displacement of people; organizations fighting against the Liberalization-Privatization-Globalization (LPG) policies of the reactionary rulers; those which boldly confront the growing authoritarianism and unbridled state repression resulting in fake encounters, mass murders, and violation of all fundamental rights of the people; and so on, as part of this broad-based non-parliamentary democratic people's front.

There are also a large number of intellectuals and other democratic individuals who are concerned about the well-being of the people and the sovereignty of our country at large. We consider all these as genuine patriotic forces that are deeply concerned about the future of our country, about the well-being of the overwhelming majority of the Indian people rather than that of a tiny parasitical class that runs the country through the so-called mainstream parliamentary parties.

I am obviously leaving out the names of the organizations and individuals who, in our opinion could play a crucial role in the revolutionary transformation of our country into a self-reliant, genuinely democratic society. Today we are passing through a phase of Indian McCarthyism that brands every form of dissent and anyone who questions the authoritarianism of the Indian state as Maoist in order to legitimize its witch-hunting and brutal repression.

Today immense possibilities have unfolded for the rapid advance of the revolutionary war in India and the task of the revolutionary party lies in how effectively and ably it can utilize the present situation, rally all those who have become the victims of the anti-people, imperialist-dictated policies of the comprador feudal forces ruling our country, and forge a broad-based united front of all these affected sections of our society and all revolutionary, democratic and patriotic forces in the country. This task should be achieved by defeating the brutal, all-out countrywide, coordinated war unleashed by the reactionary ruling classes of our country with the aid and assistance of the imperialists, particularly American imperialists.

If we fail in achieving broader unity of all these forces, the fallout would be disastrous for the Indian people at large since the aim of this cruel armed onslaught is not only to suppress the Maoist movement, but also to suppress every form of democratic dissent and struggle of the people against the authoritarian, feudal and autocratic structure of the Indian state and sociopolitical system. As put forth by our general secretary, Comrade Ganapathi, in the same interview given recently:

> This war is principally against Maoist movement but not limited to this movement and aimed enough against all revolutionary, democratic, progressive and patriotic movements and the movements of oppressed communities of our society including oppressed nationalities. At this juncture, all these forces have to think together how to face this mighty enemy and for this how to unite to go ahead.

Now coming to your specific question regarding the CPI and CPI(M). Are they not a part of the wider democratic and patriotic forces? I would say Yes and No. As far as the rank and file cadre of these parties is concerned, there is still some amount of sincerity and zeal among a section of them to work for the well-being of the people. But the leadership has completely capitulated to the exploiting ruling classes and pursues a reformist line that would only help sustain the *status quo* albeit with a few cosmetic changes. Here too, we have to differentiate the CPI from the CPI(M). We do not place both the CPI and the CPI(M) in the same category. The CPI leadership has been critical of the policies of the CPI(M), has consistently opposed counter-revolutionary vigilante gangs like Salwa Judum propped up by the state and central governments, and is opposing the Operation Green Hunt launched by the centre.

One can witness the reactionary anti-people nature of the policies of the CPI(M), especially in states where it is in power. Singur, Nandigram, Lalgarh, and a host of other names have stripped the CPI(M) of its guise of anti-imperialism and anti-neoliberalism. The CPI(M) is not even a thoroughgoing democratic force, let alone being communist. However, we are prepared to join forces with even these revisionists if they come forth into non-parliamentary struggles on the basic issues of the people, and to the extent they uphold democratic values.

It is wrong to say we are assassinating the cadres of the CPI(M). We are confronting the armed onslaught by the stormtroopers like the Harmad Bahini and other armed [men] maintained by their party leaders by putting up courageous resistance. The struggle against the CPI (M) is part of the class struggle of the people against exploitation and oppression. We challenge them to an open debate on any issue. Despite their diplomatic and opportunistic stand that their fight with the Maoists is mainly political, they are in the forefront in the war waged by the Indian ruling classes against the Maoists. Unable to confront us ideologically and politically, their leaders and spokespersons have unleashed a vicious campaign of outright lies and slander against the Maoists.

We call upon the cadres of the CPI(M) and other so-called left parties to come forward to unite with other forces to fight against the disastrous policies of the central and state governments, to unite with others to oppose the brutal war waged by the reactionary rulers guided by the US imperialists against the Maoist movement and all forms of democratic dissent. We are prepared to unite with all sincere and genuine forces in these parties who take the side of the broad masses of people.

Varadarajan: *Why has the CPI(Maoist) decided to reach out through the columns of the* Hindu? *To use a newspaper to clarify its views* vis-à-vis *the government?*

Azad: Among the daily newspapers, the *Hindu* has a reputation for giving out serious news and less of sensational stuff that has become the genre of the media these days. Our party leadership has given interviews to this paper earlier too, such as my interview on the developments in Nepal, which was covered in two parts. On a lighter vein, I think it will reach out to our direct Enemy No. 1 at the present juncture, Chidambaram, too.

I think the media can play a role in carrying the views of a banned party to the government and the people at large, particularly at a time when facts regarding our party are distorted, misinterpreted, and obfuscated in a meticulously planned manner. And when there is no scope for a dialogue given the determination of the rulers to carry out their pre-programmed war offensive that was worked out a year ago, we think it appropriate to reach out to the people at large through the media too.

Finally, I thank the *Hindu* for the thought-provoking and incisive questions it has placed before our party. We look forward to more of such interaction with the media in future. On behalf of our Central Committee and our entire party, I welcome any questions related to our ideology, political programme, strategy, tactics, and practice. I hope through regular and active interaction between organizations like ours that are proscribed by the government and the media, an opportunity is provided to the people to arrive at a correct judgement and seek truth from facts. Or else, truth is certain to become a casualty in this world dominated by corporate sharks that control virtually every source of information that is fed to the people.

CHAPTER 25

Maoist: Jagesh talks to Suvojit Bagchi

I met Jagesh somewhere between Bastar and Abuuj Madh in Narayanpur on a stormy monsoon evening. The camp where I was put up was located at the top of a hill and on arrival I noticed several plastic tents, placed along the ridge and at the steps. Jagesh was a very strong and tall man with a genuinely happy smile. He had a heavy Telugu accent. He used to laugh often while answering my questions. Before we started the interview, I briefed him about the nature of the questions and our broadcast plans. He tells me what he may or may not discuss. Then he shows me a small film on an mp4 player. I see women guerrillas crawling on the ground like alligators. I don't know why Jagesh showed me the video. We plan for an extensive interview—first on audio and then bits and pieces on video. We agree not to make public any personal or non-recorded remark. It was 19 August 2010, 8:21 p.m.

SB: *Should I introduce you to our listeners as the director of the only Maoist training school in Chhattisgarh?*

J: (Laughs) Call me an instructor . . . .

SB: *You are also a member of the state secretariat of the DKSZC and State Military Commission (SMC)?*

J: That's right.

SB: *Are you the head of North Regional Command?*

J: Can't tell you that (laughs).

SB: *You were telling me about three kinds of ambushes [that you conduct] on security forces. Can you please tell me a little about those, on record?*

J: Sure. There are three kinds of ambushes: deliberate ambush, opportunity ambush and mobile ambush. To conduct a deliberate ambush, we need to do a thorough reconnaissance of the terrain. We need to find out if it is forest, semi-forest or plain land. We need to find out how the enemies may come there—in a car, a motorcycle, a jeep, or on foot. On the basis of this information we chalk out a plan—a plan that decides if we can set-up landmine, claymore or pressure bombs. Then we wait. But the crucial thing is, without a reconnaissance . . . a deliberate ambush is not feasible.

SB: *So who conducts the reconnaissance—militia, PLGA or villagers?*

J: The villagers and the militia tell us. Then on the basis of their information, we go for a reconnaissance. The militia always has more information about the movement of police—how they will come and where they may go. They help us.

SB: *I think these things [deliberate ambush or militia's role] are clearly directives of Mao. . . .*

J: Yes, true. Mao said guerrilla warfare is a fighting technique which the less powerful use against the more powerful. It is literally a people's war. You have to constantly integrate the people with the political movement. And then while fighting you have to find out if the enemy is more powerful than you are. If they are, then you have to assemble more people—may be ten times the enemy—and attack. Also, [you have to] make sure to attack when the enemy is exhausted. But if they are really big [in size], you retreat. On the other hand, if enemy starts retreating, [you] follow them. Basic Mao (laughs).

SB: *We were talking about three ambush strategies. . . .*

J: Yes. Opportunity ambush. You don't need much planning for this. If we get some information about the enemy's advances, we go to the spot and wait [at the anticipated location of the security force]. We go there with whatever basic equipment we have. No question of planting mines, claymore, etc., we get fifteen to thirty minutes. You have to adjust yourself to whatever terrain you have . . . you won't get time to structure your formation either. Just fight—with whatever you have (laughs).

SB: *And mobile ambush. . . .*

J: (Thinks) . . . They [security] have changed their tactics . . . we no longer get enough time for deliberate or even opportunity ambush. Now we have to plan a lot around mobile ambush. That is to chase them and while they are running, to involve them in a fight and ambush them. The attack on Kongera on 29 June 2010 was partly this . . . and partly an opportunity ambush.

SB: *What about Chintalnar on 6 April 2010 [when 76 paramilitary police were killed]?*

J: I don't know—that was under a different regional command.

SB: *About Kongera. . . .*

J: Yes, I can tell you about that. . . .
(At this point Jagesh brings out an A-4 size plain white sheet and draws the map of the ambush point to explain how it all happened in Kongera, where 27 paramilitary personnel were killed.)

SB: *Did you give these people an opportunity to surrender according to your policy?*

J: Yes. But they pretended that they were giving up arms and again started firing. So it didn't work. We do let members of police forces go after arresting them. We tell them about our objectives and release them, asking them not to remain in the force.

SB: *If you can now, tell me about the PLGA. First, the command structure. . . .*

J: Ok. Let's start from the lowest level. First we have the village level command. The Panchayat Command, we call it. On top of that we have the Area Command.

SB: *Sorry to interrupt . . . but it follows the party structure?*

J: Yes. Almost. Now, in the Area Command level, which is above that of the Panchayat Command, we have the Area Militia Command. It is formed by using the resources of 3-4 villages. As you know, these villages form a *Janatana Sarkar* [JS] or RPC. From these RPCs Area Militia Command is formed. Area Command is above Militia Command.

SB: *Now, you also have small squads—the Local Guerrilla Squads [LGS]. I know that [LGS] is the formation and you are talking about the command structure. But how many squads are there in the Area Command level . . . or, do you have squads at Panchayat Command level also?*

J: No. At the Area Command level.

SB: *How many squads are there in an Area Command?*

J: One or two LGS with an Area Command. Then there is the LOS (Local Organizational Squad) and militia platoons.

SB: *And on top of that you have Divisional Command?*

J: Yes.

SB: *Formation-wise, do you have platoons in Divisional Command or Companies?*

J: Platoons and LGS.

SB: *And then Regional Command?*

J: Yes, and it has companies to support it. The companies also are part of the SMC.

SB: *Then there is CMC on top of SMC?*

J: Yes.

SB: *The squad has a leader. . . .*

J: Yes, the LGS Commander. It also has a Deputy Commander. Now the LGS Commander or Deputy Commander stays with the Area Committee to run the LGS. There is a different Area Committee member who looks after LOS. And a third person looks after the mass organization. Normally there are 15-20 members in an Area Committee entrusted with different responsibilities.

SB: *How many members are there in a squad?*

J: Seven to eleven.

SB: *Tell me about other formations like platoons or companies. . . .*

J: Told you: one squad has seven to eleven members. Now, in a platoon, there are normally three sections. Sections are nothing but squads, we call them sections when they join together to form a platoon . . . each has a platoon commander and a deputy.

SB: *More or less similar to a conventional formation, I guess. . . .*

J: In structure, not in size. A guerrilla army has to be smaller than a conventional army for manoeuvrability.

SB: *But the squads vary from seven to eleven in strength? Across the world?*

J: Yes, but not the platoon or company. We have 25 in a platoon. It could be less. A company has 70-5; even that is far less [than a conventional company].

SB: *So platoons form companies?*

J: Right . . . two or three platoons form a company with respective commanders [for the platoon]. Company has its own commander.

SB: *Company Commander reports to whom?*

J: To the Company Secretary, who reports to the SMC.

SB: *You also have battalions, after the companies?*

J: (Laughs) won't be appropriate to discuss that. . . .

SB: *And how many platoons or companies do you have in DK?*

J: (Laughs) can't tell you really. . . .

SB: *I believe your party thinks that in Andhra Pradesh you failed to raise similar formations . . . and that was one reason why you were wiped out?*

J: Yes, of course. The party gave reports also. LGS, platoon, company . . . we could not form these units there in a long time. But in DK, whenever there is an attack on us we raise new platoons . . . companies. If the government forces are increasing their strength, we are enhancing ours too. We couldn't do that in AP. Besides, we could not fight the policies—the LIC [Low Intensity Conflict] policies of the state. We took a lot of time to understand what LIC policy is and how to counter it. Meanwhile government penetrated. Then we went into a negotiation with the state and exposed ourselves [to the state]. So it was not only a military failure.

SB: *People's War Group came in the 1980s to DK, but the military was not in place. . . .*

J: Yes, after coming to DK, we had a mere organizational force. PLGA was not there. Organizational forces like LGS-LOS were there. Then the pressure slowly increased [from the state security forces]. Party felt government forces cannot be allowed to have a free run. Now how will you do that [stop the state forces] if you do not have a bigger force? So the party decided to bring 30 or 40 people together in an area. That is to put three or four LGS together. They were told to get united during an operation and then decentralize, when the operation got over. This is how a bigger force came into existence. But then we realized even a big group of 30 or 40 is not good enough; so we started building small platoons. That was in 1995. Then the number of platoons increased. Companies were formed in similar ways.

SB: *How many platoons or companies do you have now?*

J: Can't really disclose . . . (laughs)

SB: *I am very keen to know about the supply of weapons. . . .*

J: Majority of weapons come from police. We snatch it from them or recover them after an ambush. We get some from outside and make some as well. But that also is very little.

SB: *Do you think, other than a few military theories which are relevant in any underground operation, Mao is still relevant?*

J: I was not sure about that, really. But when Salwa Judum [SJ] happened . . . we realized how relevant Chairman Mao is. Mao said the people cannot survive without their army. Now, after SJ, the people started requesting us to keep a platoon in the village to give them protection. We realized the relevance of Mao. People started joining us. Five, 10 or 15 boys joined from each village. We had a shortage of space even, at one point.

SB: *So SJ helped the movement in a way. . . .*

J: People felt the repression. They learnt to defend themselves, they learnt how to live in the forest . . . to leave villages and fight. But they [SJ] tortured also . . . they harmed us . . . immensely.

SB: *So more soldiers joined during this period?*

J: Yes, of course.

SB: *What about recruitments now . . . are they still coming?*

J: Yes.

SB: *How many . . . approximately how many have you recruited in 2009?*

J: Between 300 to 500. That's a broad average that we are getting each year. Can't tell you the exact number.

SB: *How do you select them?*

J: They need to work in the organization first. They have to work in the mass fronts or as militia. They have to win the trust of the people in the village. If the person is not a lumpen and the public has no objection he is inducted in the party and PLGA. We also check his physical condition and class background.

SB: *What if someone comes from an upper class background?*

J: Will take him, but he will have to go though the process [mentioned above].

SB: *You recruit child soldiers as well . . . I could see many young boys and girls.*

J: Never, you cannot see them with guns. Those who come are children of the comrades. Or those . . . whose parents have been killed. We take them but never send them to fight or to work for the party. They stay in camp with other kids, go to party school and are never given a gun or military training. They only get trained after 16, if they want.

SB: *You can win this war. . . .*

J: It depends on people. If we can involve more people and strengthen PLGA and United Front [made up of four classes] we can. We also need artillery . . . more equipments, which we don't have at the moment. But the important thing is people's support.

SB: *You have a family?*

J: Used to have . . . last saw them in 1998. They were brought here by the party comrades from Andhra. But the party is not there any more, so they can't be brought now. So no chance of seeing them. . . .

CHAPTER 26

Maoist: Gudsa Usendi *alias* Sukhdev talks to Suvojit Bagchi

I met Gudsa Usendi *alias* Sukhdev on Day One of my stay in DK. In fact, he was the first top leader of Dandakaranya Special Zonal Committee (DKSZC) whom I met. He was smart and urban; spoke English, Hindi, Telugu, and Gondi. He was the spokesperson of the party in DK and also a member of the state committee. He had a good understanding of life outside the forest and had attended college in Andhra. He was warm and friendly, and I interviewed him in several installments. While he talked a little more than the average Maoist comrade, he almost always managed to substantiate his claims. He also had a very strong interest in life in the city and asked questions often. I stayed with him for a week and the interviews were between 1 and 7 August 2010.

SB: *You have a strange name. . . . How did you get that?*

G: It is a common name here. However, Gudsa Usendi was a party member from Abuuj Madh. He was killed on 26 April 1999. I think he was the first martyr from this area [Orchha]. Now of course you know that in any underground organization the members cannot use their family or original names. That will easily identify the person, so we use various names. In the party we have this tradition of using Gondi names and names of martyrs. There was another comrade who used to work here—in my place—before me. He took the name and then it was passed to me. Also this name is recognized by the media and my job is to interact with the media, so I decided to stick to it. . . .

SB: *In DK, the topmost committee is DKSZC and at the lower end you have the Area Committee . . . that is what I gather. . . .*

G: The topmost committee is DKSZC, but at the lower end, under Area Committee, we have Gram [Village] Party Committee and village-level party cells.

SB: *How many members are there in DKSZC?*

G: 20.

SB: *You are one of them?*

G: Yes. Someone looks after military, someone else looks after mass fronts. Likewise, there is education or women's issues. I look after publicity. The state secretary is Comrade Khosa.

SB: *What is United Front?*

G: It is a front of four classes. The poor, the peasant, small and medium capitalists. It is basically the JS. Both party members and non-members are part of JS.

SB: *Who runs JS—party or the people?*

G: Both. It runs on the party's directions but people—as in the traditional Gram Sabha [village assembly]—also play a very important role. I would say party and Gram Sabha both run JS. However, let us not forget that we call it Revolutionary People's Committee [RPC] outside DK. Here we wanted to have a Gondi name for it and hence we call it JS.

SB: *Party or army has a clearly defined hierarchy and levels. JS also has similar levels?*

G: Yes. The lowest level is JS-Panchayat [village council]. On the basis of population and geographical position one can form a JS in a Panchayat. However, the population has to be between 500-5,000. Several villages come under one JS. Then we have area level JS and district level JS. Under the Panchayat level JS, there are nine wings or departments to take up/see to the issues of the people.

SB: *How do you select these people's representatives, the JS governing council?*

G: JS selection is done by the Gram Sabha. They can select a party or a non-party member. Selection of candidates is not a very big problem. These are very small hamlets and people know each other. However, the party's mass organizations structure a panel of the candidates and propose it to the Gram Sabha. Mass organizations suggest the names.

SB: *Suggests or imposes?*

G: Suggests. Because this person who will be selected will have to work in the village, in the JS and not in the party . . . he/she has to be accepted by the people. So our intervention is minimal. The villagers can and they do object if they don't like a candidate. Mass organizations work as steering committees.

SB: *How are they elected then?*

G: There is a voting system. On an agreed date the Gram Sabha votes.

SB: *How?*

G: They raise their hand and select a candidate for the JS-Panchayat. Now, if it's unanimous, there may not be a voting. The elected JS members will then be given a department each. They will also be provided with a team to look after all the villages under the JS. Now this department [or portfolio] distribution is done on basis of serious consultation among JS members and the party.

SB: *There are nine departments?*

G: Yes.

SB: *How do you make sure that you do not impose your will on the people?*

G: See, the tribals have been running a democratic, egalitarian society for a long time. They have a clear understanding of democratic norms. Now, party is working among tribals for a very long time in DK. So the candidates who are getting selected by the people have been known in their respective areas for a very long time. People are familiar with them. Secondly, people can also recall elected candidates if they think someone is not doing a good job. They do that as well. See, Gram Sabha is an established important organization . . . so we cannot impose anything whimsically. Nor do we want to.

SB: *You are not against voting . . .*

G: No. We are against the system. The New Democracy or People's Democracy that we are talking about will have a system of voting—no doubts.

SB: *But how will you achieve that (revolution) . . . it seems you are getting surrounded from all sides. The government has this policy of increasing the number of police stations. . . .*

G: That is the main challenge of revolution . . . if it was not there then possibly we would not have called this a revolution. Yes, we are getting surrounded. Like this road (pointing on map) between Orchha and Narayanpur—a distance of 55-60 km—has seven or eight police stations. The plan is to set-up police stations at 5-km intervals. And this entire area of Narayanpur to the southern fringe of Chhattisgarh, Konta, is dotted with police stations. However, as we have always said, if people want us we will survive or we won't.

SB: *But the allegation is you kill people . . . won't that reduce your support?*

G: Now being a journalist you can deduce your own conclusion. If we were killing innocent villagers, would they have been with us? So many kids, women, young and old men? You are seeing things here—locals feed us, shelter us, are even happy to see their son or daughter getting married to a guerrilla—do you think it is because of fear? Do you think it is possible to garner this kind of support and love by fear?

SB: *I have seen photographs of your people killing the villagers. . . .*

G: Yes. We kill the informers. If we don't we can't survive. You can't sit here and talk to us. Nobody can. Even before killing them we repeatedly request him or his family not to inform the police about the events in the village, not to identify the cadres. But if even after four or five warnings the informer keeps divulging information and we keep getting caught, we kill them. Don't you think the police do not kill our boys if they can get hold of them? The difference is we even talk to the informer's family and give him the chance to stop; the police does not give that.

SB: *But what about killing hundreds of security personnel. . . .*

G: What we are doing is not violence, it's counter-violence. These people were getting the most brutal and violent treatment from revenue collectors, forest guards, contractors, landowners—all agencies of the state or those who are close to the state. Women were getting raped. Children died without food or health care for decades. Wasn't that violence? Where was your state then? For the last 50 years the people were exploited in the most ruthless ways but since there was no resistance so you couldn't hear it and never came to cover it. . . . Now there is retaliation and hence—anyone with any idea of resistance—is 'virus', that is what the prime minister is [saying] . . . the fact is the Indian state has historically refused to listen when a movement or a community has remained non-violent.

SB: *You are getting angry. . . .*

G: No, I am not. . . .

SB: *You sure?*

G: Yes.

SB: *So, now what is the plan . . . I guess you are quite powerful in the two divisional areas—North and South—above and under National Highway 16 and also in Gadchiroli. But if we look to the east of National Highway 43, connecting Raipur to Jagdalpur . . . you are pretty weak . . . isn't it?*

G: Yes. We are not powerful there. But now we are trying to build up some base. A relatively new area committee—Mainpur—has been formed to monitor the area.

SB: *Is it not a fact that where you have the advantage of the terrain, [there] you are more powerful?*

G: Yes and no. There is an advantage of terrain but on the other hand we have more cadres coming from areas that are not part of a difficult terrain, like Abuuj Madh . . . [cadres are coming] from plain areas or areas where there is less forest. Rather I would say we have penetrated those areas where class contradictions are more acute. Like in South Bastar or East Bastar.

SB: *But how is it that the more remote the place is, or more precisely in areas where the market could not penetrate . . . you are far more powerful. . . .*

G: That is not correct. I told you we are powerful in areas where market has penetrated. Because market does bring in its own class contradictions and it is based on systematic violence and exploitation . . . hence people have joined us from areas where market has entered.

SB: *You are running the party—the cadres and the army—this is an expensive affair. How do you get so much money?*

G: Any fighting force identifies its funding sources. We have two main sources of funding. Primary source is people. During seasonal work like bamboo cutting or *tendu* leaf collection the people donate a *chanda* [monetary contribution]. There is no rule as in who is going to give how much, it depends on one's ability . . . it's an entirely voluntary contribution . . . they donate a part of their income to the party to ensure that we stay here and protect them. It is called *shramdan* [contribution from labour]. We also call it Work Day.

Then there is contribution from contractors and small businessmen. Again, this [contribution] is a voluntary contribution when it comes from small . . . [businessmen]. Now there are big contractors. We fix an amount for them. We tell them, you have to contribute this [particular] amount of money, if you would like to operate in our area.

SB: *This is a kind of extortion. . . .*

G: I don't want to go into the technical jargon . . . if it's extortion or not. We can say, we try to ensure that whoever is doing trade here can't exploit people after a point. Like if the contractor is dealing with *tendu* leaves then we try to make sure that he gives a reasonable rate to the cultivators. Same for those who are buying forest produce from the local people. Only after ensuring these conditions, do we try to get some contribution from them.

SB: *There is a fixed rate. . . .*

G: Yes. We get different rates from small and medium or big businessmen. While it's a voluntary contribution for the small business, it's a fixed amount for the medium or big business.

SB: *You take money from the mining industry as well?*

G: No, never. We oppose mining and don't accept money from them.

CHAPTER 27

Maoists: Badri and Rupi talk to Suvojit Bagchi

I used to feel perennially sleepy in the camps. So one afternoon after lunch when Badri and Rupi came to visit me, after my systematic requests to interview them, I was quietly dozing. They are in their forties or late thirties and are reasonably urban. Both of them have been staying in DK for more than a decade now. Badri speaks only Telugu, and Rupi speaks Hindi as well as Telugu. We had a triangular conversation. Badri is in the education cell and Rupi is the techie. However, both take keen interest in the party's intellectual growth and women's issues. We had a three-hour conversation, excerpts of which are below. They discussed almost all their answers with each other in Telugu before replying to me. It can be said that what follows is the joint response of Badri and Rupi. The interview was on 21 August 2010 in the same camp in which the interview with Jagesh was conducted.

SB: *There are various types of schools that you run. . . .*

B-R: Education Department [EDC] runs. . . .

SB: *Yes. Can you give me a rough idea?*

B-R: One you have already seen—the Basic Communist Training School. It mostly has very young students. Those who have a basic idea of mathematics or language join this school, as you know.

SB: *How do they have this elementary understanding of mathematics or language?*

B-R: Some of them go to the government's residential schools called ashrams or learn it from party comrades. Students of the schools have to work in the villages alongside their studies. Like they have to participate in cleaning villages, etc. They don't come to school during harvest time. A broad framework to develop a socialist ideology is there but the focus is on social science, science, mathematics, some history, health and well-being and anthropology. We also would like them to acquire a basic competence in the mother-tongue. But of course all at a very elementary level.

SB: *Do they have a system of grading or promotion to the next level?*

B-R: No, not at all. That is unscientific and so much so that even in city schools now it is challenged. However, there is a system of evaluation when kids are asked to give solutions to questions . . . problems . . . but it is done in a very friendly way. . . .

SB: *Do you admit kids of rural landlords. . . . I mean can all 'classes' join these schools?*

B-R: Ideally they can. But rich people don't send their kids here. They send them to city schools. We will not have a problem if they send.

SB: *What are the other schools?*

B-R: There are two more types—MAS [Mobile Academic Schools] and MOPOS [Maoist Political School]. This is to give primary education to those who are joining the PLGA. A lot of people learn to read or write at this level. The MAS teachers keep travelling and the party decides which division he/she will visit. Local AC decides which cadres are going to go to which session.

SB: *What are the subjects?*

B-R: Language, mathematics, human sciences, *Raj-yantra*. These are grown-ups, above 16, who go to MAS.

SB: *What is Human Sciences?*

B-R: Let's say a bit of anthropology, a bit about the evolution of the human race and the evolution of the universe as well. But again at an elementary level.

SB: *What is Raj Yantra?*

B-R: Study of society. Broadly, you could call it political science. How the society evolved from primitive communism to a slave society. And then to a feudal society. Evolution of capitalism and of a socialist society. Then how state, class and struggle evolved. How the society got divided into classes and when. What is a state and what are its components. How the state changes itself and which class it works for. And how the constitution evolved and changed with the modern state.

There's a chapter on India. Indian parliament, state assemblies, and especially the relationship between state and the centre.

Political geography, we call it. . . . One more thing would be how our government [JS] is different from the Indian government.

SB: *That is all. . . ?*

B-R: There is a second round or second session for MAS, a little advanced. The important subject in this session is the history of DK. Like people's history, history of the tribals of the area. We talk about production—how was it in DK, how things changed, how people resisted the state—which is a hallmark of DK. . . .

SB: *This history of DK . . . dates back to when?*

B-R: We don't have a written history that dates back more than 100 years. We try to give a broad outline of tribal society—its democracy and people's resistance against the British forces. We tell them how the people fought against the British [in 1910]. . . .

SB: *The history you are talking about could well be a bourgeois history. I mean the history that we study is the history of the winner . . . do you have any source to study the alternative history . . . which possibly is not written by the winners. . . .*

B-R: We have very, very limited resources to research and dig out material. We rather base ourselves on recent history written by people like Rahul Sankritayan or even by B.D. Sharma. There are some local books on day-to-day life in Bastar—written by ordinary people. We read that also. We try to interview a lot of old people and tally their versions with these accounts, but the point of view is necessarily Marxist.

SB: *Are there other subjects in MAS?*

P: Tribal culture. Especially because there is an attack on the culture. Language, clothes, livelihood, living style, farming style, collective labour, leisure, agriculture, weapons . . . and of course song and dance forms. We also try to establish through our day-to-day researches, whether the cultural practices are individualistic in nature or socialistic. . . . Their modes of productions are also analysed. Medicine is also studied and discussed. We try to tell people whatever we learn in our researches, observations. I won't say outsiders have not done that, but may be [their accounts are] . . . a wee bit romantic.

SB: *You mean you document things. . . .*

P: Well, Chaitanya Natya Manch [CNM] does some documentation of the song and dance forms. They record stuff. But this has nothing to with party's work. It is documented without really thinking how it will help the revolution . . . it's an independent project.

SB: *Is that all. . . .*

B-R: Physics, chemistry and biology basics are also taught. Because to understand Marxism it is mandatory to understand basic sciences.

SB: *Do you document your struggle?*

B-R: Not really. Someone has written a few things but that is up to 1995.

SB: *You have another form of school. . . .*

B-R: Yes MOPOS. This is the political school. Party's tactics, strategy are discussed here on basis of Marxism-Leninism-Maoism [MLM]. The school's responsibility is to give political education to all. MOPOS gives education on the basis of party documents. They mostly train the party cell members, regular cadres and mid-level leadership. They travel in DK and go to divisions and the divisions decide about the members—like whom to send to specific sessions of MOPOS.

[The lecturers of MOPOS often are very senior leaders of the party. The slain member of CC, Azad, was one of the course conductors. An interview of the party secretary, Ganpathy, released by the party to the press on 16 May 2011 suggests that. Ganpathy said: 'He (Azad) was to participate in the political education training programme planned for the party leadership cadres there.']

SB: *This is also a six months' course?*

B-R: No. They take 10-15-day short courses. Their subjects—like philosophy or political economy—are taught in 2-3 days. They spend time with AC and DC members. But while the subjects remain the same, the depth varies. Yesterday you saw a class that was for platoon members.

SB: *Saw some books as well. . . .*

B-R: Printed material. Strategy to run a war—how to fight a protracted war. It is MOPOS's duty to teach that as well. Deconstructing this ongoing war—Operation Green Hunt [OGH]—is also something they do in such classes. And how to take the Marxist-Leninist ideology forward is also what MOPOS deals with. There is a lot of personal level, completely informal guidance and teaching between comrades as well. Now that brings us to the end of the three forms of schooling.

SB: *One last question and that has nothing to do with education . . . about women. There are so many women in the party but none in Central Committee [CC]. Anuradha Ghandy was there and she passed away . . . but this is one allegation against even the mainstream left that they also have almost never promoted women to their highest leadership . . . the same thing, it seems, is in the revolutionary party as well. . . .*

B-R: The party's every policy decision says women should be brought forward, especially Dalit women, since they are under pressure from all sides. However, this process did not start right from the beginning—I mean, it was not like that [that women should be brought forward] at least till the mid-1980s. Women did not get equal opportunity. It was not in the form of patriarchy but the effort was limited. Now some people, and some women comrades, have played a crucial role to raise this issue. Eventually, after 1985, things changed and women got a lot of prominence in the party. Now everywhere, in every front of the party, even in the military, there are special programmes . . . special efforts . . . for women so that they can be brought forward. But it will take more time.

There is another problem. A large number of top women comrades have been martyred over the last decade. Like Naliyala, Rajita in north Telangana, Kurnulu Adunimi *alias* Padma in Thirupati and Lalitha, Suguna . . . they were all capable women leaders. Now it is not an easy thing to become a CC member. You have to grow over the years to be one. You have to have a good understanding about a whole lot of things. Once you lose such important women comrades—it takes time to replace them . . . to bring up new leaders who have good grasp over every aspect of the revolution. And even Anuradha Ghandy passed away. . . . That is one reason why we don't have a woman at CC or PB level. May be the CC can tell you more. . . .

CHAPTER 28

Maoists: Four Comrades talk to Suvojit Bagchi

SUNIL, A 19-YEAR-OLD GONDI FROM ORCHHA IN NARAYANPUR, WHO WAS SUVOJIT BAGCHI'S GUARD FOR A WEEK

I used to stay at home and work in the farm land. I joined the Bal Sangham [children's wing of the Maoists] at eight or nine and then later I joined the PLGA. I used to participate in various sporting activities organized by the Bal Sangham. I didn't have much of an idea about the party. But the police came looking for me. They arrested my first cousin and beat him. They constantly asked my cousin about me and one officer told him that they will beat me to pulp. There was a family friend who used to work in the police. I got convinced that he will inform the police about me. So I left home and came to the forest and joined the party. Since I was with Bal Sangham, so after a few years they inducted me into the PLGA. I studied in government residential schools till third standard and would have loved to study, if the police would not have chased me. I wanted to go to the city as well at some point. But I will have to stay with the party.

BHIMA, 24, A PLGA MEMBER FROM DANTEWADA

It was 2003. I had just completed school and was looking for a job. I was well respected in my village for being a good cricket and football player. Now, one evening when we were playing cricket, some SPOs and police came and asked us to stop the match. We had an altercation and they used very bad language. I protested and they picked me up. They told me that they will watch me. Then I went to the Orissa border for a job, couldn't find one and I came to know that the police has blacklisted me as a Naxalite. I tried to get into a college so that I could get back to a decent life but I didn't have the money to support myself in a city. Neither could I support my studies. It was around that time, in 2004, that the Maoists came to the village and asked me what I was doing. I said I am quite free. They asked me to distribute their magazines and pamphlets and listen to them. In any case, I had a lot of time and was doing nothing. I started visiting them. Initially I was very guarded as I was convinced that they were goons. But slowly I changed my mind and became one of them and am now considered to be one of the best shooters. In 2005, SPOs and Salwa Judum came to our village to look for me and killed my two brothers. I think my chances of going back to a civilian life ended that day, forever.

RAJMON, MID OR LATE THIRTIES,
SECRETARY, MADH DIVISION, CPI (MAOIST)

We will not harass the government employees if they come here to facilitate health care or to educate kids. We never did that. We never killed any doctor, health worker, *anganwadi* worker or teacher—you can't find one case when we have abused anyone of them. But our demand is, before you start working here please make a survey of the area. A survey which will tell you and us how much destruction has taken place because of the Maoists and how much for security forces and Salwa Judum. How many villages they have burnt, how many women raped, how many people killed—please make a survey of that. Please also let us know how many quintals of food grain looted or destroyed and how many chickens, cows, goats or buffaloes killed or taken away. Please do that survey. We will cooperate and hence we will also cooperate with you in making schools and hospitals. But, let me tell you, that is not the intention [of the government]. The intention is to build roads to bring in the army. Is it unreasonable to oppose that?

COMRADE DEVE, A VERY SENIOR
COMRADE AND MEMBER OF STATE
SECRETARIAT OF THE DKSZC

I joined the party like most of us in the city, decades back, as a student activist. I was a member of the Radical Students Union [RSU] . . . so were all our friends at that time. Andhra has a fascinating history of radical student movement throughout the 1960s, 1970s or even in 1980s . . . that kind of pulled us into the movement. In fact, we used to call the Regional Engineering College . . . Radical Engineering

College (laughs). However, I am not from AP. The party came here [DK] in the 1980s. Comrades like Sukhdev [not Gudsa Usendi], Ramanna, Lachnudada, Khosha were part of it. There was another person Pandanna and (laughs) Lanka Papi Reddy, who surrendered a few years back. Comrade Sonu of Central Committee also came around the time. There was a decision taken by the party that we have to develop a base area here—it was taken in the 1980s. Kondapalli Seetharaamiah took the decision and, I would say it was a collective decision. It was called 'August Resolution'. In Bastar, we have lost Sukhdev, Rammana and Lachnudada . . . three important comrades in the first decade. They built the party here. Their initial movements were for increase of daily wage for *tendu patta* cultivators . . . or for other forest produce . . . and to stop the exploitation of [by] the forest guards, revenue officials, etc. The movements gave us a base . . . we gained people's confidence.

Now that [is] what made the regional big landholders hostile against us. The big landowners—who are called Mangujars here [DK], they are bit like the Bhumihars of Bihar or Bhuswamis of Andhra—they started forming groups against us. Because people like Mahendra Karma or Vikram Usendi felt that the land they hold—a few hundred or even thousand of acres—will be taken away as we started distributing land among landless people. So they united with local Patels, *gaitas* [religious headman of village], etc., to remove us. There was another reason. The women. The women, in spite of this society being quite an egalitarian one, were badly exploited by the men in the community. They had limited access to father's property, forced to stay with men whom the village elders would select, were not allowed to wear a blouse to cover the upper part of the body after marriage and even thrown out of villages when the menstruation starts. The local landowner, *gaitas* and the *kotowals* (rural police) used to decide the fate of a young girl, at times in connivance with the male members of the [girl's] family. I have witnessed this. The party clearly provided a platform to these kids . . . girls . . . women and hence you would find more women in the squads, platoons or even in mass fronts. Besides, the women have a dedicated mass front of their own—KAMS—that is a huge success.

In brief, we have managed to influence the people by being one of them. They can see that we are living and dying with them . . . so they love us now. That is our strength. This has become our home, we have become a family.

CHAPTER 29

Social Scientist: Nandini Sundar talks to Robin Jeffrey

RJ: *Tell us how you came to be involved in what we're calling the Maoist movement. What is your own background and connection? You've written extensively about Bastar district, which is now one of the hotbeds of insurgency. How did you arrive at this particular point?*

NS: I'm an anthropologist and I've been working in Bastar since the early 1990s. I've been working on the lives of people and what happens to them in times of conflict. So that's how I happened upon this because this was my field area and the Maoist issue overtook my field area.

RJ: *Tell us about your first book on Bastar. What kind of a book is it?*

NS: It's a historical ethnography of the region. And it looks at the development of the state through various moments of rebellion. So I look at the rebellion in 1876, the one in 1910 and in 1966, at the ideology and social practices that underpinned these movements and what the colonial state did to make those rebellions necessary and also to repress them.

RJ: *Tell us about Bastar itself. What kind of a place is it?*

NS: To start with, it's the most incredibly beautiful place. If you look at it in geographical terms, it's heavily forested, rich in mineral resources. People there are fairly multicultural in the sense that there are several different tribal [groups]—what are called Scheduled Tribes in India.

RJ: *You describe it so nicely but why then has there been an insurgency and unrest? What are the forces driving the excesses and conflicts that we've seen in the last four or five years?*

NS: Some of these conflicts have roots going back to the colonial period, starting from the reservation of forests when people's resources were taken away from them and given over to the Forest Department. One of the big problems has been that people who were cultivating land, which was taken over by the Forest

Department, did not have title deeds to this land. And so, they were subject to harassment by the Forest Department.

So when the Maoists came, one of the big things that attracted people to the Maoists was the fact that they guaranteed freedom from the Forest Department and also helped people to cut down forest and occupy forest land, where there was land hunger.

The Maoists also redistributed land. That's been the single most important reason why people have supported the Maoists in addition to factors such as the low rates people received for forest produce. They were cheated—they still are cheated by traders. And one of the reasons why they needed help from the Maoists was in order to get higher prices [and] be organized to demand better wages.

RJ: *Is it that the forces of modern, industrializing India have increasingly encroached on Bastar, is that part of it? That there's an impingement of outside forces into an area that was once fairly isolated and pristine? Or is it something different from that?*

NS: It's both. I think there's a great deal of exploitation of the resources that exist. And obviously, that draws in a lot of outsiders. I've seen the way in which the demographics of Jagdalpur, which used to be the district headquarters of the entire undivided district, have changed. You know, it used to be a reserved seat for Scheduled Tribe MLAs and now it's become a general seat. The whole area has been flooded by immigrants and they've taken over the festivals, etc. But beyond that, because of the mineral resources, there's a lot of interest in mining. One of the reasons why the government has seriously been pushing counter-insurgency measures is to reclaim this entire territory and open it up to mining

RJ: *But who are the Maoists? Who are the leaders? Who are the followers? Where do they come from? Are they arising indigenously or are they coming from other places?*

NS: The leaders have all come from Andhra Pradesh, a neighbouring state. They came in the early 1980s in small squads of two to five people. Since then, they have established a large indigenous cadre. But the top leadership is still from Andhra.

RJ: *And what are their origins? What kind of people are they? Do we know?*

NS: I think most of the leadership come from middle peasant or poor families. There are a few leaders, people like Kobad Gandhy, who come from a well-off family. Among the ones that I know about, some come from agricultural labour families, some come from small peasant families, some have engineering degrees and so on. But I wouldn't say they're the elite of the society.

RJ: *Do you feel you know about their intellectual roots? How have they learned about Maoism? Why have they chosen to call themselves Maoists and not something else? Marxist-Leninists for example, or even pick the good old Indian term Naxalite?*

NS: I think they call themselves Maoist because of the roots of the Naxalbari movement in Maoism. In the 1960s, that was the ideology that the Naxalites were following. And so that's the intellectual trajectory of all the Naxalite groups.

But if you look at the Andhra leaders of the People's War Group (PWG), which is the group that came into Bastar in the early 1980s, there was this major campaign, a go-to villages campaign. There were places like Warangal and Karimnagar which also had traditions going back to the Telangana struggle of the 1940s which was again a communist-led struggle for land and freedom from feudal exploitation. . . . Some of the Maoist leaders come from these families who had links—these families were also involved in the Telangana struggle. And in the early 1980s, there was this whole movement in colleges and schools to join the struggle. And in fact, one of them who's now left the party said that at that point, if you didn't join the PWG, there was something wrong with you. So, there was this wave of student idealism. And many of them come from that period. All the current leaders, I think, trace back to that period.

RJ: *The responses of the Indian government seem to have been ineffectual. Would you agree and why has that been so? A lot of governmental agony has gone into thinking about this problem but without much effect.*

NS: I think more than just ineffectual, they have been actually counterproductive because I think the single biggest reason for the expansion in Maoist spread and violence right now is government injustice through its counterinsurgency measures. So the more you repress people, the more you fire upon peaceful people protesting against land acquisition, the more you create sympathy for the Maoists. In terms of 'ineffectual', clearly the biggest failure of the government has been in governance and bringing development—and I mean by development services, not industry.

RJ: *Given where we stand now, in September 2010, what can happen to make things worse and what's necessary to make things better?*

NS: I think there are two options. One is the government can enter a long, protracted war, send in more paramilitary forces, make life so difficult for ordinary people, burn villages as they've been doing, destroy grain—which is a classic tactic: you make life so difficult for people that they stop supporting the Maoists and they come over to your side.

But that could take years and it's going to destroy the entire society in that area. Or they could engage in peace talks and negotiate and hope for some de-escalation of violence by providing basic justice. I think justice is the most important thing. If you recognize what you've done through counterinsurgency measures, apologize, give people compensation, it'll automatically de-escalate.

RJ: *The government talks about having a strategy of control, hold and build. Would that have some of the desired effects if it were carried out sincerely and vigorously?*

NS: I'm not sure how they would control, hold and build because from what we have seen they could have provided services in the camps in Chhattisgarh when they forcibly evacuated people into camps. But there's a lot of corruption in the camps. People were starving and so they would much rather go back home than stay in these government-held camps. So, I'm not sure that given the existing structure of exploitation and given the existing machinery that they would be able to hold it very long.

RJ: *What's your prognosis then, long-term? How do you see this unfolding?*

NS: As I said, there are two options. I would hope for everybody's sake that both the Maoists and the government decide to negotiate and get serious about it.

RJ: *And the initiative lies with governments. . . .*

NS: The initiative does lie with the government because it *is* the government. I mean the Maoists are just one kind of party so the government has to be the main initiator. But also because the government has recently lost a lot of credibility because of the killing of the top Maoist interlocutor[1] who was actually going to provide dates for peace talks to begin and he was killed.

RJ: *Are there other things you think we should be talking about?*

NS: I think the problem is that because of high rates of economic growth, there's not enough attention given to how governance actually works on the ground. And in a way, the Maoist issue has focused attention on that. So rather than seeing that as a threat, the Indian government should actually use this as an opportunity to change its structures of governance. But instead we have the same old kind of modernization theory: that you'll have industry and things will trickle down.

NOTE

1. This was the Maoist leader known as Azad, killed in July 2010. See the interview with him in Chapter 24.

CHAPTER 30

Security Analyst: P.V. Ramana talks to Robin Jeffrey

RJ: *In your view, what are the forces driving the unrest? What made the Naxalites effective in Chhattisgarh and other places today?*

PVR: Here, we have to understand two things. The realities on the ground facilitate the Naxalites being able to mobilize their support. The reasons why they draw supporters and sympathizers is completely disconnected with the ultimate objective of the Naxalites.

While the ultimate objective and the immediate goal is the capture of state power through an armed revolution and protracted people's participation on the lines of guerrilla warfare, they mobilize support on the basis of perceived and genuine grievances of the people and the socio-economic disadvantages that the people face in a given society.

The socio-economic conditions within a particular state would be [conducive] for the Naxalites to mobilize support. This is what has happened in all the states in the country where the Naxalites have a presence today.

RJ: *You're suggesting there's a considerable division between followers and leaders. What do we know about the leadership of the Maoist movement, the Communist Party of India (Maoist) in 2010?*

PVR: What is more striking and quite ironical is that in Andhra Pradesh, the Maoist movement began on two or three very important social issues. One of them or the most important of them was the social oppression committed by the Velama landlords on the disadvantaged and downtrodden sections of the masses. Today, the Maoist group in the country is led by Muppala Lakshamana Rao *alias* Ganpathy, himself a Velama landlord.

The leadership is highly committed. The leadership does not belong exclusively to the forward caste or even [the] backward caste. There has been one lady member in the Politbureau of the CPI Maoist who died a couple of years back of cerebral malaria. The leadership—most of them are very highly educated. For example, Ganapathi was a school teacher. The founder of the Naxalite movement in Andhra Pradesh, Kondapalli Seetharamaiah, the General Secretary of the People's War Group, was also a school teacher. Nambala Keshava Rao *alias* Basava Raju, the lynchpin of the Central Military Commission, has an M.Tech [degree]. They're very highly educated [and] very committed.

RJ: *How do you explain the fact that so many of them are Telugus? Does that go back to the Telengana insurgency of 1949?*

PVR: It was the Telangana armed struggle, and not the insurgency, of the 1950s. They're separate. When the Naxalite movement in its current phase began in the country in 1980, the People's War was founded in Karimnagar district. Soon it spread to Nizamabad. At that point in time, the people who initially got involved later rose in ranks and are now in the Central Committee, the Central Military Commission and the Politbureau—the higher decision-making bodies of the Maoists. It is for this reason that you find more Telugus in the highest leadership in the Maoists, because the movement began in the state [Andhra Pradesh].

RJ: *What do we know about the intellectual foundations of these leaders? What have they read? Why do they call themselves Maoists and not Marxist-Leninists or even Naxalite?*

PVR: There were two most lethal Naxalite groups in this country. One was the Maoist Communist Centre of India (MCCI) and the other was the Communist Party of India, Marxist-Leninist People's War. At the merger on 21 September 2004 of the People's War and the MCCI, it was decided that they would firstly call themselves the CPI (Maoist) and secondly, they wanted to be distinct from all other communist groups.

They are committed to waging an armed revolution on the lines propounded by Mao Zedong of China, adhering completely to the teachings of Mao. Therefore, they call themselves CPI Maoist. In a symbolic sense, you have the Communist Party of India, then you have the Communist Party of India (Marxist) and now, it is the Communist Party of India (Maoist), which gives them [the image] of being an all India political party and which gives them countrywide presence; that is the symbolic importance that this name has.

RJ: *Have many of the works of Mao Zedong been translated into Telugu, for example?*

PVR: Most works of Mao Zedong have been translated into Telugu. The *Red Book* is compulsory reading for every recruit. They read quite a lot. Some of the highest Maoist leadership are extremely versatile in ideology, literature and in explaining the Maoist ideology and interpreting it for the common masses. They're very clear theoreticians, very clear in their minds.

RJ: *The responses of the government to the Maoist movement seem to have been ineffective up until now. Is that true in your view and if so, why has it been ineffective?*

PVR: I would not call it ineffective. I would rather say they were not as effective as they should have been. When we speak of responses, we should look at two levels. One of the Union Government and two, of the governments in their respective affected states.

In the respective affected states, Andhra Pradesh has been the most successful and today, the Maoists have a miniscule presence in the state of Andhra Pradesh. They can certainly not commit an action at will at a place of their choice anywhere in the state. Their total [cadre] has dwindled and is a little over 100 now. They've all fled to neighbouring Orissa, Maharashtra and Chhattisgarh.

In a state such as Jharkhand where coalitions have been fluid and where the chief minister is busy everyday protecting his own chair, he does not have the time to look at the Maoist insurgency. Political maturity does not exist among all the leaders in all the affected states. They do not foresee the intensity that the problem could become four, five or ten years down the line and tend to ignore it.

But then at the time that they wish to address this challenge, it becomes that much more difficult because the Maoists are by then entrenched within that state. However, I see a turnaround in the perception of leadership in the various affected states.

There is a lack of consensus among the political leadership in the various affected states, within the states, and among the states.

I even see the latter two emerging gradually. This would take a few months more if not a few years. Once this consensus emerges within the states and among the states, then there will be political will and coordinated action against the Maoists.

On the other hand, the Union Government has initiated a two-pronged approach to deal with the Maoist insurgency, which is security and development. This is what Prime Minister Manmohan Singh said in December 2007 about the approach of the Union Government—that development and security are two sides of the same coin and that the government's response shall be walking on two legs—development and security.

RJ: *The Union Government has talked about 'control, hold and build'. Do you think that strategy—the notion that you control an area in security terms, you hang on to it and then you build development—if executed justly and effectively, is going to make a difference to reducing the appeal of Maoist ideology?*

PVR: I would look at it in a broader fashion. Rather than uniformly apply this strategy of control, hold and build, the government's response should be varying from district to district, even within a state.

There should be judicious mix of control, hold, as well as develop. That is, there should be a judicious mix of using the right quantum of force, legitimate force that is necessary in an area, rather than under-utilize or over-utilize the quantum of force and also have adequate development response.

For example, in north Chhattisgarh, which is not as affected by the Maoist presence, it is quite possible and is all the more desirable to have more of a development response than a security response. The unnecessary dumping of large quantities of force would only be to the advantage of the Maoists and not to the State.

But certainly, this strategy of control, hold, develop, in the right mixture at the right place is going to yield results. For this, the government machinery has to deliver and there has to be sincerity and strict monitoring in the implementation. I am positive that it is possible to defeat the Maoist challenge in seven to ten years.

RJ: *What is your medium and long-term view? How will matters unfold in the next two to three years and in the next five to seven years?*

PVR: In the next two to three years, there will be a jump in the number of fatalities. That is because security operations are certainly going to intensify. Then there will be retaliatory attacks by the Maoists on the security forces and those helping the security forces.

This is what the Union Home Secretary already indicated more than twice—that the levels of violence are going to rise. The reason is that security operations would intensify and there will be retaliatory action by the Maoists on the security forces. That's one. Two, gradually, political consensus and political will, will emerge within the next two to three years.

From then on, it is too early to say now. But what is desirable and what I hope shall happen is that there should be an appropriate mixture of the security response as well as the development response.

Even as the security response succeeds, the significance of the security response or the prominence that you could get would decrease and the development response would pick up. This is how I see the next five to seven to ten years.

RJ: *Is there anything we haven't touched on?*

PVR: A couple of things that we need to look at is that the Maoists are in no hurry. They'll follow a classic Maoist dictum of one step forward, four steps backward, they're willing to wait for eternity.

It is perhaps not possible that the entire bunch of Maoists present in the country would have vanished or withered away. Some of these elements will remain but they will be confined to a very narrow pocket or pockets in the country. The challenge then would be to ensure that they would not expand from that.

CHAPTER 31

Police Chief: Vishwa Ranjan talks to Suvojit Bagchi

Vishwa Ranjan is the charismatic chief of the Chhattisgarh police. He has worked in Indian central intelligence (Intelligence Bureau) for more than two decades. But unlike other senior IB officials he spends less time extracting information from journalists. Rather, he loves to talk about his life and work and has a sense of humour. He has a fabulous collection of books on a range of subjects: 'I have read everything on Mao and his strategies', he said twice. He claims he is the grandson of Urdu poet Firaq Gorakhpuri. Vishwa Ranjan is a chain-smoker and has written several books of poems in Hindi. He obliged me, when I requested him to read one of his poems for the camera. Titled *Ek Nayee Puree Subaha* (One New Complete Dawn), the poem had a couple of lines in the middle that can be translated as:

> When we speak the same language and eat the same bread
> Why do I become half grotesque and you become a half beauty?

When he finished the recitation, the interview began.

SB: *Who is this 'grotesque'—in one half of you—the Maoists?*

V: (Laughs) You see poems are not written like that. Poems are very deep experiences at the level of emotions which then try to find words and idioms because the emotions are non-verbal in nature. You try to find words for them. A poem cannot be written by the words and meanings of the dictionary, so you juxtapose images, you juxtapose sometimes fantasies, sometimes similes . . . metaphors to make the reader come close to what you felt . . . at a non-verbal level again but through the words . . . a lot of people think that poems are a piece of narration . . . it's not that . . . a non-verbal explosion of emotions . . .

Now the police chief of Chhattisgarh can go on and on like this . . . he can keep talking about poetry . . . and make you forget that you went there to ask him questions on Maoists . . . he actually spoke like that to me in a couple of two-hour sessions, but he finally gave an interview on the third day. I have encountered police officers who spoke about classical music for a week and finally refused an interview. So on the third morning I shoot my questions.

SB: *What do you think are the reasons for such a huge movement in central India—the Maoist uprising?*

V: This is an invalid question. The question should be, how did the Maoists gain hold in Bastar. What were the circumstances in which they were able to come and somehow convince the tribals that they want their welfare. We have to go back to the 1960s and 1980s to understand this movement. The tribals used to consider the forest as their own. When restrictions were imposed in the form of a forest act by the king of Bastar, there was a revolt in 1910. It was crushed by the king with the help of the British army. When the country became independent there were three distinct schools that discussed what could be the right policy to deal with the tribals. One idea was to assimilate them in the mainstream and that is how growth takes place. All of us were tribals—at some point or the other—we slowly became an agrarian society and eventually an urban society. That view was insisting, growth is an evolutionary process . . . you have to embrace development . . . you can't keep the tribals the way they are . . .

SB: *So you accept that they were kept outside development?*

V: There are many reasons for that. Tribals have an 8,000-10,000 year-old history. You have to go into that. . . .

It has been discussed repeatedly how to deal with them. There was this second idea. To integrate them with the Indian state politically but to allow them to retain their identity. That is what is known as an integrative approach.

Then there was this isolationist approach. It says you must allow them to remain what they are, and only when the demand comes from them for development, you interfere. There was great concern that if they come in contact with a more advanced culture, they would undergo traumatic experiences. [The British anthropologist] Verrier Elwin was of this view and he was advising the then prime minister [Jawaharlal Nehru] that any other method will be very traumatic for them.[1]

SB: *Does that mean that in these areas—in long stretches—there is a lack of health care and schools, and is not that one of the main reasons for the rise of Maoism?*

V: That is not the reason for rise of Maoism. The reason for rise of Maoism is ideology which wants to take over power in India. It wants to destroy the democratic fabric and establish a totalitarian regime.

SB: *You mean a communist ideology that believes in armed struggle?*

V: A Maoist ideology which believes in protracted armed struggle to gain power. . . .

SB: *But it would not have been possible without . . . sheer poverty. . . .*

V: That [poverty] will exploit any socio-economic contradiction and, in a developing society or for that matter in any society, you will find socio-economic contradictions . . . had to be. . . . It is not a static society, it's a dynamic society and there will be traumas of transition. Now tensions in such areas can be resolved democratically, or there can be ideologies that want to exploit them and educate the people to take up arms. At the same time there was a lot of international concern to save the environment. Bastar, you must realize, had 70 per cent forest cover and the Forest Act came, all over India, in 1982 [*I think he is talking about Forest Conservation Act of 1980*] and made it very difficult for the tribal population to cut trees. After the introduction of the act, there was a problem of land for the tribals. On the other hand, there was a growing population which found it difficult to maintain the kind of livelihood they used to have. They couldn't even hunt as there was a lot of concern for the protection of animals. So he [the tribal] was encircled by various concerns which were international and felt he was not responsible for it. . . . [so he must be thinking] why was he being isolated.

Now the act did not allow for any developmental work because the forest could not be used for non-forest activities.

SB: *Do you feel that this act gave rise to a new clan—the nakedars or forest officers. They started exploiting the villagers . . . while implementing the law. . . .*

V: How have they [tribals] been exploited when they did not have land. . . .

SB: *They [forest officers] were arresting people . . . harassing them. . . .*

V: But that is not harassment . . . that is ensuring law. The law says you cannot cut the trees. . . .

SB: *But that is exactly the allegation of the tribals across central India, not only in Chhattisgarh, that they were seriously harassed by forest officers and forest guards . . .*

V: Who will implement the law, if not the forest guard?

SB: *By constantly harassing the people?*

V: They [tribals, law breakers in this case] have to be arrested. . . .

SB: *It was not arrest, it was . . . loot of forest land [by forest guards]. . . .*

V: That area could not sustain that kind of a thing [loot]. You have not seen the Bastar of the eighties . . . the poor tribal had nothing. He was deprived of land, he virtually had no money to bribe. There were beatings for the cutting of trees, it was traumatic for him [the tribal].

SB: *Cows and goats were taken away, tribals alleged. . . .*

V: Oh . . . yes . . . yes . . . cows were scarce . . . but goats and chickens, they [forest guards] might have been taking. . . .

SB: *Harassing the women also. . . .*

V: Harassing the women is projected by the Maoist sympathizers. Tribal society is extremely egalitarian in many things. There is a lot of freedom for women and even if women want to get out of the [tribal] society and have affairs . . . they are always allowed to do so . . . even within tribal society there are lots of pre-marital relationships. Their sense of fair play is very different from ours.

SB: *But can that be a reason for . . . [sexual violence] . . .*

V: That cannot be the only reason for such a big movement . . .

SB: *One of the reasons. . . .*

V: I don't think so. The reason was survival. They were trying to survive and they were not getting enough land to do so . . . they could not get *pattas* [deed that is an evidence of one's right over property] and the national parks were coming up. The tribal villages had to be uprooted from the forest area. You didn't have land to give them. So you got into a great vicious circle.

SB: *So, the government should have thought about these three million people before going for such measures . . . which possibly pushed these people to take up arms. . . .*

V: That time it was not only government. Still you find a lot of concern for the environment . . . still you find high-powered committees that clears things. It's not easy. You have to balance survival of the individual on the one hand and survival of the planet on the other . . . cannot see things in isolation. Environmentalists are putting a lot of pressure to save the green cover, to save animals, the flora, the fauna. . . .

SB: *Is it reasonable to save the animals first and not the indigenous population. . . .*

V: You have to understand the historical background. You cannot jump to questions . . . that would be the most unacademic thing to do [*a bit excited*]. Government can't work in isolation . . . in a democracy they have to listen to every one and reach a consensus. Environmentalists are a major pressure group today. In this situation a party [Maoists] appears that tells you they will give you everything free . . . the tree, the forest, everything . . . that is how initial foothold was gained by the Maoists.

SB: *There should be consensus . . . Between the government and the tribals also, I assume. . . .*

V: Of course, they had their representatives. They were politically involved . . . there were elections and tribals were involved . . . they were becoming MPs and MLAs.

SB: *So are you saying tribals were kept in isolation and that is what gave the Naxals a breeding ground. . . .*

V: That gave them a breeding ground but you can't have a sequential cause and effect story . . . it is far more complex. . . .

SB: *We now change the topic. Let's talk about human rights abuses. There have been cases of human rights abuses committed by the police in the region [south Chhattisgarh] and how do you react to that?*

V: As a general case it is . . . nonsense. Individual cases have always been dealt with. Even before National Human Rights Commission [NHRC] initiated an enquiry into these allegations we had already registered cases against some of our officers who indulged in human rights violations and sent them to jail. Hundreds of allegations were made and we proved to the NHRC that they are false. They could identify only nine in which they felt the possibility of rights abuse cannot be ruled out. So an investigation should be launched.

But, I must tell you one thing . . . under no law in the world, except may be in a totalitarian system where party leaders decide who is guilty . . . nowhere, is allegation a proof.

SB: *I have been to a village, north of Indrawati river, Takilore. Seven families, with five widows, each one gave me a graphic description of how her husband was murdered on the morning of 3 February 2010. The villagers, the poorest of the poor, told me they were killed by the men in khaki uniform . . . not by the vigilante force. . . .*

V: No, no, there are no vigilante forces there . . .

SB: *Exactly, it was men in uniform. The case was not reported, neither was it investigated—not that I know of. They were not Maoists. May be they used to work in small ways for the party which, I guess, is natural in such an area. Now, how do you defend that?*

V: I am not defending that. I am just saying allegations do not prove anything. It has to be enquired into. I can take you to areas controlled by non-Maoist forces and they will give you a very different picture. You go to the Maoist areas, you will get another picture. . . .

SB: *Complete polarization. . . .*

V: It is not polarization, it is fear. A person can't afford to say anything other than what the Maoists want them to say. . . .

SB: *And the same thing in the police-controlled areas. . . .*

V: In other areas you can get both the pictures . . . people support [in police-controlled areas] Maoists also . . . that is the difference between total control by fear . . . [and control where there is a democratic government]. . . .

SB: *So are you saying in Takilore no one has been killed by security forces?*

V: No one is saying that. I am saying allegations are not proof.

SB: *But these are more than allegations. . . .*

V: These are allegations, this must be investigated.

SB: *Who is going to do that?*

V: They have to lodge a complaint. . . .

SB: *With the police?*

V: Obviously. All over India you cannot have a police to police the police and then have another set of police to police that police and keep repeating that . . . we are talking out of our head. I am saying allegations against the police have been investigated . . . and policemen have been convicted.

SB: *Rarely. . . .*

V: Not rarely. Throughout the state.

SB: *But that's really very rare. . . .*

V: It's not very rare, it has to be proved . . . one has to prove allegations in the court of law. That is the rule in India, that allegations have to be proved. Or do you suggest to do away with the judiciary and act on the basis of allegations by human rights activists. . . .

SB: *Let's bring in another issue. There is an allegation of human shielding . . . using ordinary citizens as human shields . . . administration has been doing that. . . .*

V: Administration has not been doing that. . . .

SB: *I can again give you another example.*

V: You give me any example. . . .

SB: *I was traveling in a bus . . . CG17F0752 . . . from Gidam to Jagdalpore on National Highway 16 and it was a passenger vehicle and it was a bus full of children and women. The bus was carrying Special Police Officers [SPOs] with guns . . . how can security personnel carrying arms be ferried in an area which is a conflict area. . . .*

V: So what . . . so what happens. . . .

SB: *Can you use a passenger vehicle to . . . [ferry security men].*

V: Why not? All over the world it is done.

SB: To use a passenger vehicle. . . .

V: It happens all over the world. I have been issued a weapon and I am going from one place to another—I'm not even talking about SPOs—What will I do [other than traveling in public vehicle]?

SB: *But this is human shielding . . . isn't it?*

V: Its not human shielding. Why is it human shielding?

SB: *Because Maoists may target this bus. . . .*

V: But you are not questioning the Maoists as to why do they do that. . . . You have *ipso facto* accepted that they have the right to do that. You question them. . . .

SB: *Of course, I will question them . . . but can you do that?*

V: You can travel anywhere with weapons . . . in trains, in bus . . . it's not human shielding . . . it's transportation from one place to another. . . .

SB: *But should they not be going in their own vehicle . . . convoys may be. . . .*

V: Not always . . . not always . . . they can go on foot also. That is an invalid question. It happens all over the world, even in the most insurgent areas; that doesn't mean I am using the public as human shields. In most places armed policemen use public vehicles. Because if they travel unarmed there is more possibility of them getting killed. I can show you photos of common man being killed by Naxalites. Nobody questions that . . . why?

They put IDS, mines in civil areas and no one questions that. People talk about Geneva Conventions, UN Charter. But there is also a convention that you can't put mines in civilian areas . . . but that is never questioned by the human rights activists who always question the police.[2]

SB: *About Salwa Judum [SJ]—the vigilante group. . . .*

V: I don't consider it a vigilante group. The moment you say that I refuse to talk.

SB: *Then how do you define it?*

V: It was a movement against the Naxalites. People have [been] totally confused between SPOs who were trained by a special protection group and the Salwa Judum people. Actually, there are three things. One, people in the relief camp [who left villages allegedly because of Maoists]; two, the people who have joined the SJ movement of Mahendra Karma; and then there are SPOs. Let us not merge all three. Now, the group which joined the SPOs initially to protect the camp because we didn't have enough force and hence trained [SPOs]. . . .

SB: *The local tribals. . . .*

V: The local tribals who have been living there. . . .

SB: *Was it justified?*

V: (Surprised) Why was it not? SPOs are accepted all over the world, they are trained to do their job. . . .

SB: *So do you expect something like SJ to come up in the next few months. . . .*

V: See SJ does not come up . . . you can't fabricate a movement . . . it can't be sustained. . . .

SB: *It is a movement?*

V: It is a movement. SPOs are different. SPOs were accepted in the old Police Act of 1861.

SB: *So the movement [SJ] was funded by the Government of India [GOI]?*

V: No movement was funded by GOI.

SB: *Then why is the collector of the district announcing . . . SJ is no more. . . .*

V: I will tell you. I think that kind of question emanates when we either try to hide things or do not understand the whole situation.

The SJ was not funded by the government. The relief camps (of SJ) were . . . [and the camps are] where you have the people, the SJ members and the SPOs. SPOs are given an honorarium through a different head—a state head and a central head. SJ movement stopped because in 2007, when I came, I decided they won't take out processions. A lot of force is required to protect them. They were subjected to retaliation by the Maoists—it is difficult to protect such large groups. Rather they can do symbolic meetings.

SB: *SJ polarized the tribal society. . . .*

V: Don't think so . . . there were always movements against the Maoists. The Maoists started interfering in their day-to-day life, they started taking away children to become their soldiers from Bal Sangham.

SB: *So forces like SJ may revive. . . .*

V: We don't know . . . but they cannot be allowed to go out . . . we are not in a position to escort them with adequate force. Our force is now committed to fighting the Naxalites. . . .

SB: *Was Operation Green Hunt [OGH] . . . a term coined by you?*

V: No . . . no . . . first of all it is Project Green Hunt [PGH] not OGH. It's a multifaceted project that involves identification of ambush points. Now, we know the ambush points so, in the last few years, they have not managed to give us any major reverses. [I think, what he meant was ambushes against police, as hundreds of paramilitary personnel died in 2010.]

SB: *So identifying ambush points is OGH. . . .*

V: One part of the project. . . .

SB: *So there is OGH . . . however, the central government is saying that it does not exist. . . .*

V: But people are saying that it is a central government project . . . the joint operations . . . that is Green Hunt . . . that is what the media is saying . . . that is absolutely nonsense . . . the joint operation was built around a different strategy altogether. . . . We started Project Green Hunt in 2008. It [PGH] was like this . . . gradually entering the area, identifying the ambush and pressure points, i.e. crossing points of the Naxalites when they move from one point to another, de-mining of the most important roads—which is a constant exercise and still going on—as you de-mine the area, they again mine it. . . .

And, of course, winning the hearts and minds of the people

which went through big *jan jagran aviyan* [mass awareness campaign], both in district towns and in smaller villages and in bazaars, and this whole thing is PGH.

SB: *What is identifying of ambush point?*

V: See you have to understand the terrain. You must keep moving in the terrain and gather information to find out that this is a dangerous area, a killing zone; field formations have to change or you may get trapped. If there is an ambush you got to have a clear idea of what will be the nature of the counter ambush and you have to implement that immediately. How to cross the ambush area with minimal damage and maximum riposte. This is trying to familiarize yourself with the area . . . identifying ambush points, pressure points, camping sites . . . all of them should be plotted on the map for future reference.

SB: *But Maoist camps are always on the move. . . .*

V: But you know where they camp . . . you know the areas and can plan. . . .

SB: *What really is the government policy in these areas . . . can you give an idea?*

V: It is three-layered. One, for those who surrender, there is a surrender policy. Then the Naxalites have virtually destroyed the entire infrastructure of the area. So a lot of rebuilding has to be done, but rebuilding can't be done in a combat zone. You have to control the area so that development engines can move in.

SB: *So you mean to clean the area. . . .*

V: I don't mean to clean the area. How do you clean the area?

SB: *To drive away these Naxalites. . . .*

V: Naxalites will leave . . . If they find it's not conducive for their stay they will leave. . . .

SB: *Strategic hamleting. . . .*

V: No, no . . . hamleting is a very different thing . . . these are the words used by the supporters of the Maoists to confuse people. People who do not understand what hamleting means get something from the internet and start parading these terms. . . .

Hamleting is surrounding the area with such villages whereby you stop any movement of food, etc., inside and you starve them into submission. This is not possible because Maoists are not the only people living there. Villagers are there so you can't stop food from going inside.

SB: *But that is happening now. . . .*
V: Nowhere it is happening. . . .
SB: *But the food is controlled. . . .*
V: Where is it getting controlled. . . . ?
SB: *The ration is now given from the police station . . . from Narayanpur. . . .*
V: No, no, no . . . Public Distribution System [PDS] is a different thing and that [PDS] is what the police is interested in . . . that if a village requires 200 quintals of rice, they should not take 300 quintals. . . .
SB: *So how will you determine this requirement. . . .*
V: We know how many people live there. . . .
SB: *And how much they can eat. . . .*
V: They will get food according to the fixed ration . . . not how much they can eat. In public distribution system people have fixed portions of rice. No one is stopping private persons from taking the food grains and selling. We are only trying to see that the government ration is not wasted. . . .
SB: *This allegation is also there that they can't take sufficient amount of food inside. . . .*
V: If merchandise is going to the remotest areas of Dantewada . . . [that means] PDS is working . . . how can you say food is stopped from entering . . . no food was stopped from entering the area. These kinds of allegations are made to give a bloated figure [of the amount of food required] so that a part of that food can go to the Maoists.
SB: *How will you control the area . . . what is the plan?*
V: That I won't tell you. The Maoists will design a counter-strategy in that case.
SB: *Many . . . many thanks really for giving such a long interview over a few days. . . .*
V: Tell me something: why you guys are so sympathetic to the Maoists . . . ? Anyway, thank you too.

NOTES

1. Verrier Elwin denied this allegation of being an 'isolationist' in an article written much later. It was reprinted in *Seminar* magazine. See http://www.india-seminar.com/2001/500/500%20verrier%20elwin.htm.
2. On 17 May 2010 the Maoists blew up a bus close to a place called Chingavaram on the Dantewada-Sukma road killing more than 40 people.

In an interview released by the party on 16 May 2011, secretary Ganapathi said: 'Near Chingavaram, our targets were clearly the Koya Commandos and SPOs. These bloodthirsty forces had raided a village named Kutrem, killed three *adivasis*, raped women and were returning. But we did not know that there were people inside the bus. The information we had was that SPOs had got into the bus after forcing the people to get down. On the roof top of the bus too it was these armed killer gangs who were traveling. So we considered it a military target and attacked it.' Allegations and counter-allegations continue while Bastariyas—as the people of the region are called colloquially—keep getting killed.—S.B.

CHAPTER 32

Special Police Officer: Dileep Sethia talks to Suvojit Bagchi

Dileep Sethia, the Maoist-turned-SPO-turned-constable, in charge of one wing of Koya Commando, a force created out of local tribal youths to combat Maoists, was interviewed in October 2010 in Dantewada.

SB: *Your name is Dileep. . . .*

D: Yes, Dileep Sethia.

SB: (*Pointing at guy sitting next to him*). . . . *Your bodyguard?*

D: Yes, Yogesh Kumar.

SB: *You were with the Maoists earlier?*

D: Yes.

SB: *Tell me from the beginning . . . how it all happened. . . .*

D: Actually I was in a hostel in Dornapal [in Dantewada]. I was a student. I was a good writer, so they [Maoists] used to call me to write pamphlets. They used to have frequent meetings in the area. Then they [Maoists] made me a complete fool. They told me to go with them for a fortnight. They called me to a village called Dulher. So I went there . . . it was in July . . . and from there I was straightaway taken to Andhra Pradesh and kept for one and half years.

SB: *When was it?*

D: 1994.

SB: *How old are you now?*

D: 35.

SB: *You were 19 then. . . .*

D: Yes. . . .

SB: *Okay. And did you join the SPO?*

D: I surrendered in 1996. There was no SPO at that point, it was called *gopniya sainik* [secret army]. It was basically a police informer's job. I got that job in 1998. Then in 2005 Salwa Judum [SJ] happened and I became an SPO. Then I performed well and [was] taken as a constable.

SB: *When was that?*

D: 2006.

SB: *You had to appear in a departmental test for that?*

D: Yes. Actually it was given to me generally . . . I was promoted. Because I took part in lot of Naxal operations . . . killed them also in various places. . . .

SB: *Killed the police, you mean?*

D: No, not police. After joining the police I took part in various encounters. . . .

SB: *You mean you have killed Maoists in various places?*

D: Yes, I have a group. I led the group to operations . . . we did that in various places . . . so we were promoted . . . like two-three boys . . . we were made constables from SPO. . . .

SB: *People you killed were Naxalites?*

D: Yes, Naxalites. . . .

SB: *How many have you killed so far?*

D: I have lost count [of how many I have killed]. Killed in several places. Entered Andhra and killed them . . . with Greyhound force . . . killed them in Maharashtra. . . .

SB: *In Gadchiroli ?*

D: Yes. In our neighbouring district . . . Bijapur . . . killed them there also two-three times. Here also [Dantewada] . . . killed them in the liberated zone. . . .

SB: *Which area is a liberated zone?*

D: Jagargunda and down south. Police hardly enter there. Even if they get in, they do a basic survey and come out. . . . We have a group here Koya Commando and a Delta team . . . we work here actively. . . .

SB: *What is Koya Commando?*

D: The tribals are called Koya . . . it's a society. Now Koya Commando is the name given to the group of SPOs. The young boys who can fight are taken from tribal society and imparted special training. They are made fit for operations. Through them anti-Naxal operations are mounted in the district. Naturally, we are in the most wanted list of the Naxalites. Anything can happen to us . . . but we are not scared. If we fight we will die, if we don't fight then also we would die.

They have killed two of my brothers after I joined the police. My father went mad. My house was destroyed . . . in the village . . . I have said this before. This is the truth.

SB: *The police tell you to convey these to the journalists . . .?*

D: No, this is the truth. I am not speaking on behalf of the police.

SB: *You are unsafe. . . .*

D: Yes . . . totally . . . if I leave the force I can't survive for a day. . . .

SB: *How do you know they are targeting you?*

D: They go to the villages and tell about us. They announce our names from their list. They tell the villagers such and such persons were involved in operations. . . .

SB: *You have your informers in the villages?*

D: Yes. . . . Then we got diaries and pamphlets of the Maoists where they have written about us . . . that they are looking for us . . . they know us by name. . . .

SB: *What kind of protection do you have?*

D: There are five armed bodyguards. Don't move much . . . carry a 9 mm revolver . . . got 12 bullets . . . we will get 25 lakh [Rs. 2.5 million rupees—about US $55,000] if we die. . . . Naxalites will get nothing.

SB: *So how many people work under you?*

D: 65 . . . even the Naxalites are scared of us . . . because we know the terrain . . . nobody can fight the Maoists without our support.

SB: *You mean the local boys' support. . . .*

D: Yes (points at paramilitaries) . . . look at them, how [they] are walking . . . casual, slow, unfit . . . look at us. We are fast, fit and we know the area . . . you can't win this war without us. I am genuinely fight prone . . . am never scared . . . if they [the force] get 50-60 like me things will change. . . .

SB: *They don't have 50-60 like you?*

D: Lots are there but they got to have the same thinking . . . philosophy. . . .

(*We reached an SJ Camp in Kasuli, while talking.*)

SB: *You worked for Salwa Judum [SJ] also?*

D: Nope. But SJ was a great thing. All the villagers got united against Naxalites through SJ. With their bows and arrows . . . they started moving from village to village and kept adding [including SJ] *sanghams*. It was a peace movement . . . and a successful movement. SJ should have been allowed to continue in DK. Naxalites were in trouble, they could not survive . . . no way.

But SJ was politicized. Political leaders got into it and the problem started. Politics and political leaders should have been kept out of it, they spoilt it [in order to gain a] vote bank. Rumours were spread against SJ . . . that SJ is torturing people. That was a big lie . . . they [political leaders] bad-mouthed a good movement . . . they said SJ goons are putting houses on fire. . . .

SB: *But that was true . . . isn't it?*

D: Nope, I can't tell you . . . nothing of that sort happened in front of us. Well, this much happened . . . those who were with the militia or *sangham* . . . they never used to accept [SJ] . . . never used to participate in the SJ activities . . . used to harass [SJ] . . . so finally [SJ] used to kill them . . . those who were particularly close to Naxalites and villagers know about them . . . those persons [used to get killed]. And in lot of places the Naxalites used to kill villagers and put houses on fire and blame us. . . .

SB: *You report to whom?*

D: SP [Superintendent of Police] and anyone who is in charge of operations. We contact them directly. We walk in the path shown by them. . . .

SB: *Who is the DIG-Operation here?*

D: Kolluri *Sahab* [S.R.P. Kolluri, the ex-police chief of Dantewada].

SB: *Is he the DIG [Deputy Inspector-General]?*

D: No, he is the SSP [Senior Superintendent of Police]. . . .

SB: *So no DIG here, separately. . . .*

D: No, he does it . . . alone . . . we take orders from him only. There is one DSP-Operation under him.

CHAPTER 33

Collector: R. Prasanna, Ex-Collector of Dantewada, talks to Suvojit Bagchi

I recorded a telephone interview with Dantewada's ex-collector R. Prasanna in March 2011, right after the attack on villages in Dantewada, organized by the police and the SPOs. At the time of the interview I was not aware of the attack on the villages. As a result of this attack Prasanna, who was reportedly doing a commendable job to implement the government's developmental policies in Dantewada and was thus creating a roadblock for the Maoists, was transferred. Interestingly, he was also implementing the Supreme Court order to remove the security forces from schools and government buildings when he was sent to Raipur. In this interview, given when he was working as the collector of Dantewada, Prasanna spoke at length about the developmental policies undertaken by the government in Dantewada.

SB: *Reportedly, loads of developmental activities are going on in Dantewada—can you give me an outline?*

P: We are giving emphasis on all kinds of work. First priority is infrastructure, especially roads. . . .

SB: *Roads?*

P: Yes. There are some important roads like Dornapal to Jagargunda via Chintalnar, then Palnar to Jagargunda via Arangpur. These are important roads and there is lot of resistance in building these roads. But we are giving them priority.

SB: *How lengthy are these roads?*

P: Dornapal to Jagargunda is 50 km and Palnar to Arangpur is 18 km. Now, regarding Palnar-Jagargunda road, we will construct up to Arangpur in the first phase and not the entire stretch [in the first phase].

SB: *You have said you were facing resistance . . . what kind of resistance?*

P: This is a sensitive area. Naxalites are here. Dornapal-Jagargunda is the same road where 76 CRPF soldiers were martyred [in 2010]. Lot of police personnel have been martyred. Same for Palnar-Arangpur road. We have limited reach . . . it's a sensitive area. . . .

SB: *Who is funding the road project—state or centre?*

P: State government so far. We have issued tenders several times for construction of these roads but no contractor was ready to take up the projects. So we had to raise a Zila Nirman Samiti [committee to build the district]. Collector, SP, DFO [Divisional Forest Officer], Zila Panchayat, PWD [Public Works Department] and some other departments are members. Now the committee is responsible for the road construction.

SB: *You are building the road . . . there are no contractors?*

P: Depending upon our requirement we hire small-time contractors, small-time vendors . . . PWD does the quality check. On the basis of their evaluation we make the payment.

SB: *What is the budget?*

P: Dornapal to Jagargunda, around Rs. 90 crore. Palnar to Arangpur around Rs. 40 crore.

SB: *Since there is a resistance [from the Maoists] in the construction of these roads, what kind of measures are you taking to complete the project?*

P: We are taking a few strategies. There are villages on the road. We are reaching those villages and talking to the *sarpanch* [village council head], *mukhiyas* [village head] of these villages and educating people. We are making them aware of the importance of the road. We have formed teams of police, CRPF and SPOs to give protection.

SB: *Like you are giving protection to the road constructors. . . .*

P: Yes.

SB: *Can you give an example like how you are doing that. . . . to each group or individual?*

P: We won't give protection to every individual. The force will do area-domination exercises and conduct small operations. We will also give inner-cordon protection to the places where men and equipment are located.

SB: *There is one allegation, especially from the Maoists, that the roads are constructed to take forces inside . . . what will you say about that?*

P: These roads are not important for the police because normally police use helicopters to commute. Especially around that area. . . . Dornapal-Jagargunda road, they mostly use helicopters. So road construction and ferrying forces are not connected. They [Maoists] don't want the road because if roads are constructed there will be development and the movement will become completely irrelevant.

SB: *What are the other forms of development?*

P: We are trying to provide electricity. We are hopeful by the end of the year all villages will have electricity. And the basic facilities like health, education, ration, water supply . . . we are giving special attention to all those. There's a huge shortage of doctors. Now through NRHM [National Rural Health Mission] we are giving special pay package [to the doctors]; we have recruited a lot of MBBS doctors. Then we have managed to get RMA [rural medical assistants] posted in remote areas in the health centres. We are talking to a few NGOs to set-up mobile ambulance facilities in the interior areas. We have signed an MOU regarding that [with the NGOs].

SB: *This has nothing to do with* Médecins Sans Frontières *[MSF] project. . . .*

P: They have a separate project. Nothing to do with our project.

SB: *There was some controversy regarding their functioning . . . are you opposing them?*

P: No. They are working in the area.

SB: *What is the budget this year?*

P: If you put all infrastructure development project[s] plus salary, it will be Rs. 800 crore.

SB: *Rs. 800 crore [US $180 million]?*

P: Yes.

SB: *Can you give a broad idea—what was this amount, two or three years back?*

P: Just Rs. 300-400 crore . . . around. . . .

SB: *That is like more than 100 per cent increase in development budget in a short period. . . .*

P: Since this is one of the most backward regions of India the government is gracious enough to take special care so that the region can catch up with rest of India.

SB: *Rs. 300-400 crore increase is a very substantial increase in developmental budget for a district. Will you be saying it all happened because of the movement led by the Maoists?*

P: I don't know whether there is any correlation between Naxal menace and government funding. The Government of India officials can answer the question. But definitely since there was a governance deficit, they [government] are now trying to fill in the gaps by providing additional incentives.

CHAPTER 34

Journalist: Kunal Majumder talks to Robin Jeffrey

RJ: *Tell us about growing up in Dhanbad in Jharkhand. There were a lot of tribal people there, tribal people who now are seen as being some of the main backers of the Maoist movement. What was it like?*

KM: I grew up in Dhanbad, particularly in a place called Jharia, which is the heart of the coal mining industry in the region. What is funny about Dhanbad is [that] it's supposed to be [the] heartland of Jharkhand, which was itself formed on the lines of empowering the tribals. Dhanbad, as such, doesn't have any tribal population. So it seems that over the years, as the mining industry grew, the tribals or the indigenous people were sort of ejected from their main place. Dhanbad has ended up becoming a place with people from outside—Bengalis, Marwaris, Biharis.

There are very few tribal people. So when I see a situation in which I see the tribals hitting back with help of the Maoists, I'm not quite surprised, to be honest.

RJ: *In some ways, Dhanbad in those days was an enclave in a tribal area. Would that be a fair description?*

KM: Yes, it was a place which attracted a lot of trade. It still continues to attract a lot of trade. People from different parts of the country would come down and there was [a] cosmopolitan culture in that sense.

RJ: *Tell us then a little bit about the assignment you had in April when you went to visit some of the Maoists in Bastar.*

KM: There was a phone call inviting us to go down. There were instructions what to take, what time to land, which bus to take, where to get down, what sort of hotel to stay [in]. After that there was a person who escorted us to the entrance of the jungles where the CRPF [Central Reserve Police Force] weren't tracking us. From there, it was a 30-km, almost eight-hour walk inside the jungles.

We weren't told whom we were meeting and we weren't told what the purpose was. We were just told to please come if we were interested in visiting the camps. In the jungles, once we reached our particular destination, we ended up meeting the mastermind of the 76 attacks [the ambush that killed 76 police in Chhattisgarh in April 2010], Ramanna.

I think two weeks before the meeting, he had planned the whole incident. And along with him was Ganesh who I think is the general secretary of south Bastar and also a political strategist for CPI (Maoist).

RJ: *What kind of men were they? Did you get a sense of their background?*

KM: Both of them are from Andhra Pradesh. Ramanna is from a farm labourer's family. His father was a farmhand. Not even a farmer but farmhand. He studied through school and then dropped out and started participating in revolutionary movements among the labour union movements. Ganesh is a B.Sc. in chemistry from Osmania University, one of the most prestigious [universities] in India. He also started participating in the student union movement.

RJ: *What about the people around them, the people who escorted you to the camps? Were they tribal people or were they also Telugu people?*

KM: They were tribal people. The leadership of the Maoists is Telugu. But 30 years back, [leaders like] Ramanna and Ganesh came to Chhattisgarh and the Bastar area. The followers are indigenous tribal people from Chhattisgarh.

RJ: *What language do they use to communicate?*

KM: What's interesting is that all of them learnt Hindi and communicate in Hindi. The tribal people communicate in Hindi as well. But I'm told that lately they [the leaders] are also learning Gondi, which is the local language so that it could become a two-language thing.

Their [the tribal people's] mother tongue would be Gondi and of course radio is probably the only modern equipment with them. But I do understand from my sources that they are given classes in Hindi. The Telugu leadership also speaks in Hindi.

RJ: *What are the forces driving the unrest in the so-called Maoist tracts today?*

KM: I personally think that the Maoist movement is a political movement. It must be [differentiated] from the tribal issue. Maoists would pick up any sort of reason to propagate their ideology. Ramanna, Ganesh—they themselves acknowledged that they have been working in the area for 30 years. So if it was just a tribal issue, it should have come up in the national media or violence should have started 30 years back. But it did not.

Poverty need not necessarily lead to violence. It seems that over 30 years, these people have been—if I may use the word—instigating or they have picked up the cause of the tribals and mobilized them. And it's now that they are in a position of strength, not extreme strength, but in somewhat a position of strength. And they are working on it. They're challenging the state.

RJ: *After 30 years, what has been the catalyst for an explosion of violence in the last three or four years?*

KM: People would like to say that. But my reading is that they just reached a position of strength. If they had reached it 15 years back, they would have done the same thing.

So, at the moment they are capable of mobilizing people, attacking armouries and looting ammunitions. Most of the guns they use are looted from the Indian ordnance factories. They are now able to attack and use them.

To your question [of] why now and why not 30 years back: we had violence in the 1960s in Bengal. Then subsequently, there was violence in Andhra Pradesh. Now after 2004, the Andhra police and the Greyhounds, the anti-Naxal forces in Andhra, drove them out. So now, the next place they possibly could prosper is Chhattisgarh.

RJ: *What are the grievances of the tribal people in Chhattisgarh?*

KM: This is the issue that Ramanna [the Maoist leader] made the reason for the attacks. One of course is Green Hunt, the anti-Naxal operation launched by the central government, which is a coordinated operation. But Chidambaram, the home minister, completely disowns this. He says that there was nothing called Green Hunt.

But [regarding] the reasoning of the local people, Ramanna

says [that facts such as] the state government, headed by Dr. Raman Singh who is the chief minister, signing 96 MoUs [Memoranda of Understanding] with mining companies [are grievances].

The Maoists would like to say that the tribal people have grievances with the mining companies because the mining companies are taking away land and water from the indigenous tribals.

RJ: *Government responses to these events seem to have been pretty ineffective up until now. Would you agree?*

KM: The government response has been ineffective primarily for two reasons. Somewhere down the line, I think the government does mess up things. For example, the forces that the government is sending out. The first thing is that they think it's a law and order problem.

Second, when they are sending forces to all these insurgency-infected areas they tend to think that the tribal people are equal to the Maoists. I'm not saying Chidambaram thinks this, but the people at the base cannot differentiate between a tribal and a Maoist. They end up harassing the poor tribal who might not be a Maoist, instead of targeting the right person. So there's a failure of intelligence on the ground.

The first thing I mentioned is the problem of law and order because they think it's a law and order situation when it is clearly not so. It's a political ideology that's been propagated which has to be countered through development. Of course, force could be a part of it. But force cannot be the only element.

RJ: *What events can happen that will make things worse and what is necessary to make things better?*

KM: One of my colleagues made this statement to me. He said that the Maoists need not do anything. The pace at which the Government of India is moving or the things that it is doing are enough to heighten this tension because it seems that the government is not in touch with what's happening at the ground.

The CRPF when they are sent down, the Cobra forces, which are the elite of the CRPF, the paramilitary, they've [all] lost contact with the reality because the strategy is made in Delhi.

And people have no connection. This is the monsoon time so this is a peaceful sort of time because it's an informal sort of agreement between government forces and the Maoists that they would not attack each other. But once the monsoon is over, there's a possibility of an attack on the Maharashtra side. That's the input I have been getting.

What you need to do is that you need to get the fodder of the Maoists, the tribals, away from the Maoist ideology.

RJ: *The government describes its strategy as control, hold and build. Is that a practical strategy?*

KM: How long can you control a population in a democratic country? Sometimes I think the way the government addresses the issue seems as if we are in some communist nation, which is ironic because we are trying to take control of the Maoist situation.

RJ: *What about the 'build' part of that equation? What's necessary in these areas to give people a better life and reconcile?*

KM: What's necessary in these areas are clean water, vaccines, health care, education. What's not necessary is signing dozens of MoUs with mining companies. What's not necessary is diverting the water. What's not necessary is getting all these multinationals into Bastar. That's not necessary.

If we can allow the people in the Andaman and Nicobar [islands] to have their own lives, why can't we allow the people in Bastar to stay the way they want?

RJ: *Is there anything else you think we should be talking about?*

KM: Whatever the government representatives say, they acknowledge that there is an inherent problem with the armed forces on the ground. Their violence, which includes some of the experiences of *Tehelka* reporters in which the paramilitary has been involved in violence, rape, burning down houses which, though acknowledged, is brushed aside. But that's according to social scientists and people—civil activists. That's one of the reasons why tribals are moving towards the Maoists.

What I hear is that, 'Oh, in seven to ten years, this is going to get over.' But how is it going to get over? Somewhere in the middle something is missing.

Contributors

ISHTIAQ AHMED is a graduate of the University of Punjab, Lahore, with a Ph.D. from Stockholm University. He has taught in Sweden for many years while maintaining ties with his native Pakistan. He writes regularly for Pakistani newspapers and in 2011 edited *The Politics of Religion in South and Southeast Asia*. He is an Honorary Senior Fellow in the Institute of South Asian Studies at the National University of Singapore and an Emeritus Professor of Stockholm University.

SUVOJIT BAGCHI has been a correspondent with the BBC World Service since 2004 and a journalist for more than 15 years. Keenly interested in subaltern insurgencies and Islamic societies, he has travelled and reported from all over India, including the conflict areas of Kashmir and central India, where he spent five weeks in 2011 with the Maoists in their forest hideouts. Previously based in Kolkata as a print journalist, he lives and works in New Delhi.

SUMANTA BANERJEE is a former journalist, political and civil rights activist and translator of Bengali books into English. He is the author of several books, including *In the Wake of Naxalbari* (1980), which has been reprinted several times and is considered a classic on the subject.

SUDEEP CHAKRAVARTI is the author of *Red Sun: Travels in Naxalite Country* (2008; updated 2009). An analyst of socio-political and security issues in South Asia, novelist and a professional member of the World Future Society, Washington D.C., he was a journalist and senior editor with several media organizations, including the *Asian Wall Street Journal*, *India Today* and HT Media. He lives in Goa and New Delhi and is working on a non-fiction book set in India's Far East.

SHOMA CHAUDHURY is managing editor of *Tehelka*, an investigative news magazine. Having worked with the *Pioneer*, *India Today*, and *Outlook*, she joined Tarun Tejpal and the team that started Tehelka.com in 2000. After the government forced the closure of Tehelka.com, she stayed on to fight *Tehelka's* battles and relaunch it as a national print weekly. She has written on various areas of conflict, including the Maoist insurgency. Among her distinctions are the Ramnath Goenka and Chameli Devi awards and selection by *Newsweek* in 2011 as one of 150 'women who shake the world'.

CHITRANGADA CHOUDHURY is a Fulbright-Nehru Fellow at Columbia University. She has worked with two of India's leading national dailies, the *Indian Express* and *Hindustan Times.* Probing power and marginality in a country in flux, she has won national and international awards for her journalism. In 2009-10, she co-researched the status of the PESA legislation and the Maoist movement for a public study commissioned by India's central government.

IFTEKHAR AHMED CHOWDHURY was foreign minister of Bangladesh from 2007 to 2009. He served as a civil servant in both wings of pre-1971 Pakistan, completed a Ph.D. at the Australian National University and represented Bangladesh as a senior diplomat and as ambassador to the United Nations. He is a Senior Research Fellow at the Institute of South Asian Studies at the National University of Singapore.

AJAY DANDEKAR is a professor of social sciences at the Central University in Gandhinagar, Gujarat. He has written books on ancient Indian history and on the Warli tribe, and numerous papers on rural development. He served on a committee to advise the central government on the rehabilitation of India's 'denotified tribes' and conducted a study for the Bombay High Court on farmer suicides. In 2009-10, he co-researched the status of the PESA legislation and the Maoist movement for a public study commissioned by India's central government.

PRASENJIT DUARA is director of the Asia Research Institute and of Research in Humanities and Social Sciences at the National University of Singapore. He studied in St Stephen's College and Jawaharlal Nehru University, Delhi, and Harvard University where he received his Ph.D. Fluent in five languages, including Mandarin and Hindi, he has published widely on Chinese and Asian history. *Culture, Power and the State: Rural North China, 1900-1942* (1988) won prizes from both the American History Association and the Association for Asian Studies.

AVIJIT GHOSH works as a senior editor at the *Times of India* in New Delhi. Born in Agartala, he grew up in different small towns of

Bihar and Jharkhand. He is addicted to films, music, cricket and football. He has written two books: *Bandicoots in the Moonlight*, a novel, and *Cinema Bhojpuri*, which earned a special mention for best writing on cinema in the 58th National Film Awards. He is working on his second novel.

HARIVANSH is chief editor of *Prabhat Khabar*, a Hindi daily based in Ranchi in Jharkhand and publishing from nine centres in central and eastern India. He has worked as a journalist in the region for more than 30 years. A native of Ballia district in Uttar Pradesh, he has an MA in economics from Banaras Hindu University and began his newspaper career with the *Times of India* group.

JOHN HARRISS is director of the School for International Studies at Simon Fraser University. He trained as an anthropologist at Cambridge and the University of East Anglia. His widely admired research has focused on the politics of economic development, particularly in rural India. He has led academic units at the University of East Anglia and the London School of Economics and directed the South Asia office of Save the Children (UK).

DIVYA IYER is an experienced television journalist and a senior special correspondent with CNN-IBN, India's leading English news channel. Her documentary on India's condemned prisoners called *On Death Row* won the Best Crime Show in the News and Television Awards 2011. She has led the metro team of CNN-IBN and has been a recipient of a CNN International Fellowship during which she worked at CNN in Atlanta, Georgia.

DAYAN JAYATILLEKA is the Sri Lankan ambassador to France, with accreditation to Spain and Portugal, and Sri Lanka's Permanent Delegate to the UNESCO. He is Honorary Senior Fellow of the Institute of South Asian Studies at the National University of Singapore and has served as ambassador/permanent representative of Sri Lanka to the United Nations at Geneva. A Ph.D. from Griffith University, his most recent book is titled *Fidel's Ethics of Violence: The Moral Dimension of the Political Thought of Fidel Castro.*

ROBIN JEFFREY is a visiting research professor at the Institute of South Asian Studies and the Asia Research Institute at the National University of Singapore. A student of Indian politics and history since 1967, he is the author of *India's Newspaper Revolution*, 3rd edn. (2010).

KUNAL MAJUMDER is a current affairs correspondent with *Tehelka*, an independent Indian weekly news magazine. He grew up in Dhanbad, the coal-mining region of Jharkhand, and has covered Maoist activity in Chhattisgarh and Jharkhand since 2009, along with writing stories on environment, child rights and politics. He is the winner of UNFPA Laadli Media Award 2011 for Best Feature story on gender sensitivity.

AKANKSHA MEHTA is an associate research fellow at the S. Rajaratnam School of International Studies at the Nanyang Technological University, Singapore from where she has a Master's degree. She began researching the Maoist movement in India in 2008 and has written commentaries, articles and reports on the trends and organization of the movement.

S.D. MUNI is a visiting research professor at the Institute of South Asian Studies at the National University of Singapore. A scholar with 33 years' service to Jawaharlal Nehru University, a diplomat and former Indian ambassador to Lao PDR, he is the author and editor of two dozen books on politics and international relations, among which is *Maoist Insurgency in Nepal* (2003).

S. NARAYAN is the head of research and visiting senior research fellow at the Institute of South Asian Studies at the National University of Singapore. In public service for nearly four decades, he was economic advisor to the prime minister in 2003-4. He has authored and edited numerous books including *Growth Opportunities in Indian States: Issues of Governance and Economic Development* (2005).

OM PRAKASH is an assistant professor at Zakir Husain College, Delhi University. He worked on the theme 'Dialogue and Democracy: A Study of Engagement between Indian State and CPI (Marxist-Leninist) Groups' for his Ph.D. in the Department of Political Science, Delhi University, from 2004-9.

P.V. RAMANA is a research fellow at the Institute for Defence Studies and Analyses in New Delhi. A security specialist who has focused on Maoist questions for many years, he is the editor of *The Naxal Challenge: Causes, Linkages and Policy Options* (2008).

RONOJOY SEN is a visiting research fellow at the Institute of South Asian Studies at the National University of Singapore. A Ph.D. from the University of Chicago, he was Senior Assistant Editor with the

Times of India and has held visiting fellowships at the National Endowment for Democracy and the East-West Center, Washington. He is the author of *Articles of Faith: Religion, Secularism, and the Indian Supreme Court* (2010).

PRATIMA SINGH is a research associate at the Institute of South Asian Studies at the National University of Singapore. A graduate of the Singapore Management University, she writes on different aspects of economic development in India and works on issues of politics and governance in the country.

NANDINI SUNDAR is professor of Sociology, Delhi School of Economics, University of Delhi, and co-editor, *Contributions to Indian Sociology*. Her publications include *Subalterns and Sovereigns: An Anthropological History of Bastar* (2nd edn., 2007), published in Hindi as *Gunda Dhur Ki Talash Mein* (2009), and *Branching Out: Joint Forest Management in India* (2001). She is editor of *Legal Grounds: Natural Resources, Identity and the Law in Jharkhand* (2009) and also co-editor of *Anthropology in the East: The Founders of Indian Sociology and Anthropology* (2007), and *A New Moral Economy for India's Forests: Discourses of Community and Participation* (1999).

SIDDHARTH VARADARAJAN is one of India's most respected journalists. One of the *Hindu's* most senior editors, he began his journalism career with the *Times of India* after having studied at the London School of Economics and Columbia University. He has reported from Europe, central Asia and throughout India and compiled and edited *Gujarat: The Making of a Tragedy* on the communal riots of 2002.

Index